Sex, Law, and Society
in Late Imperial China

Law, Society, and Culture in China

EDITORS
Philip C. C. Huang and Kathryn Bernhardt

ADVISORY BOARD
*William P. Alford, William T. Rowe, Hugh Scogin, Jr.,
Jonathan Spence, Alexander Woodside*

THE OPENING OF archives on legal case records and judicial administration in China has made possible a new examination of past assumptions about the Chinese justice system. Scholars can now ask where actual legal practice deviated from official and popular conceptualizations and depictions. In the process, they can arrive at a new understanding not only of the legal system, but of state-society relations and the nature of the Chinese social-political system as a whole.

Studies of Chinese justice also permit the joining together of social and cultural history. Historians of society and economy, on the one hand, and of mentalities and culture, on the other, have long tended to go their separate ways. Law, however, is a sphere of life in which the two are inseparable. Legal case records contain evidence for both practice and representation. A study of law can tell us about the interconnections between actions and attitudes in ways that segmented studies of each cannot.

The series comprises major new studies by the editors themselves, as well as other contributions from a new generation of scholarship, grounded both in the archives and in new theoretical approaches.

Sex, Law, and Society
in Late Imperial China

Matthew H. Sommer

STANFORD UNIVERSITY PRESS, STANFORD, CALIFORNIA

Stanford University Press
Stanford, California
© 2000 by the Board of Trustees of the
Leland Stanford Junior University

Printed in the United States of America
CIP data appear at the end of the book

For my parents,
Donna M. Sommer, M.D., and
John L. Sommer, M.D.

Preface

I HAVE LONG LOOKED forward to the day when I could thank in writing the many people who have helped me. First of all, Philip Huang was the best adviser a graduate student could possibly hope for; he gave me free rein to find my own way, but was always there when I needed him. He has remained a constant source of encouragement and inspiration in the years since I received my doctorate. In addition, Kathryn Bernhardt and Elizabeth Perry both played a vital role as informal advisers and mentors, reading multiple drafts of dissertation chapters and offering valuable counsel throughout my graduate years. I also thank my other teachers at UCLA: Francesca Bray, Herman Ooms, Hugh Scogin, Richard von Glahn, and Scott Waugh. Haun Saussy graciously stepped in at the last minute as an outside reader, and his incisive comments helped me understand, among other things, that Qing jurists were not hypocrites for not having been feminists.

Several other teachers have my deep appreciation for their gifts to me. The late Maureen Mazzone stimulated my early interest in history, and Lillian Li, the kind mentor of my undergraduate years at Swarthmore, deserves the credit for getting me hooked on the history of China in particular. Their faith in me played an important role in whatever success I have enjoyed. Kent Guy introduced me to the study of Qing documents, imparting basic research methods that have become second nature. Jing Junjian opened up the world of imperial legal codes and commentaries and taught me the rudiments of the Qing judicial system; his influence will be obvious to any informed reader of this book, and even where I disagree with him, it is in a spirit of profound respect. My language teachers are too many to list here, but three will always claim a special place in my heart: Yuan Naiying ("Tang Tai-tai") of Middlebury's Chinese School and Chen Shunzheng of National Taiwan University, who taught me to read classical Chinese; and Tatematsu Kikuko of the Yokohama Stanford Center, who tutored me in reading Japanese scholarship on Chinese legal history.

In graduate school, I learned as much from my peers as from my professors. Brad Reed played a vital role in every stage of the project, and he has stood by me for over a decade as a trusted friend and intellectual sparring partner. Most of the ideas in this book had their genesis in conversations with him, and I will always treasure the time we spent together in Seattle, Los Angeles, and Chengdu. Chris Isett and Karasawa Yasuhiko both influenced my thinking on many important issues, and their friendship made life in Los Angeles a real pleasure. David Wakefield helped get me started at UCLA, and it was he who convinced me that I could actually write a dissertation about sex; moreover, his indomitable spirit in fighting cancer inspired me to persevere at many points when my own confidence wavered and it all seemed impossible. Other friends at UCLA who supported me with camaraderie and advice are Cheng Hong, Clayton Dube, Eugenia Lean, Liu Chang, Lu Hanchao, Lu Zhongqi, Jennifer MacFarlane, Meng Yue, Pu Guoqun, and Zhou Guangyuan.

A number of other scholars supplied valuable criticism at early stages of my dissertation: Benjamin Elman, Joseph Esherick, Harold Kahn, Robert Kreider, James Lee, Lindy Li Mark, Jonathan Ocko, John Shepherd, Giovanni Vitiello, and Wen-hsin Yeh. Richard Gunde has my gratitude for telling me bluntly how silly the first draft of the first chapter of my dissertation sounded, and for helping me in countless other ways. Later, while I was revising my dissertation into the present book, the following people did me the honor of commenting on all or part of the manuscript: Charlotte Furth, Gail Hershatter, Kishimoto Mio, Dorothy Ko, Susan Mann, Paola Paderni, William Rowe, Shiga Shûzô, Terada Hiroaki, Sophie Volpp, and Judith Zeitlin. I also wish to thank my reading circle friends here in Pennsylvania, who treated me to a lively discussion of my final draft over dinner: Hugh Clarke, Maris Gillette, Lillian Li, and Paul Smith. A number of people helped me to acquire important sources and to translate difficult texts: Chang Che-chia, Ih-hae Chang, James Cheng (of UCLA's East Asian Library), Karl Kahler (of Penn's East Asian Library), Karasawa Yasuhiko, Dorothy Ko, Liang Min-min, Liu Chang, Terada Hiroaki, and Zhou Guangyuan. Two in this category deserve special mention: my colleague Paul Goldin, for assisting with the early texts I cite in Chapter 2, and Wai-yee Li, for checking my translations of Ming literature in Chapter 6. The readers for Stanford University Press—Valerie Hansen and an anonymous scholar—have my sincere thanks for their valuable comments, and especially for the exceptional speed with which they reviewed my manuscript.

I should also mention my colleagues and students at the University of Pennsylvania. Bruce Kuklick, Lynn Lees, and Marc Trachtenberg kept me out of trouble during my first years at Penn; Warren Breckman, Kathleen Brown, and Drew Faust improved my manuscript with their comments; and Jeff Fear was always willing to have one more beer while I hashed over the whole project one more time. Most important, Lynn Hunt offered wise counsel about how to turn my dissertation into a book, and she generously nurtured my intellectual growth during the unforgettable semester we taught a graduate seminar together.

The Sichuan Provincial Archives in Chengdu and the First Historical Archives in Beijing have my sincere gratitude for making available most of the Qing legal cases that made this study possible. During my visits to these archives, I received especially kind and effective assistance from Yang Jian and Wen Jingming in Chengdu, and from Qin Guojing, Yin Shumei, and Zhu Shuyuan in Beijing. My hosts at People's University and Sichuan University provided excellent support (especially in the Kafkaesque aftermath of a bicycle accident in Chengdu), as did Keith Clemenger of the Committee for Scholarly Communication with China.

I am fortunate to have had the opportunity to present preliminary versions of my work in the following venues: the Center for Chinese Studies, UCLA; the Center for Chinese Studies, UC Berkeley; the history faculty seminar at The Johns Hopkins University; the East Asian Law Colloquium at NYU Law School; the Center for East Asian Studies, University of Pennsylvania; the annual conference of the Association for Asian Studies (Honolulu, 1996); and the conference on "Law, Society, and Culture in Late Imperial China: A Dialogue Between American and Japanese Scholars" (Kamakura, 1996). Many thanks to the organizers and to all who offered comments and questions.

The help of all these mentors, friends, and colleagues would have gone for naught had I not received generous financial support from the following: the Committee for Scholarly Communication with

China; the History Department and the Center for Chinese Studies at UCLA; the American Philosophical Society; the History Department and the Faculty Research Foundation of the University of Pennsylvania; my parents, Donna M. Sommer, M.D., and John L. Sommer, M.D.; and Luca Gabbiani.

My wife, Ih-hae Chang, has sustained me with her confidence, and our daily conversations about this or that legal case helped drive the project along. I do not have the skill to express in writing the depth of my affection and gratitude, and it would embarrass us both if I tried to do it here. My children Anne and Joseph contributed absolutely nothing to this book; in fact, they slowed it down quite a bit. But they have made my life all the richer, by giving me a life *outside* the book. The same can be said of my brother Andy, who helped keep things in perspective by reminding me that most people don't spend their time on such arcana as eighteenth-century Chinese law.

This book is dedicated to my parents, with profound gratitude for all the moral and material support they have provided over the years. My mother and father imparted to me at an early age their passion for different languages and cultures. One of the many rare opportunities they gave me was a trip to China in 1978, when I was seventeen: that trip changed my life. In addition, I am sure I owe to my father, who practiced urology for more than thirty years, a certain lack of squeamishness in talking about sex and the body. He was always happy to discuss his cases with me, which made for some remarkable dinner conversation during my childhood. I remember an episode from my high school physiology class, when each student was assigned to present an oral report on some disease. I chose syphilis and gonorrhea, and I can still visualize the reaction of my more socially active classmates to the interesting slides that my father had lent me.

Last but not least, my sincere thanks to Muriel Bell, Nathan MacBrien, Sally Serafim, and their colleagues at Stanford University Press, for shepherding my book into print with such calm and reassuring competence.

Two important articles came to my attention too late to be incorporated in the present study. Paola Paderni, who was one of the first scholars to use a large sample of Grand Secretariat memorials to study legal issues, has published an article in Italian (which I cannot read) based on several cases of sodomy ("Alcuni Casi di Omosessualità nella Cina del XVIII Secolo," in *Studi in Onore di Lionello Lanciotti* [Naples: Istituto Universitario Orientale, Dipartimento di Studi Asiatici, 1996], 961–87). At the time, she and I were working in ignorance of each other's research, and she tells me that her findings confirm some points I made in my dissertation. More recently, Michael Szonyi has published the first persuasive evidence I know of that there actually existed in Fujian a sodomitical subculture with its own religious cult to correspond to the well-known stereotype of that province ("The Cult of Hu Tianbao and the Eighteenth-Century Discourse of Homosexuality," *Late Imperial China* 19, no. 1 (1998): 1–25). Readers who wish to pursue further the issues treated in Chapter 4 should consult both of these valuable articles.

In closing, a word of warning may be in order. This book recounts many shocking crimes, crimes that have lost little of their horror despite the passage of centuries. I have not glossed over the details and have avoided euphemism, and at times my treatment may seem detached, if not callous. I have included such painful details for two reasons. First, many of these cases turned on the physical specifics of what had occurred. Second, it seems to me we do no honor to the victims of these crimes by shying away from the brutality they suffered.

Contents

A Note on Conventions

WHEN ADULT WOMEN are mentioned in Chinese legal texts, usually only their surnames are given. To be perfectly accurate, only the surnames of their fathers and/or husbands are given, followed by *shi* (the very rough equivalent of "Ms."). (For gender distinctions in Chinese names, see Watson 1986.) For example, a woman whose husband's surname is Wang and whose father's surname is Li would be referred to as "Wang Li *shi*." Sometimes the two surnames would be distinguished by using the logograph *men* after the husband's and *shi* after the father's (see, for example, the widow remarriage contract translated in Chapter 5)—thus, "Wang *men* Li *shi*" would be the equivalent of "Mrs. Wang née Li." I have generally given women's names in the manner they are recorded in primary sources, using one or two surnames followed by *shi*.

Where possible, I have provided the ages of protagonists in legal cases (the age given at the first recorded deposition or, in case of homicide victims, at the inquest). Ages are expressed in *sui*, which is not the same as the Western "years old." A person is one *sui* at birth, and ages another *sui* at every new year thereafter; therefore, an age expressed in *sui* would be one or two more than the same number of "years old" (for example, fourteen *sui* would be reckoned twelve or thirteen years old).

Each Chinese date is converted to the likely equivalent year according to the Western calendar. Appendix E lists major dynasties mentioned in the text, as well as reign periods for the Ming and Qing dynasties.

All translations are my own, except where noted. For source abbreviations, see the References, pp. 369–70.

Sex, Law, and Society
in Late Imperial China

Map 1. Provincial Boundaries of China Proper, Late Eighteenth Century

CHAPTER ONE

Introduction

The Issues

The Manchus who conquered the Ming empire in 1644, founding on its ruins the Qing ("pure") dynasty, have been vilified in many ways. Perhaps the most novel accusation leveled at them is that they took all the fun out of sex and made prudes of the Chinese. R. H. Van Gulik writes, "With the crumbling of the Ming Empire the robust pleasures of these full-blooded men and women faded away, their buoyant spirit evaporated, sex tending to become a burden rather than a joy" (1974, 333). The charming pornography so warmly appreciated by Van Gulik gave way to puritanical Confucian tracts. Other scholars tell us that the "homophobic" Qing dynasty destroyed an old culture of tolerance toward same-sex love; that it modified rape law in order to suppress women more effectively; that it allowed the high arts of the courtesans to fall into decay; and that it largely succeeded in supplanting "a world of robust popular practicality and sensuality" with a state religion of female chastity.[1]

I have long wondered about this image of the Qing, especially about the extraordinary efficacy it attributes to a supposedly alien regime of sexual repression. Given the vast territory of the empire and the limited technology and communications available to any premodern regime, the Qing must have been a fantastic engine of repression, centuries ahead of its time, to achieve such dramatic results. I have wondered too about all that "robust" sensual pleasure and license attributed to the conquered society, which after all consisted overwhelmingly of poor peasants who depended on family farming for survival. To the Sinologist of a certain persuasion, seventeenth-century China resembles some exotic Tahitian shore as seen through the eyes of one of Captain Bligh's lonelier sailors. With the Qing legal archives open for research, it's time we took a closer look both at the regulation of sexuality, and at the sexuality being regulated, during the late imperial period.

I first began reading Qing case records with an eye to their potential as sources for social history. I found, however, that I had to clarify the legal issues before I could see through to the social ones, and this prior task became my principal focus. I then decided to present a synchronic snapshot of the regulation of sexuality in the Qianlong reign (1736–95), a period when the Qing state functioned as effectively as it ever did, and from which the richest sources survive.[2] But it soon became clear that the eighteenth century was a time of radical change in the regulation of sexuality; my "snapshot" of a system in motion was likely to blur. I found I could not avoid pushing my project back in time in order to make sense of what I saw in the Qianlong case records.

My basic goal is empirical: to explain the regulation of sexuality in late imperial China, especially legislation and central court practice during the Qing. What principles informed this judicial project, and how did it work? What changed, and why? I hope to understand the Qing regulation of sexuality in terms of broader historical changes, and also to locate such regulation in a wider social context. How did it relate to attitudes and practices not necessarily limited to official or elite circles—let alone Manchu ones?

The Western Paradigm of Progress in the Law

Most scholarship has portrayed law in imperial China in largely static terms. The implied standard against which it appears static is the Western paradigm of historical progress in the law, which emphasizes the development of individual rights, contractual obligation, and constitutional limits to government power over the last few centuries. This legal paradigm is a subset of the "metanarrative" of modernity, which interprets history since the Enlightenment as linear progress toward a better, freer, more scientifically advanced future.[3] Many in the West appear to assume that the expansion of individual liberty constitutes the essence of historical change in the legal-political sphere, and that the future will witness the inexorable spread of human rights and democracy around the globe.

This paradigm captures an important dimension of recent Western history and should not be dismissed lightly, especially by people who embrace the basic values of the Enlightenment. But did anything like this progress affect late imperial Chinese law? The most likely candidate might be the Yongzheng Emperor's elimination of a number of hereditary debased-status categories, beginning in 1723 with the "music households" (*yue hu*) associated with sex work and other stigmatized entertainment. This initiative has generally been characterized in the historical literature as an "emancipation," but its real significance is far from clear. At least one scholar suggests that the emancipation actually had a significant liberating effect on the people in question (Hansson 1996). Another applauds the "progressive spirit" of this "excellent policy" but concedes that it failed to achieve any concrete effect (Terada 1959). Still others dismiss it as meaningless (Ch'ü 1965; Jing Junjian 1993). Through this literature runs the unspoken assumption that the Yongzheng initiative should be evaluated as success or failure according to whether it promoted the unfolding of individual liberty and opportunity; the main yardstick these scholars use is whether the "emancipated" people gained access to the civil examination system, which they assume to be a "right" of commoner status.[4] Overall, one gets the impression that the Yongzheng initiative might be important, but it's not entirely clear why—perhaps its importance is mostly symbolic, as a missed opportunity to chart a more modern course for China in the critical century leading up to the Opium War.

A more sophisticated view sees the Yongzheng policy as symptomatic of the "slow erasure of old status barriers" being driven by socioeconomic change (Mann 1997, 43). This interpretation is no doubt correct, and some of the Yongzheng edicts indeed fit a larger eighteenth-century trend in which commercialized, contractual relations of production replaced the few isolated examples of serfdom that remained (P. Huang 1985; Kuhn 1990, 34–36). But we are left wondering about the purpose and real effects of this policy. In particular, an analysis that focuses on the emancipation of labor fails to explain why the emperor accorded first priority to prostitutes and musicians. From the perspective of Qing legal archives, the outstanding feature of this Yongzheng policy was the *criminalization of prostitution*—but this fact has been entirely missed by previous scholarship.

The Western paradigm of progress in the law does not seem particularly useful for understanding Chinese legal history.[5] Indeed, as the red herring of "emancipation" suggests, this paradigm may blind us to other kinds of change that did in fact take place. For example, T'ung-tsu Ch'ü's classic *Law and Society in Traditional China* (1965) downplays whatever changes did occur, for the sake of arguing the uncontroversial point that "legal modernization" along Western lines did *not* occur. He assumes that if Chinese law did not experience this particular kind of progress, then there must have been no significant change at all, because the Western model represents the only kind that matters.[6]

The Western paradigm of progress in the law is especially important for the regulation of sexuality, because the concepts of rights and privacy that have emerged imply individual sovereignty over the body—and over the last century, a number of Western nations have greatly expanded individual freedom in decisions related to sex, marriage, and reproduction. Michel Foucault opens his introductory volume to *The History of Sexuality* with a shrewd critique of the notion that the last century has witnessed a liberation from "Victorian repression" (1978, 3–12); but his own unconventional life is itself powerful testimony to the erotic liberation that has taken place. This ideal of erotic liberation has influenced some historical studies of sex in China, which seem to assume that the only important story is one of a struggle between individual freedom and narrow-minded repression. Thus, the Qing dynasty (with its officially sponsored cults of domesticity and female chastity) is seen as imposing a sort of Chinese "Victorian" regime that repressed an earlier culture of sensual license, and that later persisted in the guise of Communist neo-puritanism. After Mao's death this repressive regime began to crumble, and one can now hope that (to borrow Foucault's words) "tomorrow sex will be good again" (1978, 7).[7]

But there are other stories to be told. In this connection, Foucault's critique of the stereotyped view of the Victorian era is highly relevant. What happened, he argues, was not "repression" so much as a fundamental shift in configurations of "power-knowledge": instead of enforced silence, there was a "proliferation" of new discourses centered on sex, and "sexuality" emerged as the key to modern identity. Specifically, the authority to define and to judge shifted from the Church to the newly emerging medical and psychiatric professions, so that what had been sin was now "medicalized" as pathology: for example, the *sodomite* who had confessed his acts of sin to a priest for absolution became the *homosexual* who confessed his symptoms to a doctor for diagnosis and treatment (1978, 42–43, 66–68). In the process, new social "species" were invented as foci for anxiety and regulation: the perverse adult, the masturbating child, the hysterical woman, and the Malthusian couple (1978, 104–5).

I intend nothing so ambitious as a Foucaultian analysis of Chinese sexuality, and late imperial China was emphatically different from the Europe that Foucault describes. (In particular, nothing like "medicalization" occurred until the early twentieth century, when China's modernizing urban culture and new mass media were so strongly influenced by the West—see Dikötter 1995.) Still, there are certain parallels. If the history of Chinese law does not involve the progressive unfolding of individual freedom, then what happened in the Qing was not a simple repression of the individual, either. Instead, Qing innovations (especially of the eighteenth century) represented a fundamental shift in the organizing principle for the regulation of sexuality: from *status performance*, whereby different status groups had been held to distinct standards of familial and sexual morality, to *gender performance*, in which a uniform standard of sexual morality and criminal liability was extended across old status boundaries and all people were expected to conform to gender roles strictly defined in terms of marriage. This reordering of priorities prompted an intensified surveillance, which aimed to rechannel sexual intercourse in order to enforce a uniform marital order, to defend it against internal subversion and external attack. It also provoked a proliferation of discourse of practically Foucaultian proportions, as new crimes were invented, old criminal categories were reinterpreted and expanded, and a new cast of characters emerged as objects of apprehension and regulation.[8]

The Old Paradigm of Status Performance

Throughout the imperial era, legally defined duties and privileges varied, depending on one's position in hierarchies of family and status. T'ung-tsu Ch'ü (1965) identifies three broad levels of status that framed the law until the end of the imperial era: officials, commoners, and mean persons. But within that overall framework, both social structure and legally defined status hierarchy underwent considerable change. Chinese society gradually became more "egalitarian" over the last centuries of the imperial era, in conjunction with the emergence of imperial autocracy.[9] The Period of Division (A.D. 220–589) and the Tang dynasty (618–907) had been characterized by relatively weak imperial houses, surrounded by elaborate hierarchies of hereditary aristocrats, who reproduced their wealth and status through legally defined birthright to lucrative office, and who were served by a variety of hereditary laborers (slaves, serfs, and bondservants) whose unfree status defined them in legal terms as debased or mean people (*jian min*). The proportion of free commoners (*liang min*) was relatively small, consisting mostly of peasants taxed directly by the imperial state, which claimed ultimate title to their lands (in a sense, the imperial house was simply the biggest aristocratic family, and the "free" peasantry its serfs). Most people were fixed in place, both geographically and socially, and function matched status in ways that were transparent and obvious to all.

People at different status levels were held to different standards of sexual and familial morality. Indeed, the guiding principle for the regulation of sexuality from at least the Tang through the early Qing dynasty[10] may be termed *status performance*: the assumption that one must perform the role conferred by a particular legal status. Status performance took other forms: for example, sumptuary law imposed particular kinds of dress on different status groups, and adornment above one's station was a criminal offense. Hierarchy was further enforced by the differential weighting of penalties for acts of violence involving persons of different status. But sexual standards were a critical factor; in particular, the stigma attached to unfree, mean status derived in large part from the assumption that such people did not live according to the Confucian ritual norms (*li*) that regulated proper relations between the sexes. Sexual immorality can be seen as the defining factor in debased-status stigma.

The most obvious manifestation of this principle is the question of female chastity. From antiquity, a sex offense was defined basically as heterosexual intercourse outside marriage (see Chapter 2). But this definition *always* deferred to the principle of status performance. At root, mean status meant *unfree* status, unfree in the sense of owing labor service (Niida 1943, 959 and 963–64; 1962, 1/16); and for women, such service had a distinctly sexual dimension. Commoner and elite women were expected to remain absolutely chaste, and sexual intercourse between a commoner woman and a man not her husband was always considered a serious offense. People of mean status were not expected to conform to this standard; more accurately, they were not *entitled* to conform to it. Female slaves and bondservants, married or not, were sexually available to their masters, a fact explicitly recognized by law. The only offense identified in this area was intercourse with a female slave belonging to another man, suggesting that the offense was not against the woman herself but against her master; even this crime was punished rather lightly, however. Males and females of debased status were prohibited from extramarital sexual intercourse with each other, but this offense was punished more lightly than commoner adultery (see chapters 1 and 2).

In addition, certain debased-status groups (notably the *yue* households) were expected to perform sexual and other entertainment services. This was not exactly "prostitution" (which implies a commercial sex market), but rather a form of hereditary penal servitude or slavery to the imperial state. Sexual intercourse between commoner males and women of such status was never defined as a crime, regardless of whether the women were married. Moreover, legal codes from Song through Qing held it a crime for a commoner husband to pimp his wife (or otherwise acquiesce to her infidelity), punishable by a beating and compulsory divorce; by contrast, among the *yue* households and other mean-status groups associated with sex work, many prostitutes were pimped by their husbands or fathers, an arrangement deemed normal and not interfered with by the authorities (see Chapter 6). Nor would a male slave whose wife was "favored" (*xing*) by their master be held to the commoner standard of husbandly responsibility for her chastity.

Thus female chastity, and the norms of marriage that went along with it, were assumed to be attributes of free-commoner (*liang*) status. A mean-status husband did not have the exclusive claim to his wife's sexual labor, nor the obligation to guard that claim, that a commoner husband had. Moreover, if a male of debased status offended *upward*, by engaging in sexual intercourse with a woman of higher status (especially a woman of his master's household), that act was punished far more severely than would illicit intercourse between commoners (let alone that between mean persons).

In some respects, officials (and their families) were held to an even stricter standard of sexual and familial morality than commoners. From at least the Song dynasty, they were prohibited from marrying or even sleeping with prostitutes. Officials who committed illicit intercourse with women in their jurisdictions would be stripped of rank and degree, after which they would receive the regular corporal penalties. Commoner widows were allowed to remarry after completing three years' mourning for their husbands; however, from the Yuan dynasty forward, the widows of degree-holding officials were prohibited from ever remarrying. In Yuan law, an official's wife who eloped with one of her retainers would be executed.

To sum up, sex served as a key marker of status distinction, and the regulation of sexual behavior amounted to the regulation of status performance: that is, it ensured that people behaved in a manner appropriate to their station. The contrast between different standards of sexual morality (especially the relative availability of women) played a fundamental role in marking status strata as distinct from one another. Indeed, the term *liang*—which literally means "good" but was used to denote free commoner status—always carried a moral dimension, and the sexual immorality attached to debased status helped define, by contrast, all that was "good" about the "good people" (*liang min*)—that is, free commoners.

The New Paradigm of Gender Performance

By the eighteenth century, all but a tiny percentage of the population could be considered free commoners.[11] Aristocracy had disappeared entirely (except for a minuscule layer of elite Manchus). Instead, the dominant social class was a landlord gentry that could claim nothing as birthright and feared downward mobility through property division. This gentry sought wealth and prestige through competition in civil service examinations (now requisite for office-holding), which had been introduced by centralizing emperors in order to break down independent aristocratic power. Gentry were treated as ordinary commoners, except for office-holders and higher level degree-holders; even this upper gentry could not reproduce its legal privileges except through new examination degrees. Moreover (to quote Francesca Bray):

The aristocratic elite of pre-Song China had protected their status and maintained the social order through practices of exclusion: their status was transmitted through descent, and their marriage practices, family rituals, and other markers of status were forbidden to commoners. From the Song, however, the new political elite were meritocrats who worked through a strategy of inclusion. They strove to build an organic social order, ranked but open to all, that would bind the whole population into a shared culture of orthodox beliefs, values and practices. (1997, 42)

A free peasantry, bound by contractual obligation (if any at all), comprised the overwhelming majority of the population. There remained a small proportion of mean persons (including some domestic slaves), but commercialization and social mobility had blurred the traditionally fixed connections between legal status and occupation—a phenomenon especially obvious in the area of sex work, where an archaic system of official penal servitude had been transformed by the rise of a pervasive commercial sex market (see Chapter 6 and Wang Shunu 1988). Servile labor no longer played an important role in the agrarian economy; mean status gradually came to be associated less with bonded servitude per se than with certain stigmatized occupational or regional subethnic groups, whose members were not slaves despite their hereditary mean status. Accordingly, the original meaning of the *liang/jian* dichotomy as free/unfree was gradually displaced by the nuance of moral judgment, and fixed, hereditary status labels became more of a legal fiction than an accurate description of social reality.[12]

The Qing dynasty—especially the Yongzheng reign (1723–35)—marks a watershed in the regulation of sexuality, when the age-old paradigm of status performance yielded to a new one, gender performance. This new paradigm sums up the cumulative effect of a whole range of legislative initiatives of the Yongzheng reign, shored up by complementary legislation of the Qianlong reign that followed. To summarize broadly:

1. Prostitution was entirely prohibited, in conjunction with the elimination of the debased-status categories associated with tolerated sex work (notably the *yue* households); these people would henceforth be held to a commoner standard of female chastity and criminal liability. At a stroke, prostitutes, their pimps (often their husbands), and the commoner males who had enjoyed their services as a perquisite of status all became criminals (see Chapter 7).

2. The sexual use of servile women by their masters was sharply curtailed, and the law obliged masters to arrange timely marriages for female domestic slaves. The law implied that if masters wanted to sleep with their female slaves, they should promote them to legitimate concubine status. These measures extended commoner norms of marriage and chastity to servile women and, in conjunction with the ban on prostitution, extended the prohibition of extramarital intercourse to *all* women (see Chapter 2).

3. Qing lawmakers increased the basic penalties for "consensual illicit sexual intercourse" (see appendixes A.2 and A.3), but they also further relaxed the conditions for immunity from punishment for a husband who murdered his wife (or her partner) if he discovered she had committed adultery (see Meijer 1991). The Qing judiciary also consistently defined wife-selling as a form of adultery, even if no illicit intercourse preceded the transaction (see Chapter 2; Sommer 1994).

4. Lawmakers imposed new draconian penalties on a number of variations of rape. The worst-case scenario was reformulated not in

terms of the old status transgression (that is, a male slave assaulting his master's women, as in the Tang code) but rather as the pollution of a chaste wife or daughter of humble family by a rogue male outside the family order. A plethora of new measures aimed to suppress the "rootless rascals" (*guang gun*) who were now imagined as sexual predators (see Chapter 3).

5. Consensual anal intercourse between males had been prohibited since the Ming dynasty; now, for the first time, lawmakers defined an explicit crime of homosexual rape, for which they imposed harsh penalties. Sodomy offenses were assimilated to the previously heterosexual category of "illicit sexual intercourse" (*jian*) by mapping a new hierarchy of offenses and penalties that precisely matched those for the "parallel" heterosexual offenses. The homosexual rapist was imagined as the same "rootless rascal" feared to threaten the pollution of chaste women, and the male rape victim was imagined as an adolescent male of good family. The Qianlong judiciary also issued unprecedented legislation on self-defense against homosexual rape, which became a mitigating factor in the punishment of homicide (see Appendix B.2). These measures implied a new anxiety over vulnerable masculinity, corresponding to the new anxiety over female chastity, as well as a new imperative that males act as husbands and fathers, corresponding to the imperative that females act as wives and mothers (see Chapter 4).

6. The imperial chastity cult was greatly expanded over its Ming and early Qing precedents, and the Yongzheng Emperor pointedly shifted the distribution of honors from elites to humble commoner women, praising especially the poor widow who struggled to support her children without compromising her chastity (Elvin 1984; Mann 1987). Lawmakers and propagandists invented new categories of chastity heroine and martyr, as well as new crimes against chastity; moreover, the penalties for old crimes against chastity were greatly increased. But instead of greater diversity, this proliferation involved a further reduction of different female roles into "wife," implying an even stricter expectation that every female act the part of a chaste wife, regardless of her stage in life (see Chapter 5).[13]

The cumulative thrust of these initiatives was to extend a uniform standard of sexual morality and criminal liability to all. This uniform standard, based on rigid interpretation of the normative marital roles expected of commoners, left less room for variation and exception than before. Previously tolerated spaces for extramarital sexual intercourse were eliminated from the law, and the imperial center mandated that local officials intensify their surveillance of sexual behavior and gender roles (for example, administrative penalties were imposed on magistrates who "failed to detect" and eliminate any prostitution within their jurisdictions). Much of the old status-based legislation remained on the books, but it was displaced in practice by the new measures. Out of 56 new substatutes related to sex offenses promulgated by 1780, only three had any direct connection with status difference—and all three had the effect of *reducing* the privileges of hierarchy (see chapters 2 and 3).[14] This shift of emphasis is equally clear in the Qing archives: central cases from the Shunzhi reign (1644–61) include a fair number involving status transgressions of some sort that are judged according to the old Ming statutes, but such cases are unusual in the Qianlong and later reign periods. Moreover, *every single one* of my county-level sex offense cases (the earliest of which date from 1758) involves offenses between legal status equals. Even the ubiquitous agricultural laborers in central cases from the late eighteenth and early nineteenth centuries are almost always treated as the legal status equals of their employers.[15]

The heightened emphasis on stereotyped gender roles demanded their *performance*, sometimes on the stage of a magistrate's court. This demand is most obvious in the area of female chastity (as we see in chapters 3 and 5). The prosecution of rape required a prior exoneration of the female victim, based on intense scrutiny of her conduct before, during, and after the rape attempt itself. For a widow to preserve her independence and her control of property and children required a very public performance of the role of "chaste widow" that had to meet specifically coded expectations. But appropriate gender performance was also required of males, as seen in the prosecution of sodomy, wife-selling, prostitution, and other crimes.[16]

With the shift in paradigms, old dangers yielded to new ones. No one worried much anymore about the rebellious slave who might violate his master's wife—instead, people feared the rogue male outside the familial order altogether who might covet the women and young sons of better-established householders. A new cast of characters appeared in legal discourse as targets for suppression: the "bare stick" or "rootless rascal" (*guang gun*), the homosexual rapist, the pimp, the morally lax husband. Others appeared as new objects of protection or even quasi-religious veneration: the adolescent male, and the chaste wife or daughter of *humble* family. Certain familiar figures took on greatly heightened significance: the lewd widow, the chaste widow, and the avaricious in-law. Other familiar figures were slated for elimination: for example, the penetrated male and the legal prostitute, along with her husband/pimp and the commoner male who enjoyed her services as a privilege of his status.

Gender Anxiety and Fear of the Rogue Male

What else was happening in the eighteenth century that can help us understand this shift in the regulation of sexuality?[17] Fixed, heritable status had by and large become an anachronism by the Yongzheng reign, and the shift in the regulation of sexuality represented in part an effort to update the law to fit a changed social reality: the *de jure* extension of commoner standards of morality and criminal liability followed, after a certain delay, the *de facto* expansion of commoner status. Moreover, the eighteenth century witnessed a broader shift in Qing jurisprudence to focus on *conduct* as the most useful way to distinguish between individuals for purposes of law. One is tempted to compare it to that in the early modern West: "a progress from *status* to contract in which men's duties and liabilities came more and more to flow from willed action instead of from the accident of social position recognized by law" (Pound 1954, 150). But that is only part of the story; and it does not help us explain the new obsession with fixing and policing family-based gender roles, or the growing anxiety about that new bogey of the Qing judiciary, the "rootless rascal" outside the family order altogether.

One long-term factor behind the revolutionary upheaval of the late nineteenth and early twentieth centuries was a gradually worsening subsistence crisis among much of the peasantry, driven in part by overpopulation and agricultural involution. A rising proportion of men lacked the resources to marry and reproduce, and so fell through the cracks of society. By the nineteenth century, the proliferation of surplus males was fueling endemic low-level violence in poor regions. Elizabeth Perry (1980) has shown that in rural Huaibei (where perhaps a fifth of adult men never married), such violence in "predatory" and "protective" forms played a critical role in peasant survival strategies, and at times might explode into open rebellion against the imperial state. Eventually, such men—for whom "liberation" meant wives and farms of their own—would play a major role in the Red Army and in violent land reform. But the problem of a dangerous underclass of surplus males was already evident in the eighteenth century.[18]

The demography of premodern China is notoriously difficult; we simply do not have precise population figures before the Communist era, except for isolated examples. But there is consensus on a few basics. Between 1700 and 1850 the empire's population roughly tripled, from about 150 million to about 430 million, while cultivated acreage only doubled (Ho 1959; Perkins 1969). One result was further intensification of an already labor-intensive agriculture, at the cost of diminishing returns (the vicious circle of "involution" analyzed by P. Huang 1985 and 1990). A related development was (in the words of demographic historian Ted Telford) "a chronic shortage of marriageable women—an endemic 'marriage crunch' felt most keenly by lower-class males" (1992, 924). The precise dimensions and causes of the shortage of wives are open to debate, but widespread crisis strategies included female infanticide and the sale of daughters and wives (to become prostitutes, servants, concubines, and so on). These strategies skewed the overall ratio between the sexes and removed countless females from the pool of potential wives for poor men. There is evidence of female infanticide skewing the sex ratio as far back as the Song dynasty; even without infanticide, the longstanding practice of polygyny among the elite would have reduced the supply of wives for poor men (since concubines came from poorer backgrounds than their husbands). But the situation was worsening in the Qing. By the eighteenth century, the proportion of males who never married had almost certainly begun to rise; but even if the *proportion* of surplus males in the overall population did not rise, their *absolute numbers* surely did, in concert with the steady population growth that continued until at least the mid-nineteenth century.[19]

Philip Kuhn (1990) has commented eloquently on the paradoxical character of the eighteenth century as an age of both prosperity and anxiety. The Qing state was at the height of its powers, and both economy and population grew to unprecedented levels. At the same time, there was a creeping awareness of fundamental problems, symbolized by growing fear of the swelling underclass of vagrant males; this fear, shared by both the imperial state and settled communities, at one point crystallized in a mysterious sorcery panic that swept across some of the most prosperous regions of the empire. Kuhn's evidence that a large vagrant underclass existed in China's most prosperous regions as early as the mid-eighteenth century—and that imperial officials feared such vagrants as a grave security threat—bears special relevance to our understanding of the paradigmatic shift in the regulation of sexuality. The sexual predator imagined by the eighteenth-century substatutes was stereotyped as a "rootless rascal" (*guang gun*), that is, the superfluous rogue male who threatens the household order from outside. The term *guang gun* appears in legal discourse for the first time in the late seventeenth century, and the eighteenth century witnessed a flood of new edicts and substatutes (including many related to sex offenses) that explicitly targeted the *guang gun* for suppression.[20]

Eighteenth-century demographic trends implied not just rising competition in the marriage market but also the growth of a crowd of rogue males who lacked wives, family, and property. Left out of mainstream patterns of marriage and household, they also lacked any obvious stake in the normative moral and social order: no wonder the imperial state regarded such men with fear and loathing. Indeed, Kuhn stresses that anxiety about this vagrant underclass was not limited to official circles; on the contrary, the sorcery panic that he recounts afflicted ordinary members of settled communities, and expressed their deep fear of outside, rogue males (1990).

Kathryn Bernhardt has recently argued (in regard to marriage and women's property claims) that between the Tang-Song and Ming-Qing periods, the emphasis of codified law shifted away from aristocratic priorities toward those of ordinary commoner peasants. She characterizes this process as the "peasantization" of the law (1996, 56–58). Something similar seems to have occurred in criminal law, at least in the area of sex offenses. In Tang-dynasty law, female chastity applied to the unfree status categories no more than did aristocratic standards of succession and inheritance, and the irrelevance of the one was directly linked to the irrelevance of the others. The "peasantization" of these civil law questions paralleled the extension of commoner standards of sexual morality and criminal liability.

From this standpoint, Qing innovations in the regulation of sexuality can be interpreted as the defense of a generalized normative family order against the predations of males left out of that order. This new priority reflects the leveling of social structure that had taken place, and may reflect the genuine fears of the settled peasant household as well. (It seems probable that new terms like *guang gun*/"rootless rascal" and *ji jian*/"sodomy" entered legal discourse from the vernacular, since they do not appear in legal texts prior to the Qing dynasty but can be found in Ming vernacular fiction.) The heightened stress on fixed gender roles, especially among ordinary commoners, implies a strengthening of household defenses in which the chaste wife stood on the frontlines to defend the familial order.

The sexual choices and experiences of poor women became the subject of countless memorials and imperial edicts.

The very vehemence of exhortation about female chastity in the eighteenth and nineteenth centuries suggests increasing alarm at the breakdown of moral and social order under the pressure of socioeconomic realities. Such exhortation—and the legislation that gave it force—implies an effort to enroll women as "moral police" to guard the family's fragile boundaries against assault by the growing crowd of rogue males at the bottom of Qing society.

How the Other Half Lived

The best recent work on women in late imperial China has focused on the Yangzi Delta elite, because only in that privileged stratum did some women enjoy the resources to write and publish. The contributions of this research are enormous (as my frequent citations testify), but it helps us to understand the lives of the poor majority only in the most tentative and indirect ways.[21] In contrast, Qing legal cases tell us precious little about the elite, who (one suspects) had better ways to solve their problems than going to court. Instead, the legal archives provide an unprecedented opportunity to glimpse the lower strata of society, to look beyond the state and elite to learn something firsthand (or close to it) of the lives of peasants and marginalized people.

For example, most studies of prostitution in the Ming and Qing focus on elite courtesans whose appeal to their upper-crust clients was more cultural than carnal (Ko 1994; Mann 1997; Widmer and Chang, eds., 1997). I have yet to see a courtesan appear in the archives. Instead, we find peasant women pimped by their husbands or working in urban brothels—or "music households" (*yue hu*), found in early Qing legal cases, offering services quite unrelated to music. The same is true of same-sex union: in legal cases, we find not the refined setting of opera patronage or the wealthy libertine who sodomized his adolescent pages for diversion, but rather alliances among beggars, mendicant monks, laborers, and the like that probably had more to do with sheer survival than with pleasure per se.

In a separate section below, I address the challenges of using the ethnographic evidence in Qing legal cases as the basis for social history. For now, I wish to emphasize that such evidence offers the clearest view we are ever likely to get of how peasants and marginalized people actually lived in the late imperial period, and of how they thought about sex, gender, marriage, and family. Such evidence gives us our firmest basis yet for assessing the connections between imperial law and wider social practices and perceptions.

For example, many scholars have wondered whether the dramatic expansion of the chastity cult in the eighteenth century really had any impact on the ordinary people who were its target. Did they know or care about it? Did it reflect or influence their morality? Was it a success in any meaningful way? A similarly contentious issue has been Qing legislation against anal intercourse between males (*ji jian*, "sodomy"). Did what Vivien Ng (1987 and 1989) and Bret Hinsch (1990) call the "homophobia" of the Qing state have anything to do with contemporary popular perceptions? Or was this legislation simply imposed by an autocratic conquest state on a preexisting and widespread culture of tolerance? What did ordinary peasants in the eighteenth century think about male homosexual union? The ethnographic evidence in legal cases enables us to answer such questions in a satisfying way for the first time.

Most important, this evidence sheds new light on the role sex played in survival strategies of poor and marginalized people. A subplot of this book is the story of people excluded from accepted patterns of marriage and household because of poverty and other factors bonding with each other in unorthodox ways to satisfy a range of human needs. Legal case records reveal a variety of scenarios, including same-sex unions among marginalized males; covert relationships between independent widows and their hired laborers; sexual triangles that developed when a patron moved in with a poor couple, paying to support them in exchange for sexual access to the wife; and relationships in bands of itinerant beggars, in which one or more women allied with a group of men. For such people, sexual relations deemed illicit by the state combined with coresidence, pooling of resources, emotional bonds, and sometimes fictive kinship ties to become the basis of unorthodox household patterns. In these scenarios, we see the role played by sexual bonding in the survival strategies of marginalized people in a Hobbesian world unkind to individuals on their own. In many ways, these arrangements mimicked normative marriages and households, but they were stigmatized and illegal all the same—and frequent appearance in criminal records underscores the vulnerability and instability of such bondings.

This evidence reveals a previously invisible dimension of Qing social practice, one that involved a large and growing number of people and was viewed with alarm by everyone with a stake in the established, normative order. Legal archives show us the picture seen by Qing officials as they engaged society in the arena of county and central court adjudication. Official perceptions of social trends may not have been perfectly accurate, but they mattered: eighteenth-century innovations in the regulation of sexuality typically resulted from the proposals of provincial officials, based on their perception that problems they encountered in the courtroom required statutory redress.[22]

Sources

The principal source for this study is Qing-dynasty legal case records, which became available in large numbers only in the nineteen-eighties and nineties, with the opening of archives in the PRC and the publication of documents held by the Academia Sinica in Taiwan. Most of the cases cited here I collected during research trips to the PRC in 1991–92, 1996, and 1997. They represent both the very bottom of the judicial hierarchy (the county level) and the very top (central courts at the provincial and palace levels).

County Case Records

The county- (*xian*) level yamen (that is, government office) was the court of first instance in the Qing judiciary. The richest collection of county cases by far is the Ba County Archive, held at the Sichuan Provincial Archives in Chengdu, which includes over 100,000 files (*juan*) of legal records dating as far back as the mid-eighteenth century. Ba County centered on the city of Chongqing (Chungking), which also served as the capital of Chongqing Prefecture and the headquarters of the Eastern Sichuan Circuit Intendant. The far smaller Shuntian Prefecture Archive (held at the First Historical Archives in Beijing) and Danshui-Xinzhu Archive (widely available on microfilm) together contain no more than a few thousand files of all kinds, mostly from the last fifty years of the dynasty. Many local archives in China hold a dozen or so files, but these scattered materials have yet to be systematically surveyed by historians. The paucity of county-level records is stark testimony to the scale of destruction that afflicted China intermittently from the Taiping Rebellion through the Cultural Revolution. I have heard, for example, that the Taiping rebels burned down the yamen in every county seat they occupied; it is probably no coincidence that the three major archives to survive come from regions unvisited by the rebels.

County-level case files typically include plaints and counterplaints, magistrates' responses, summonses and warrants, runners' reports, transcripts of court hearings, contracts and other documents submitted by litigants, magistrates' final decisions, and so on (see P. Huang 1996 and Allee 1994 for detailed discussion). Such files enable us to follow the development of a case from inception through the various stages of adjudication (although many files are incomplete). My sample includes some 500 Ba County cases from the period 1758–1852;[23] and 160 Shuntian Prefecture cases (almost all from Baodi County, located about 80 kilometers southeast of Beijing), mostly dating to the first half of the nineteenth century.[24]

Central Case Records

By "central case records" I refer to two categories of documents: (1) routine memorials reporting on capital crimes committed in the provinces, which were processed for the emperor by the Grand Secretariat (*Neige xingke tiben*), and (2) records of crimes that occurred within the imperial capital of Beijing and for security reasons were subject to "immediate examination" (*xian shen*) by the Board of Punishment.

Routine criminal memorials almost all fall into two groups: (1) those from provincial governors reporting serious criminal cases, which were referred to the Three High Courts of Judicature (*San fa si*);[25] and (2) those from the Three High Courts either confirming or rejecting the sentences recommended by governors. Though ostensibly directed to the emperor, these memorials were actually handled by the Grand Secretariat. Each records the entire process of review that a case underwent since first being investigated by the county magistrate. It includes a transcription of the magistrate's original report detailing his opinion of what happened, quoting confessions and testimony, and concluding with recommended sentences for offenders. Each stage of review is represented in another layer of opinion added by reviewers (prefect, judicial commissioner, and the like), which sometimes includes additional evidence. The provincial governor (and sometimes the governor-general) would add his own summary and recommendations and submit the whole for the emperor's scrutiny. Memorials from the Three High Courts of Judicature simply recapitulate the contents of governors' memorials, adding their own layer of review. The cover of each memorial bears a vermilion rescript giving (supposedly) the emperor's orders, written neatly in the hand of some secretary. On all the memorials

I have seen, the rescript either refers the case to the Three High Courts (or occasionally to one of the Six Boards) or simply confirms the Three High Courts' recommendations; it seems that even an energetic executive like the Qianlong Emperor rarely intervened at this stage of the routine judicial process.[26]

The First Historical Archives in Beijing holds an enormous number of routine memorials on capital crimes, covering the entire length of the dynasty; the vast majority date from 1736 or after. The Academia Sinica in Taipei has a smaller yet still considerable collection of such memorials (MQ). It is an especially valuable source of cases from the Shunzhi and Yongzheng periods, only a few hundred of which remain in Beijing (almost nothing survives from the Kangxi period in either collection). I was able to copy some 600 memorials in Beijing (most date to the Shunzhi, Qianlong, and Jiaqing reigns), all from the archival category "marriage, sex offenses, and family disputes"; I have found many other valuable examples in the Academia Sinica's published series.

On my first research trip to Beijing in 1992, I concentrated on memorials from the Qianlong reign. Later, I realized that the Yongzheng reign had been a key watershed in the regulation of sexuality; on subsequent trips, I focused my search on the seventeenth century and was able to gather enough early Qing evidence to give a clear picture of the situation prior to the important initiatives of the Yongzheng. Early Qing case records are especially important in understanding the changing treatment of prostitution, as will be seen in Chapter 6.

"Immediate examination" cases originated in Beijing (and those that survive are all held at the archives there); any serious incident that took place within the capital or its immediate environs would be referred by the security forces directly to the Board of Punishment, without passing through the normal intermediate levels of review. In effect, the board served as court of first instance for such cases, dividing them up among its different provincial bureaus (*si*) for adjudication (Na Silu 1992). Immediate examination cases run the gamut from fairly trivial incidents to the worst capital offenses; such files often include the same sorts of evidence found in county-level case records. I copied 80 of them, mostly from the early to mid-nineteenth century, all from the archival category of "marriage, sex offenses, and family disputes."

Comparison of Local and Central Case Records

The main difference between local and central cases is how they show the law being applied. Much local adjudication was characterized by an informality that reveals the priority of practical solutions over rigid imposition of formal law. The vast majority of litigation in county courts involved relatively minor offenses and concluded at the county level, without being sent up through the bureaucracy for review. In the records of such cases, magistrates usually did not bother explaining their decisions in terms of specific laws and meted out (or withheld) penalties on a case-by-case basis without direct reference to the code.

This does not mean that local adjudication was arbitrary or unconnected with the principles embodied in codified law (see P. Huang 1994 and 1996 for a demonstration of this point in regard to civil law); magistrates consistently denounced conduct that was banned by the code, even if they did not necessarily punish it according to the detailed specifications of formal law. Nor should we assume that magistrates broke the rules by taking a flexible approach to routine cases. In Ba County, for example, disgruntled litigants could appeal magistrates' decisions to the Chongqing Prefect or to the Eastern Sichuan Circuit Intendant (whose headquarters were both right next-door to the county yamen), and there are many examples of such appeals having a decisive effect on judicial outcomes; for this reason, we can safely assume that no Ba County magistrate could have gotten away with violations of accepted procedure for long. It seems, rather, that the petty nature of routine cases gave local officials a great deal of leeway in how they put general principles into practice—and this practical flexibility helps account for the success and longevity of the late imperial legal system. In Chapter 7, we examine how Ba County magistrates enforced the prohibition of prostitution, a good illustration of the flexible yet meaningful implementation of central directives on the local level.

One gains a radically different impression of Qing adjudication from central court records, especially Grand Secretariat memorials. When judging routine cases, the county magistrate faced his social inferiors within his own jurisdiction; when judging capital cases, however, he faced Beijing, from the lowest position on the bureaucratic totem pole. Therefore, in capital cases being prepared for central review, magistrates matched every possible offense uncovered in the course of investigation to a statute (*lü*) or substatute (*li*) in the code, and sentenced every offender to the exact penalty mandated therein.[27] Even the most trivial secondary offenses were judged and sentenced "by the book." The magistrate's own report would be included in every review document on the case, including the governor's memorial to the emperor. The level of detail in these documents seems to exceed any conceivable practical purpose: for example, a memorial will duly report that a beggar's dirty socks stolen by his murderer have been recovered and turned over to his family, in accordance with the code's requirement that stolen property be restored to its owner. "Immediate examination" cases handled by the Board of Punishment often involved nothing more serious than prostitution or adultery, yet they, too, were always handled with strict and meticulous reference to the code.

It seems, then, that the packaging of central cases carried a meaning as much symbolic and ideological as anything. Every transgression, however minor, was carefully named and punished according to the code's meticulously calibrated scale of penalties. At the end of the process, no doubt would remain: the truth had been discovered, every offense identified and requited, and balance restored. This process proved to the judicial system its own efficacy, serving perhaps more as a mirror for the self-regard of the center than as a didactic public exercise. The ritual labor of matching offense to statute had a disciplining effect on the judiciary, requiring each bureaucrat to conform to protocols mandated by the center, with his performance scrutinized at succeeding levels by his superiors—and finally by the emperor himself, who in the Legalist paradigm held his laws like reins, the better to manipulate and overawe his ministers.

Because of this meticulous matching of offense to code, central cases are of far greater utility than county-level cases for examining the orthodox constructions of the state. A basic method of this book is to use central cases (and occasionally, official casebooks) to trace "by the book" application of codified law to situations of concrete fact. Imperial legal codes imposed a carefully calibrated scale of penalties, adjusting their weight to reflect differences of status between offender and victim (including relative seniority within the family, if the parties were related) (Bodde and Morris 1967, chaps. 1 and 3). In the area of "illicit sexual intercourse," penalties could also be weighted to reflect degrees of chastity and sexual virtue. Therefore, the explicit application of codified law in central cases enables us to establish in some detail how judicial orthodoxy balanced competing priorities to define and promote an ideal social order. In contrast, county-level cases are far more revealing of the practical problems faced by local magistrates, and of the strategies of ordinary people who interacted with authority during the less formal adjudication of routine cases.

Of course, this book does not cite every one of these cases I have gathered, either from the county or central courts; nor have I attempted any quantitative survey of the entire sample (I do not believe the material lends itself to quantitative analysis for most purposes). Nevertheless, in a fundamental way I have drawn on my experience with the entire body of material in writing this book. To use this archival material effectively, I believe it is vital to read in it as widely as possible. Only then can the historian develop a clear sense of the difference between "boilerplate" and spontaneous testimony. One must also acquire a textured feeling for context in order to notice important silences, to read seemingly insignificant details for their larger implications, to get a sense of what a "typical" case in a given area looks like. It is by reading widely that one gains a nuanced understanding of contemporary legal reasoning and even a certain empathy with what passed for common sense in the era in which the cases were recorded.

The Late Imperial Tradition of Legal Commentary

This study also depends on the legal codes of various dynasties, including several critical commentaries on the Ming and Qing codes by senior jurists of those dynasties. Case records from Qing archives cast this other material, which has long been available, in an entirely new light.

The Ming-Qing tradition of legal commentary involved tracing change over time by comparing current law with earlier codes and commentaries, using the Tang code as a baseline (because it was the earliest code to survive intact, and had provided the basic vocabulary, concepts, and hierarchy of penalties employed by its successors). The great commentators of the Ming—such as Lei Menglin in the Jiajing era and Wang Kentang in the Wanli era—and of the Qing—Shen Zhiqi in the Kangxi era, Wu Tan in the Qianlong era, and Xue Yunsheng in the Guangxu era—were active senior jurists who approached the judicial problems of their day through historical analysis. Each of these commentators provided a "snapshot" of the law current when he was writing, and also looked back in time to see how it had evolved. What was the logical coherence of the current law? Had inconsistencies or contradictions crept in over time? Did an old measure retain any use, given changed circumstances? Sometimes, the real purpose of such analysis was a thinly veiled criticism of recent innovations.[28]

Xue Yunsheng is the greatest exemplar of this tradition of critical commentary. Writing at the end of the nineteenth century, Xue was an ardent reactionary who advocated a return to the first principles of the Tang code. His *Lingering Doubts After Reading the Substatutes* (*Du li cun yi*) questions the value of many of the eighteenth-century substatutes that overlaid the original Qing code of 1646 (which had consisted almost entirely of Ming-dynasty statutes). His *Combined Edition of the Tang and Ming Codes* (*Tang Ming lü he bian*) pushes this argument farther back in time, contrasting the simplicity and clarity of Tang law with a Ming code that he believed had been significantly distorted by the influence of the alien Yuan dynasty. Xue Yunsheng's reactionary polemic failed: after his death, the reform designed by his protégé Shen Jiaben abandoned much of Chinese tradition in favor of Western models. However, Xue's commentaries retain enormous value for legal history.[29]

Some of the best historians of Chinese law have appropriated, more or less consciously, many of the techniques of late imperial commentators (for example, Jing Junjian 1993 and 1994); doing so is entirely fitting, since everyone studying Chinese legal history depends on these valuable sources at least to some extent. (My own tracing of judicial concepts on the level of codes, using the Tang code as baseline, basically follows the approach of the Chinese commentators.) But the Qing jurists who did this work assumed their readers to be other Qing jurists, thus taking for granted an intimate knowledge of the living law current when they were writing. Equally, as serving officials who had themselves tried cases, they assumed an understanding of how that law actually worked in practice. There is much they did not bother to explain, because they assumed their readers already knew it. But that knowledge has been lost—and the unavailability, for many decades, of actual case records meant that legal historians could not recover it.

Attempts were made to compensate for the lack of case records: Japanese scholars like Shiga Shûzô (1967 and 1984) have made great contributions on the basis of published collections of magistrates' judgments; and Western scholars like Bodde and Morris (1973), Marinus Meijer (1981, 1985, and 1991), and Vivien Ng (1987) have used officially authorized casebooks to estimable effect. But both collected judgments and official casebooks have important limitations.

Collected judgments were usually published by magistrates themselves or by filial sons or protégés, and one cannot help suspecting
that the cases they summarize have been selected (and edited) in order to manifest the benevolence and sagacity of their authors. Moreover, as Philip Huang points out (1996, 17), such sources may lead
us into mistaking the Qing state's idealized representations of itself
for empirical fact. On the other hand, official casebooks such as
Conspectus of Legal Cases (*Xing an hui lan*) and its sequels are limited in a somewhat different way. Intended as reference works for
sitting magistrates, they provide brief summaries of decisions by
central courts on cases that required application of the law to tricky
or unusual fact situations (not unlike the casebooks used in American law schools today)—and casebooks are most useful for the examples they provide of the hairsplitting logic necessary to balance
competing principles or to apply the law by analogy to unanticipated
scenarios. Many of the cases are highly exceptional, which is why
they were included in these collections; their summaries provide no
testimony and little if any evidence of how each case was originally
worked up at the county level. Moreover, these casebooks concentrate on recent decisions that set new precedents and thus present a
slice of central court reasoning in a specific, brief period only. For
example, almost everything in *Conspectus of Legal Cases* dates from
the two or three decades prior to its publication in 1834; it tells very
little about seventeenth- or eighteenth-century jurisprudence.

The Opportunity Afforded by Qing Legal Archives

The availability of original case records offers the prospect of a
quantum leap in our understanding of law and society in the Qing
dynasty. Considerable new research has already resulted, although
we are just beginning to tap the potential of these records. Most important, Philip Huang's recent work (1996) uses cases from the
county level to transform our understanding of civil adjudication
and to illuminate the paradoxical combination of representation
and practice that characterized Qing government in general.[30]

The principal focus of the Qing code proper was crime and punishment, while civil adjudication was mostly left to county-level
courts, so it is obvious that county case records are necessary for
any real understanding of Qing civil law.[31] But we should not assume that the code is a straightforward, unambiguous guide to
criminal practice, either. Out of filial deference to dynastic founders, old statutes were left in the code as a formality even after they

became obsolete and were no longer cited, or had been entirely supplanted by new substatutes. Old laws and legal terms often remained superficially unchanged but were interpreted and applied in radically new ways. This superficial appearance of stasis makes it easy for a casual reader of the code to miss the real dynamics of Qing law, especially during the eighteenth century. Even simple empirical questions can become hopelessly confused.

An illustration is the question of how Qing law punished "consensual illicit sex" (*he jian*). The 1646 edition of the Qing code simply preserved the fourteenth-century Ming dynasty statute, which prescribes 80 blows of the heavy bamboo if the woman were single, and 90 blows if she had a husband; if the woman were married, then her husband might keep her or sell her in marriage, as he pleased (Appendix A.2). This statute always remained the opening passage of the Qing code's chapter on sex offenses, thus misleading even scholars with impeccable standards into thinking that it continued in force throughout the dynasty. In the third year of the Yongzheng reign (1725), however, a new substatute was added to the code punishing any "illicit sexual intercourse between soldiers or civilians" (*jun min xiang jian*) with 100 blows of the heavy bamboo and a month in the cangue. The title of this law is confusing, because it seems to mean soldiers having sex *with* civilians; in practice, though, it was applied to *all* cases of consensual illicit sex (few of which involved military personnel). From 1725 on, the Ming statute's penalties and its distinction based on marital status were no longer applied (although the husband of an adulteress would still be authorized to sell her). But this change is far from obvious if one reads only the code; one discovers it only by reading central cases of adultery that postdate 1725—and they have to be *central* cases, because local magistrates rarely cited the code when judging routine cases.

What may seem like a trivial change in fact matters quite a bit. Other central cases show that starting in the Yongzheng reign, prostitution was punished in exactly the same way, according to the same substatute—and a new substatute of 1734 extended the same treatment to consensual homosexual sodomy as well. In other words, the Yongzheng judiciary began to interpret prostitution and sodomy as being equivalent or parallel to ordinary adultery (a policy followed until the early twentieth century). This had not been the case before—in fact, the three scenarios had always been seen as fundamentally different—and grasping the new parallel drawn between them is critical to understanding the Yongzheng judicial reforms as a whole. But one cannot make this connection without actual case records that show how these offenses were punished in practice.

This illustration points to a larger problem of interpreting the Qing code. Some of the best work in the field has tended to treat Qing law as a static system, whereas in fact it underwent profound change, especially in the eighteenth century. Such change was especially critical in the regulation of sexuality. Legal case records highlight this dynamism by showing that the substatutes promulgated in the eighteenth century indeed constituted the living law of the dynasty. Philip Huang points out that key operative principles for civil adjudication are usually found in the secondary substatutes (rather than in the statutes themselves), and thus their real importance cannot be determined without evidence of actual magisterial practice. In his view, statutes often embodied timeless moral ideals, whereas substatutes gave the principles to be applied in practice (1996, 104–7).[32] In criminal law, the situation was starker: a new substatute often completely nullified the relevant statute (as well as any earlier substatute on the matter in question). Thus, Xue Yunsheng entitled his critical commentary on the Qing code *Lingering Doubts After Reading the Substatutes*, because it was precisely the substatutes that really mattered.

In sum, legal case records provide the essential means for understanding both judicial practice and the dynamics of late imperial law. They enable us to restore in some measure the practical knowledge that Qing commentators assumed on the part of their readers.

"Ethnographic" Evidence in Legal Cases

Official constructions aside, legal case records from both central and county courts contain a great deal of valuable evidence of an ethnographic nature, making possible a social history of previously invisible aspects of illiterate people's lives. For example, to sentence a murderer accurately, a magistrate had to determine the exact circumstances and motive of the murder; this background information often tells us much more than just which law the magistrate should cite.

Most of the ethnographic evidence in both local and central cases can be found in records of testimony by witnesses at court hearings, including the confessions of convicted criminals. These records are probably as close as we will ever get to the "voice" of the illiterate in late imperial China. But they are usually not verbatim transcriptions of witnesses' utterances; rather, they are summaries of testimony crafted from witnesses' answers to questions posed during interrogation. The answers were strung together in the form of a monologue in the "voice" of the witness—the questions are usually not recorded. These statements were shaped by the priorities of the magistrate, and should not be mistaken for purely spontaneous declarations.

The transcription of witnesses' answers to questions invariably required some measure of translation, since throughout the empire such documents were written in standardized Mandarin vernacular—a somewhat artificial written language based on the northern dialect group *guan hua*. In regions where some form of *guan hua* was spoken, such written records may approximate quite closely the actual words used by witnesses; in southeastern dialect regions, a greater degree of translation would have been necessary.

In the process of transcribing answers and shaping them into monologues, witnesses' statements were edited to some extent, especially in the reports of serious crimes to be forwarded for review. The purpose of this editing was to improve internal consistency, thus enhancing the impression that the truth of the crime had been uncovered. Another related purpose was to put the name of the crime into the mouth of the offender, underscoring the accuracy of the match between the offense confessed and the statute cited. For example, the confessions quoted in this book almost invariably use the legal term "illicit sex" (*jian*) (used as a noun or transitive verb) when referring to illegal acts of sexual intercourse. We do not know whether witnesses actually used this term, but at least some must have said something a bit more colloquial when they testified in court. This term also served as a euphemism: legal secretaries were instructed to avoid "obscene" language and excessive detail when recording testimony on sexual matters. It was enough to establish that the criminal act had been committed and confessed (Karasawa 1992; Zhou Guangyuan 1993).

But it would be a mistake to dismiss such records as falsification or fraud. Rather, they represent what magistrates took to be accurate statements of witnesses' testimony that stressed what was relevant for judicial purposes. Summaries of testimony were read back to witnesses to confirm their accuracy, and legal secretaries' handbooks counseled against recording false statements, warning that they would be exposed during the review process. Indeed, the practical function of the review system was to detect malfeasance and error. Prefects retried serious criminal cases, and the principal offenders (and sometimes witnesses) would accompany a case report as far as the provincial capital, to be reinterrogated at each stage of review. This procedure also guarded against the arbitrary extraction of confessions with torture.[33] If a prisoner recanted upon reinterrogation, his case would be retried by a different lower court, and the discrepancy would have to be explained. If a judgment was found unconvincing, reviewers would return the case for further investigation. Review was a tool of autocratic centralization: the whole point of the review system was to ensure that no bureaucrat or yamen functionary abused his authority or arrogated to himself power beyond his station.[34]

If we are aware of how the judicial process produced these records, it is possible to read them for insight into far more than just the official categories of the law. By keeping in mind the purposes for which a magistrate elicited testimony, we can reread that testimony from different angles, for other purposes.

Chapter 4 illustrates both the difficulty and the value of getting beyond official constructions through this ethnographic evidence. In the representations of same-sex unions found in such records, there is little information about emotional content or variation in sexual practice, because the judicial priority was to prove crimes of sodomy. Hence, the investigative process tended to reduce an entire relationship to particular acts of anal intercourse, without leaving much sense of the deeper meaning of that relationship to its participants. At the same time, however, such records provide persuasive evidence that the judicial construction of phallic penetration derived from more widespread notions of gendered hierarchy that were shared even by the men who participated in such acts.

Historians of early modern Europe like Carlo Ginzburg (1983) and Natalie Davis (1987) have pioneered the creative use of seemingly inconsequential details of legal records to reconstruct popular attitudes. An example of this approach can be found in Chapter 4. In surveying cases of sodomy, I noticed by comparing confessions that the penetrator was invariably older than the partner whom he penetrated. This information was not singled out for specific comment, though, and given my limited sample, I could not be sure whether I had detected a significant pattern or a simple coincidence.

But then I found a case in which the penetrator was *younger* than the man he penetrated—and in this case, the magistrate followed up the latter's confession with specific questions about the relative ages of the sexual partners. (Such follow-up questions were sometimes added to the written report after confessions to satisfy reviewers that apparent inconsistencies had not been missed.) The magistrate did not believe that an older man would allow himself to be penetrated by a younger man. Then it was explained that the older partner had been blackmailed into submitting by threat of public exposure of his "passive" sexual role with a third man, who was older than them both. This explanation satisfied the magistrate.

This interrogation helped the magistrate understand the motive for a homicide in order to determine the appropriate sentence. It helps us understand that hierarchy of age was perceived (by the sexual partners themselves, and by the magistrate and his reviewers) as naturally conforming to a parallel hierarchy of roles in acts of penetration. Only the violation of that congruence required special explanation. The successful blackmail also indicates the powerful stigma associated with being penetrated—it was preferable to submit to a younger man in secret than to have it publicly known that one had been penetrated at all.

This is just one example of how Qing legal cases can be excavated for evidence of popular attitudes and practices separate from purely judicial constructions. One of my priorities in writing this book has been to translate extensive passages from courtroom testimony and judicial summaries, in order to let such material speak for itself as much as possible. Specific research questions aside, I hope to share with readers some of the richly textured, unquantifiable sense of ordinary life that these documents convey.

CHAPTER TWO

A Vision of Sexual Order

Definitions and Boundaries

This chapter sketches a preliminary definition of *jian*, the basic term used for sex offenses in legal codes of the late imperial era. English has no exact equivalent of this word, which one finds used as a noun, a transitive verb, and a modifier. The closest approximations of the noun—"sexual intercourse out of place" or "illicit sexual intercourse"—are both awkward and imprecise. But also, the sexual dimension captures only part of the term's wider range of meaning, just as anxiety about intercourse out of place was only a subset of a more general fear of moral and political disorder.

The framework of sexual orthodoxy throughout the imperial era was an ideology of social control that linked propriety in personal relationships to political order. This linkage lies at the heart of Confucianism, which, like many moral systems, cherishes the hierarchy of the patriarchal family as a natural model for legitimate political authority. The first chapter of the *Analects* tells us: "Those who in private life behave well towards their parents and elder brothers, in public life seldom show a disposition to resist the authority of their superiors. And as for such men starting a revolution, no instance of it has ever occurred" (Waley 1938, 83). As this passage suggests, Confucianism closely identifies the filial piety a son owes his parents and ancestors with the loyalty a subject owes his ruler. Sex, as part of procreation, was always understood to play a central role in filial piety. As Mencius famously commented: "There are three things which are unfilial, and to have no posterity is the greatest of them" (Legge 1970, 313). T'ung-tsu Ch'ü elaborates: "It may be said that the family had to be maintained so that the ancestors could be sacrificed to. Ancestor worship was then the first and last purpose of marriage. It is therefore not difficult to understand why a bachelor or a married man without a son was considered unfilial" (1965, 91). Moreover, subordinating procreation to filial piety implied controlling sexual access to women, in order to keep descent lines clear—and a third link seen as homologous to both filial piety and political loyalty was the sexual chastity a wife owed her husband. The Neo-Confucianism promoted by late imperial dynasties placed heightened emphasis on this third link, and during the High Qing, an extraordinary propaganda campaign politicized female chastity to an unprecedented degree. Women who had made exemplary sacrifices to remain chaste became the objects of imperial propaganda and ritual that explicitly emphasized the parallels between political, filial, and sexual loyalty.

Sexual Disorder and Political Disorder

From an orthodox perspective, then, sexual intercourse out of place implied multiple and complementary levels of disorder. The key words that Chinese jurists and moral philosophers have used since antiquity to characterize sexual offenses all contain a nuance of political danger. For example, *jian* could connote the crime of "illicit sexual intercourse," as well as treachery or betrayal of a political nature—as in the Ming and Qing codes' statutes against "treasonous factions" (*jian dang*) at court. A wife who betrayed her husband was termed a *jian fu* (literally, "wife who has committed illicit sexual intercourse"); a minister who betrayed his sovereign was a *jian chen* ("treasonous minister").

The Han-dynasty dictionary *Shuo wen jie zi* defines *jian* as *si* (Xu Shen 1994, 265). What does *si* mean? In the twentieth century, *si* has come to be used to represent the imported concept of "private," and that is the easiest translation, but the Chinese language traditionally included no term with the positive or even value-neutral connotations of this English word; *si* carries a strongly pejorative connotation, and in most traditional texts, it might be more accurately translated as "illicit," "unauthorized," or "selfish"; it is the opposite of the adjective *gong* (now used for "public"), which refers to all that conforms to common interests and public order. Classical moral discourse held that the proliferation of "private ways" (*si dao*)—idiosyncratic standards of right and wrong that vary from individual to individual—leads to social and political chaos (*luan*).

Therefore, individuals should conform to the "All-Encompassing Way" (*gong dao*) in their personal conduct.

Like *jian*, *si* could have both sexual and political connotations: *si tong*—literally, "illicit intercourse"—could mean either treasonous communication with an enemy or adultery. In legal texts of the late imperial dynasties, *si* often appears in conjunction with *jian*, to stress the illicitness and criminality of that conduct. In the Ming dynasty, for example, some prostitution was legal and even conducted under official auspices; however, it was a criminal offense for commoners "to sell illicit sex privately" (*si zi mai jian*)—that is, without official authorization (see Chapter 6).

Similarly, the term *luan* (often translated as "disorder" or "chaos," and rendered as "revolution" by Arthur Waley in the passage from *Analects* quoted above) implies the perversion of sexual, familial, and political order; it appears in compounds meaning "incest" (e.g., *luan lun*) and "rebellion" (*pan luan*). One of the "Ten Abominations" (*shi e*) enumerated at the beginning of every legal code from the Tang dynasty forward is *nei luan*, literally, "internal disorder." In a legal context, *nei luan* refers to incest, but it can denote rebellion or civil war as well. The director Kurosawa Akira captured this range of nuances in his 1985 film *Ran* (the Japanese pronunciation of *luan*), which is loosely based on *King Lear*. In Kurosawa's vision of *luan*, when sons are set over their father, feudal order falls apart—devolving into a nightmare of fratricide, patricide, incest, betrayal of husband by wife, and finally civil war.[1]

This connection between sexual and political disorder was not just a question of semantics or of Confucian abstraction. Late imperial officials expressly associated improper sexual and gender relations with politically suspect tendencies in popular culture. For example, both Ming and Qing dynasties made repeated efforts to ban the free mixing of men and women at religious gatherings, and to suppress "licentious books" (*yin shu*)—that is, drama and vernacular fiction that were sexually explicit or seemed in other ways disrespectful of traditional mores and authority figures.[2] Nor should we dismiss these suspicions as mere prudishness or paranoia: a basic feature of the millenarian movements that repeatedly challenged the imperial state was some alternative approach to sex and gender relations. This heterodox tradition reached back at least as far as the Yellow Turbans revolt of the second century A.D., whose adherents practiced Daoist sexual disciplines en masse (Van Gulik 1974, 84–90). The late imperial era offers a number of notorious examples. The

White Lotus sects that staged several major uprisings worshiped a female deity and often were led by women; some congregations encouraged free sexual relations among their members (Naquin 1976). In the mid-nineteenth century, the Taiping rebels (whose crusade to found a "Heavenly Kingdom of Great Peace" cost 20 to 30 million lives) banned foot binding, prostitution, and polygyny, divided families into separate military units segregated by sex, forswore all sexual intercourse until final victory, promoted women to leadership roles, and (according to some accounts) opened their heterodox civil service examinations to female candidates. Imperial officials singled out these appalling violations of sexual and gender order for particular censure (Michael 1966; Ono 1989).

Defining a Sexual Offense

But what, precisely, did jurists consider to be a sexual offense? Legal codes from imperial China provide none of the specific taxonomy of bodily positions and erotic gestures familiar from the Western legal tradition. In the West, it has been common for particular sexual acts, such as oral, anal, or intercrural (that is, between the thighs) intercourse, to be prohibited even to married couples (Brundage 1987; Ruggiero 1985). In contrast, the Chinese legal tradition determined the legitimacy of a sexual act primarily by its relational context, not by the particular nature of the act itself.

Late imperial jurists sought the authority of early classical texts for many of their deliberations, including the definition of sex offenses. An important and frequently cited source is the second century B.C. "Great Commentary" (*dazhuan*), attributed to Fu Sheng, on *The Book of Documents*; the relevant passage appears in the chapter about the ancient mutilating punishments, under the punishment *gong*. The exact nature of *gong* depended on the sex of the offender: for men, it meant castration, but for women, it meant to be sequestered in a room and never let out. In his commentary, Fu Sheng explains what crime *gong* was designed to punish, thereby providing the classic definition of a sexual offense: "If a male and female engage in intercourse without morality (*nan nü bu yi yi jiao*), their punishments shall be castration and sequestration [respectively]" (Lau, ed., 1994, 5.22/22/22).[3]

We should note, first of all, that Fu Sheng specifies a heterosexual context: the crime he is talking about took place between a male and a female. (In fact, I know of no clear-cut prohibition of male homosexual acts until the sixteenth century. Such acts were not included in the criminal category *jian* until the Qing dynasty—see Chapter 4.)[4] But how did jurists interpret the phrase "intercourse without morality"?

An important clue is that many later texts paraphrase Fu Sheng by replacing *yi* (morality or righteousness) with *li*. For example, an edict of 348 A.D. mandates that, "If a male and female engage in intercourse without *li*, they shall both be executed" (*nan nü bu yi li jiao, jie si*) (*Wei shu*, 2873). *Li* means rite or ritual—and, by extension, the Confucian concept of the moral norms that should regulate conduct in specific relationships. What was the connection between *yi* (morality) and *li* (ritual) when judging an act of sexual intercourse? The seventh-century classicist Jia Gongyan explains that: "To engage in intercourse *with* morality (*yi yi jiao*) means intercourse between a man and woman who are married according to the six rites of matrimony (*liu li*)" (Jia Gongyan 1966, 36/1a). The "six rites of matrimony" were the basis of a gentleman's marriage—that is, marriage that was legitimate and proper. The basic elements of the six rites (outlined in *The Rites of Zhou*) were negotiating the marriage contract through an intermediary; presenting gifts to the bride's family; comparing the name and birth date of the bride with those of the groom for purposes of divination; choosing an auspicious date for the wedding; notifying the bride's family of that date to secure their approval; and finally transporting the bride to the groom's home to consummate the marriage. With some variation, these remained basic features of the customary procedure for acquiring a wife right down to the twentieth century. Where in the early empire they had defined an aristocratic ideal of legitimate marriage, over the late imperial era they were generalized as part of a more broadly inclusive Confucian family orthodoxy (Gao Chao and Ma Jianshi, eds., 1989, 209).[5]

In short, for heterosexual intercourse to conform to morality, it had to take place within legitimate marriage, sanctioned by the appropriate rites; outside legitimate marriage, it should be considered a crime. This basic principle set down in antiquity was taken for granted in the deliberations of late imperial jurists—and, indeed, the most straightforward definition of the crime *jian* is simply heterosexual intercourse outside marriage. But before the eighteenth century, at least, jurists always understood that there were certain status-based exceptions to this generalization. As we shall see, Qing jurists would eliminate what remained of these status-based exceptions, interpreting the ancient principle more literally and applying it more uniformly than ever before.

In the formative and early imperial eras, the term *yin* ("licentiousness") was often used to denote the crime defined as "intercourse without morality/ritual." For example, the early dictionary *Xiao erya* (which probably dates from the Han dynasty) states: "If a male and a female engage in intercourse without ritual, it is called '*yin*' (*nan nü bu yi li jiao, wei zhi yin*)" (guang yi 4/4a). Some early texts (including Qin and Han statutes) use *jian* to mean offenses of a specifically sexual nature, but this term often carried a broader meaning of depravity, villainy, or criminality. Legal codes from the Tang dynasty on use *jian* in a more exclusive and exact way, to mean illicit sexual intercourse or political treachery. Still, late imperial legal texts sometimes use *yin* as a synonym for the sexual meaning of *jian*, and in Qing dynasty case reports, it is the arousal of *yin xin*, a "licentious heart," that provokes people to commit *jian*. The Qing also banned "licentious songs" (*yin ci*) and "licentious books" (*yin shu*); moreover, classical Confucian discourse warned of the political dangers of "licentious music" (*yin yue*), and one priority of the Yongzheng Emperor's elimination of the debased-status group "music households" was to purge the imperial music establishment of moral taint (see Chapter 7).

Why should extramarital heterosexual intercourse be considered a crime? We find an early explanation in commentaries on the "Annals of Emperor Wen the Filial" (in Sima Qian's second century B.C. *Records of the Grand Historian*). It is said that Emperor Wen, an enlightened sovereign of the Han dynasty, abolished all the ancient mutilating punishments, with the single exception of *gong*. Zhang Fei (a third century A.D. jurist) explains: "Licentiousness (*yin*) makes chaos (*luan*) of the order of other men's lineages (*zu xu*); for this reason, Emperor Wen did not eliminate *gong*." In other words, the essence of the crime that *gong* punished was disruption of the descent order of another man's lineage, resulting in *luan*; this crime constituted a unique threat that even the benign Emperor Wen believed should continue to warrant mutilation (*Shi ji*, 10/29).

To sum up, the early texts cited by late imperial jurists identified three basic elements that defined a sexual offense. First, it was intercourse between male and female. Second, it was intercourse outside legitimate, normative marriage. Third, it represented an assault by an outside male that threatened to disorder another man's lineage—and therefore presented a dangerous threat to social order as a whole. In spite of many changes over time, these three elements would inform all later discussion of the crime of illicit sexual intercourse. For example, when introducing the Tang and Ming dynasties' statutes against that crime, Xue Yunsheng simply quotes Fu Sheng and Zhang Fei, and concludes: "This is what later ages have called the crime of '*jian*'" (TM, 26/14b). A second Qing commentator explains the harm caused by *jian* in similar terms: "A man who engages in illicit sexual intercourse debauches the wife or daughter of another man; he ruins the inner female quarters (*gui men*) of another man's household" (Yao Run et al., eds., 1878, 33/1b commentary). Here, a woman's social identity is defined by her relationship with husband or father, and it is the interests of these men—and by extension, the authority of the state—that were at stake in prohibiting illicit sexual intercourse.

The Prerogatives of Father and Husband

Having outlined the classic elements of "illicit sexual intercourse" (*jian*), we now examine several specific scenarios to see how late imperial jurists defined this crime in practice. Not all of these scenarios constituted crimes or, even if they did, necessarily fell within the category of *jian*. When jurists define a crime, they draw boundaries that identify the licit as much as the illicit; thus it can be useful to look just outside the territory of the crime itself, at acts that are somehow related but remain legal nonetheless. The purpose here is to gain a clearer sense of the interests and authority the late imperial state sought to uphold in prosecuting this crime.

Unfilial Marital Intercourse

Could anything that took place *within* marriage be considered a sex offense, punishable by law? From the previous discussion, it would seem not. But the Tang code declares it a crime for a man to impregnate his wife during the mourning period for his father or mother, punishable by a year of penal servitude (TL, 12/7a). *Collected Statutes of the Yuan* records a case from 1298 in which a battalion commander consummated his new marriage (*cheng qin*) during the mourning period for his father; he was stripped of his post and ordered divorced from his wife, for the crime of "unfilial conduct" (*bu xiao*) (YD, 41/2a).[6] Similarly, the Ming and Qing codes proscribe marrying or taking a concubine during mourning, and they mandate extra penalties for offenses of illicit sex if committed during mourning (DC, 105-00, 372-00). Some Ming commentators also urge punishment for unfilial timing of marital intercourse (although the Ming and Qing codes contain no such law). For example, the sixteenth-century jurist Wang Kentang suggests that begetting a child during mourning for parents should be punished with a beating, in application of the statute against "doing inappropriate things" (TM, 26/24a).

A contemporary of Wang Kentang's goes further, urging that the Tang code's heavier penalty be revived. None of the texts cited above classify the unfilial timing of conjugal relations as "illicit sexual intercourse" (*jian*). But this commentator proposes an apparent paradox: "A husband who commits *jian* with his wife is guilty of a crime." How could anything between husband and wife possibly constitute *jian*?

The definition of *jian* is marriage without ritual (*hun bu yi li*), and that is precisely the way to characterize the situation when a wife conceives during the mourning period for her husband's father or mother. It is by forgetting his parents to indulge in licentiousness (*yin*) that her husband has made her conceive; he should receive 60 blows of the heavy bamboo and a year of penal servitude. Therefore, it can be said that "a husband who commits *jian* with his wife is guilty of a crime."   (XF, ming li fu juan/12b–13a)

In the phrase "marriage without ritual," we hear echoes of Fu Sheng and Jia Gongyan. This commentator's use of the criminal term *jian* may be ironic, but his point is that the basis of sexual relations should be *li*, rather than desire—and he means *li* not simply as legalistic formality, but as the moral standards that govern human relations. In the Confucian family scheme, the paramount *li* is filial piety, which should govern even the sexual relations of husband and wife, especially since the ostensible purpose of such relations was to secure patrilineal descent and continue the ancestors' incense fire. When filial piety was sacrificed to licentiousness, then even the sexual relations of husband and wife might be considered immoral and criminal. It was subordination to Confucian morality, not just the external forms of ritual, that rendered sexual relations legitimate.[7]

Perhaps the best illustration of this thinking in Ming and Qing law is the question of sexual relations between a betrothed couple prior to the approved date for their wedding. A Ming "statute applied by analogy"[8] that continued in force during the Qing provides: "If a male and female are betrothed but have not yet been married, and they privately engage in illicit sexual intercourse (*si xia tong jian*), then they shall receive 100 blows of the heavy bamboo by analogy to the statute against 'a son or grandson violating [a parent or grandparent's] instructions'" (Huang Zhangjian, ed., 1979, 1042; DC, 5/1311). Here, the premature intercourse is defined as *jian* not simply because it takes place outside marriage, but because it defies the authority of the couple's parents, on whose approval the legitimacy of the marriage depends.

A complementary example comes from the imperial chastity cult of the Qing dynasty. In 1742, an adopted daughter-in-law[9] was canonized as a chastity martyr: her betrothed had tried to consummate their union prematurely, and she died fighting off his advances. Since the groom's parents had not yet approved, such premature union lay outside the strict bounds of female chastity: the canonization edict praises the "self-discipline in accordance with ritual" (*yi li zi chi*) the girl demonstrated in rejecting "her husband's attempt at private illicit intercourse" (*fu zhi si jian*). This language resonates with the classical references that informed late imperial treatment of sex offenses, affirming the principle that what legitimized sexual intercourse was "ritual" (*li*), namely filial deference to parental authority; such deference even took priority over a bride's submission to her future husband (QHS, 403/508).

Forcible Intercourse Within Lawful Marriage

Ideally, then, even the conjugal bed was supposed to be ruled by an internalized Confucian morality. If so, what was the legal standing of a husband who used coercion to engage in intercourse with his own wife, against her will? Did such coercion count as a violation of the morality (*yi*) or ritual norms (*li*) that classically defined legitimate sexual relations?

In fact, imperial law did not punish husbands who coerced their wives—just as Western legal systems have not done so until very recently. A brief comparison with the "marital exemption" in Western rape law may help clarify what was distinctive about the Chinese variant of this more general pattern. Since ancient Rome, the Western legal tradition has held the "free consent" of both bride and groom to be an essential prerequisite for legitimate marriage. This basic doctrine was much strengthened by the church courts of medieval Europe, which defined marriage as a sacrament freely undertaken by two equal souls before God. Even private verbal promises might constitute valid and binding contracts of marriage, regardless of parental dismay. In this way, the canon law of marriage established the "free consent" of contracting parties as the *sine qua non* of modern contract law (Berman 1983, 226–30; Brundage 1987; Ingram 1987).

Ironically, the doctrine of a woman's right to withhold consent *to marry* underlay what became known as the "marital exemption" in Western rape law. According to canon law, a woman's consent to marry had to be given freely, but once given, could not be retracted. Moreover, once bound to each other, husband and wife owed each other a "marital debt" of sexual service that neither could refuse to honor. In theory, this debt bound both partners equally, but one finds no learned discourse about why a wife could not be prosecuted for raping her husband. Rather, until recently Western jurists consistently held it to be impossible for a husband to "rape" his wife because it was impossible for her to withdraw the consent she had freely given when they married. A wife's legal status *vis-à-vis* her husband rendered her incapable of the "nonconsent" that defined rape (Brundage 1987; Temkin 1986).

Imperial Chinese law achieved much the same practical result, but on a very different ideological basis. In law and in custom, the contracting parties to a marriage were the fathers (or appropriate patriarchal stand-ins) of the bride and groom; there was no formal requirement to consult the couple's wishes at all. The difference between Chinese and Western traditions has found expression in their respective marriage rites: since Roman times, it has been customary practice in the West for couples to exchange vows in public (Brundage 1987, 88); in contrast, the typical Chinese practice involved transporting a bride to her new husband's home, where the couple would bow silently before his family's ancestral altar. In China, marriage rites symbolized not the free will of individual souls exercised before an omniscient God, but rather the submission of maturing children to family roles and filial duty. Hence, there was no need for Chinese legal theorists to pretend that a wife's consent played any role in legitimizing sexual intercourse within marriage. In fact, a woman's "consent" (*he*) bore legal relevance exclusively as a form of crime: "consensual illicit sex" (*he jian*). No Chinese jurist seems to have felt compelled to ponder the concept of "marital rape," even as a theoretical absurdity to be explained away.

A case from Mayi County, Shanxi, memorialized in 1747 illustrates the legal irrelevance of the coercion of a wife by her lawful husband. A peasant girl named Wang Shi (thirteen *sui*) had been married to Ren Tianfu, the son of Ren Shun. According to the judicial

summary of the case, "every night Wang Shi went to bed wearing
her clothes." One night, after four months of this, "Ren Tianfu
wanted to make Wang Shi take off her clothes and go to bed, but she
did not obey. Angered, Ren Tianfu beat her with a piece of firewood,
injuring her left arm, left shin, left wrist, the left side of her groin,
etc." The next day, the girl's mother, Huang Shi, came to fetch her
for an opera performance being held in her home village. No one
else was home at the Ren household when she arrived. Seeing that
her daughter looked upset, Huang Shi asked what was wrong. Then,
"Hearing what had happened, she took Wang Shi back to her own
house; because her groin had been beaten, Wang Shi had difficulty
walking. . . . When they arrived home, Huang Shi took off Wang
Shi's clothing, and seeing her daughter's many injuries, she became
incensed, and wanted to beat Tianfu in order to vent her anger." She
took the girl and her nephew, Wang Chang, back to the Ren house.
A fight broke out between the two families, and Wang Chang beat
Ren Shun to death.

For purposes of law, this was a homicide case, and Wang Chang
was sentenced to strangulation after the assizes for "homicide in a
fight." Huang Shi had not participated in the killing, the magistrate
decided, but her behavior had still been inappropriate, because
"telling her nephew to accompany her, she went and started the
quarrel." Therefore, she was sentenced to 80 blows of the heavy
bamboo according to the statute on "doing inappropriate things; severe cases."[10] As for her son-in-law, "the injuries Wang Shi received
when Ren Tianfu beat her involved no broken bones or teeth, so according to the statute [on wife-beating], he is not liable for punishment." Nor was he held liable for fighting with Huang Shi. Her
daughter, Wang Shi, could be treated leniently, since "she is young
and, besides, has been beaten and injured."

The term *jian* never appears in this case record, let alone the legal
term for rape, *qiang jian* (literally, "coerced illicit sexual intercourse"). Because the marriage of Wang Shi and Ren Tianfu was legitimate, having been approved by the fathers on both sides (this
point is made clear at the beginning of the judicial summary), "illicit sexual intercourse" was not at issue. The experiences of the girl
were reported simply to explain the background to the homicide.
Ren's actions lay well within a husband's legal prerogatives with regard to his wife. On the contrary, it was Wang Shi's defiance that
was objectionable, since it had provoked her mother's involvement
and, indirectly, the homicide (MQ, 150-106).

Nevertheless, there was a limit to how violently a husband could handle his wife with impunity, even if she defied him. As this memorial implies, a husband was authorized to beat his wife, but only so long as he inflicted no "breaking injury" (*zhe shang*—i.e., broken bones or teeth, or worse). If a husband *killed* his wife, then under most circumstances, his initial sentence would be strangulation, subject to review at the Autumn Assizes. At this annual review, most death penalty convictions were reconsidered and mitigating circumstances weighed with a view toward delaying or commuting execution to a less severe penalty (usually some degree of exile). The Qing dynasty's rules for the Autumn Assizes mandated that if a husband had killed a wife who had been "defiant" (*bu shun*) or "unfilial" (*bu xiao*), then his death sentence would be radically commuted.[11] "Defiance" certainly included refusing intercourse, but even this sort of defiance did not justify wanton sadism. A reprieve was justified only when the husband's violence somehow accorded with the normative basis of marriage.

In 1784, the Qianlong Emperor addressed this question by contrasting two husbands whose convictions for "intentionally killing" (*gu sha*) their wives were under review at the Autumn Assizes. In the first case, Chen Minggui's wife Lin Shi had resented his poverty, had argued with his mother, and had repeatedly expressed her desire to leave him. When Chen scolded her, she insulted and cursed his mother—so he strangled her. In the emperor's view,

The law truly cannot tolerate such a perverse, rebellious, and immoral woman. . . . Chen Minggui's killing of his wife was truly caused by her own unfilial rebelliousness, and is different from a cruel "intentional killing." The basic purpose of taking a wife is to care for one's parents, and the purpose of enlightened punishment is to assist in moral instruction. . . . [Therefore,] We shall *not* approve Chen Minggui's execution.

In the second case, after Wang Tianfu's wife, Yu Shi, had refused sexual intercourse, not only did he beat and kick her, but he used a fire tongs to burn her genitals with such savagery that she died soon after.

This criminal was already in his thirties, but Yu Shi was only seventeen *sui*. Just because she refused to go to bed with him, he was filled with murderous purpose, and he both beat and burned her—this was extreme cruelty indeed! [Wang Tianfu] should be slated for execution, and We *shall* approve the sentence, so as to admonish the violent and cruel.

The emperor concluded by noting that "one crime was motivated by righteous anger (*yi fen*), and the other by licentious cruelty (*yin xiong*). The differences must be weighed and each case judged accordingly."

The contrast drawn by the emperor is critical. The wife in the first case should herself be considered a criminal because she had grievously flouted the moral norms that govern marriage, especially filial piety; thus, her husband was perfectly justified in becoming angry and violent (although killing her was going too far). The emperor characterized his anger as "righteous" or "moral" (*yi*), the same quality that defined legitimate sexual intercourse. But in the second case, the husband's only motive had been licentiousness, an unacceptable guide to marital relations. True, Yu Shi had refused intercourse, but no other defiant behavior is mentioned (had there been any, it would be listed in detail); however, it appears that this episode took place on the couple's wedding night, so her refusal might be attributed more to chaste modesty than to perverse defiance. This mature man should have chastised his young bride with restraint, to teach her her proper role ("moral instruction"); instead, he tortured her to death. But notice that the emperor's indignation has nothing to do with any violation of the woman's own will or consent. Rather, it is the extreme disproportion between the wife's transgression and the husband's violence that provokes his ire (Gang Yi 1889, 1/51a–b).

A sense of moral proportion mattered greatly to judgments of wife-killing. For example, Ming and Qing law provided that if a husband caught his wife in the act of adultery, he could kill her (and her partner) with complete impunity (if he acted at once). In other words, to kill one's wife was not necessarily wrong, as long as a husband acted out of "righteous anger" against a wife who had threatened the basic integrity of his household and lineage.[12] This was one of the very few situations in which anyone other than the emperor himself was legally authorized to take life. It recalls the tradition that when Emperor Wen of the Han dynasty abolished the dreadful mutilating punishments, he made a unique exception to retain *gong*, because he believed it necessary to deter licentious people from disordering other men's lineages.

To sum up, a wife's consent was not a prerequisite for legitimate intercourse. In fact, the norms governing marriage required submission from a wife, just as they required moral guidance from a husband. Therefore, if a husband forced his wife, that act did not fall within the purview of "illicit sexual intercourse." Nevertheless, marital relations, including both sex and violence, were properly governed not by lust or other egocentric impulses but rather by deference to one's place in a larger familial order. A husband might employ violence only to a degree consistent with enforcing that order.

Marriage by Abduction: "Consummation" or "Illicit Sexual Intercourse"?

Usually, marital context was clear, so there was little question whether sexual intercourse, if it occurred, was "illicit." But what if the marital context itself were in dispute, and a man claimed he had legitimately married a woman whom he had forced to engage in sexual intercourse?

A case from Lu Department, Sichuan, memorialized in 1740 illustrates the problem. Wu Ying claimed that his daughter Wu Danü (fifteen *sui*) had been abducted by a large gang of men and "raped" by their leader, Yang Denggao (Wu's petition uses the legal term for the crime, "coerced illicit sexual intercourse"). In a countersuit, Yang insisted that Wu Danü was his legitimate wife. Therefore, the magistrate's investigation concentrated on clarifying not whether Yang had engaged in sexual intercourse with Wu Danü—that was not in dispute—or whether he had used coercion to do so, but instead whether he had established a legitimate claim to her prior to that act.

Investigation revealed that Yang had asked Ma Xizuo, the father-in-law of Wu Ying, to act as go-between to find him a wife. Ma, in turn, had asked Liu Shixue to arrange for a relative's daughter to marry Yang. Liu had received from Yang—via Ma Xizuo and Wu Ying—ten taels of silver for the "bride-price." Liu then spent the money and absconded, and it turned out that the woman's own father had never agreed to the marriage in the first place. Yang tried to recover his money from Liu's father, with no luck, but finally Wu Ying guaranteed that he would be repaid.

But three years went by, and Yang still had neither money nor wife. As Yang described in his confession, his uncle told him: "Wu Ying himself has a daughter about the right age. Now, if you spread it around that the woman agreed upon was his daughter, then you can wait until he sues you, bribe several people to be firm witnesses, and engage him in litigation. You needn't fear—in the end, he'll give you his daughter." Yang tried spreading the rumors, but Wu ignored him. "So I talked it over with my uncle, and he told me to go kidnap Wu Ying's daughter." Yang agreed. To gain accomplices, he held a drinking party for fifteen friends; he told them that "my marriage was paid for and all settled, but the woman's family wouldn't let me take her in marriage, and I asked them to go help me fetch her home."

The men agreed, and they accompanied him with a sedan chair on a predawn raid on Wu Ying's home. Wu was away in Chengdu on business; only the girl and her mother were at home. Wu Danü later testified:

It was still dark, and I had just gotten up. Yang Denggao grabbed me and carried me out of the house, tied me to a sedan chair, and carried me to his house. There, two women took hold of me and made me go through the wedding ritual of bowing before the ancestral altar with Yang Denggao. Then they shut me up in a room. That night, I was raped (*qiang jian*) by Yang Denggao.

At a second hearing, she elaborated: "That night, Yang Denggao pulled and tore my clothing, and used coercion to consummate illicit sex with me (*qiang bi cheng jian*). During the daytime, they always kept me locked inside the room."

In these passages, Wu Danü used vocabulary that fit the legal definition of rape (it is possible that her testimony was edited slightly to improve the internal consistency of the written case report). But even in his final confession, Yang Denggao used very different language to describe what happened. He admitted having abducted the girl by force, but then, after they got back to his house: "My grandmother Hu Shi and my sister-in-law Wen Shi took hold of Danü and had [us] go through the wedding ritual of bowing before the ancestral altar; that night we consummated the marriage (*cheng qin*)."

The magistrate, however, found that Yang had no legal claim to Wu Danü, despite his efforts to approximate the rituals of legitimate marriage (the procession with the bride in a sedan chair, bowing before the ancestral altar . . .). It appears Yang had hoped that by presenting the Wu family with a *fait accompli*, he would pre-empt any legal action on their part; he seems to have assumed that Wu Ying would prefer to accept the "marriage" rather than go through all the public humiliation and aggravation of having him prosecuted for abduction and rape.

Yang ended up being sentenced to strangulation after the assizes under the statute on "coercively seizing (*qiang duo*) a wife or daughter of good family and using her for illicit sex as a wife or concubine (*jian zhan wei qi qie*)"; the penalty was the same as that mandated for rape, and was upheld by imperial rescript. The language of the statute is telling. It uses the legal term "coercion" to underscore the illegitimacy of the offender's *acquisition* of the woman: she had not been taken in legitimate marriage, which required her father's approval. The point is reinforced by the term "illicit sex," which signifies how the offender has used the woman, *as if* she were his wife or concubine (XT, 68/QL 5.10.27).

The focus of legal concern in this case was the marital context, and that is how "coercion" was relevant. In the medieval canon law of Europe, the judgment of analogous cases hinged on whether the *woman*'s consent to marry had been freely given prior to intercourse (Brundage 1987, 470–71). In China, the salient question was whether the woman's father had agreed to a legally binding marriage contract: it was *his* consent that empowered the husband. In both legal traditions, however, the legitimacy of the marriage determined the legitimacy of the sexual intercourse. The woman's own experience of the sexual act in itself held no legal relevance.

Sexual Relations Between Masters and Servile Women

Can we conclude that all intercourse outside legal marriage was punishable as a sexual offense? There were two important status-based exceptions. One was intercourse with debased-status prostitutes, which we shall address at length in Chapter 6. Here, let us examine the legal standing of sexual relations between a master and his female servants and slaves.

Two legal principles applied to such relations, involving the two kinds of particularism identified by T'ung-tsu Ch'ü (1965) as definitive of traditional Chinese law. The first is legal status difference: any free commoner (*liang min*) possessed legal status superior to slaves and other persons of mean or debased (*jian*) status.[13] The second principle is hierarchy within the household: relations between master and servant or slave were treated as an extension of family-based particularism. Imperial law privileged any head of household *vis-à-vis* the subordinate members of his household (for example, a husband or father compared with his wife or children). If the subordinate member of household happened to be a slave, servant, or long-term hired laborer—so that the two axes of hierarchy coincided—then his or her legal subordination was all the greater.

Jurists assumed that any act of sexual intercourse implied hierarchy and domination, the fundamental paradigm being gender hierarchy (with the male penetrating and thereby subordinating the female). Therefore, legal codes consistently mandated increased penalties for acts of illicit sex in which a male slave (etc.) crossed status lines *upward* with a female of his master's own family; examples of such weighted penalties survive from as early as the third century B.C. (Zhang Jinfan et al. 1992, 424). Such punishments were significantly harsher than those mandated for offenses between unrelated persons of the same legal status. Codes from the Tang dynasty through the Qing mandated death even for consensual acts, if the woman in question were the wife, daughter, concubine, or other first-degree relative of the head of household (e.g., DC, 37-00, -01, -02, -03; 373-00). Such acts contradicted status hierarchy by setting up an opposing hierarchy of penetration, so that sexual and gender domination moved against the "current" of status domination.

The Master's Privilege

What if the master crossed status lines downward? For many centuries, something like the marital exemption operated to protect his sexual privileges.[14] But the legal conceptualization of sexual relations between masters and servile domestic women did change over time.

The Tang code prescribed penalties for engaging in "illicit sexual intercourse" with female slaves only if they belonged to someone else; this criminal term was not used to refer to relations between a master and *his own* slaves: "If [a commoner male] commits illicit sex with a government or privately owned domestic female slave (*bi*), the penalty shall be 90 blows of the heavy bamboo. . . . Whoever engages in illicit intercourse with the wife of someone else's *bu qu*, or with a wife or daughter of *za hu* or *guan hu* status, shall be sentenced to 100 blows of the heavy bamboo."[15] These penalties are considerably lighter than the one and a half years of penal servitude prescribed for consensual illicit intercourse with a status equal. According to the official commentary on the Tang code, "it is obvious from this language that there is no penalty if it is the wife of a *bu qu* in one's own household" (TL, 26/15a–b). In addition, Xue Yunsheng notes that the absence of any mention of domestic female slaves (*bi*)[16] of one's own household in either the statute or the official commentary shows that it would never have occurred to a Tang-dynasty jurist to apply the laws against "illicit sexual intercourse" to a master's use of his own slaves (DC, 370-01, commentary). Indeed, Tang statutes refer to sexual relations between masters and their domestic slave girls with the very positive-sounding verb "to favor" (*xing*). For example, one statute specifies that "whoever engages in illicit intercourse (*jian*) with a female slave who has been sexually favored (*xing*) by his father or grandfather shall receive a penalty reduced by two degrees."[17] The contrast between *jian* and *xing* in this sentence highlights the illegitimacy of the former and the legitimacy of the latter.

Evidence of Change in Legal Thinking

We can detect a subtle change in legal discourse between the Tang and Yuan dynasties. *Collected Statutes of the Yuan* states that "it would be inappropriate to sentence" to any punishment "masters who engage in illicit sexual intercourse with the wives of their slaves" (YD, 45/1b). The difference from Tang law is that here such sexual relations are termed "illicit sexual intercourse," even as they are exempted from penalty. Yuan law did specify that if the daughter of a slave (*nu*) had been betrothed to a commoner, then she herself should be considered a commoner; thus, her father's master was prohibited from "bullying her into engaging in illicit sexual intercourse" (*qi jian*), and he would be liable for 107 blows of the heavy bamboo, which was the ordinary penalty for a commoner who raped an unmarried commoner female (*Yuan shi*, 2655). Of course, this measure implies that a slave's daughter who was *not* betrothed to a commoner remained fair game for her master, and that "bullying" her into intercourse would not count as rape. As in Tang law, there is no mention of sex with a master's own domestic female slaves (*bi*). However, Yuan law did prohibit masters from forcing their female slaves to work as prostitutes, and any abused in this way were to be "freed to become commoners" (*fang cong liang*). Thus, while the chastity of free commoner women did not apply to female slaves, they were to be sexually available only to their own masters, and could not be forced into the "parallel" debased-status category of hereditary sex workers (TM, 26/25a).

The Ming code makes no mention of "illicit sexual intercourse" between masters and their female slaves or servants; again, according to Xue Yunsheng, "probably the reason it is not mentioned is that there is no crime to be judged" (DC, 370-01, commentary). The sixteenth-century jurist Lei Menglin offers a more detailed explanation:

Probably, the reason why the statute does not mention a head of household engaging in "illicit intercourse" with the wife of his slave or worker-serf (*gugongren*) is that a head of household's status *vis-à-vis* his slaves and worker-serfs is not based on the moral principles that define human relations (*ben wu lun li*); they serve him solely on the basis of difference between free commoner (*liang*) and debased (*jian*), and between superior (*zun*) and inferior (*bei*).

In other words, illicit sexual intercourse was a violation of "moral principles" that constituted the normative basis of relations between free commoners, but the term did not apply to a master's relations with the debased, servile labor of his household. Indeed, Lei Menglin is quite explicit in pointing out that servile status disqualified female domestic slaves (*bi*) from having any chastity that could be recognized by law: "As far as domestic slave girls are concerned, they are persons who must serve the head of their household; they are ruled by this circumstance, and must submit, regardless of their own wishes. Therefore, the code prescribes no penalty [for masters who engage in intercourse with them]."

Nevertheless, Lei Menglin expresses considerable contempt for a head of household who would stoop to such behavior: "If a head of household engages in illicit intercourse with the wife of his slave or worker-serf (*gugongren*), then as a superior he makes himself inferior (*jiang er zi bei*), and as a commoner he debases himself (*jiang er zi jian*); with such behavior, he does considerable insult to his own person." Here, Lei Menglin's contempt stems not from the violation of the women's chastity or of their husbands' prerogatives, but from the master's unseemly lack of self-control. He is sufficiently disgusted to propose that such sexual relations be punished: "In either case [i.e., intercourse with married servile women or with *bi*], it would be appropriate to sentence [the master] to a beating under the statute against 'doing inappropriate things'" (cited in DC, 370-01, commentary). Lei Menglin's disapproval contrasts strongly with the Tang code and its official commentary, which express no ambivalence whatsoever about the prerogatives of status hierarchy.

Curtailment of Masters' Sexual Privileges in the Qing

Qing lawmakers may have been influenced by Lei Menglin's commentary. At the very beginning of the dynasty, the Board of Punishment ordered that "anyone who engages in illicit sex with a married servant woman (*you fu zhi pu fu*) shall receive a whipping of 27 blows" (QHS, 825/994). After a number of modifications, this policy evolved into the following substatute, added to the code in 1725:

If a head of household engages in illicit sex with a married woman subordinate to his household (*jia xia you fu zhi fu*), then he shall receive 40 blows of the light bamboo [in accordance with the statute against "doing inappropriate things: petty cases"]; but if he is an official, then instead his case shall be referred to the Board [of Personnel] for deliberation of administrative sanctions. (DC, 370-01; QHS, 825/993–94)

In an exception to the standard pattern for measures against illicit sex, this substatute makes no distinction between "consent" and "coercion"—tacit admission, perhaps, that the distinction carried little meaning, given the power relations involved in this scenario. Moreover, the lightness of the penalty, one of the lightest in the Qing code, makes it clear that this sort of sexual offense was considered far less serious than one that occurred between status equals, let alone one that crossed status lines upward (the penalty for rape of a status equal being strangulation). Nevertheless, this Qing measure must be considered a major departure from statutory tradition, which from Tang through Ming had explicitly exempted such sexual relations from any punishment at all.

This law applied only to *married* women. The same was true of a separate substatute promulgated in 1738:

If a head of household indecently seizes and occupies (*wang xing zhan duo*) the wife of his slave or servant (*nu pu zhi qi*), or seeks to engage in illicit sexual intercourse with her and fails, and for either reason cruelly beats the slave or servant, or kills his wife, and if clear and definite proof is established, and the head of household himself admits his crime, then regardless of whether he is a commoner or an official, he shall be deported to Heilongjiang to serve as a runner.   (QHS, 810/845)[18]

The implication of these measures is that even a husband of servile status should enjoy at least a token sexual monopoly over his own wife.

Should we assume, however, that *unmarried* women of servile status continued to be fair game? The legal standing of female domestic slaves in the Qing dynasty is somewhat ambiguous. Certainly, they continued to be sexually available to their masters; however, in Qing law, a *bi* who had been sexually intimate with her master was no longer considered an ordinary slave but rather a sort of secondary spouse, regardless of whether he himself recognized her as such. This had been the case back during the Tang dynasty only in the extremely limited sense of the incest taboo, which rendered such a slave off-limits to her master's male relatives. Tang law is very clear about the fixed status of these slaves. In general, a master was even prohibited from formally elevating his *bi* to the status of concubine (*qie*). If a *bi* had been "favored" by her master and bore him a child, then "he may be allowed to take her as his concubine." But even bearing a child did not entail any *automatic* change in her status. It simply gave her master the legal option of promoting her if he chose to do so, and this move had to be preceded by the woman's formal emancipation from slavery (TL, 12/14a).

By the Qing dynasty, however, the legal position of a *bi* who slept with her master appears to have changed, as a central case from 1655 illustrates. A Manchu banner officer stationed in Nanjing had acquired a Han Chinese *bi* while campaigning in Fujian. When she learned that her master already had a wife, she became intensely jealous and used black magic to make the other woman ill and to try to make her master prefer her instead. But he discovered what she had done and turned her over to the authorities for punishment, saying that he did not want her anymore. In Qing law, using black magic to harm someone was punished by analogy to the statute against "planned murder";[19] the initial judgment was that as a slave who had attempted to harm her master's wife, she should be beheaded. But when the Three High Courts of Judicature reviewed the case, they commuted her sentence to a beating and exile. They reasoned that "since this woman has obviously already been intimate (*qin hou*) with her master, she cannot be sentenced as a slave"; instead, she should be sentenced under the statute against "planned murder of a senior family member within the mourning system of fifth or closer degree [excluding the first and second degrees]" (DC, 284-00). In other words, by sleeping with her, this *bi*'s master had *automatically* promoted her to legal membership in his family, whether he recognized it or not. What sort of family member did she become? Not quite a concubine, since a concubine's relation to her husband's main wife fell within the second degree of mourning (so a concubine who attempted the planned murder of a main wife would suffer death).[20] Despite this ambiguity, the ruling suggests that to Qing jurists, sexual intercourse with a female domestic slave amounted to the consummation of some sort of secondary spousal relationship (XT, 1007/SZ 12.4.13).

Another Qing innovation is found in a substatute of 1735 that imposed a new responsibility on the masters of domestic female slaves:

Among degree-holding or commoner households, if any [head of household] fails to arrange a marriage (*bu xing hun jia*) for his female domestic slave (*bi nü*), so that she ends up alone, then he shall be sentenced to 80 blows of the heavy bamboo, according to the statute against "doing inappropriate things: severe cases." If he is a commoner, the beating shall be carried out, but if he is a degree holder, then he shall be allowed to redeem the beating with a cash fine, as provided by statute. He shall be ordered to arrange her marriage. (DC, 117-01)

This law was definitely enforced, at least when violations came to the attention of central courts. For example, in a central case from Guizhu County, Guizhou, memorialized in 1738, a head of household was punished for failing to arrange a marriage for one of his female domestic slaves (she was twenty-five *sui*). This woman had engaged in illicit sexual relations with two different men, one of whom became jealous and murdered the other. The presiding magistrate and his superiors held her master indirectly responsible for these crimes, on the assumption that a timely marriage would have prevented her adultery and the consequent murder (XT, 155/QL 3.3.27).

By the end of the Yongzheng reign, then, Qing law required a head of household to arrange marriages for his female domestic slaves when they reached maturity, and he was forbidden from sexual intercourse with any married women subordinate to his household. In addition, if he slept with his unmarried slave himself, she would automatically become a member of his family, a sort of secondary concubine, at least for legal purposes. Taken together, these Qing rulings imply that a master should abstain from sexual relations with his *bi*, and arrange her proper marriage to another man, unless he intended to marry her himself. In this way, the imperative that every woman be a wife was extended further than ever before.

Moreover, in the eighteenth century, when the imperial chastity cult was dramatically expanded to include women of humble background, *bi*, "wives of servants" (*pu fu*), and wives of "worker-serfs" (*gugongren*) were all made eligible for honors as chastity heroines (if they met evidential requirements). A payment would be granted to finance a memorial arch for the woman; however, no tablet would be erected for sacrifices in the local temple of chastity and filial piety (erection of a tablet was standard in ordinary cases). This exclusion from the temple preserved the sense that these women were somehow tainted by inferior status (concubines, in contrast, would receive full honors). Nevertheless, the fact that servile women were honored under any circumstances suggests that they were being credited with something like a *liang* standard of wifely chastity (QHS, 403/508, 513–16).[21]

This conclusion is reinforced by a central case from Longxi County, Fujian, memorialized in 1748, in which a *bi* named Chunmei (eleven *sui*) was raped by a neighbor of her master's.[22] At trial, her master presented the girl's contract of sale (*mai qi*) in order to prove her age[23] and Chunmei referred to herself in testimony as "this humble *bi*" (*xiao bi*), instead of the terms typically used by commoner girls in this context (e.g., "this humble daughter," *xiao nüzi*). The key point here is that Chunmei's *bi* status in no way mitigated the penalty of her rapist, who was sentenced to strangulation under the same statute that applied to the rape of an ordinary commoner (MQ, 154-19).

Now there was an old Ming statute still on the books against "illicit intercourse between commoners and mean persons" (*liang jian xiang jian*). It provided that "if a commoner engages in illicit intercourse with another man's *bi*, then the penalty shall be reduced one degree [from that applied for intercourse with another commoner]." In 1740, however, this statute had been amended with the following interlinear commentary: "but if *coercion* is used, then the ordinary statute should apply, and the rapist should be sentenced to strangulation after the assizes" (QHS, 825/994). In other words, the rape of another man's *bi* would now be punished with the same severity as the rape of a commoner wife, implying that a single standard of chastity applied to both categories of women.

Hierarchy between masters and servants remained a matter of basic importance in the daily life of the Qing elite, and it may be that in practice a master's privileges underwent little erosion, regardless of change on the level of formal law. A 1738 case from Zhili reinforces this note of caution. Late one night, a wealthy man named Huang Xuan ordered Lu Shi, the wife of one of his male servants, to wait on him in his room while he drank wine. After some time, he grabbed her and tried to rape her, but she resisted. "Struggling, the two fell to the floor. Huang forced himself on top of Lu Shi, and she screamed. The whole household was alarmed, and assuming there was a thief, [the servants] took up weapons and came running to the scene." Lu Shi's brother-in-law, Zhao Long, arrived first. Entering the room, he saw his master grappling with his sister-in-law on the floor. "He was immediately filled with shame and anger, so he struck Huang Xuan on the head once with a staff. Then his father, Zhao Ru, shouted for him to stop, so he did." Huang recovered from the injury; nevertheless, he pressed charges against Zhao Long, who was sentenced to immediate beheading according to the statute on "a servant striking his master."

Upon review, however, Zhao Long's penalty was commuted to beheading after the assizes, which left open the possibility of a reprieve; the reason was that the reviewers found his motivation to be understandable, even if they could not completely excuse his effrontery in striking his master's head with a weapon. Then, when the case came up for review at the assizes, the Qianlong Emperor spared Zhao Long, and ordered his sentence *further* reduced, expressing sympathy for his attempt to rescue his sister-in-law. But the Board of Punishment remonstrated: "Even though Zhao Long saw his own sister-in-law being raped (*qiang jian*) by their master, and struck him in anger only once, this is a case of a servant striking his master, and involves the principle of status difference; therefore, the sentence should [at most] be postponed [rather than immediately commuted]." Zhao Long probably ended up with a sentence of exile rather than execution.[24] It appears that Huang Xuan was not charged with any offense (even though the board's memorial characterizes his sexual advance as "rape" and the woman he attacked was married), probably because the rape attempt did not succeed (cited in Wei Qingyuan et al., 1982, 133–34).

One is tempted to conclude that when push came to shove, the state backed the privileges of the ruling class. Nevertheless, from a longer historical perspective the remarkable feature of this case is the degree to which senior jurists (including the Qianlong Emperor himself) seem to have agonized over how to balance the servant's righteous defense of his sister-in-law's chastity—of which they approved—against the age-old principle of protecting a master's status and authority in his own household. The fact that Huang Xuan pressed charges shows how sure he felt of his privileges. But the official response shows how much judicial thinking had changed since the Tang dynasty, when it would have been unimaginable for an emperor to express concern about the chastity of a servant.

To summarize, the Tang code simply assumed that a master's sexual access to the servile women of his own household was a normal privilege of his position; such relations did not fall within the purview of "illicit sexual intercourse," even for purposes of nomination. But over time, the legal standing of such sexual relations changed: by the Ming, it had become a gray area, with the formal law prescribing no penalties, but an influential jurist like Lei Menglin advocating punishment all the same. Qing-dynasty lawmakers began by criminalizing sexual relations with servile women who were married, and later mandated that masters arrange marriages for all who were *unmarried*. They further held that a master's sexual relations with *bi* implied the consummation of a quasi-spousal relationship; although her exact status remained vague, she no longer counted as a slave outside the family. In addition, rape law and canonization in the eighteenth century credited *bi* with a standard of chastity that approached that of commoner wives.

Taken as a whole, the clear trend in late imperial law was to extend the free-commoner norms of marriage and family (especially female chastity) to include servile women, thereby narrowing and finally eliminating a context outside formal marriage where sexual intercourse had been legally permissible. This process accelerated in the Qing, with key measures being promulgated during the Yongzheng and early Qianlong reigns. The practical impact of such measures is open to question. But they were clearly part of a larger trend of extending uniform standards of sexual morality and criminal liability to all.[25]

Breaking the Moral Bond Between Husband and Wife

We have seen that a husband's legal authority over his wife, including the right to use violence, was neither absolute nor arbitrary; he was empowered only to the extent that his treatment of her conformed to the interests of the larger Confucian familial order. Even the wifely duties of deference and sexual submission were conditioned by this more fundamental imperative. Two scenarios included by late imperial legal codes under the rubric of illicit sexual intercourse further clarify our understanding of the contingent nature of a husband's "sexual monopoly." This monopoly was his to enjoy himself, but not to share with others.

Illicit Sexual Intercourse Approved by the Husband

What if a husband permitted his wife to engage in sexual relations with another man? The chapters on prostitution will treat this question at length, but it is worth previewing the argument here. Until the eighteenth century, prostitution was legally tolerated as long as such work was confined to women of hereditary debased status, especially the *yue hu*, or "music households." Case records from the early Qing (and other sources) show that many such women had husbands who acted as their pimps. The laws against "illicit sexual intercourse" did not apply to such people, who were considered beneath the law, and commoner males who engaged their services were not guilty of any offense.

In contrast, any act of extramarital intercourse involving a free commoner female was punishable as "illicit sexual intercourse." Moreover, for a commoner husband to pimp his wife or concubine (either with her consent or by force) was considered a fundamental betrayal of the moral basis of their marriage: that is, it counted as "intercourse without morality/ritual." As early as the twelfth century, an edict (of the Southern Song dynasty) mandated that any commoner couple guilty of such offenses be divorced (QY, 80/24b), and compulsory divorce remained part of the punishment for this crime until the end of the imperial era. In the Yuan dynasty, if a commoner husband "abetted his wife to act as a prostitute" (zong qi wei chang), they would be punished in the same manner as ordinary adulterers: the husband, wife, and customer would all receive the standard penalty for "consensual illicit sex" with a married woman, 87 blows of the heavy bamboo. The couple would be divorced, and the woman would be returned to her natal family to be married off to someone else (YD, 45/8a–9b; cf. Yuan shi, 2644). The Ming and Qing codes punished this crime in precisely the same way (although the number of blows was rounded up to 90) (ML, 25/1a; DC, 367-00). Payment of money for the woman's sexual services did not warrant any extra penalty: it was the sexual promiscuity that was being punished, not the use of money to facilitate it.

We should bear in mind that compulsory divorce was a serious penalty, at least for the husband. To be married was (and perhaps still is) the mark of social adulthood in China, and among the poor peasantry marriage served as an important status symbol for men— one that could only have gained in importance as the shortage of wives worsened (for this reason, in wife-selling cases it is not uncommon to find that the wife was more eager to be sold than the husband was to sell her—see Sommer 1994, 379–85). The men affected by these laws were already desperate enough to consider pimping their wives; once divorced, how many of them would ever manage to recoup the resources necessary to marry again?

What was the rationale for prohibiting such sexual relations, and further, for mandating the divorce of the couples involved? The Yuan judiciary's position on the matter is representative of its successors as well. In 1303, a senior official characterized "husbands abetting their wives to act as prostitutes" as "commoners debasing themselves" (liang wei jian)—that is, acting in the manner of debased-status prostitutes. In the same year, the Yuan Board of Punishment issued the following statement: "The bond between husband and wife is vital to the moral foundation of human relations, and a husband who abets his wife to act as a prostitute gravely injures the public morality (da shang feng hua). . . . If a husband accepts money to have his wife engage in illicit sexual intercourse with other men, then the bond of moral duty between them has already been broken (*yi jue*). . . . " The board characterizes this conduct as "breaking the bond of moral duty" between husband and wife (*yi jue*), a legal condition that indicated compulsory divorce in the code of every dynasty from Tang through Qing. In considering the range of human relations, Chinese jurists distinguished between "unions made by Heaven" (*tian he*), such as the relationship between father and son, and "unions made by men" (*ren he*), such as marriage and adoption. Both kinds of union were characterized by *yi*—or "morality," a moral bond that conferred different responsibilities on each partner to the relationship. This morality (*yi*), of course, is the same condition that legitimized sexual intercourse, according to Fu Sheng's classic definition of a sex offense. It was possible to offend against moral duty in Heaven-made relationships (for example, unfilial conduct), but for legal purposes, the moral bond in such relationships was irrevocable, and could not be "broken" (*jue*). Thus, for example, Qing-dynasty case records show that if a commoner pimped his daughter, he would be punished; nevertheless, his daughter would return to his custody in the end (XT, 194/DG 5.10.23). But in man-made relationships, the moral bond could be broken; therefore, if a husband abetted or forced his wife's illicit sexual intercourse, the couple would be ordered divorced.[26]

The term used in Yuan, Ming, and Qing law for "abetting" a wife's illicit sexual intercourse, *zong*, implies active complicity on the part of both husband and wife. The literal meaning of *zong* is "to release" or "give rein" (to a horse); it can also mean "to indulge." In the Confucian scheme, it is up to a husband to discipline his wife, to provide moral guidance and set limits on her behavior. The image of the statutory language, then, is of a husband failing in the duty conferred by his position, when he lets his wife indulge herself in sexual promiscuity. By this failure, he forfeits his claim to his wife.

If instead of "abetting" his wife's illicit sexual intercourse, a husband had *forced* her to sleep with another man, then the same basic principles applied, except for the punishment of the wife. In Yuan law, a wife "forced" (*le*) to act as a prostitute might or might not be punished, "depending on the circumstances of the case" (YD, 45/9a–b; *Yuan shi*, 2644). In the Ming statute against this crime (which the Qing continued to use), a wife "forced to engage in illicit sexual intercourse" (*yi le tong jian*) was exempted from any punishment, and would simply be returned to her natal family; her husband would receive 100 blows of the heavy bamboo, and the man who slept with her a mere 80 blows (ML, 25/3a–b; DC, 367-00). Here, the preponderance of blame went to the husband—it was *his* consent and the force *he* employed that were decisive—instead of being spread evenly among the three, as in cases of "abetting." Even so, the penalties for both men are far lower than the penalty mandated for rape of a status equal, strangulation after the assizes. In fact, Yuan, Ming, and Qing statutes against a husband forcing his wife to sleep with another man all assiduously avoid the key word "coercion" (*qiang*) that defined rape ("coerced illicit sex"—*qiang jian*). The difference between this scenario and legally defined rape is that the woman's husband has authorized another man to rape her. As the 1715 commentary of Shen Zhiqi notes: "In cases where a wife, concubine, [etc.] is forced (*yi le*) by her husband to engage in illicit intercourse with another man, then even if the woman refuses to submit, and for this reason the man who engages in illicit sex with her uses coercion (*qiang*) to do so . . . it would be inappropriate to punish him for the crime of rape (*qiang jian*)" (cited in Yao Run et al., eds., 1878 33/7a). This offense constituted a form of illicit sexual intercourse that took place against the woman's will, but the husband's authorization made it a very different and far less serious offense than rape.

Wife-Selling as Illicit Sexual Intercourse

Another crime that broke the moral bond between husband and wife was "to sell a divorce" (*mai xiu*)—that is, for a husband to sell his wife in marriage to another man. As far as I know, the earliest mention of *mai xiu* appears in Yuan-dynasty law. Yuan law apparently distinguished between two different variants of the crime, but the matter is a little ambiguous. The "household and marriage" chapter of the Yuan code states that "it is forbidden for a husband who does not get along with his wife to sell a divorce, or for any man to buy a divorce from him (*mai xiu mai xiu*); violators shall be punished." The measure does not spell out the penalties; it adds, however, that "those who separate by consent (*he li zhe*) shall not be punished" (TM, 26/17b–18a; YD, 18/29a). The "offenses of illicit sex" (*jian fei*) chapter of the Yuan code gives the second variant of the crime:

Any who engage in consensual illicit sex (*he jian*), and then conspire together to use money to buy a divorce (*yi cai mai xiu*), so that [the man who has engaged in illicit sex] can marry [the wife who has engaged in illicit sex] as his own wife, shall each receive 97 blows of the heavy bamboo; the wife who has engaged in illicit sex (*jian fu*) shall be returned to her husband. (TM, 26/18a; *Yuan shi*, 2655)

The first measure does not mention "illicit sex"; it simply forbids a husband who does not get along with his wife to sell her to another man. The second statute explicitly bans a transaction motivated by adultery—that is, in which a man buys his lover from her husband. In this second measure, adultery is the focus of judicial interest, rather than wife-selling per se: only the adulterers are to be punished, and the woman is to be returned to the husband who sold her.

An edict of 1301, however, asserted that if a husband "sold a divorce" (*mai xiu*) to another man, then "the bond of moral duty has already been broken (*yi jue*)," and it ordered that his wife be "divorced and returned to her natal lineage." The case that prompted this edict does not seem to have involved any adultery prior to the sale of the woman; nor does the edict spell out any penalties, other than confiscation of the money paid for the woman (YD, 18/30a). Since the edict does not specify one or the other variant of the crime, it would seem that either would break the bond of moral duty between husband and wife, thus indicating her compulsory separation from both men.

There was strong continuity between Yuan and Ming law in the treatment of wife-selling, as in many other matters. The Ming code contained the following statute:

If money (*cai*) is used to buy or sell a divorce (*mai xiu mai xiu*), so that one man marries the wife of another with consent (*he qu ren qi*), then the original husband (*ben fu*), the wife (*ben fu*), and the man who bought the divorce (*mai xiu ren*) shall each receive 100 blows of the heavy bamboo; the wife shall be divorced [from both men] and returned to her natal lineage, and the bride price (*caili*) shall be confiscated. . . .

If the man buying the divorce and the wife use some scheme to force the original husband to divorce her, then if the husband otherwise has no desire to sell a divorce, he shall not be punished. The man buying the divorce and the wife shall each receive 60 blows of the heavy bamboo and one year of penal servitude; the wife's extra penalties [i.e., the penal servitude] shall be redeemed with a fine, and she shall be given to the original husband, who may sell her off in marriage (*jia mai*).

In cases involving concubines, the penalties shall be one degree lower. In all cases, any go-between shall receive a penalty one degree lower than that of the offenders.   (Huang Zhangjian, ed., 1979, 934; DC, 367-00)

This law seems to incorporate the logic of the 1301 edict by ordering that all three parties to the transaction be punished equally, and by separating the woman from both men. The second clause spells out the one scenario in which the "original husband" is guiltless—when he is the victim of a conspiracy between his wife and her buyer.

This statute appears in the Ming code's chapter on "offenses of illicit sex"—in fact, it is a separate clause of the measure that prohibited a husband from "abetting" or "forcing" his wife to engage in adultery. Unlike Yuan law, there is no measure in the Ming code's chapter on "household and marriage" that uses the term "to buy or sell a divorce" (*mai xiu mai xiu*). The placement of the statute in the "illicit sex" chapter suggests that it was intended to cover transactions resulting from prior adultery between a wife and her purchaser, an impression strengthened by the language of the statute's second clause. Nevertheless, the word *jian* appears nowhere in the text of the statute itself. During the sixteenth century, that ambiguity (which derived, perhaps, from the ambiguity of Yuan law) helped provoke a controversy within the Ming judiciary over the exact nature of the offense and its relationship to the larger criminal category of "illicit sex." Specifically, it was debated whether a wife-selling that involved no prior adultery should be prosecuted.

One school of thought called for a broad reading of the statute to prohibit all unauthorized wife-selling, regardless of motive. For example, Lei Menglin makes the following argument:

The statute itself is one of the measures on "illicit sex" (*jian*). Nevertheless, it does not say "the man who committed illicit sex" (*jian fu*), but rather "the man who bought the divorce" (*mai xiu ren*); it does not say "the wife who committed illicit sex" (*jian fu*), but rather "the wife" (*ben fu*). Therefore, it is certain that the definition of "buying or selling a divorce" is not necessarily limited to [wife-selling] that results from prior illicit sexual activity. [Even if illicit sexual activity does not precede the transaction], this is not the legitimate way to give or take a wife in marriage (*fei jia qu zhi zheng*), and any kind of illicit union constitutes "illicit sex" (*fan gou he jie wei jian ye*). For this reason, the statute has been included in the chapter on "illicit sex." (TM, 26/17b)

In other words, buying a wife from her husband did not constitute a legitimate marriage; thus, the sexual union that *resulted* from the transaction counted as adultery. Whether the wife-selling had been *preceded* by adultery was beside the point: morally, it was all the same, and should all be prosecuted in the same way.[27] This broad interpretation of the statute on "buying or selling a divorce" would seem to fit the classical definition of sex offenses as "intercourse without morality/ritual"; moreover, it appears to make sense in terms of wider contemporary perceptions. According to Ogawa Yôichi, the term "illicit sexual intercourse" (*jian tong*) as used in a Ming collection of vernacular stories simply meant "illegal marriage"—namely, the union of male and female without proper marriage rites (1973, 148).

A second school of thought, however, called for a much narrower application of the statute. For example, a 1568 memorial from an official of the Court of Judicial Review complained about widespread confusion in the application of the statute:

> If a husband and wife do not get along, then according to law they should divorce; if a wife engages in illicit sex, then according to law, [her husband] is allowed to sell her off in marriage. In either case, when a second husband goes through a matchmaker and pays money to take the woman as his wife, then [their union] does not constitute "illicit sex," and is not prohibited by the statute. But these days, the statute against "buying or selling a divorce" is always cited [indiscriminately].

In short, there were some situations that warranted divorce, remarriage, and wife-selling, but even these legitimate actions had been confused with the crime of "buying or selling a divorce." Only wife-selling directly motivated by prior adultery should be punished. In response to this complaint, an imperial edict approved the narrow interpretation, but debate continued nevertheless. The following year, the Censorate reaffirmed the narrow interpretation and proposed specific ways to implement it:

> The clear meaning of the statute is that the crime is a form of "illicit sexual intercourse." . . . The language of the statute itself . . . does not include the word "illicit sex"; for this reason alone has controversy arisen. . . . Henceforth, whoever sells his wife in marriage out of greed for money (*tu cai jia mai*) should be punished according to the statute against "doing inappropriate things," and, depending on the circumstances, the amount paid should be recovered and confiscated. Whoever sells his wife in marriage out of poverty or illness should not be punished; nor should any second husband be punished if he has used money to buy [another man's wife] in marriage, but [whose case] otherwise involves no "buying or selling of divorce" because of illicit sex.

In other words, wife-selling motivated by purely materialistic concerns was a separate matter, and should be punished only lightly, if at all; a man who acquired a wife by purchase from her first husband should be punished only if he had slept with her in advance. This memorial received imperial endorsement (TM, 26/18a–b; *Ming shi*, 2290–91).

In spite of these clear statements from the center, advocates of the broad interpretation persisted—and it was this interpretation of the statute which prevailed in the Qing dynasty. The first edition of the Qing code preserved the Ming statute on "buying or selling a divorce," but it attached the following interlinear commentary: "If a husband does not report [his wife's] adultery [to the authorities], and instead sells her in marriage to the man who engaged in illicit sex with her, then the original husband shall receive 100 blows of the heavy bamboo, and the man and wife who engaged in illicit sex shall each be punished to the full extent of this statute" (DC, 367-00). The inclusion of this commentary left no doubt that prior adultery was only one of the scenarios to which the statute applied. All unauthorized wife-selling should be prosecuted as "buying or selling a divorce," because in essence it all constituted adultery. In 1715, Shen Zhiqi explained the connection this way:

A man who "sells a divorce" is himself discarding his wife, so he has lost the moral bond of husband and wife (*shi fu fu zhi lun*); a man who "buys a divorce" is scheming to marry another man's wife, so he, too, ignores the legitimate way of marriage (*shi hun yin zhi zheng*). Such behavior is of the same ilk as illicit sexual intercourse, and for that reason the crime is listed not with the statutes on "marriage," but rather here [in the code's chapter on "illicit sexual intercourse"]. (Cited in Yao Run et al., eds., 1878, 33/7a)

Central case records from the eighteenth century show that the statute against "buying or selling a divorce" was rigorously applied to a wide range of scenarios of wife-selling that included no prior adultery. In fact, poverty seems to have been by far the dominant motive behind such transactions; nevertheless, the Qing Board of Punishment was quite strict in considering wife-selling as a form of "illicit sexual intercourse," at least until the late Jiaqing reign (Sommer 1994, 377–94).

Authorized Wife-Selling, and the Sold Wife as Adulteress

Their differences aside, both sides to the sixteenth-century debate agreed that the criminality of "buying or selling a divorce" depended on some essential connection with "illicit sex"; that connection was what rendered such transactions incompatible with the norms of legitimate marriage. In other words, the problem was adultery, rather than wife-selling itself.

Indeed, as the 1568 memorial quoted earlier points out, there were occasions when the law explicitly authorized a husband to sell his wife to another man in marriage; in such cases, the statute on "buying or selling a divorce" did not apply. Ming law provided that a wife "may be sold in marriage by her husband" (*cong fu jia mai*) in at least three situations: if she had been convicted of adultery (DC, 366-00), if she had run away (DC, 116-00), or if she had conspired to force her husband to "sell her divorce" to another man (DC, 367-00). Each scenario was defined as a criminal betrayal of the husband, and thus the law authorized him to sell her (or to keep her if he chose) after reporting her to the magistrate for prosecution. The righteousness of the husband, betrayed by his wife, was what distinguished authorized wife-selling from the crime of selling a divorce.

As far as I can tell, formally authorized wife-selling was largely an innovation of the Ming dynasty. The scant evidence in surviving Yuan case law suggests that if a husband no longer wanted a wife who had committed adultery, he was required to divorce her and return her to her natal lineage; he might sell her off in marriage only if she had committed adultery more than once (YD, 45/15a and 18/31a–32a; *Yuan shi*, 2654). In effect, the Ming code added being sold to being beaten as part of the routine punishment for a wife's adultery.

Qing lawmakers preserved the Ming code's authorization of wife-selling, adding a single qualification: if a husband caught his wife and her lover in bed but killed only the lover, then his wife was to be "sold in marriage under official auspices (*dang guan jia mai*), and her body price (*shen jia*) confiscated by the state."[28] The homicidal husband would not be punished, but he would lose the option of either selling or keeping his wife; moreover, the amount paid for the woman would be kept by the authorities (DC, 285-00). The purpose of this Qing amendment seems to have been to deter the use of entrapment to get an excuse for murder.

A fundamental condition that Ming and Qing law placed on authorized wife-selling was that the betrayed husband could not sell her to her partner in adultery. The original Ming statute on "consensual illicit sex" (*he jian*) provided that: "If [the original husband] sells her in marriage to the man who has engaged in illicit sex with her, then that man and the husband shall each receive 80 blows of the heavy bamboo; the wife shall be divorced [from both men] and returned to her natal lineage, and the bride-price shall be confiscated" (DC, 366-00). This measure applied when a husband had had his wife and her lover prosecuted, and then sold her to him anyway

(Yao Run et al., eds., 1878, 33/1a). A husband who sold his wife to her lover without even reporting the adultery for prosecution was guilty of "selling a divorce" and was to be prosecuted under that statute (as the interlinear commentary added in the early Qing made explicit).

The authorization of wife-selling in some circumstances highlights the underlying consensus of the Ming debate about the crime of "buying or selling a divorce": the problem was not commodification per se, but rather "intercourse without morality/ritual." (This is a theme we will return to in the chapters on prostitution.) Hence, the rule that a betrayed husband could not sell his wife to her lover—the point was to punish adultery, not to promote it. The husband's right to sell his wife was limited to specific circumstances in which he retained his moral authority. If he acquiesced to adultery after the fact, then he lost that authority—and thus would lose all say over his wife's fate.

Authorizing a betrayed husband to sell an adulterous wife satisfied two priorities. It would enable the husband to recoup some of his family's investment in the woman (the bride-price originally paid for her), supplying him the means to remarry and start anew.[29] Also, it would find an appropriate place for the woman in a different household: late imperial dynasts hated and feared individuals outside the family system.

On a more fundamental level, however, authorized wife-selling seems to have been based on the logic that an unchaste wife might be treated legitimately as a commodity, like a slave or a prostitute. In fact, while the code specifies that a wife convicted of adultery should be "sold in marriage" (jia mai), implying that she be given a second chance with a new husband, it was not unheard of for such women to be sold as slaves—or for magistrates to accept such an outcome.[30] A similar logic informed a Yuan law that permitted a "wife of commoner household who has been discarded by her husband because she committed illicit sexual intercourse" to become a prostitute (in effect relinquishing her commoner status and the mandatory chastity that went with it): the moral norms of commoner society no longer applied to a woman who had so debased herself (TM, 26/25a). This logic derived from the age-old paradigm of an intrinsic link between sexual morality and legal status.

The Ming-Qing statute on "buying or selling a divorce" mandated that the sold wife receive 100 blows of the heavy bamboo.[31] What was the rationale behind this sentence? The Qing judiciary consistently held that a sold wife, in principle, was an adulteress. As Shen Zhiqi explains, a wife's "consent" (*he*) to being sold was essentially the same as the "consent" of an adulteress to illicit sexual relations:

The phrase "to marry the wife of another with consent" (*he qu ren qi*) [in the statute on "buying or selling a divorce"] implies that the man buying the divorce first has a consensual agreement (*he tong*) with the wife; in other words, the wife herself intends to submit happily [to her buyer] (*yue cong*). . . . The term "consent" (*he*) in the phrase "to marry [the wife of another] with consent" is like the "consent" in "to engage in illicit sex with [a woman's] consent" (*he jian*), so the primary blame must be placed on the wife.[32]

Shen's focus on a wife's *consent* underscores her criminal culpability, because in late imperial law, the concept of a woman's consent to sex existed only as a category of crime: "consensual illicit sex" (*he jian*), as opposed to "coerced illicit sex" (*qiang jian*). Moreover (as explained in the next chapter), Qing magistrates viewed anything short of active, violent resistance as "consent" by default. In this light, Shen's analysis implies that the proposal to sell a wife constituted a challenge to her chastity that demanded militant resistance; a passive attitude was no better than active agreement. He concludes: "The man who buys a divorce craves sex (*tan se*), while the man who sells a divorce craves money (*tan cai*); if there were no prior consent of the wife, then why would she deserve the same penalty as they?" In short, the wife's "prior consent" was a prerequisite for the transaction—without it, no wife-selling could succeed (Yao Run et al., eds., 1878, 33: 7a). As the Board of Punishment stated in 1828, "For women, a reputation for chastity is more important than anything else. If a wife is perfectly willing to have her divorce sold—to be remarried in spite of already having a husband—then this is in no way different from engaging in illicit sexual intercourse" (XA, 8/7b–8a).[33]

We see, then, that a wife who was sold was considered unchaste, no matter whether her sale had been illegal, or authorized by a magistrate. A wife's prior unchaste behavior is what entitled her husband to sell her. But even in illegal transactions, any wife who consented to be sold thereby demonstrated her lack of virtue. The sexual union that followed simply confirmed it.

Every Woman a Wife

We conclude this chapter with a first approximation of what "illicit sexual intercourse" (*jian*) meant in late imperial law. The early texts cited by late imperial authorities like Xue Yunsheng single out three elements of importance: heterosexual acts are the focus of scrutiny; intercourse is criminal if it occurs outside legitimate marriage, defined by proper rites but also by internalized Confucian morality; and the danger of this crime is that it represents an attack by an outside male that threatens to disorder another man's lineage. In other words, this offense threatened the larger family order, and therefore the political order as well. Sex out of place was a danger to the patrilineal family and to an imperial state that conceived of itself as the family writ large.

What of individual will? Because a woman's willful consent was not necessary to legitimize sexual intercourse, *jian* excluded what we now call "marital rape." But her *father's* consent was necessary to legitimize marriage, and thus the sexual consummation of a disputed or illegal marriage did constitute *jian*. Moreover, there were limits to a husband's legitimate sexual use of his wife. Marital intercourse that violated the dictates of filial piety was considered criminal by the jurists of several dynasties. In addition, *jian* included acts endorsed by the husband that broke the moral bond between him and his wife: for example, abetting or forcing his wife's intercourse with another man, or selling her to another man in marriage. The criminalization of such acts recalls Fu Sheng's classic definition of a sex offense as "intercourse without morality."

The boundaries of the illicit shifted over time. We have seen at least two examples of how the compass of the criminal category "illicit sexual intercourse" expanded, especially during the Qing. The inclusion of some wife-selling in this category appears to have been an innovation of the Yuan dynasty; the broad reading of the Ming statute received full implementation by central authorities in the Qing. As a result, even wife-selling motivated by poverty came to be classified as a form of adultery. Something similar happened to the legal standing of sexual relations between masters and their female slaves and servants; by the Qianlong reign, what had long been a basic perquisite of status had been more or less ruled out of legal existence, as the commoner standard of marriage and chastity was extended to include servile women. As we shall see, the Yongzheng judiciary also eliminated the other status-based exception to the prohibition of extramarital intercourse, namely prostitution. "Every woman a wife" might have been the slogan of the Qing judiciary, as it worked to extend the *liang* standard of familial and sexual morality to all.

CHAPTER THREE

The Evolution of Rape Law: Female Chastity and the Threat of the Outside Male

The Credentials of the Victim

The Chinese legal term translated into English as "rape"—*qiang jian*—literally means "coercive illicit sexual intercourse"; its counterpart is *he jian*, or "consensual illicit sexual intercourse." The first thing to note, then, about late imperial rape law is that for an act to count as *qiang jian*, it first had to count as *jian*—and we have already seen that this prior category excluded many acts that would be defined as "rape" in Western law today. (But for convenience, I shall continue to use the English term to denote the Chinese legal concept.) The second thing to note is that "consent" carried no positive connotation: a woman's consent to illicit sex meant that she shared the guilt and therefore the punishment for that crime.

If the legitimacy of a sexual act did not depend on a woman's consent or willing participation—if, indeed, her consent bore relevance only as a crime—then how did jurists define rape? When I first began to study this topic, my gut reaction was righteous indignation at the huge gap I perceived between my own notion of women's rights and the standards employed by late imperial jurists in judging rape cases. (The same indignation animates Vivien Ng's widely cited 1987 article on Qing rape law.) It is commonplace today to define rape and other cruel acts as criminal precisely because they violate a person's rights; this definition, however, assumes that an individual's freedom of body and will is the standard against which crime offends. In the West, much of the effectiveness of the women's liberation movement, including the reform of rape law, has depended on the ability of activists to point out the hypocrisy of a judiciary that claims to protect individual rights but has failed in practice to extend equal protection to women. Still, there is no point in accusing Qing jurists of such hypocrisy, for they were no hypocrites; they never pretended that the purpose of criminal law should be to protect individual rights, let alone women's bodily freedom. In fact, such heterodoxy would have horrified them, if they could be persuaded to understand it.

Late imperial jurists thought of rape in terms of pollution: the pollution of descent lines, of commoner status, and especially of female chastity. But could not the same be said of *consensual* offenses? Indeed, the distinction between coercion and consent, which implies that the attitude of the woman herself somehow matters, seems to have held relatively little importance in earlier dynasties. In the Tang code's statutes against illicit sex, the clear priorities are transgressions of status order and family order; coercion is mentioned almost as an afterthought. The main difference between coercion and consent was that a woman who had been coerced would receive no punishment; an offender who used coercion would receive a penalty raised by only one degree over that for consensual illicit intercourse. An increase of one degree meant an extra half-year of penal servitude, added to the one-and-a-half year penalty for consent if the woman were single, or to the two years mandated if she were married (TL, 26/15a).

An extra half-year does not seem like much of a difference, especially when compared to Ming or Qing dynasty law, in which the basic penalty for coercion was strangulation, as opposed to a beating for consent. The importance of the distinction between coercion and consent increased dramatically after the Tang, as this contrast suggests, reaching its apogee in the eighteenth century. In effect, rape was lifted out of the background offense and accorded central prominence, and thus a woman's attitude toward sexual intercourse took on a new importance for the law. What was it, exactly, about a woman's attitude that mattered so much to late imperial jurists?

The Rising Priority of Female Chastity

An official commentary on the basic Ming-Qing statute against illicit sexual intercourse includes the following statement: ". . . For a man who engages in illicit sexual intercourse (*jian fu*) to succeed in accomplishing this crime, it is necessary that the wife who engages in illicit intercourse with him (*jian fu*) be licentious, depraved, and without shame. . . . Therefore, the man and woman receive the same penalty." Consent represented a shameless wife's betrayal of her husband with an outside male, a combination of internal sub-version and external attack. In contrast, the coercive variant con-sisted of an outside male's violation of a wife who had remained *loyal*: "If a woman has maintained her chaste purity (*zhen jie*), and a man uses coercion to violate her sexually, then he wantonly gives rein to his own lecherous evil in order to pollute (*wu*) her chastity (*jie cao*). For this reason, in severe cases when the rape is already consummated, the offender should be strangled" (Yao Run et al., eds., 1878, 33/1b commentary). We find a similar statement in Huang Liuhong's influential 1694 handbook for magistrates, *A Complete Book Concerning Happiness and Benevolence*:

> Why is the penalty for "coercion" uniquely severe? In the context of illicit sex, "coercion" refers to the sudden pollution of a female, who has previ-ously maintained her chaste purity (*zhen jie zi shou zhi nü*), by means of violent coercion (*qiang bao*). The purpose of imposing the death penalty is to reward [the victim's] resolve to maintain chaste purity (*zhen jie zhi cao*), and also to shame wives who are evil and licentious.   (1973, 19/21b)

The prerequisite for sentencing a rapist to the full penalty of stran-gulation was that his victim had "maintained her chaste purity." It was the pollution he inflicted on her chastity that defined his crime, but she must have been "pure" in order to suffer that pollution, in order for the rape to have caused significant harm.

The judiciaries of earlier dynasties had probably shared the basic assumption that the harm caused by rape depended on the victim's previous record of chastity. Indeed, this assumption appears to be a regular and even definitive feature of patriarchal legal systems. But over the course of the late imperial period, the ideological import of female chastity increased precipitously, and in the process, the legal discourse of rape was transformed.

Here I agree with Vivien Ng's argument that Qing rape law "was intended to help further promote the cult of chastity," and thus re-alize "the Neo-Confucian social order" (1987, 69). Ng is mistaken, however, in her assertion that this phenomenon represented a sud-den and radical departure from earlier judicial practice, motivated by the early Qing regime's desire to garner legitimacy among the conservative Han Chinese elite (1987, 57–59). The transformation of the legal discourse of rape accompanied the development of im-perial chastity cults from the Yuan dynasty through the Qing. In the Yuan cult, which later inspired that of the Ming dynasty, the classic object of imperial veneration was the "chaste widow" (*jie fu*)—the wife who neither remarried nor committed adultery after her husband's death (YD, 33/17a; Elvin 1984). By the early sixteenth century, however, the Ming government had also begun to canonize (*jing biao*) "chastely martyred wives and daughters" (*zhen lie fu nü*) who died by homicide or suicide while resisting rape. Such martyrs were to be commemorated with official monuments and their burial expenses paid by the state (MH, 79/457). The Ming cult was inherited by the Qing state and much elaborated, especially during the eighteenth century (QHS, 404; Liu Jihua 1991). The Ming-Qing cult established as the highest standard of chastity a woman's willingness to die rather than suffer pollution through sexual contact with someone other than her one husband.

One feature of this chastity discourse was a tendency to collapse all females into the category of wives. From the Song through the Qing, historians have detected a growing tendency to stigmatize widow remarriage (Ebrey 1993; Mann 1987; T'ien Ju-k'ang 1988). In the eighteenth century, we also find that the ranks of eligible chastity martyrs began to include young girls who committed suicide to follow deceased fiancés to the grave, without their marriages ever having been consummated. If a young girl remained alive after her fiancé's death, but insisted on serving his parents as a chaste widow, then she would be granted the same honors as chaste widows who had actually been married (QHS, 404; Liu Jihua 1991). In other words, even widows and girls who were not yet married were increasingly pressured to submit to the sexual monopoly of a single husband (be he future, present, or past).

We can detect this same tendency in the penalties prescribed during successive dynasties for sex offenses. From the Tang through the Yuan, the penalties for rape consistently remained one degree more severe if the victim were married than if she were not; in Ming and Qing law, this distinction disappeared, along with the *lesser* of the two penalties. So, too, with consensual offenses: up through the early Qing, the prescribed penalties were always one degree more severe if the woman were married (TL, 26/15a; SX, 26/18a; YD, 45/1a; DC, 366-00). Then, in 1725, the marital distinction was eliminated for this category as well; a new substatute imposed a single stricter penalty for consensual illicit sex, regardless of the woman's marital status (see Appendix A.3). In both instances, the result of eliminating the marital-status distinction was that illicit sex with an unmarried woman came to be punished just as severely as that with a married woman.

The most obvious manifestation in rape law of the growing fixation with chastity was a systematic increase in the penalties for rape. During the Tang-Song period, the rape of a female of equal legal status as the rapist had been punished by penal servitude (TL, 26/15a; SX, 26/18a; QY, 80/21a). The penalties for rape then increased after the Northern Song, culminating in the imposition of death penalties.[1] During the Yuan dynasty, the rape of a married woman or of a girl ten *sui* or under was punished by strangulation. (If the victim was an unmarried female over ten *sui*, the penalty was a beating and penal servitude—YD, 45/1a–5a.) If three or more men together raped a female, they would suffer death as well (*Yuan shi*, 2654). The Ming code mandated strangulation after the assizes for any rape, regardless of the victim's age or marital status (DC, 366-00). Qing lawmakers preserved the Ming statute, and strangulation remained the basic penalty, but in the eighteenth century, many new measures were promulgated to add harsher penalties for specific scenarios of rape. For example, laws of the Yongzheng reign cited the "substatute on rootless rascals" (*guang gun li*) to punish gang rape (*lun jian*), or rape by one offender if the victim was aged ten *sui* or under; the penalty for these crimes was immediate beheading and, in some instances, public exposure of the head. Other Yongzheng substatutes mandated beheading after the assizes for rape of a girl between ten and twelve *sui*, and for any rapist who also injured his victim with an edged weapon, and strangulation for any man whose *unsuccessful* rape attempt or noncoercive sexual proposition (*tiao xi*) provoked a woman to commit suicide out of "shame and indignation." These are just a few of the situations for which new laws mandated extra penalties beyond those in the Ming code.[2]

Thus, by the Ming-Qing period, the growing ideological importance of chastity had raised the stakes in rape cases: for the victim, because of the heightened emphasis on chastity as the definition of her worth, and for the rapist, because his life now hung in the balance. The imposition of the death penalty for rape was explicitly justified by the pollution of chastity suffered by the rape victim. A Ming-dynasty commentator stated the connection plainly: "If a woman originally maintained her chastity, and a man used coercion to engage in illicit intercourse with her, then the rapist should be executed by strangulation" (XF, 13/16a). But the late imperial judiciary was exceedingly chary about executing criminals, requiring a strict standard of evidence (including confession) and multiple stages of review for every capital case (Bodde and Morris 1967, 131–43; Conner 1979; Shiga 1984). As Huang Liuhong observed in 1694, "Among offenses of illicit sexual intercourse, coercion is the only one punished by execution; therefore, in judging coercion one must be particularly cautious, because to do otherwise means to consign men to death [without proper cause]" (1973, 19/18b). Therefore, prosecution for rape became a process of scrutinizing the victim's record of chastity—her credentials, as it were—to determine if she truly was chaste enough to justify putting her rapist to death. Huang Liuhong: "If the victim is a wife who has committed offenses of illicit sex (*fan jian zhi fu*), then [the male] cannot be given the penalty for coercion" (1973, 19/19a).

The result was that, as Vivien Ng has put it, "the victim's chastity was put on trial" (1987, 63). This no doubt had always been true to some extent; but the focus on the victim's record of chastity and her conduct during the rape itself reached the level of an obsession by the Ming dynasty. What really stands out in the historical record is the elaborate and explicit discourse on rape in Ming-Qing law, compared with the laconic coverage of the crime in earlier legal codes.

Chastity as a Function of Free Commoner Status

The rising priority of female chastity accompanied the declining significance of clear-cut status differences in the law. What was the connection between the two trends? One way to look at the problem is through the changing meaning of the legal term *liang*. The literal meaning of this adjective is "good" or "respectable," but it is difficult to translate precisely, because its usage in the context of sex offenses conflates legal status with morality. To complicate the matter further, the balance between these two meanings changed over time.

In the early imperial era, *liang* referred to the free status of commoners and their superiors, as opposed to the unfree status of debased groups like slaves, bondservants, and music households (Niida 1943, 959, 963–964). The moral norms of marriage and family, especially female chastity, were attributes of free, *liang*, status; to be perfectly accurate, *liang* status was a prerequisite for a woman even to aspire to chastity. As we have seen, female slaves (even married ones) possessed no legally recognized chastity—they were sexually available to their masters, whether they liked it or not. Chastity was even less relevant to hereditary mean groups like the music households, who were enslaved into sexual and other entertainment services by the imperial state. In the centuries before the rise of the gentry and a large free peasantry, a major proportion of the empire's population consisted of unfree labor and other debased groups for whom the supposed virtues of *liang* status simply bore no relevance.

Therefore, in Tang-dynasty statutes against illicit sex, it is the offenses involving free women that really matter, especially if the male offender is a member of one of the many unfree, debased-status categories—and even more so if the woman is a member of his own master's family (which would mark her as a member of the aristocracy, since peasants did not own slaves and bondservants). At this early date, the law emphasized clear-cut status differences rather than virtue; moral expectations depended entirely on legal status. Thus, a master's use of his own slaves did not count as illicit sexual intercourse; moreover, illicit sex between two slaves, or between a *liang* male and a slave belonging to someone else, was punished much less severely than that involving free women. The Tang statutes against illicit intercourse simply do not address chastity in any explicit way—for example, the very brief discussion of coercion makes no distinction between victims who are chaste and those who are unchaste (see Appendix A.1).

We see a remnant of this archaic order in Qing laws that envision the rape victim as a *liang ren fu nü* or *liang jia fu nü*: these phrases literally mean "the wife or daughter of a commoner" or "a wife or daughter of commoner family," but in High Qing usage, their essential meaning is a *chaste* wife or daughter. One of the notable features of Qing substatutes against rape is that they so consistently use such phrases to identify the rape victim, even though the rapist too is clearly envisioned as a commoner. (The lawmakers of earlier dynasties did not find it necessary to say *liang* over and over again when talking about sex offenses between persons of equal status.) Moreover, Qing substatutes tell us who did *not* qualify as their ideal rape victim: "a wife or daughter who has committed illicit sexual intercourse" (*fan jian fu nü*) or "a wife who has committed illicit sexual intercourse" (*fan jian zhi fu*). These phrases do not appear in the rape laws of earlier dynasties. In other words, by the High Qing, the *liang* rape victim came to be constructed primarily in contrast with an unchaste woman—it was taken for granted that both were free commoners.

What all this means is that in Qing laws on illicit sex, certainly by the mid-eighteenth century, the term *liang* almost always means *chaste*, and no longer has much to do with formal status distinction.

By that time, practically everyone in the empire was considered a commoner before the law; the elaborate aristocracy, multiple categories of hereditary unfree labor, and relatively small free peasantry that had characterized medieval social structure were a dim memory. It makes sense that the legal term *liang* would come to refer primarily to the putative *moral* attributes of free commoner status, if it were to continue to have any use at all.

Rape of an Unchaste Woman of Commoner Status

In Ming-Qing law, even if a woman could prove the rapist's coercion and her own resistance, an unsatisfactory record of chastity meant that if prosecuted at all, her attacker would not receive the full penalty of death prescribed by the statute on rape. One of many clear statements of this principle appears in the *jian shi* commentary by Ming jurist Wang Kentang; this passage was transcribed as an interlinear commentary for the basic Ming statute on "illicit sex" when it was added to the Qing code:

If an offender, seeing a woman engaging in illicit sexual intercourse with another man, subsequently himself uses coercion to engage in illicit intercourse with her, then because she is already a woman who has committed an offense of illicit sex (*fan jian zhi fu*), it would be inappropriate to sentence him to the penalty for coercion. Instead, the statute's provision on "luring a woman to another place for illicit sex" should be applied.

The resulting penalty would be 100 blows of the heavy bamboo for the man, and likely for the woman as well, since "luring a woman . . . " was defined as a consensual offense. This penalty was slightly more severe than that prescribed for ordinary consent, but many degrees less than the strangulation mandated for rape (see Appendix A.2). This provision applied if the rapist himself had witnessed his victim's illicit sexual activity before attacking her. Writing in the late nineteenth century, Xue Yunsheng observes that the Qing code contains no general statute on the rape of "a wife or daughter who has previously committed offenses of illicit sex" (*fan jian fu nü*), but he notes that "in the past, offenders in such cases have had their penalties reduced [by one degree] and have been sentenced to life exile." For a rapist to receive the full penalty of strangulation, his victim had to be "a chaste wife or daughter" (*liang ren fu nü*) (DC, 366-12, commentary).[3]

This judicial practice was codified in a number of different Qing substatutes. One example is the 1725 substatute against gang rape, which identified the victim as "a chaste wife or daughter": the ringleader of a gang rape should be beheaded immediately and have his head exposed, and secondary accomplices should be strangled after the assizes (DC, 366-02). Nevertheless, as in cases of rape by a single offender, these death penalties would apply only if the victim were chaste. The principle was made even more explicit by a substatute of 1801. It reaffirmed the penalties for gang rape but added that if the victim was "a woman who has previously committed offenses of illicit sex" (fan jian fu nü), then the rapists would receive penalties reduced by several degrees: military exile in a malarial region for the ringleader, and life exile at a distance of 3,000 li for his followers (DC, 366-12). These penalties were severe—in part, no doubt, to punish the threat to public order represented by collective violence—but they confirmed the principle that even gang rapists deserved death only if their victim had been chaste. The same principle guided an 1805 substatute prescribing reduced penalties for the "coercive abduction" (qiang duo) of "a woman who has previously committed offenses of illicit sex" (DC, 112-06). (For this purpose, a wife who had been sold by her husband counted as "a woman who has previously committed offenses of illicit sex" as well.) Actually, the purpose of these 1801 and 1805 measures was to make sure that gang rape and kidnapping would be prosecuted *even if* their victims were unchaste women; I suspect that previously, such offenses against women known to be unchaste would not have been prosecuted at all.

We perceive the issue of victim chastity from a different angle in a substatute of 1775. This measure added extra penalties to the basic ones for homicide if the offender had been attempting to rape his victim when he murdered her. But it includes the following exception: "If the victim has previously engaged in consensual illicit sex with the offender, but later for some reason rejects him, so that he kills the [victim], then all such cases shall simply be judged according to the basic statutes on [homicide]." The point of this clause was to distinguish such a scenario from the rape and murder of a chaste woman, which would carry extra penalties beyond those mandated for murder alone. If the murdered woman had previously engaged in "consensual illicit sex" with her rapist-murderer, then the rape itself did not need to be punished, only the homicide (DC, 366-10). In other words, as far as the law was concerned, it was impossible for a man to rape a woman who had previously "consented" to sleep with him; her consent, once given, could not be withdrawn. (This measure recalls the reasoning behind the "marital exemption" that protected husbands in the Western legal tradition.)

To sum up, the penalty for rape in Ming-Qing law was determined in proportion to the standard of chastity that had been violated. The assumption was that prior unchaste activity to some extent approximated the pollution inflicted by rape. But it seems likely that any woman known to be unchaste who was raped simply would not qualify as a rape victim, in that the crime would not be taken seriously at all; I have yet to see these substatutes on the rape or kidnapping of an unchaste woman applied in actual archival case records. A far more important question in Ming-Qing rape law was how a woman—assumed to be a commoner with no record of sex offenses—responded to the *challenge* of a rape attempt. What standard did she meet, when put to the test? Did she *prove* her chastity through exemplary resistance? We shall return to this question when we address how judges distinguished coercion from consent in practice.

Rape of a Chaste Woman of Mean Status

The term *liang* never lost the nuance of legal status altogether; this is one reason why the word is so hard to pin down. What changed was the word's *emphasis*, as chastity came to outweigh status difference in the great majority of sex offense cases. Qing society continued to include a few slaves, as well as professional entertainers and prostitutes, against whom the judiciary would discriminate right down to the end of the dynasty (Jing Junjian 1993). Indeed, given the double meaning of *liang*, the rising value of chastity relative to status difference suggests a hypothetical question that we can safely assume a Tang jurist would never have asked: how should the judiciary treat a rape victim of *mean* status (not *liang*) who happened to be *chaste* (*liang*)? I have never seen a case in the archives that would answer this question; fortunately, however, the *Conspectus of Legal Cases* reports an incident that occurred in Beijing in 1849 and was referred to the Board of Punishment for "immediate examination." The facts of this unusual case were not in dispute: a woman named Liu Shi had been gang-raped by three bannermen.[4] The problem was how severely to punish the rapists, given Liu Shi's particular status: she earned a living by singing and performing music, having been trained in this profession by her adoptive mother, and having married another musician-actor. Therefore, she was an entertainer, a member of a despised occupational group;

she was not a prostitute, however, and there was no indication that she had ever had illicit sexual relations.

As we have seen, a 1725 substatute mandated extreme degrees of the death penalty for the gang rape of a *liang ren fu nü*—literally "the wife or daughter of a commoner," but generally interpreted to mean a chaste woman. Also, an 1801 substatute mandated reduced penalties for the gang rape of "a woman who has previously committed offenses of illicit sex." But neither provision exactly fit Liu Shi. (The judgment nowhere mentions the old Ming statute on "illicit sex between commoners and mean persons" [DC, 373-00], which apparently had become obsolete, though it remained on the books.) As the Board of Punishment explained:

Liu Shi, who was raped, performs and sings music, and so possesses the status of a professional actor (*you ling*); therefore, it would be inappropriate to treat her as "the wife or daughter of a commoner." Still, she has not personally committed any lascivious evil, so it would also be inappropriate to judge her case according to the provision on gang rape of "a woman who has previously committed offenses of illicit sex." The code contains no specific substatute covering her situation.

[The ringleader in this case] gathered a gang of men in the middle of the night on the streets of the very capital, and employed coercion to gang rape a woman. . . . [For such crimes,] he surely cannot escape death. Yet, in the final analysis, the woman who was raped is different from a commoner (*jiu yi liang ren*); the hasty application of the most severe penalties to this case would provide no means of manifesting the distinct levels of legal status which are involved.

The board struck a balance: the ringleader of the gang rape was sentenced to strangulation after the assizes, and his followers to slavery in the military forces stationed in Xinjiang. These penalties were *more* severe than those mandated for leaders and followers in the gang rape of "a woman who has previously committed offenses of illicit sex," but *less* severe than those for the gang rape of "the wife or daughter of a commoner." This hairsplitting provided adequate punishment for such a heinous crime, while honoring the old principle that illicit intercourse with a mean-status female was less of an offense than that with a commoner. Evidently, a mean-status female who was chaste could suffer more pollution than an unchaste commoner, but not as much as a chaste commoner.

The intriguing feature of this case, from a historical perspective, is that we see the judiciary explicitly weighing the *moral* content of *liang* against its status content, treating the two as separate variables instead of assuming that they automatically went together—

and calibrating the penalties for commoner rapists in order to give a mean-status woman credit for a high standard of chastity. These calculations would have been unthinkable in earlier dynasties (XAX, 28/14a–15b).[5]

The Importance of Penetration

As we have seen, the polluting threat of an outside male was fundamental to the definition of illicit sexual intercourse (whether coercive or consensual). Ming-Qing law mandated that any offspring of illicit union should become the responsibility of their father, the male offender; as the polluted fruit of outside penetration, such children should be excluded from the lineage of the mother's husband (see Appendix A.2). Similarly, if a wife committed adultery or ran away, her husband gained the right to expel her or to sell her off in marriage; she lost all claim to his property and children. (If a widow committed adultery, then her husband's family gained the same rights—see Chapter 5.) A husband who caught his wife in the act of adultery could kill her and her partner with impunity. Each of these measures aimed to safeguard descent and inheritance against the polluting threat of the outside male.

Penal and Ritual Consequences of Penetration

Accordingly, it makes sense that late imperial law distinguished between acts of illicit sex that were "consummated" (*cheng*) and those that were "not consummated" (*wei cheng*). The verb translated here as "to consummate" also carried the nuances of "to complete" or "succeed"; this verb's function in the phrase "to consummate illicit sex" (*cheng jian*) directly parallels that in contemporary terms meaning "to consummate marriage": *cheng hun* and *cheng qin*.

A basic legal principle throughout the late imperial period was that rape which was not consummated deserved a penalty one degree lower than that which was consummated. The earliest explicit statement of the principle that I have seen appears in a twelfth-century edict of the Southern Song dynasty: "Anyone who commits illicit sexual intercourse but does not consummate the act shall receive a penalty one degree lower than that for illicit sex that has already been consummated" (QY, 80/22a). This edict refers to illicit intercourse generally, but later legal texts usually apply the distinction only to coercion. Aside from this Southern Song edict, I have no evidence of how much importance courts attributed to the issue of consummation prior to the adoption of death penalties for rape in the Yuan dynasty. It is certain, though, that the death penalty would have greatly heightened the legal significance of this distinction (just as it heightened the importance of the rape victim's record of chastity), since a one-degree reduction would for the first time mean the difference between life and death for an offender. Indeed, Yuan law provided, in reference only to coercion, that "if illicit sexual intercourse is not consummated, then the penalty shall be reduced by one degree." Also, more specifically, "any father-in-law who bullies (*qi*) his daughter-in-law into illicit sexual intercourse shall be put to death if the act has already been consummated; if it has not been consummated, then he shall receive 107 blows of the heavy bamboo [and penal servitude]" (i.e., a reduction of one degree) (*Yuan shi*, 2653). As in the Song, the penalties differed by only one degree, but now the life of the rapist hung in the balance.

The Ming code's basic statute on illicit sex provides that "Whoever commits rape shall be strangled; if the rape is not consummated, the offender shall receive 100 blows of the heavy bamboo and life exile at a distance of 3,000 *li*" (i.e., a reduction of one degree). The Qing code preserved this portion of the Ming statute intact (adding only a phrase to make it explicit that strangulation should occur "after the assizes"—see Appendix A.2). The reduction below the death penalty also applied to variations of the crime (covered by separate measures of the code) when they were not consummated—for instance, rape of a girl under the legal age of consent, gang rape, and the like. A Ming commentary explains that if a rape were not consummated, then "fortunately, the woman's chastity has not yet been polluted (*wu*), so the offender receives a reduced penalty" (XF, 13/17a). In other words, a woman's chastity would suffer pollution only if rape were consummated; as we have seen, it was this pollution that warranted death for the rapist.

Criminal penalties aside, the distinction between rape that was consummated and that which was not gained a new formal prominence during the Ming and Qing dynasties, when it acquired a key role in determining eligibility for chastity-martyr canonization. When the Ming government began to honor "chastely martyred" rape victims (by the early sixteenth century), it specified that the only women eligible were those who "avoided pollution by their attackers" (*bu shou zei wu*) (MH, 79/457). Beginning in 1672, the Qing state also canonized martyred victims of attempted rape, using legal terminology to set the condition that a woman would be eligible only if her rape were not consummated (QHS, 404). Eighteenth-century memorials on rape cases show that the evidence mustered to prosecute rapists simultaneously enabled judges to evaluate the eligibility of dead victims for canonization, a key question being whether the rape had been consummated; in effect, the judgment of a rapist determined the judgment of his victim, and vice versa. In these memorials, recommendations for canonization immediately follow the recommended sentences of the rapists.

From the perspective of imperial *ritual*, then, chastity was an absolute, objective condition, rather than a nuanced measure of a woman's subjective intent. If the boundary of consummation had been crossed during rape, then the victim had been polluted irrevocably, regardless of her previous record of chastity, the intensity of her resistance, or the violence or numbers of men by which she had been subdued. Such was the policy on canonization eligibility from the early sixteenth century through the early nineteenth century.[6]

Standards of Evidence for Consummation

Qing case records show that consummation meant something very specific: the penetration of a woman's vagina by a rapist's penis. This is not surprising; the definition of rape in these terms (distinguishing it from other kinds of sexual assault) appears to be a regular feature of patriarchal legal systems (for example, the Anglo-American common law tradition; see Blond et al. 1991, 121). As with the question of a rape victim's chastity, penetration no doubt always played some role in Chinese rape law, but its importance must have increased with the rise of chastity cults and the imposition of death penalties for rape. What stands out in legal texts from the Yuan dynasty on, but especially from the eighteenth century, is the great significance attributed to consummation, and the precision with which courts scrutinized evidence and inscribed boundaries.

In a 1739 case from Wei Department, Zhili, a man named Su Wang (twenty-two *sui*), who worked at a temple weaving mats, agreed to weave a little mat as a toy for Li She'er, a girl of eight *sui*, if she would "play" with him. According to Su's confession, "I told her to take off her pants and crouch on the ground, and she obeyed, taking her pants off herself and crouching. I pulled open my own pants, squatted on the ground, and violated (*jian*) her from behind. . . . She felt pain and started crying, so I stopped without finishing (*mei you jian wan*), and helped her put on her pants." The girl's father heard her crying, ran to the scene, and saw blood on her pants.

She told him what had happened, and he seized Su and took him to the authorities. The girl was examined by a court midwife, who reported: "Li She'er's vagina is polluted (*wu*) by blood, it is swollen, and inside it has been broken (*po*). . . . She has truly been polluted by illicit intercourse (*jian wu*) with a man." Determining that illicit sexual intercourse had been consummated, the magistrate sentenced Su Wang to the full penalty of immediate beheading for "luring away a girl not yet ten *sui* and sexually polluting her by coercion (*qiang xing jian wu*)." (The girl's age meant that the act automatically counted as coercion.) We can conclude from this example that consummating rape required penetration of the vagina, but did not necessarily require the rapist to continue to the point of ejaculation (XT, 71/QL 4.7.11).

But it had to be penetration with a penis; other body parts could not consummate rape. For example, in 1812, the Board of Punishment issued the following opinion to the governor-general of Zhili, who had reported his provisional judgment of an attempted rape:

> Fan Youquan wanted to rape Li Erjie, who was only fourteen *sui*. Seeing that she was young and short of stature, he feared that it would be difficult to penetrate her (*kong nan xing jian*), so first he tried thrusting his finger into her vagina, scratching (*kou*) it so that it broke (*po*) and bled.
>
> In the records of their testimony, Li Erjie, her father Li Deyi, and the other witnesses all state that she was not polluted by illicit sex (*jian wu*). In addition, according to the midwife's examination, Li Erjie is a virgin (*chu nü*); she has not had her body broken (*ceng wei shen po*). The governor-general has sentenced Fan Youquan to life exile [at a distance of 3,000 *li*], according to the code's provision on "rape that has not been consummated." The sentence is appropriate. (XA, 52/5a–6b)

This judgment shows that penetration by a finger did not count as consummated illicit sexual intercourse—the girl remained a virgin because her body had not been "broken" (*po*) by a penis, even though it had been "broken" by a finger (this verb means "break" in the sense of puncture, split, or tear). Significantly, the word used here for "body"—*shen*—implies chastity, as in a phrase often used in legal texts for "to lose chastity": *shi shen*. Manual penetration, however violent, could not "sexually pollute" a woman's chastity. This case also suggests the social significance of virginity, quite apart from questions of imperial ritual and law: it seems to have been important to the father to establish that his unmarried daughter had not been polluted by the attack.[7]

It appears that the distinction between different body parts was not so absolute in earlier periods. *Collected Statutes of the Yuan* reports a case from Jiangxi, dated 1297, in which the Yuan judiciary apparently interpreted the manual penetration of a young girl as consummated rape. Yuan law provided that the rape of a girl aged ten *sui* or younger be punished by strangulation, but it made an exception for men of "advanced age," who would receive a reduced penalty of 107 blows of the heavy bamboo and penal servitude (with no option to redeem the penalty with a fine) (*Yuan shi*, 2654). In the 1297 case, a man named Li Gui sought to "pollute by illicit sex" (*jian wu*) a girl of nine *sui* named Pan Maoniang in order to take revenge on her father, against whom he bore some grudge. The offender began by "using the second finger of his right hand to thrust into her vagina, gouging (*wan*) it so that it broke (*po*) and bled." The girl screamed in pain, so he released her and she ran home, whereupon her father reported the assault to the authorities. The magistrate determined: "Li Gui is reported to be seventy-five *sui*; therefore, even though he used his hand to damage Pan Maoniang's nine-*sui* body (*shen*), it would be inappropriate to sentence him [to strangulation] for 'coercive illicit sexual intercourse.' Li Gui shall receive 107 blows of the heavy bamboo [and penal servitude]." This judgment was confirmed by the Secretariat.

Now if Li Gui's assault on Pan Maoniang were *not* judged to be consummated, then presumably the offender would have received a reduction of his sentence by one degree, instead of the full 107 blows and penal servitude mandated for "a man of advanced years." Therefore, it would seem that the Yuan judiciary considered this assault the equivalent of *consummated* rape. The conclusion is reinforced by the title of the case summary: "A Man of Advanced Age Pollutes a Young Girl by Illicit Sexual Intercourse" (*nian lao jian wu you nü*) (YD, 45/2b). This is the opposite of the conclusion reached by the Qing Board of Punishment when judging the same scenario, which suggests that the standard for judging consummation became stricter over time, along with the penalties for rape. (Ming-Qing law also made no age-based exceptions to the death penalty for rape.)

The importance of phallic penetration of the vagina to defining the "sexual" component of sexual assault in Qing law is underlined by a 1739 case from Qianjiang County, Guangxi. In this example, Wu Maode, his cousin Wu Maojue, and a servant, Lu Texi, murdered Maode's sister-in-law, Huang Shi, and another servant, Chen Telou, who were suspected of having a sexual relationship. According to the official account, the men smashed Chen's genitals with a rock, and then tied a large stone to his chest and drowned him in a lake. Then, Maojue and Lu "pulled off Huang Shi's pants and tied her ankles. Wu Maojue loathed her adulterous licentiousness (*jian yin*), and so, ordering Wu Maode to hold her down, he thrust a stick into her anus, forcing her skirt up inside it." Then they drowned her.

The Wu cousins were sentenced to strangulation after the assizes for "purposely killing a younger female relative within the mourning system" (Lu escaped arrest). The official judgment denounces the murderers' cruelty; nevertheless, in spite of the sadistic acts specifically targeted at the offending zone of the victims' bodies, neither man was accused of any offense of illicit sex. The subject of "coercive illicit sexual intercourse" never comes up in the memorial; the term *jian* appears only in reference to the purported affair of the murdered couple (which proved to be an unfounded rumor).

The Qing code contains many detailed provisions mandating extra penalties for homicides that involved offenses of illicit sexual intercourse, especially rape. In this case, if the murderers had used their penises to penetrate Huang Shi, that fact would certainly have been specified in the judgment and different laws would have mandated even more severe penalties. But because phallic penetration had not occurred, the sadistic acts that preceded the woman's drowning were interpreted simply as part of the way she was murdered, rather than as a separate category of specifically sexual assault (XT, 68/QL 4.4.11).

Contact with a rapist's penis would not necessarily pollute a woman's chastity, as long as penetration did not occur. In fact, contact with the penis in the context of resisting rape might even be interpreted as evidence of chastity, for purposes of canonizing a martyr. In a case from Chaoyang County, Guangdong, memorialized in 1739, Lin Qimao tried to rape Liu Shi with the assistance of her mother-in-law, Xie Shi (Lin and Xie Shi were having a sexual affair and, fearing that the younger woman would expose them, agreed that Lin should rape her in order to guarantee her silence through shame). Carrying a knife, Lin crept into Liu Shi's bedroom. According to his confession:

I climbed onto the bed and felt for Liu Shi, who was startled awake and cried out "Thief!" Xie Shi pressed the blanket over Liu Shi's face and mouth, and I straddled her body and pulled open her pants. Just as I was about to penetrate her (*xing jian*), Liu Shi grabbed my penis with her left hand. I was in pain, so I punched her in the stomach with my fist, but she just wouldn't let go. So I reached out, picked up the knife, and cut her hand.

She still didn't let go, so I cut her again. She still wouldn't let go, so I grew anxious and put my strength into it and cut her one more time—then she finally relaxed her grip [having died].

Lin Qimao was sentenced to immediate beheading for killing a woman in the course of a rape attempt. Xie Shi was sentenced to 100 blows of the heavy bamboo and life exile at a distance of 3,000 *li*; this was the penalty prescribed by the statute on "one offender seizing a woman by force, and a second raping her" (in the end she escaped punishment because of an amnesty). Since she had committed adultery with Lin, her husband was given the choice of keeping her or selling her off in marriage (see Appendix A.2).

Liu Shi was found worthy of canonization as a chastity martyr, her aggressive resistance being interpreted as proof of a determination to die rather than allow herself to be polluted. But if Lin had succeeded in inserting his penis in Liu Shi's vagina, then she would not have qualified for canonization, despite her tenacious resistance. (Ironically, as in many rape cases, the rapist's testimony to her chastity was what decided the question—XT, 72/QL 4.?)

What about rape in which a different orifice was penetrated? In a 1735 case from Zhuo Department, Zhili, the rapist penetrated the anus of a girl aged eight *sui*; the case record refers to this act as *ji jian*, a Qing legal term that usually denoted anal intercourse between males (see Chapter 4). As the memorial notes, "there is absolutely no provision in the code which states how the coercive sodomy (*ji jian*) of a young girl should be punished." In other words, the definition of "coercive illicit sexual intercourse" in the code's many provisions against that crime covered vaginal penetration only. Therefore, the judiciary sentenced this rapist by *analogy* to a substatute on the (vaginal) rape of a young girl, which mandated immediate beheading for "luring away a girl not yet ten *sui* and polluting her by rape" (DC, 366-04). The victim had not been murdered, so the judiciary did not have to confront the theoretical question of how anal penetration might affect eligibility for canonization as a chastity martyr (MQ, 61-23).

A revealing detail is that magistrates ordered midwives to make pelvic examinations only of alleged victims who were unmarried. As jurist Shen Zhiqi stated in 1715, "In cases of young daughters (*you nü*) [being raped], it is necessary to have a midwife examine clearly to make certain whether they have ever actually been penetrated" (literally, "actually had their bodies broken"—*shi ceng po shen*) (cited in Yao Run et al., eds., 1878, 33/1a). Pelvic exams were also performed on Buddhist nuns who had been raped, as long as they were presumed to have remained celibate prior to the assault (XT, 119/QL 10.12.10). Even if a married woman had been murdered in the course of a rape attempt, her genitals were not routinely examined; magistrates would instruct coroners not to expose the "lower body" (*xia shen*) of such homicide victims, as a concession to their families. If a living rape victim were a married woman, the judgment of whether rape had been consummated depended on the testimony of rapist and victim. In other words, pelvic trauma resulting from violent penetration had no legal significance when viewed apart from a woman's marital context. Since trauma in a married woman might conceivably have resulted from her husband's legitimate actions, it could not be considered evidence of rape. It was useful as forensic evidence only if the victim was unmarried and presumed to have been a virgin; in that context, evidence of penetration constituted evidence of "breaking" prior to marriage—that is, illicit sexual intercourse.

To sum up: for rape to be consummated, the vagina had to be penetrated by a penis. Ejaculation was not necessary: even momentary penetration crossed a boundary that could not be recrossed. Thus, for purposes of high ritual during the Ming and Qing dynasties, the victim's chastity suffered irrevocable pollution. She could not be canonized as a chastity martyr if she had died during the assault. For purposes of criminal law, the perpetrator of such irreparable harm deserved the full penalty of death. But at least by the Qing dynasty, penetration with fingers or objects did not count as consummated intercourse.

Some value specific to a woman's vagina could be destroyed by a pollution specific to the penis of someone other than her husband. Concern with penetration no doubt long predated the Ming-Qing period, given the danger of pregnancy and the classic fear that outside males would disrupt patrilineal descent. In the late imperial dynasties, the heightened obsession with female chastity promoted penetration to a life-and-death crisis of moral and political imperatives.

Coercion Versus Consent

The fundamental dichotomy of "coercion" (*qiang*) and "consent" (*he*) has an ancient provenance, being expressed with the same terms in the laws of the Qin (221–207 B.C.) and Han (206 B.C.–A.D. 220) dynasties. All offenses of illicit sex fell into one category or the other. Zhang Fei, a third-century A.D. annotator of the Han code, explains that coercion and consent were defined in terms of each other: "if [a woman] does not consent, then the act is called 'coercion'" (*bu he, wei zhi qiang*) (Zhang Jinfan et al., 1992, 424, 444). The key here is the woman's response to a challenge to her chastity, the agent of action being imagined as male. Did she consent? Or did he have to use coercion?

Age of Liability for Consent

Consent possessed legal relevance only as a form of crime, but a woman had to be capable of betrayal for her consent to carry criminal weight. A twelfth-century edict of the Southern Song provided that in cases of illicit sexual intercourse, "if the female is ten *sui* or under, then even if she consents, the offender shall be punished in the same way [as for coercion]" (QY, 80/21a). Yuan law contained the same provision (YD, 45/1a, 2a). A Ming statute, maintained in the Qing code, raised the legal age of consent by two years: "whoever engages in illicit sex with a young girl of twelve *sui* or under shall receive the penalty for coercion even if she consents" (DC, 366-00). By raising the age of consent, Ming-Qing jurists in effect expanded the scope of illicit intercourse to which the death penalty for coercion applied.

A Ming commentary explains the rationale behind the legal age of consent: "young girls of twelve *sui* and under have not yet developed a capacity for lust (*yu xin*)" (ML, 25/2a). This opinion was echoed by a Qing commentator: "In young girls of twelve *sui* and under, sexual awareness has not yet bloomed (*qing dou wei kai*), so they still have no capacity for licentiousness (*yin xin*)" (cited in Yao Run et al., eds., 1878, 33/2a commentary). It was this "capacity for licentiousness" or "licentious heart" that made effective consent possible. In other words, the development of sexual awareness engendered the possibility of betrayal, which was the only reason a woman's sexual awareness held any relevance for the law.

Evidence of Historical Change

We have already noted the rise in the severity of penalties for rape over the late imperial period, as well as an apparent intensification of the judicial fixation with a rape victim's previous record of chastity and with phallic penetration of the vagina. We can also detect a related increase in the strictness of standards of evidence for coercion, so that the burden of proof bore ever more heavily on the female victim, who was held to an ever-stricter standard of conduct both during and after the rape attempt. The focus of change was the relationship between coercion and consent; in effect, the balance between them shifted.

Early texts seem to suggest that active, voluntary participation was what defined consent. Zhang Fei's formula (cited above) implies that in the absence of a woman's active consent, an act would count as coercion, by default. Similarly, the official commentary on the Tang code defines consent in positive, reciprocal terms: "'Consensual illicit intercourse' refers to when both offenders are in mutual consensual agreement (*he jian wei bici he tong zhe*)" (TL, 26/18a). Indeed, it was this mutuality or symmetry of consent that originally justified equal penalties for both sexual partners. By the Ming-Qing period, however, the balance had shifted, and jurists defined consent largely in negative terms: what failed to meet the high evidentiary standard for coercion counted, by default, as consent. In Ming-Qing law, the male was considered innocent of coercion until the female was proven innocent of consent.

The aspect of this change most readily documented concerns the concept of "coercion followed by consent"—either during a single act of intercourse, or over the course of a series of acts engaged in by a single couple. I have found only sketchy evidence for the earlier dynasties. A twelfth-century edict of the Southern Song is the most suggestive: "If a man first coerces a woman but she later consents (*xian qiang hou he*), then the man shall be punished according to the law on coercion, and the woman shall receive a penalty one degree lower than that for consent" (QY, 80/21a). In other words, the initial rape would deserve the full penalty mandated for that crime, regardless of subsequent events. The woman would be punished for her consent, but the mitigating circumstance of the initial coercion would indicate a reduction in her penalty. The Tang code served as the basis for Song jurisprudence, and, like the Tang code's official commentary, this edict suggests a distinction between a woman's active, voluntary participation—which would deserve the full penalty for consent—and her less than enthusiastic submission under circumstances not of her own choosing.

Yuan-dynasty rape law appears to have occupied a transitional position, being somewhat stricter on women than Southern Song law but less so than Ming-Qing law. Again, the evidence is fragmentary yet suggestive. *Collected Statutes of the Yuan* reports a case from present-day Hebei, dated 1304, in which a married woman named Gao Watou accused one Ai Wenyi of raping her; he denied the charge. Investigation determined that Ai had engaged in illicit intercourse with her several times: "the first time, he coerced her; later, he again engaged in illicit sex with her, and she submitted." Therefore, the presiding official reasoned, "it would be inappropriate to judge this crime in the same manner as coerced illicit sexual intercourse; it appears to have been consensual illicit sexual intercourse." But that sentence, too, seemed inappropriate: "On the other hand, the woman herself filed charges against the man"—which suggested to the magistrate that her "submission" had not been enthusiastic. Therefore, as a compromise, he sentenced the woman to only 57 blows of the heavy bamboo, rather than the 87 blows prescribed by Yuan law for the consensual illicit sex of a married woman. He further ordered that her husband "be allowed to divorce her and return her to her natal lineage." Ai Wenyi died before sentencing, so we do not know what his exact penalty would have been. But the magistrate's comment indicates that the woman's "submission" after being raped would have spared Ai Wenyi the full penalty (strangulation) mandated by Yuan law for the rape of a married woman. Nonetheless, the treatment of the woman Gao Watou seems to follow the policy outlined in the Song edict cited above: the fact that sexual relations began with coercion indicated a reduction in the penalty for the woman's subsequent consent (YD, 45/15a).

What kinds of evidence were required to prove coercion? The Tang and Song codes are silent on this matter, but the death penalties mandated beginning in the Yuan no doubt required a stricter standard of evidence. *Collected Statutes of the Yuan* briefly summarizes a test case of the rape of a married woman dated 1269, from present-day Henan, for which the death penalty was imposed. It states that the rapist tore out his victim's hair, beat and kicked her, and "used words to intimidate and terrify her," so that he was finally able to consummate the act. This summary suggests that evidence of considerable violence was required to prove coercion, at least when the offender's life was at stake (YD, 45/2a).

The Ming dynasty codified a strict and highly specific standard of evidence for coercion. In 1587, the Board of Punishment presented a memorial concerning the great gap that had emerged between the penalties for coercion and consent: "The statute states that whoever commits illicit sex with consent shall be beaten with the heavy bamboo, while whoever commits illicit sex by coercion shall be strangled. There is such a wide gap between the severity of the two punishments that the offenses must be distinguished clearly." In order to avoid confusion, the Board of Punishment proposed precise criteria that would have to be met before a man could be sentenced to strangulation:

Henceforth, for coercive illicit sexual intercourse to be prosecuted, [it shall be required that] the illicit intercourse was consummated only because a weapon was used to threaten the woman, or because she was overpowered and tied up, so that even though she wished to struggle free she was unable to do so; [it shall be further required] that the woman cried out and cursed, and that she exhibit evidence such as torn clothing and broken skin. Only then shall the offender be sentenced to strangulation.

In a third passage, the board listed several ambiguous scenarios in which coercion might be present to some degree but which would not count as rape for purposes of law:

If a man approaches with coercion and the woman responds with consent (*qiang lai he ying*), or if he begins with coercion but in the end she consents (*shi qiang er zhong he*); or if the woman denies having consented and claims that she was coerced only because someone has seen them together, or if she fears exposure and therefore falsely accuses him of coercion in order to conceal her consent; or if the offender is caught elsewhere than where the offense took place, or if the only evidence of illicit sex is a third party accusation—under none of these circumstances shall the man receive the penalty for coercion.   (TM, 26/14a–b)

The board's memorial received imperial endorsement. The third passage, in particular, stands in strong contrast with the Song edict cited above: in Ming law, initial coercion was completely negated by subsequent consent. It is less clear whether the second passage, on the types of evidence necessary to prove coercion, represented a significant departure from early judicial practice; even so, that seems likely, since the lawmakers of earlier dynasties apparently did not feel compelled to spell out their criteria in such concrete, specific terms. Earlier dynasties were simply not as fixated on rape as were the Yuan and, especially, the Ming and Qing. Nor, it seems, did the lawmakers of earlier periods necessarily see rape as an all-or-nothing test of a woman's chastity, as later became the rule.

The 1587 memorial formalized the standard by which rape cases were judged under Ming law; we find similar language in authoritative commentaries on the Ming code (XF, 13/16a; also see citations in TM, 26/14a, and Wu Tan 1992, 950). The Qing judiciary adopted the Ming standard, adding it to the basic Ming statute on illicit sex as an interlinear commentary. This commentary, which appeared in the first edition of the Qing code in 1646, includes the following statement:

> In prosecution for rape, there must be evidence of violent coercion (*qiang bao*), and the situation must have been such that the woman could not struggle free; there must also be persons who heard what happened, as well as evidence such as physical injury or torn clothing. Only then shall the offender be sentenced to strangulation. If an offender joins with a woman by coercion, but consummates the act by means of her consent (*yi qiang he, yi he cheng*), then it does not count as coercion.[8]

In Ming and Qing law, then, any act of illicit sex that failed to meet the standard of evidence for coercion was automatically regarded as consensual. For legal purposes, consent might include anything from active enjoyment to terrified submission. A woman had to resist actively and even violently for her attacker's conduct to be defined as coercion. This Ming-Qing standard appears to reverse the formula proposed by Zhang Fei in the third century, which had implied that anything short of active consent counted by default as coercion.

The net result of change had been to narrow the definition of rape to include only violations of women whose impeccable chastity could be proven by their conduct in response to the challenge of rape, as well as by previous sexual history. In Ming-Qing law, the harm caused by rape depended on the chastity of the woman raped; it was the court's judgment of the victim, ultimately, that determined her rapist's penalty.

Distinguishing Coercion from Consent in Qing Practice

An 1828 case summarized in *Conspectus of Legal Cases* illustrates the difficulty of fitting human relations into the stereotyped categories of consent and coercion. The governor of Guangxi reported to the Board of Punishment that in this case, instead of "joining by coercion, but completing the act by means of the woman's consent" (*yi qiang he, yi he cheng*)—a scenario defined by the interlinear commentary as the equivalent of consent—the *opposite* had happened: the man had "joined with the woman with her consent, but had consummated the act only by means of coercion" (*yi he he, yi qiang cheng*). The governor asked the board for advice, since nothing in the code seemed to cover such a scenario.

The board replied with a caustic reprimand. First, it summarized the legal principles involved:

The statute mandates strangulation [only] in cases of rape (*qiang jian*) where there is evidence of violent coercion from beginning to end. If the man first joins with the woman by means of coercion, but then consummates the act by means of her consent, the case should still be judged according to the provision on consensual illicit sex (*he jian*).

But this notion of "first joining with the woman with her consent, but then completing the act by means of coercion" simply defies common sense (*qing li suo wu*). That is why the statute contains no specific language to cover such a situation. It is the responsibility of the investigating official to resolve the question of whether it was coercion or consent by determining the facts and assigning penalties according to statute. It is intolerable to judge a serious criminal case so irresponsibly, vacillating between the two alternatives.

The Board then summarized the facts *as reported by the governor:*

In this case, Deng Zhangpang, seventeen *sui*, lived in the same village as Deng Niangmei (of the same surname but unrelated), who was only thirteen *sui*. Seeing that Deng Niangmei was at home alone, Deng Zhangpang seduced (*hong you*) her into dallying and engaging in illicit sex (*xing jian wan shua*). Deng Niangmei agreed (*yun*); Deng Zhangpang helped her remove her pants and, embracing her on a pile of hay, was just about to engage in illicit intercourse (*zheng yao xing jian*), when she became fearful and refused. So he forced her down with his hands and used coercion to consummate the illicit sexual act (*qiang xing cheng jian*). Deng Niangmei felt pain and began to weep and cry out, so Deng Zhangpang became afraid and ran away.

The board rejected this version of the facts. It made no legal sense to take seriously any claim of second thoughts on the part of the girl after she had allowed Deng to remove her pants and embrace her: "Since Deng Zhangpang had elicited her agreement to play around and engage in illicit sex, why would she suddenly become fearful and refuse, after he had already taken off her pants, but had not yet started the sex act? The presentation of facts in the original record of testimony is incoherent and disjointed."

Therefore, the board weighed the only two possible situations, given the procrustean dichotomy of coercion and consent:

Deng Zhangpang was already seventeen *sui*, and so was hardly immature and ignorant. Deng Niangmei was already thirteen *sui*, and therefore not "a little girl of twelve *sui* or younger" [i.e., she was not below the legal age of liability for consent]. Nevertheless . . . if Deng Niangmei really were too young to understand what illicit sex is, and the criminal took advantage of her ignorance to trick her into taking off her pants and to rape her, then he first plotted the seduction, and then proceeded to consummate the illicit sex by coercion. In that case, he should be sentenced to strangulation according to the statute on rape. It is impermissible to say that he "joined with the woman with her consent, but consummated the act by coercion," thereby distorting the situation so that he escapes justice.

But, if Deng Niangmei first agreed (*yun*) to have illicit sex, then by the time she felt pain the consensual illicit sex had already been consummated. In that case, even though the criminal gave rein to his lust and continued the illicit sexual intercourse in spite of Deng Niangmei's weeping and cries of pain, it would still be inappropriate to sentence him according to the statute on rape.

The board closed with this admonition:

If the governor in question can only determine the correct facts, the code indeed contains clear language specific to this case, and there should be no difficulty in citing it in order to determine the appropriate sentence. But the [governor] has not investigated with care, allowing the criminal to vacillate in his confession.

The only way the board might have considered the incident rape was if the girl had been so immature that she was incapable of effective consent. However, even that was a stretch, since she had already reached the legal age at which a female became liable for consent. Otherwise, the episode could not be considered coercion, because Deng Niangmei clearly had not resisted from the start. Having allowed Deng to remove her pants and embrace her on the haystack, the only conceivable reason for her to protest was physical pain—but if she felt pain, then it was already too late. The act had been consummated, her chastity was gone, and her subsequent feelings about the matter were irrelevant. While it was legally conceivable for coercion to be followed by consent—which then negated the initial coercion—the opposite situation defied reason. For consent to give way to coercion would imply that a woman's freedom of body and will was the standard used to define rape (XZ, 14/5a–b).

Just as consent did not necessarily imply active, voluntary participation, a judgment of coercion depended less on what the rapist did than on how the woman reacted. That judgment and the extreme penalty that went with it were measures of the woman's extraordinary vigilance in defense of her husband's sexual monopoly. In an important sense, they were rewards to the woman for having met such a difficult test of her chastity.

A central case from Taikang County, Henan, memorialized in 1739 shows how the Qing judiciary treated rape that was followed by the victim's submission to her rapist (a scenario, it will be recalled, that

Song lawmakers had treated as coercion, at least for purposes of punishing the rapist). Ding Da, his wife, Ma Shi, and their daughter Ding Dajie (eighteen *sui*), were itinerant beggars, and they pooled resources and traveled with Ding Er, with whom Ding Da had sworn brotherhood. Unbeknownst to Ding Da (who was blind), Ding Er and Ma Shi had begun a sexual affair. Shortly thereafter, the gang took up with another beggar, Wang Wu, who also began sleeping with Ma Shi.

One day, Wang Wu and Ding Dajie were left alone together. According to Dajie's testimony, "Wang Wu used force to violate me (*ying ba xiaode jian le*). I told my mother, but she didn't say anything, and since my father is blind, I didn't tell him. Afterward, Wang Wu often slept with me (*tong shui*)." Significantly, this passage does not use the legal term "coercion"—*qiang*—which almost certainly would have been added to the edited transcript of her testimony if it were being used to convict Wang Wu of rape. Ding Er found out and was jealous; according to his testimony, though, "since I, too, was having illicit sex with Ma Shi I was afraid to make a scene, because if Ding Da found out it would cause trouble for everyone, including me." For this reason, he murdered Wang Wu and disposed of his body in secret, telling the others that Wang had simply left on his own. A couple of weeks later, the band was staying at a ruined temple; according to Ding Dajie, "Then, Ding Er also violated me (*ba xiaode jian le*). Afterward I told my mother, but she didn't say anything. Ding Er violated me (*jian guo xiaode*) about four or five times."

Eventually, the band was arrested and Ding Er was sentenced for the murder. The two women had not been involved in the murder, but they were punished for their illicit intercourse with Ding Er and Wang Wu, which was all treated as consensual. Each woman received a sentence of 100 blows of the heavy bamboo and one month in the cangue, under the substatute on "soldiers or civilians engaging in illicit sex" (which by the eighteenth century was being cited to punish consensual illicit sex instead of the old Ming statute—see Appendix A.3).

Were Ma Shi's relations with the two men really "consensual," in any sense other than that of Qing law? She depended on them because of her husband's blindness, and she probably had no real choice other than to sleep with them. But Ding Dajie clearly did not welcome the men's advances, and she seems to have resigned herself only after realizing that her mother could or would do nothing to help her (neither woman seems to have thought telling Ding Da would do any good). Dajie's testimony makes it plain that in every instance, intercourse was something the men did to her against her wishes. But the presiding judges never treated this as a case of "coercive illicit sexual intercourse"—the term nowhere appears in the case record. There is no sign that any official asked her for evidence of the violent coercion used, or of her resistance, in order to weigh application of the statute on rape. The penalty Ding Dajie received shows that her response to the challenge to her chastity counted as consent for purposes of law. Had her case been judged by the Song or Yuan judiciary, she would likely have received a reduced sentence for consent with mitigating circumstances. By the Ming-Qing era, judges consistently treated subsequent consent as completely negating initial coercion (XT, 73/QL 4.10.15).

Judicial considerations aside, this case offers an excellent example of the instrumental nature of sexual relations among the marginalized people (such as beggars, hired laborers, poor peasants, mendicant clergy, and demobilized soldiers) who appear in so many Qing cases involving sex offenses. In this Hobbesian milieu, sexual relations deemed criminal by the state combined with coresidence, pooling of resources, and sometimes emotional bonds and fictive kinship, to become the basis of what might be called "unorthodox households." The judiciary's stereotyped dichotomies (coercion/consent, chaste/unchaste) seem inadequate to capture the reality of sex as a survival strategy at the bottom of Qing society.[9]

Stereotypes of the Dangerous Male

This glimpse into the lower depths of eighteenth-century society leads us to the question of how late imperial jurists imagined the hypothetical rapist, the dangerous outside male against whom the family order had to be defended. From antiquity, illicit sexual intercourse had been defined as an assault on family order by an outside male, with or without the treacherous collusion of an inside female. But the jurists' image of that outside male threat changed over time, in conjunction with change in social structure and legal status order.

The Old Stereotype of the Mean-Status Rapist

By considering the scale of penalties in the Tang code's statutes against illicit sex, we can deduce what sort of rapist Tang lawmakers feared the most. The severest penalty in these statutes is beheading;

apart from some spectacular variations of incest, beheading was reserved for a male slave (*nu*) or "semi-slave" (*bu qu*) who used coercion to have intercourse with a woman of his master's immediate
family (see Appendix A.1 and TL, 26).[10] This dangerous male was an
outsider in terms of status, class, and blood; nevertheless, he was a
familiar figure, a member of the large mean labor force attached to
every elite household in that era. The priority accorded this particular scenario reflects the anxiety of an aristocracy over its ability to
subjugate its own slaves, and suggests comparison with the American slaveholder's paranoia about black men raping white women:
in both systems, the worst-case scenario represented an inversion of
the actual state of affairs (in which masters enjoyed free sexual use
of their female slaves), and reflected the ruling elite's insecurity
about the possibility of class rebellion. Indeed, one of the highest
priorities of the Tang code as a whole is to control mean-status labor.

The new substatutes against rape promulgated by Qing jurists,
especially in the eighteenth century, portray a very different dangerous male. His defining characteristics are not mean status or servile
attachment to an elite household. On this subject, it is possible to
be confused by the structure of the Qing code, which preserved almost all the old Ming statutes long after many were no longer applied in practice. If one looks only at those statutes, which date
from the late fourteenth century, one sees little of the living law
that Qing jurists actually applied during the eighteenth and nineteenth centuries. The living law is represented by the substatutes;
and one of the clearest indications of the declining importance of
status transgression is that very few of these new substatutes had
anything to do with intercourse between mean-status males and
commoner females.[11]

The old statute against "illicit intercourse between commoners
and mean persons" (*liang jian xiang jian*) was never amended by
substatute, and it closely resembled the Tang-dynasty original on
which it had been based (DC, 373-00). In the Qing archives, I have
seen no cases in which this statute was cited to punish a mean-
status male.[12] The old statute against "a slave or worker-serf (*gugongren*) engaging in illicit intercourse with his master's wife" (DC,
370-00) was amended in the eighteenth century by three substatutes; however, two of these imposed new penalties for *masters* or
their relatives who sexually abused the wives of slaves and servants
(DC, 370-01 and 02). The third confirmed the old statute's penalty
of beheading for a slave or worker-serf who raped his master's wife

or daughter. In addition, it added the explicit requirement that the strict standard of evidence used in ordinary rape prosecution must be applied to these cases as well: "investigation must establish firm proof of physical injury and torn clothing, and there must be neighbors who testify that they saw or heard [the rape]." In effect, this substatute extended to slaves and worker-serfs the protection of being assumed innocent of coercion until the alleged rape victim was herself proven innocent of consent (DC, 370-03). All three substatutes can be interpreted as having a *leveling* effect, in that they reduced the harshness of legal discrimination against servile labor.

What about case records? In the Qing archives, I have seen only a single case of a slave (*nu*) being executed for intercourse with a woman of his master's family, and it dates from the very first decade of the dynasty.[13] The situation of hired laborers is more complicated. Ming laws inherited by the Qing defined *gugongren* (which Huang translates "worker-serf") as the status inferiors of their employers, to be discriminated against accordingly in criminal judgments. Over the course of the eighteenth century, however, the Board of Punishment sharply narrowed this legal category to exclude the great majority of ordinary hired laborers; in effect, the Qing judiciary came to recognize nearly all agricultural workers as the status equals of their employers—who, by the eighteenth century, were usually peasants or managerial farmers of fairly modest means (P. Huang 1985, chap. 5; Jing Junjian 1993, 35–40).

This change did not happen overnight. A key test case in 1757 involved a laborer's rape of his employer's wife, which the board decided involved status equals (P. Huang 1985, 98). Nevertheless, three rape cases memorialized in consecutive months of 1762 reveal some of the confusion that accompanied this shift in status classification. In each case a hired laborer had tried to rape his employer's wife or concubine and, when she resisted, had wounded her severely with a knife. In the first (from Fengtian, Shengjing), Chen Tianzhang was an immigrant who had been hired by verbal agreement to work for only two months; therefore, the Shengjing Board of Punishment recommended that he be treated as his employer's status equal for purposes of sentencing. But this recommendation was rejected by the Three High Courts of Judicature, which labeled Chen a "worker-serf" (*gugongren*), without giving any specific reason for doing so (XT, 184/QL 27.2.5). In the second case (from Peng County, Sichuan), laborer Zhou Yinglong had also been hired without a written contract, and the governor-general of Sichuan sentenced him as his employer's status equal. Once again, the Three High Courts over-ruled the decision, pointing out that Zhou had agreed to work until after the new year, and thus had been hired "on an annual basis" (XT, 179/QL 27.3.7).

In the third case (from Tang County, Zhili), laborer Wang Daxiao had worked for "less than a year," without a written contract, and "had not received much wages yet"; therefore, the governor-general of Zhili sentenced him as his employer's status equal. This time the Three High Courts agreed, and asserted that the legal definition of "worker-serf" required either that the laborer had been hired on an annual basis, or that he had worked for the same employer on a more casual basis for at least five years; all others should be treated as their employers' status equals (XT, 188/QL 27.4.13). But this def-inition directly contradicted the Three High Courts' own decision just two months before in the case of Chen Tianzhang (who had agreed to work for two months only). This snapshot of 1762 reveals a marked lack of consensus among senior jurists about how hired la-borers should be treated.

By the seventeen-eighties, however, the central judiciary had de-cided that essentially all agricultural workers hired by ordinary com-moners—including those employed on an annual basis—should be treated as their employers' status equals (P. Huang 1985, 98–99). Hired laborers of one kind or another appear frequently as criminals in late eighteenth- and nineteenth-century legal cases, but they are nearly always treated as the status equals of their employers. In all other contexts, they are assumed to be ordinary commoners.

The New Stereotype of the "Rootless Rascal"

It would seem that the Qing judiciary worried less than the Tang judiciary about rapists of specifically mean status or among servile labor. The penalties for such rapists remained harsh; still, with strangulation or beheading being mandated for *all* rapists, the penal-ties for mean status males no longer stood out in the way they orig-inally had. Moreover, both the substatutes and the archives show that these males were not a major focus of either legislative initia-tives or routine rape prosecution during the eighteenth and nine-teenth centuries. Instead, the bogey of the Qing judiciary was the marginal man who stood outside of (and presumably opposed to) the family-based social and moral order that underpinned the late impe-rial state.[14] That outside male was an aggressive penetrator in sexual and symbolic terms: he ruptured the boundaries of the household and threatened to violate the women (and young boys) within.

This sexual predator was a subset of a more general stereotype of the dangerous outside male that runs through Qing legal discourse. We find this dangerous male mentioned repeatedly in the Qing code; he appears with increasing frequency and urgency in the substatutes that accumulated over time. Qing lawmakers used a number of terms in various combinations to characterize him. He was "violent" (*xiong*), "wicked" (*e*), "licentious" (*yin*), and "habitually fights" (*hao dou*); he was a "worthless, wicked reprobate" (*bu xiao e tu*), a "depraved rogue" (*diao tu*). But most frequently, he was characterized as a "*guang gun*": literally, a "bare stick."

Guang gun is an old term, but as far as I know it first appears in legal discourse in the late seventeenth century. *Gun* means a "stick" or "club"—thus, by extension, a man who stands alone (without "roots" or "branches"). The word implies both a lack of socializing ties and the roguery that resulted; a source from as early as the Tang dynasty defines *gun* as "evil village youths" who dressed disreputably, gathered in gangs, and got into fights (cited in ZD, 5/282). The prefix *guang* (bare, naked, alone . . .) emphasizes poverty and lack of a wife. The late Qing scholar-official Zhang Binglin defined *guang gun* as either "a violent man" (*xiong ren*) or "a man without wife or family" (*wu shi jia zhe*) (cited in *Ci hai*, 1/294). To sum up, then, a *guang gun* was a man with no wife, family, or property to discipline him and give him a stake in the social and moral order. A translation more idiomatic than "bare stick" might be "rootless rascal."

The Qing code's chapter on extortion (*kong xia qu cai*) is the one most explicitly devoted to the "rootless rascal" (DC, 273-00; QHS, 794/692-703). The original Ming statute that heads the chapter says nothing specific about "rootless rascals." But the substatutes appended over the course of the Qing dynasty, instead of elaborating on the theme of extortion, seek to punish habitual troublemaking by incorrigible individuals or groups of men. Many of these later substatutes have no direct link to extortion per se. Indeed, over time, as new laws accumulated, the emphasis of the chapter shifted away from that specific crime, to dangerous antisocial behavior in general, and to the different categories of marginal men considered a threat to social order. Some are "catch-all" laws that could apply very widely:

Any violent, wicked rascal (*xiong e gun tu*) who repeatedly causes trouble, commits violent acts, and without reason harasses and harms respectable commoners (*liang min*), and whose behavior is well-known to others, and for which there is firm proof, shall be exiled to the farthest frontier and held securely at a distance of 4,000 *li*.

Note that here the contrast between culprit and victim is based not on legal status difference, but on habitual wickedness versus law-abiding decency: "*liang min*" here implies commoner status less than a judgment of moral worth.

Other substatutes in the extortion chapter aim to punish (for example) "depraved rogues" (*diao tu*) who stir up trouble and extort or bully "gullible villagers" (*xiang yu*); migrants who maintain no proper registration, and who commit violent and evil acts, showing no respect for law and order; "rootless rascals" who migrate to Shengjing, and collude with locals to engage in various kinds of harassment or extortion; Miao tribesmen who practice kidnapping, extortion, and other violence on non-Miao; yamen underlings or Han civilians who intrude on Miao territory and engage in bullying, extortion, rape, and the like; eunuchs who escape palace supervision and cause trouble out in society; and bandits or sectarian partisans of different kinds who gather in gangs to intimidate and engage in violence (separate substatutes name Anhui, Guangdong, Guangxi, Guizhou, Jiangsu, Jiangxi, Shaanxi, Shandong, and Shanxi as provinces where such troublemakers need to be suppressed).

Running through the judicial discourse of the rootless rascal we find a consistent conflation of certain kinds of crime (extortion, kidnapping, rape, seduction, sodomy, intimidation, robbery, banditry, heterodoxy) with certain kinds of men (local toughs, rootless migrants in frontier areas and cities, yamen runners, male Buddhist and Daoist clergy, fugitives from justice, unsupervised eunuchs, Miao tribesmen). The distinguishing feature of these men is not formal status debasement—status difference appears to be irrelevant in this context, and the men prosecuted as "rootless rascals" are invariably treated as commoners for legal purposes. One way or another, all of these men can be seen as existing outside the mainstream pattern of settled households, the network of family and community relationships that the ideal Confucian scheme depended on to enmesh and socialize individuals. Their victims are portrayed as law-abiding commoners: "humble peasants," chaste wives and daughters, non-Han tribesmen who stay in their place, and so on. These laws mandate harsh penalties of exile and death not so much to punish individual *crimes* as to remove incorrigible troublemakers from society altogether.

The most important measure added to the extortion chapter of the code was referred to by jurists simply as the "substatute on rootless rascals" (*guang gun li*—see Appendix A.4). Promulgated in the early Qing, this substatute mandated immediate beheading for a ringleader and strangulation for his followers, who committed a variety of violent crimes mostly related to the chapter heading of "extortion." In the sixteen-seventies, jurists began to cite this law by analogy to punish an increasingly wide range of other crimes, including especially heinous scenarios of rape (gang rape or kidnapping of a chaste woman, rape combined with murder, rape of a young girl, and the like), and such use by analogy was eventually codified in a series of new substatutes (e.g., DC, 366-02, 03, 04, 08, and 09). It was cited also to punish the corresponding scenarios of homosexual rape, a subject we shall address in the next chapter (see Appendix B.1). Increasingly, Qing legal discourse characterized the violent sexual predator specifically as a "rootless rascal." For example, in a 1733 edict, the Yongzheng Emperor commented: "If a man tries to rape a woman, and kills her because she resists, then an offender of such licentious viciousness (*yin xiong zhi fan*) is truly no different from a 'rootless rascal'—and only immediate beheading is harsh enough punishment to requite his crime" (MQ, 59-10). In the First Historical Archives in Beijing, eighteenth- and nineteenth-century examples of heterosexual and homosexual rape being punished by analogy to the substatute on rootless rascals are extremely common.[15]

We should note here the phallic connotation of the term *guang gun*. A study of Beijing idioms observes that *gun* (stick) was slang for "penis"; that, it suggests, is why *guang gun* (i.e., "bare penis") was slang for a man with no wife (cited in Chen Baoliang 1993, 161). In vernacular fiction, *gun* served as a metaphor for an erect penis—for example, in the late Ming novel *Plum in the Golden Vase*, when the Daoist priest Jin Mingzong (himself a rootless rascal) prepares to rape a young man (Chen Jingji) in the bed they happen to be sharing: "He manipulated his penis until it was very hard, a stick standing straight up (*zhi shu yi tiao gun*)" (93/10a). One does not have to be a crude Freudian to sense that the repeated use of *gun* in legal texts (*guang gun, gun tu, e gun, yin gun,* and the like) reinforces the image of the rogue male as a specifically *phallic* threat to social order.

Male clergy, both Buddhist and Daoist, are singled out for special scrutiny in legal codes from the Tang dynasty forward, but especially in the Ming and Qing. By forswearing sexual relations, abstaining from marriage, and living apart from their families, these men stood outside the mainstream family order in the most basic ways. Qing officials saw such men as the very personification of the "rootless rascal" and all the dangers he represented. As Philip Kuhn has shown, the "clerical underclass" was an object of especially intense concern during the eighteenth century, because imperial officials believed that the numbers of "roving clergy" were growing rapidly, providing "a breeding ground for sedition and lawlessness"; indeed, there was strong suspicion that "many 'monks' and 'priests' were not 'really' clergy at all, but rogues who took clerical garb to evade the law" (1990, 44). The Qing dynasty made repeated efforts to subject clergy to social and political control by registering them at particular institutions, by making novices the responsibility of their superiors, by banning the wandering of mendicant clergy, and by prohibiting men from joining clerical orders without registering and receiving permission from imperial authority (for the elaborate new control measures undertaken in the eighteenth century, see QHS, 501).

Jurists seem to have been particularly inclined to suspect clergy of sexual aggression. For example, a Ming law adopted by the Qing code punishes Buddhist or Daoist clergy at temples who seduced or abducted women, or who "swindled them out of money" (DC, 161-01). Another statute increases by two degrees the severity of penalties for any sexual offense that is committed by clergy (DC, 372-00). An eighteenth-century measure cites the substatute on rootless rascals to punish "lamas, Buddhist monks, and other clergy" who commit rape and cause the victim's death (DC, 366-09). The code contains many other examples: the suspicion seems to have been that clerical celibacy was a disingenuous façade, designed to facilitate sexual aggression and other predatory behavior by disarming gullible people. (This suspicion certainly conforms to the stereotype of male clergy in Ming and Qing dynasty vernacular fiction.)

To sum up, then, the sexual predator portrayed in Qing legislation is a subset of a more general archetype of the dangerous male: the rootless rascal outside the family order, who poses a multifarious threat to that order. The rapist feared most by the Tang code was an outsider by reason of blood, status, and class, but he had a known place in the household order; indeed, one can say that the greatest danger came from *within* that order. But the Qing dynasty's judicial discourse of rape is not about legal status transgression or class tensions within the aristocratic manor—the rootless rascal and his victim are both assumed to be commoners, but formal legal status is beside the point. His danger comes from his position as an individual outside the family order that supported normative values and imperial power. Tang-dynasty aristocrats feared their own slaves, not unknown outsiders; Qing jurists feared the growing crowd of rogue males at the bottom of society, who provided the cannon fodder for banditry and rebellion, and who might covet the wives and daughters (and young sons, too) of better-established householders.

Central Court Practice in the Qing Dynasty

Let us turn now to those cases of rape that fully satisfied the orthodox standards of the judiciary. Case records in which men were actually prosecuted for rape clearly do not represent all rapes that occurred, especially if one adheres to a rights-based definition of that crime. Rather, they record specific scenarios that fit the narrowly defined official standard. A brief survey of such cases from the Qing dynasty enables us to establish with some precision the late imperial judiciary's idealized stereotype of this crime.

I have detailed records of 49 cases of heterosexual rape from the Yongzheng, Qianlong, and Jiaqing reigns (all are central cases). In each, a man was formally convicted of rape or attempted rape (and sometimes of additional crimes like homicide). (We shall profile homosexual rape in Chapter 4.) The sample includes a total of 58 rapists and 50 rape victims (one case involving two victims, and some women in other cases having been raped by more than one man). This sample may be too small for some definitive quantitative survey, and the case records do not always provide the specific details we would like to know. But there is enough information to suggest what sort of attack by what sort of man on what sort of woman would satisfy official standards sufficiently for the Qing judiciary to impose death penalties for rape.

Profile of the Ideal Rapist

Let us first examine the convicted rapists themselves. If we shift from legislative discourse to the actual prosecution of rape, we find that the rootless rascal was more than just rhetoric.

Case records report the ages of 43 of these men: most were in their twenties or thirties, the average age being thirty-one *sui*. The sample also provides the occupational status of 43 rapists. A total of 29 (67 percent) had lowly or stigmatized occupations, including 22 agricultural laborers, one beggar, one itinerant barber, one soldier, one yamen runner, and three men described as "not working at any legitimate occupation" (*bu wu zheng ye*). Of the fourteen rapists with more respectable occupations, two were tailors, one was a mat weaver, and eleven appear to have been ordinary peasants; several are described as very poor. In addition, two of the rapists are described as habitual thieves, and four others were engaged in burglary when they committed rape. It seems safe to assume that the fifteen men whose occupations are not reported did not enjoy remarkable occupations or incomes, either; otherwise that information would surely be recorded.

We know for sure the marital status of 28 men: only four were married, while 24 were single. If we are conservative, then, we can say with absolute certainty that only 24 rapists out of the entire sample of 58 were unmarried (41 percent). But it seems reasonable to infer that most, if not all, of the rapists whose marital status is not reported were single as well. For one thing, central cases during these three reign periods routinely include the testimony of immediate family members of offenders convicted of capital crimes, and in the few cases where a rapist is reported as married, his wife appears as an important witness ("Where was your husband on the night of the crime?"). The general poverty and occupational profile of the sample also suggests they were unlikely to be married, given the worsening "marriage crunch" among the poor in eighteenth- and nineteenth-century China. Moreover, in cases of rape (whether heterosexual or homosexual), magistrates seem to have felt the marital status of the defendant to be especially relevant. If a rapist is reported as married, the magistrate sometimes asks him why on earth, if he had a wife of his own, he would commit rape. Such interrogation implies an expectation that it was precisely the *lack* of a wife that would provoke a man to commit rape—an expectation reinforced by the judicial stereotype of the "rootless rascal."

We know the places of origin of 41 of the convicted rapists. Most were from the same villages as their victims (almost the entire sample is rural), but eleven were outsiders. Ten of the outsiders were immigrants from other counties or provinces.

With this information, we can construct a tentative profile of the typical man convicted of rape during the High Qing. He was in his twenties or thirties, probably of disreputable occupation, and almost certainly poor and unmarried. In most cases he would be from the same village as his victim, but there was a good chance that he would be an unknown outsider. He might well be involved in other disruptive activity, such as theft; also, several men in the sample were drunk when they committed rape. In short, he was a young man without property, status, family, or prospects—and hence, with little obvious stake in the social order.

Profile of the Ideal Rape Victim

An examination of the female victims of these rapists reveals an even clearer stereotype. The status of every female in the sample was defined by some legitimate relationship to a man. Out of the 50 rape victims, thirteen were unmarried daughters living at home; seven were young adopted daughters-in-law whose marriages had not yet been consummated; 28 were wives (including one concubine); and two were widows. Twelve victims were below the age of liability for consent; of the mature women, most were in their late teens and twenties. The oldest was thirty-six *sui*.

We know who reported 46 of the rapes to the authorities. Not surprisingly, 27 were reported by a husband, father-in-law, or brother-in-law, and one was reported by a husband's landlord; fifteen were reported by the victim's father or other natal relative. Only two were reported by the women themselves. In other words, the active support of the senior males of a victim's family was usually necessary for the prosecution of rape to occur.

Perhaps the most revealing detail is the location of each female when she was raped, which is reported for all 50 victims. Thirty-seven (74 percent) were at home, including nineteen women who were attacked at night while they lay in bed. Another six were working on family land; four others had gone out on some specific household errand (e.g., fetching water). One woman was returning from her parents' home, which she had visited with the permission of her husband's family. The remaining two rape victims were young girls attacked while they were playing outside, not far from home.

What stands out, of course, is the domestic patriarchal context. These women and girls had all remained unambiguously within the domestic sphere proper to them. They could not be blamed for provoking rape through some questionable activity of their own. The uniformity of the sample in this respect reinforces the conclusion that prosecution for rape required a preliminary judgment that the raped woman was a legitimate victim, that her rape represented as much an attack on the family order as on her own person (indeed, the need for preliminary judgment of the *victims* is precisely why we have more detail about them than about their rapists). This image recalls the literal meaning of the statutory term for the ideal rape victim, "a wife or daughter of commoner family." The great majority of these rape victims were ordinary peasants: they were chaste but humble commoner wives and daughters. To underscore the point, the stereotypical perpetrator of this attack was a rogue male dangerously free of the socializing bonds of marriage, family, and property.[16]

A final point which stands out is the role of physical injury in proving rape. Of the 50 rape victims in the sample, eighteen died by homicide or suicide; six others survived with serious wounds; another two attempted suicide but failed. Of the victims who survived without serious bodily harm, only thirteen were over the age of liability for consent (thirteen *sui*). Eleven unharmed victims were twelve *sui* or under—for these underage girls, any sexual act would automatically be treated as coercion, so the only evidence necessary was proof of the victims' ages and of consummation.

In short, two-thirds of the victims over the age of liability for consent suffered death or grievous bodily harm. This ratio points not just to the violence of rape in general, but also to the Ming-Qing standard of evidence for coercion and resistance, which placed the highest value on the injury or death of the victim.

Cases That Satisfied the Judiciary

This discussion of central court practice concludes with three examples that illustrate how the principles and standards of evidence described thus far played out in the adjudication of cases that fully satisfied the Qing judiciary. All three are drawn from memorials presented by provincial governors to the central authorities for review of the rapists' death sentences.

In the first example, a case from Pi Department, Jiangsu, memorialized in 1739, Tian Dong (forty-nine *sui*), an unmarried casual laborer from Shandong, was convicted of raping Zhang Kuijie (fourteen *sui*), an unmarried girl who lived near him in the same village. One morning, Tian saw Kuijie playing in the doorway of her house with her next-door neighbor, a girl named Xiaoyatou (also fourteen *sui*). Tian realized that the girls were alone, their families having gone to the fields to harvest grain, and related in his confession:

I deserve to die for it, but I wanted to have illicit sex with Kuijie. First I tried to persuade her to come over to my doorway to pick and eat dates, but she was unwilling. I waited awhile, and then went over and picked up Kuijie in my arms and carried her into the empty room [I rent], bolted the door, forced her down, . . . tore off her pants, and raped her. After I was finished, I went back outside.

Then, Kuijie ran crying to the field where her mother and older brother, Zhang Qi, were working and told them what had happened. Zhang Qi reported the crime to the local yamen.

At first, Tian Dong denied the charge, claiming that he had merely scolded the two girls when he caught them stealing dates from his employer's trees. His petition concluded: "Weeping, I recall that I am nearly fifty *sui*, while [this girl] is a mere adolescent. I, too, am a human being—how could I possibly do such a thing?" Therefore, in the first court hearing, the magistrate pressed Kuijie's brother Zhang Qi: "What proof do you have that Tian Dong raped your sister?" Zhang begged the magistrate to question the two girls.

Xiaoyatou testified that Tian Dong had forcibly carried Kuijie to his house; Kuijie had screamed, but Tian had pressed his hand over her mouth; carrying her inside, he shut the door, and came back out only after some time had passed. The magistrate pressed her: "When you saw Kuijie had been carried by Tian Dong into his house, why didn't you cry for help?" She replied, "At the time, there was nobody home at Kuijie's house, and my parents weren't home either. Everyone else lives pretty far away, and I was terrified—who should I have cried to for help? When my parents came home, I told them about it." The magistrate pressed Kuijie on the crucial issue of the degree of her resistance. She described what had happened: "I am young and weak, and though I struggled, I couldn't struggle free. After he raped me, he ran out first. I put on my pants, and, crying, went to the fields to tell my mother and brother." The magistrate continued to press her: "Why didn't you scream?" She replied: "I did scream, but he pressed his hand tightly over my mouth." "Did you scream while he forced you down and pulled your pants off?" "I screamed, but again he pressed his hand over my mouth, so that the sound of my screams couldn't come out." "Were your pants torn when he pulled them off?" "I was wearing a pair of blue cotton pants; he tore them."

A midwife examined Kuijie (who was not married), and confirmed that the girl was "not a virgin" because she had "already been broken" (*yijing po shen*). Zhang Qi then submitted the girl's torn pants. Tian Dong's employer contradicted the story about the date trees, testifying that they were still too young to bear fruit. And Xiaoyatou's father testified that his daughter had told him about the rape immediately after he arrived home that day. Confronted again, Tian confessed. Even then, the magistrate continued to press the question of resistance in follow-up questions recorded in the transcript of Tian's confession: "Did the girl scream?" Tian: "She started to scream several times when I first picked her up and when I was raping her, but each time I covered her mouth with my hand so that no sound could come out." Tian Dong's sentence was strangulation after the assizes, confirmed on review.

Zhang Kuijie had no physical injury that constituted evidence of her resistance. (The trauma to her vagina was not noted as an "injury," but simply as evidence that it had "already"—that is, prior to marriage—been penetrated. The language used to describe the midwife's evidence is neutral: it does not differentiate the girl's physical experience in any way from normal or legitimate sexual intercourse. This trauma served as a sort of negative evidence: if she had *not* already been "broken," then it would have been clear that rape had not been consummated.) No weapon was used by the rapist, either, but Kuijie's youth and relative weakness probably reduced the need for this kind of evidence. Otherwise, it was a perfect case. Nothing disqualified the girl from consideration as a worthy victim of rape. But the decisive point was that an eyewitness testified that Kuijie had resisted and tried to scream, and that this statement was confirmed by the rapist's own confession, as well as by the physical evidence of the torn pants (XT, 71/QL 4.7.18).

As seen in this case, it was not necessary that every single element of the standard of evidence for coercion be present, but there still had to be multiple, mutually supporting proofs. In a different scenario—known in legal texts as "stealing illicit sex" (*tou jian*) or "acting as an impostor to engage in illicit sex" (*mao jian*)—a woman might be accused of having submitted by default unless the evidence on her side were truly impressive. In this scenario, which appears not infrequently in central cases of rape, the rapist would sneak into the woman's bed while she was asleep and consummate the act before she was fully aware what was happening.

A case from Dingyuan County, Anhui, memorialized in 1762 provides an illustration. Peasant Wang Yuzhi (thirty-two *sui*) got the idea to "steal illicit sex" one night while drinking heavily; he had been lusting for some time after Wang Shi (eighteen *sui*, no relation), the wife of his neighbor Li Gouhan. He went to their house, used his knife to dig a hole in the earthen wall, and, hearing that both husband and wife were asleep, crept inside. He saw that Wang Shi was naked—it was summer—covered only by a pair of pants, so he opened his own pants, climbed on top of her, and began to rape her: "At that point, I was hoping she would think I was her husband, and I consummated the illicit sex (*cheng le jian*)." According to Wang Shi's testimony:

> In my dreams, as I was sleeping, I felt there was somebody on top of me, and I was startled awake. I thought it was my husband, but then I sensed that his body was different from my husband's, so I stretched out my foot and felt my husband still lying there asleep; then I realized that I had been violated (*jian*) by someone. I was just about to yell, when he stuck his tongue inside my mouth. I really hated that, so I bit off a piece of his tongue. Then he grabbed my throat, but I pulled at his hand; he broke one of the fingers of my right hand; at that time, I was kicking wildly, and my husband was startled awake. Then [the intruder] got up, opened the door, and ran away.

Note that in this narrative, it was not *what* the man was doing to her, but rather the realization that he was not her husband, that defined his actions as "illicit sex" (*jian*, used here as a transitive verb), that indicated she had been "violated." After a while, Wang Yuzhi came back with a knife and demanded that she give him back the piece of his tongue that she had bitten off. It was only at this point that the couple recognized him—but they were able to run out into the rice paddies and hide until he finally left. The next day, they reported the rape to the local yamen, presenting the piece of tongue as evidence. When Wang was arrested, all the magistrate had to do was note the injury to his tongue, and he confessed.

The evidence in Wang Shi's favor far outweighed any ambiguity about her having been asleep when the attack began. She had bruises and a broken finger to prove the violence of the attack, as well as the piece of Wang's tongue to prove the ferocity of her own resistance. Wang's confession confirmed her account, but she also had the most authoritative eyewitness possible: her husband. (I suspect the reason this scenario appears so often in rape cases is that the husband's testimony was considered so decisive, rather than that it actually happened so frequently.) There was also the hole Wang had dug through the wall of the house, the fact that he had returned to the scene of the crime with a weapon, et cetera. He was sentenced to strangulation after the assizes (XT, 170/QL 27.4.17).

In both of these cases, the woman was violated within her proper domestic space—Zhang Kuijie while playing with a neighbor girl in her own doorway, and Wang Shi while sleeping in bed with her husband. An 1803 handbook for magistrates addresses this issue:

> If one man acting alone tries to commit rape in broad daylight, he usually cannot succeed, even if he [and the woman] are in a remote place frequented by few people. If in such a case a woman claims that rape was consummated, then it must be that "the man joined with the woman by coercion, but consummated the act by means of her consent." Otherwise, it may be that the man simply made a pass at her and they had illicit sex.
>
> If a man plots to have illicit sex in broad daylight, it is usually when he happens to encounter a woman in some lonely village or remote empty place, and he is suddenly filled with lustful thoughts; usually the man is alone. If he encounters a young girl of fifteen *sui* or under, then he may be able to "join by means of coercion"; but if she is over sixteen *sui*, then it is unlikely that the rape will be consummated.
>
> But women who walk alone without any company are rarely chaste. If, after having illicit sex, a woman reveals this information, then chances are that the man had promised to pay her but cheated, or that she is trying to extort money from him. That is why she denies consent and alleges coercion.

The author goes on to cite the need for physical evidence of resistance and the testimony of witnesses to build a convincing case of rape (Lü Zhitian 1803, 3/12b–13a).

There were occasional exceptions, however. In a case from Luojiang County, Sichuan, also memorialized in 1762, a woman named Xiang Shi (thirty *sui*), was able to have her rape by Zhou Mingzhi (twenty-five *sui*, a single immigrant from Huguang) recognized and prosecuted as such, even though she could produce no physical injuries, torn clothing, or third-party witnesses to prove her resistance. According to Xiang Shi's testimony, her husband was away traveling on business; she had gone to visit her parents, and was walking home:

> There was no one to accompany me home. . . . Because I wanted to take the shortest route, I took a small path, where I ran into Zhou Mingzhi, who was approaching [from the opposite direction]. He forced me down on the ground and pulled off my pants. I struggled and screamed, but he pulled a knife and threatened to kill me. I couldn't struggle free from him, and he was able to consummate the illicit sex by coercion (*qiang jian cheng le*). A silver ring I was wearing was thrown off [in the struggle], and he took that, too.

She went home and, crying, told her brother-in-law what had happened. From her description, he realized that the rapist was Zhou

Mingzhi (she herself did not know him) and went with several neighbors to seize him. Searching Zhou, they found both the knife and the ring, had Xiang Shi confirm that he was her attacker, and then took him to the authorities.

In the first court hearing, the magistrate noted that Xiang Shi had no physical injuries; nor did she have torn clothing or a third-party witness to confirm her story. The magistrate pressed her, but she insisted that she had been attacked with "violent coercion": "Truly, I was sexually polluted by Zhou Mingzhi only because I am weak, and was forced down on the ground by him, and because he threatened me with a knife, so that I could not struggle free. He absolutely did not have my consent to consummate the illicit sex (*bing mei you he cheng de shi*)." Fortunately for Xiang Shi, Zhou Mingzhi confirmed her account, confessing that he had used coercion:

I took a knife with me because I was going into the hills to cut kindling. I encountered Xiang Shi walking toward me, and since we were on a small path, no one else was around, and there were no homes in the vicinity, it suddenly occurred to me to rape her. So I went up to her, forced her to the ground, and pulled off her pants. Xiang Shi wouldn't submit, and struggled and screamed, so I threatened her with my knife; she could not struggle free, and so I was able to consummate the rape (*qiang jian cheng le*). A silver ring on her hand was thrown off, and I picked that up and took it with me. . . . I freely acknowledge my crime, for which I deserve to die.

The magistrate made a preliminary judgment that rape had been committed and reported the matter to his superiors at the prefectural and provincial levels, asking for instructions. They ordered him to visit the scene of the alleged crime to see if it was a well-traveled thoroughfare, and if there were any people living nearby—if so, the accounts of both rapist and victim would have been contradicted. The magistrate traveled to the scene of the crime, together with victim and accused and his entire entourage, and held a hearing on the spot. He found no evidence to contradict previous testimony; he also reinterrogated the prisoner and his accuser, who both stuck to their stories. On this basis, he confirmed his judgment that rape had been committed, justifying it to his superiors with the following logic:

The offender has testified to the foregoing and does not deny his guilt. It is noted that Zhou Mingzhi raped Xiang Shi in a remote place out in the open; there was no one who "heard what happened," nor was there "physical injury, torn clothing, and other such evidence" [as required by statute]. Nevertheless, it was only because he used a knife to threaten her and bring her under control, so that she could not struggle free, that she ended up being sexually polluted. Moreover, the ring which was thrown off Xiang Shi's hand was discovered on the offender's person. The violent coercion of the situation is clear enough from this evidence. Zhou Mingzhi should be sentenced to strangulation after the assizes.

This judgment was confirmed on review.

If exceptional, this case is an exception that proves the rule about the need for multiple proofs of coercion and resistance. Xiang Shi's story was accepted in spite of her lack of injury, torn clothing, or eyewitness testimony because: a weapon had been used; Xiang Shi's ring and the knife were found on the rapist; he confessed freely to the crime and testified that Xiang Shi had resisted as best she could; and the magistrate could find no independent evidence or witness to contradict the testimony of rapist and victim, though he tried. Also, Xiang Shi was backed by her brother-in-law, the man with immediate authority over her, who had taken the initiative in arresting the offender and reporting the crime. He confirmed that her husband was away and that she had had permission to visit her parents: her presence outside of the domestic space could be justified (XT, 171/ QL 27.1.28).

In each of these cases, especially the last one, we are confronted with the bizarre spectacle of the rapist being asked to testify to his victim's chastity. Since a full confession was necessary for the successful prosecution of any capital offense, the woman's ability to meet the standard of evidence for coercion ultimately depended on the rapist's perception of what had occurred. The rapist himself had to testify that he had used violent coercion, that his victim had struggled and screamed, and so on. Of course, the late imperial system required confession for conviction in all capital cases; but most capital crimes other than rape involved homicide, the definition of which depended less on the subjective perception of the offender than did rape. In Qing law, self-defense did not excuse homicide, except homicide in defense against rape—but this brings us back to subjective perceptions.

Feminist scholars point out that it is not unusual for a woman to experience a rape, but for the accused to believe sincerely that his actions have been reasonable and legitimate (hence, the continuing controversy about such matters as date rape and fraternity rape). Therefore, they argue, to define rape sometimes requires the taking of sides, an abandonment of the pretension of neutrality: one must accept the standard of either the woman or the man (e.g., MacKinnon 1989, 180–83). (In recent years, some American courts have acknowledged this point by beginning to apply the hypothetical standard of what "a reasonable woman" would think, instead of the traditional common law standard of "a reasonable man," when judging cases of rape and sexual harassment.) The Qing legal system's requirement of confession for conviction in capital cases meant that the rapist's standard would always be applied in arriving at judgments of rape. This was one more aspect of the raised stakes in Qing rape law, one more reason why convictions for coercive illicit sexual intercourse lack the slightest ambiguity that might cast doubt on the woman's credentials as a worthy victim.

Conclusion

Many elements of late imperial rape law would probably have been familiar to the jurists of earlier dynasties, and indeed to jurists of other legal traditions altogether. For example, Anglo-American common law traditionally defined rape as "unlawful sexual intercourse (requiring penetration) of a woman not the rapist's wife, by force and against her will." It required that "actual force" or verbal threat thereof be present for a woman to prove that the act had been "against her will"; it required that a woman prove she had "resisted to the utmost" in order to communicate her "nonconsent" to the rapist, and held her "at fault if she did not manifest her nonconsent with sufficient clarity"; in addition, "the fact that a victim was unchaste, was a prostitute, or had a prior consensual sexual relationship with her rapist was a defense to the crime of rape" (Blond et al. 1991, 121–27). This reasoning would have made perfect sense to a Qing magistrate—and possibly to a Tang magistrate as well. These basic elements of rape law are common enough that they may be considered definitive of women's status under traditional patriarchal legal systems. It is only in recent decades that some countries have begun to reform rape law from the relatively new perspective of women's rights.

It is essential, then, that we distinguish the commonplace from what was truly distinctive in the late imperial period. In particular, to understand the regulation of sexuality in the context of broader historical trends, we must distinguish what changed from what remained basically the same. The key change is that both the ideal rape victim and the ideal rapist envisioned by jurists shifted from a status-based stereotype to a moral stereotype linked to normative family roles.

Female chastity and penetration *always* mattered—but both came to matter more, as family-based gender roles began to rival and then outweigh fixed status distinctions for judicial purposes. By the eighteenth century, the key distinction for jurists was not between free and unfree women, but rather between chaste and unchaste women. The stereotypical rapist was *always* envisioned as an outside male who threatened family descent lines with pollution and disorder—but the specifics of his identity changed over time. The old stereotype of the slave attacking his master's wife or daughter gave way to the predatory rogue male outside the family system. In this new stereotype, the key distinction for jurists was not between aristocratic master and mean laborer, but between normative householder and rootless rascal.

This shift would appear to parallel what Kathryn Bernhardt (1996) has observed with regard to the civil law questions of marriage and women's property claims: a process of "peasantization," whereby judicial priorities shifted from the aristocratic concerns reflected in the Tang code to the peasant household concerns reflected in Ming and Qing legislation. The typical victims in Qing rape cases were not members of the gentry (let alone the old aristocracy), but chaste wives and daughters of humble, law-abiding peasant families.

We should bear in mind that in the old system, people of mean status had originally played a critical role in the overall social and economic order. Even their stigma helped define, by contrast, all that was "good" (*liang*) about their status superiors. From that perspective, the stereotypical Tang rapist was a man who did not keep in his place—but he *did* have a proper place. The stereotypical Qing rapist represented something more ominous: he was an outsider altogether, who was feared as a fundamental threat to the family-based social order because he had no place in it at all. There was no room in Qing legal discourse for a decent, law-abiding "rootless rascal."

The increased emphasis on female chastity implies that the sexual choices of individual peasant women mattered greatly to the imperial state. Through legislative and propaganda initiatives, the Qing state in particular sought to enlist female agency and assertiveness in the cause of defending an embattled, normative family order. This priority reflects both awareness and growing concern about the many people who did *not* conform to that order—witness the great frequency and variety of survival strategies involving criminal sexual relations that can be found in the Qing archives. Eighteenth-century innovations in the regulation of sexuality reflect profound uneasiness at the highest levels over the moral and political implications of social and demographic change.

The Problem of the Penetrated Male: Qing Sodomy Legislation and the Fixing of Male Gender

The Issues

Conspicuously absent from classical definitions of sexual offenses were acts between members of the same sex. The earliest unambiguous prohibition of male homosexual intercourse appeared in the sixteenth century, and only in the Qing dynasty did homosexual rape become a priority for legislation and prosecution. Moreover, it is only in the Qing that lawmakers included such acts in the venerable criminal category of "illicit sexual intercourse" (*jian*). The Yongzheng reign, in particular, witnessed a major initiative to systematize the prohibition of sodomy precisely along the lines of preexisting laws against heterosexual offenses.

The task of this chapter is not only to explain late imperial anxiety about anal intercourse between males but also to locate the criminalization of such acts in a larger context. What logic guided the Qing reconstruction of sodomy law according to standards and penalties already applied to heterosexual offenses? Was this initiative an alien imposition on an older culture of tolerance? Or did Qing constructions of sodomy somehow make sense in terms of older judicial thinking and wider contemporary perceptions not limited to official or elite circles?[1]

Previous Scholarship

It is no great mystery why heterosexual acts would have concerned the Qing judiciary or its predecessors. But why prohibit sex between men? Three scholars have offered explanations of Qing laws against "sodomy" (*ji jian*).

According to Marinus Meijer (1985), consensual sex between males was not banned until the mid-Qing; in fact, its prohibition is two hundred years older than that. He also suggests that this law was simply part of a consistent effort to ban all "sexual intercourse" outside marriage (1985, 109). Depending on exactly what he means by sexual intercourse, this observation may be accurate, but it begs the question why lawmakers singled out anal intercourse between males over other possible scenarios. For example, they never banned sex between women—indeed, I find not a single mention, let alone prohibition, of female homosexual acts in any Qing or earlier legal source (not to mention other extramarital practices familiar from the Western legal tradition, such as masturbation and bestiality).

Vivien Ng (1987 and 1989) argues that Qing "homophobia" was part of a propaganda campaign orchestrated by Manchu conquerors to win the allegiance of conservative Chinese elites who had been alienated by the decadence of the late Ming court. She also claims that the penalty for "male homosexuality" was more severe than that for "unchaste female behavior," speculating that sex between men "was viewed as a direct challenge to the requirements of filial piety" because it could produce no sons (1989, 88–89). In fact, the penalty for consensual sodomy that she cites (100 blows of the heavy bamboo and a month in the cangue) was exactly the same as that for consensual heterosexual offenses (see appendixes A.3 and B.1).

Bret Hinsch (1990) adopts the conclusions of Meijer and Ng, which suit his own theory of a "general tolerance toward homosexuality" up to the Qing dynasty, when "the new Manchu morality" induced the regime to prohibit consensual sex between men for the first time in Chinese history (1990, 4, 142). Neo-Confucianism and Westernization reinforced this bigotry, resulting in the homophobia of current Chinese regimes (1990, epilogue). Hinsch offers many valuable insights—for example, that age and status hierarchies tended to parallel the hierarchy of roles in anal intercourse. Nevertheless, as Charlotte Furth has pointed out in a perceptive review (1991), his desire to recover a "homosexual tradition" to contrast with the homophobic present may obscure more than it reveals.[2] His notion of "imported Manchu concepts of sexuality" (1990, 162) also provokes skepticism. Arguably, no one was more obsessed with defending Manchu values than the Qianlong Emperor, yet he was widely reputed to enjoy erotic relations with males, as were the Xianfeng and Tongzhi emperors.[3] Manchu legal texts from the period prior to sinicization and conquest reveal no special bias against same-sex activity. Manchu tradition forbade sex in fewer contexts than did Ming law; the Qing founders even abandoned certain marriage customs to conform to Chinese incest taboos (Zhang Jinfan and Guo Chengkang 1988, 485). (In fact, I have found no evidence of ethnic Manchu influence on *any* aspect of the Qing regulation of sexuality.)

A further possibility, that desire for a member of the same sex was perceived as illness or perversion, has been ruled out by Furth's seminal investigation of contemporary medical texts: "No kind of sex act or object of desire was singled out in medical literature as pathological" (1988, 6). Qing sodomy legislation had nothing to do with the "perverse implantation" that in Foucault's view characterized the new sexuality of the modernizing West (1978).

Sexual Orientation Versus Penetration Hierarchy

Meijer, Ng, and Hinsch all identify the prohibition of *consensual* sodomy as the critical feature of Qing legislation, interpreting it as a new form of oppression, even homophobia. This focus seems to imply that the central story in the history of sexual regulation must be a struggle between individual erotic freedom and narrow-minded persecution.[4] But if one reads the Qing sodomy legislation, consent appears almost as an afterthought, and the original proposal that inspired the Yongzheng initiative does not mention consent at all.[5] Furthermore, in the Qing archives I have yet to find a single case of consensual sodomy being punished in the absence of other, more serious crimes. What bothered Qing lawmakers the most was homosexual *rape*, and it is the draconian penalties they imposed for that crime that were truly unprecedented. Also, because penalties for homosexual offenses were no more severe than those for "parallel" heterosexual ones, it would seem that persecution of sexual minorities was not the point.

These scholars also use the noun "homosexual" to denote a male who had sex with males, and "homosexuality" to denote such activity and erotic attraction for members of the same sex generally. Such usage goes to the heart of a basic controversy in historical studies of sexuality, namely, whether sexual orientation as experienced in the West today is primarily a biologically determined constant, independent of historical change, or primarily a modern social and cultural construct. Of course, homoeroticism and same-sex union are nothing new, nor are they uniquely Western. But to refer generally to "homosexuals" and "homosexuality" (or, for that matter, "heterosexuals" and "heterosexuality") risks the anachronism of assuming that a fundamental *social* identity based on the sex of a person's object of desire has always and everywhere existed and been experienced in the same way.[6]

In many societies, the sex of one's object of desire has yielded in priority to a hierarchical division between the penetrant and penetrated roles.[7] In late imperial China, legal and literary texts strongly suggest that only penetrated males were perceived as "different"; desire for another male in and of itself seems to have carried little significance for popular attitudes and none at all for law. (In legal texts, homoerotic desire requires no special vocabulary, just the same clichés used to describe heterosexual lust, such as *yin xin*.) This division of roles was understood to involve multiple hierarchies, especially that of gender, the model being heterosexual intercourse.

We have seen that the penetration of women outside marriage threatened the disruption of patrilineal family order and the pollution of female chastity. But also, penetration in its proper place initiated individuals into adult gender roles: in a fundamental way, one became socially male or female to the extent that one played a specific role in a stereotyped act of intercourse. Charlotte Furth has shown that late imperial medical literature defined "false males" and "false females" primarily in terms of inability to penetrate or to be penetrated, respectively (Furth 1988). In other words, to become a *real* male or female required successful performance of the appropriate sexual role.

Gender implied hierarchy, and since sexual roles defined gender roles, the act of sexual intercourse was seen as a gendered expression of domination. When a male penetrated a female, he put her in her place—both literally and figuratively. A fundamental concern, then, was to ensure that this pattern of domination not conflict with normative patterns of domination. That is why the highest priority of Tang-dynasty statutes against illicit sex was to prevent a male slave from penetrating the women of his master's family, an act that would violate the "natural" flow of status domination. (On the other hand, it was long taken for granted that a master should enjoy sexual use of his slaves; the diminution of such privileges implied an erosion of the legal absolutism of slave ownership.) By a similar logic, the penetration of a male upset the proper hierarchy of gender, in which masculinity was defined by the penetrant role in the division of sexual labor, corresponding to the husband/father role in the division of social labor. In late imperial China, common sense held that to be penetrated would profoundly compromise a male's masculinity; for this reason, powerful stigma attached to a penetrated male. This stigma was especially powerful, it appears, in settled peasant communities, where social status and economic viability depended above all on marriage, reproduction, and family farming.

This basic perspective had been around for a long time. But classic tales of same-sex union from the formative and early imperial eras tend to locate homosexual penetration in a context in which *status* domination apparently overrode any disturbing aspect of gender inversion. The most famous tales tell of feudal lords or emperors favoring catamites who are celebrated for youth and feminine beauty.[8] Indeed, such gender inversion in and of itself must not have troubled lawmakers of earlier dynasties nearly to the degree that it troubled Ming and especially Qing lawmakers, or they would have addressed it more explicitly. As with female chastity, masculinity took on greatly heightened significance in the late imperial era. The two developments were parallel and closely related. As traditional status distinctions became obsolete, and official anxiety over demographic trends grew, the regulation of sexual behavior focused ever more closely on narrowing and fixing normative gender roles for both females *and* males. It was this context that accorded such unprecedented priority to the penetrated male.

Legislative History

Before the Qing: A Separate Category

Sex between males, even when prohibited, was long treated as a category fundamentally different from *jian.* As we saw in Chapter 2, Fu Sheng's classic definition of a sex offense, later used to define *jian*, specifies a heterosexual context: "If a male and female engage in intercourse without morality (*nan nü bu yi yi jiao*)." The Qing jurist Xue Yunsheng confirms that anal intercourse between males "originally could not be judged according to the provisions on illicit sexual intercourse" because "there is a great difference between [sex with] a male and [sex with] a female" (*nanzi yu funü da xiang xuan shu*) (the agent of action is presumed male) (DC, 285-33, commentary).

Hence, the classic purpose of legislation against *jian* had nothing to do with same-sex acts, regardless of whether they were considered crimes. But in the Qing, the definition of this legal term expanded: new laws assimilated homosexual offenses to heterosexual ones, labeled them a subcategory of *jian,* and included them in that chapter of the code. Underlying this shift, however, we can identify a basic continuity: from the Song dynasty through the Qing, judicial interest in male homosexual acts consistently focused on phallic penetration of the anus, the division of sexual roles thereby implied, and the stigma of the penetrated male. This division of roles held far greater significance than that the object of desire was of the same sex. To my knowledge, no other act or disposition to perform such acts was ever singled out in legal discourse.

The earliest evidence I find of laws against homosexual acts in any form[9] emphasizes the gender inversion attributed to the penetrated male. Song-dynasty sources report that a law of the Zhenghe era (1111–18) punished "young males who act as prostitutes" (*nanzi wei chang*) with 100 blows of the heavy bamboo and a fine of 50,000 cash, paid to whomever reported the culprit. (*Chang* implied female gender; male prostitutes were referred to as *nan chang*—literally, "male female-prostitutes.") Another Song text mentions the prosecution of cross-dressing male prostitutes for the offense of *bu nan*—literally, "being not male" (Zhou Mi 1987, 1040/58; Zhu Yu 1987, 1038/312; also see DC, 375-03, commentary). This fragmentary evidence suggests that Song lawmakers associated the penetrated role with cross-dressing and with the debased legal status of prostitutes, and that they sought to punish males who consented to such degradation. (The texts do not mention the penetrant role, nor do they use *jian* to denote homosexual acts.) The apparent purpose was to fix boundaries: to prevent persons of free, commoner status from being degraded by occupation to mean status (which included prostitutes), and to prevent males from being degraded into females by penetration or cross-dressing.

To my knowledge, the earliest statute explicitly banning intercourse between males dates from the Jiajing reign (1522–67) of the Ming dynasty. The Ming code's chapter on illicit sex includes no reference to such activity. Instead, the Jiajing measure appears in a supplementary set of "statutes applied by analogy" (*bi yin lü*[10]), each of which cites a preexisting measure to be applied to offenses not covered in the code proper. (This supplement systematized the long-standing practice of judgment by analogy, and thus the punishment of male-male intercourse in this way may predate its Jiajing codification.) "Whoever inserts his penis into another man's anus for lascivious play (*jiang shenjing fang ru ren fenmen nei yin xi*) shall receive 100 blows of the heavy bamboo, in application by analogy of the statute on 'pouring foul material into the mouth of another person' (*hui wu guan ru ren kou*)" (Huang Zhangjian, ed., 1979, 1068). This statute contrasts sharply with those against heterosexual offenses found in the illicit sex chapter of the Ming code. First, it could hardly be more explicit about the act being punished—far more so than the illicit sex statutes, which use *jian* to stress extramarital context without reference to specific gestures or anatomy. The statute quoted above never mentions *jian* at all, let alone the Qing legal term for sodomy, *ji jian*.

Second, the statute does not employ the dichotomy of coercion and consent used to define sex offenses since antiquity. Although the analogy to assault might seem to imply coercion, my only example of this law's use in practice involves the punishment of a man who had *consented* to being penetrated (MQ, 40-73). Ming lawmakers may simply have assumed it impossible to rape a man—an assumption that continued, with some qualification, to inform legislation during the Qing (see below). At any rate, the penalty (100 blows of the heavy bamboo) approximated contemporary penalties for consensual heterosexual offenses (80 to 100 blows); it was far less severe than that for heterosexual rape (strangulation) (DC, 366-00).

The most significant feature of the statute is its analogy between anal penetration and a crime listed in the "fighting" (*dou ou*) chapter of the Ming code: "pouring foul material into the mouth of another person" (DC, 302-00). Lawmakers evidently found this a more exact analogy than any of the heterosexual offenses in the illicit sex chapter. But since the fighting chapter lists dozens of crimes, this particular choice begs analysis. It contains three key elements: penetration, "foul material," and targeting the mouth. Such assault could surely cause physical injury. But foul material suggests pollution and humiliation more than physical danger; also, most cultures associate the head and face with personal dignity. In other words, pollution and humiliation were more important than battery to defining the crime of anal penetration. Moreover, such harm clearly affected the penetrated person only: *being* penetrated corresponded to having foul material poured into one's mouth. The stigma would attach to the penetrator no more than foul material would sully the one who poured it.

Early Qing Law: The Analogy Between
Heterosexual and Homosexual Rape

Like most Ming laws, the "statutes applied by analogy" were adopted into the first edition of the Qing code in 1646. Thereafter, as new substatutes were added, many "statutes applied by analogy" became obsolete and were eliminated (DC, 52/bi yin lü). Xue Yunsheng reports that the one on anal penetration was applied during the Kangxi reign (1662–1722), and I have a 1724 case in which it was applied. It remained on the books at least until 1725 (DC, 285-33, commentary; Wu Tan 1992, 1141–44; MQ, 40-73).

By 1655, however, Qing courts had begun using the term *ji jian* ("sodomy") to refer to homosexual anal intercourse (MQ, 23-85). In 1679, a substatute against *ji jian* appeared for the first time, in the illicit sex (*jian*) chapter of the code. By the end of the Yongzheng reign, the code contained substantial legislation on the subject, superseding the old Ming analogy, which was finally dropped. This legislation represented a break with earlier practice, in that homosexual intercourse was for the first time directly assimilated to heterosexual offenses under the rubric of "illicit sex."

The origins of the term *ji jian* are not clear; I have not seen it in any pre-Qing legal text. In Qing legal sources, a logograph meaning "chicken" is used to represent the sound *ji*. This usage appears to be a later substitution for an obscure logograph, also pronounced *ji*, which may be an invention of the Ming dynasty (since dictionaries cite no earlier usage of the term). The fifteenth-century literatus Lu Rong defines this obscure logograph as "what Hangzhou people call a male who has a female appearance (*nan zhi you nü tai zhe*)" (Lu Rong 1965, 132). According to the late Ming scholar Yang Shiwei, the logograph means "to use a male as a female" (*jiang nan zuo nü*) in a specifically sexual sense.[11] The construction of the obscure logograph is suggestive: the lower half of *nan*, meaning "male," has been replaced by *nü*, meaning "female" (see Character List). The essence of the term is gender inversion, especially that imposed on a male who was anally penetrated—as implied by Yang Shiwei's definition and by the logograph's construction. It is not clear just when or why the logograph for "chicken" came into use, but it already connoted obscenity, appearing in slang terms for "penis" (*ji ba*—"chicken tail") and "streetwalker" (*ye ji*—"wild chicken"/"pheasant").

The 1679 substatute marked the first appearance of *ji jian* in the code itself:

If evil rascals (*e gun*) gather in a gang and abduct a son or younger brother of commoner family (*liang jia zi di*) and use coercion to sodomize him (*qiang xing ji jian*), then the ringleader shall be immediately beheaded, and the followers shall all be sentenced to strangulation after the assizes [by analogy to the substatute on "rootless rascals"]. If it is consensual (*he tong zhe*), then the crime shall be punished according to statute.

In 1696, the following amendment was added: "If degenerate evil characters (*bu xiao e tu*) abduct the son or younger brother of a commoner (*liang ren zi di*) and use coercion to sodomize him, then the followers shall be sentenced to strangulation after the assizes, and they shall not be granted clemency under any amnesty. If it is consensual, then the crime shall be punished in the usual way" (QHS, 825/990). This law differs from the Ming statute applied by analogy in several important ways. First of all, it introduces the dichotomy of coercion and consent to divide the newly named crime into the traditional subcategories of illicit sex—and there is no question that coercion is the focus of concern. Moreover, where the old Ming law in no way distinguished between penetrator and penetrated, except to imply the one-way pollution caused by the act, this substatute makes a strong, clear distinction between the two. The homosexual rapist is our familiar rootless rascal, who was also the target of Qing legislation against heterosexual rape; in addition, the putative victim sounds suspiciously like a *male* version of the chaste wife or daughter imagined as the victim of heterosexual rape.

The 1679 substatute specifies gang rape, but it ended up being applied to a wide variety of scenarios. In a 1733 example from Haiyang County, Guangdong, Yu Zidai (fifty-seven *sui*) lured Chen Amai (sixteen *sui*) into a sugarcane field, raped him, and beat him to death. Yu was sentenced as follows:

According to the established substatute, "If degenerate evil characters gather in a gang and abduct a young man of good character and forcibly sodomize him, then the ringleader shall be sentenced to immediate beheading." Now, Yu Zidai did not gather a gang, but nevertheless, he did lure Chen Amai away and raped (*qiang jian*) him; in addition, he killed him immediately afterwards. This is lecherous evil in the extreme! Yu Zidai should be beheaded immediately, according to the substatute's provision on "ringleaders." (MQ, 41-7)

In this instance, rape was followed by murder; however, the provision on "ringleaders" was cited to sentence rapists even if they had acted alone and committed no violence other than the rape itself (MQ, 59-10). In other words, from 1679 until 1734, the penalty for simple homosexual rape (immediate beheading) was more severe than that for simple heterosexual rape (strangulation after the assizes).

For some decades, the 1679 substatute was the only law on the books that mentioned gang rape of either male or female; therefore, central courts cited it by analogy to punish the gang rape of a *female* as well (e.g., XT, 80/YZ 1.4.26). In effect, such citation applied the "substatute on rootless rascals" to heterosexual gang rape in a two-step process, via the 1679 substatute.[12] The analogy between heterosexual and homosexual gang rape, along with the inclusion of sodomy in the heretofore-heterosexual category *jian*, implied that the sex of the victim was decreasingly relevant to how judges perceived rape.

What about consensual sodomy? The 1679 substatute confirms, as an afterthought, that consent should be punished "according to statute" or, as the amendment adds, "in the usual way." This language refers to the Ming "statute applied by analogy." The 1679 law added new penalties for rape, but confirmed the old analogy's application to consensual acts. We see an example of the latter in a 1724 homicide case involving three soldiers from Zhangpu County, Fujian. Tu Lian (thirty-six *sui*) had had a sexual relationship with Zheng Qi (in his early twenties) for four years (Tu penetrating Zheng), and they shared a bed; their roommate, Wu Zongwu (twenty-four *sui*), slept separately. One night while Tu Lian was out, Wu was bothered by mosquitoes, so he crawled in bed with Zheng, who had a mosquito net. When Tu returned, he killed Wu out of jealous rage. Tu Lian was convicted of "purposeful homicide"; more pertinent is the judgment of his sexual partner:

Zheng Qi allowed Tu Lian to sodomize him; we find that the code contains only penalties which uniformly apply to males and females who engage in illicit sex (*nan nü tong jian*); it contains no standard provision prescribing penalties for two males who engage in sodomy (*liang nan ji jian*). Therefore, Zheng Qi shall be sentenced according to the supplementary statute applied by analogy, which provides that "whoever inserts his penis into another man's anus for lascivious play shall receive 100 blows of the heavy bamboo, in application by analogy of the statute on 'pouring foul material into the mouth of another person.'"

This judgment, approved by imperial rescript, shows that the Ming statute was used to punish not only penetrators but also any male shameless enough to submit to sodomy. Its language reflects the point of transition at which it was written: the sexual activity is called *ji jian* and compared to the "illicit sex" of "males and females." But there existed as yet no illicit sex measure by which to judge a consensual offense, and thus the old Ming analogy had to be used (MQ, 40-73).

The Assimilation of Sodomy to Illicit Sex

Early Qing rape law was something of a mess. Jurists had begun to draw a parallel between heterosexual and homosexual offenses, but penalties varied, and depended on a confusing hodgepodge of old Ming laws, new ad hoc substatutes, and a number of direct and indirect analogies. It was just the sort of situation to appeal to the rationalizing impulses of the Yongzheng regime.

Earlier measures were superseded in 1734 by a substatute in the illicit sex chapter of the code which remained in force until the early twentieth century (see Appendix B.1 for translation). The initiative for this new law came in a memorial from Xu Ben, the governor of Anhui. Xu Ben argued that the 1679 substatute against gang rape lacked sufficient precision to cover the actual variety of homosexual rape cases that occurred (some involved homicide, but not all; some involved more than one rapist, but not all); nevertheless, it was being cited indiscriminately to impose immediate beheading in all types of cases, because no other law was available. Governor Xu himself had just sentenced a man to immediate beheading on the basis of the substatute, even though the rapist had acted alone and had not harmed his victim aside from the rape itself; the penalty seemed too harsh, since it would have been only strangulation after the assizes, had the victim been female. Moreover, Governor Xu observed that the Yongzheng Emperor had recently issued an edict providing detailed guidance for the punishment of different variations of heterosexual rape. "Now, it seems that the substatute against coercive sodomy should be subdivided in the same way, into specific crimes and penalties." The emperor referred Xu Ben's memorial to the Board of Punishment for deliberation. The board agreed, and offered a detailed proposal, which became the 1734 sodomy substatute (MQ, 59-10).

This law (along with complementary measures that followed) achieved a precise assimilation of sodomy (*ji jian*) to heterosexual *jian*. The breakdown into specific offenses paralleled preexisting categories of illicit sex. Moreover, the penalties for sodomy offenses now equaled in almost every detail those for corresponding hetero-sexual ones. This rationalization of penalties for sodomy was a logi-cal result of the increasingly close analogy drawn by Qing jurists be-tween sodomy and heterosexual offenses for the preceding fifty years.

Gang rape of a person of either sex was punished according to the substatute on "rootless rascals," ringleaders by immediate behead-ing and followers by strangulation after the assizes. Rape by one of-fender of a person of either sex over twelve *sui* was punished by strangulation after the assizes; rape of a child of either sex between ten and twelve *sui*, by beheading after the assizes; rape of a child un-der ten *sui*, by immediate beheading, according to the substatute on "rootless rascals."

Rape of a person over twelve *sui* of either sex that was "not con-summated" (*wei cheng*—that is, in which the vagina or anus was not penetrated) was punished by 100 blows of the heavy bamboo and life exile at 3,000 *li*. If the victim were twelve *sui* or under, the offender was enslaved to the military forces in Heilongjiang.

"Consensual" sex with a child aged twelve *sui* or under of either sex was automatically treated as "coercive" and punished by stran-gulation after the assizes. Consensual sex with a person over twelve *sui* of either sex was punished according to the substatute on "sol-diers or civilians engaging in illicit sex" (*jun min xiang jian*), by 100 blows of the heavy bamboo and one month in the cangue.[13] Prosti-tution by male or female, as well as sex with a prostitute, received the same penalty.[14]

After 1734, any sodomy offense not covered in the code was judged by precise analogy to the corresponding heterosexual offense. For example, in an 1833 case from Beijing, Du Zhuer (thirty *sui*) penetrated his half-brother (same mother, different father) Fan Erge (eleven *sui*) in exchange for a few cash. As the code did not address incest between males, Du was sentenced by analogy to the substat-ute on "illicit sex with a sister by the same mother but a different father"; because of Erge's youth, the penalty was increased by one degree (XB, FT/06194).

In a complementary process, the legal discourse of sodomy adopted key terms and standards long used in the prosecution of heterosexual rape. As we have seen, certain factors disqualified a woman from full treatment as a rape victim by automatically indi-cating lighter penalties for her rapist. This weighting of penalties shows that the law did not define rape from the victim's point of view, but rather in terms of an objective loss inflicted on the victim by penetration outside a legitimate context. After the assimilation of homosexual offenses to heterosexual ones, the same logic framed the evaluation of the *male* rape victim. The 1679 and 1734 substatutes characterize the penetrated male as a *liang jia zi di* or *liang ren zi di*—literally, "a son or younger brother of commoner family" or "of a commoner." Such characterization matches closely that of the ideal female victim of rape or abduction as *liang jia fu nü* or *liang ren fu nü*—literally, "a wife or daughter of commoner family" or "of a commoner." As we have seen, by the mid-eighteenth century, the literal meaning of *liang* as commoner status yielded to the new emphasis on female chastity; so, too, in sodomy law, the requirement that the victim be *liang* implied a judgment of his sexual history and virtue. In this way, standards for evaluating female chastity and defining legitimate access to women were adapted to measure the loss suffered by a penetrated male.

Nonetheless, Qing jurists never imagined men to be exactly the same as women! As we see below, the exact parallel between homosexual and heterosexual offenses broke down over the question of resistance to rape. The difference between the plausibly rapable male and female articulates most clearly the Qing judicial construction of sex between men.

Adaptation of Heterosexual Standards to Sodomy

The following examples show how Qing jurists adapted the concepts of consummation, status distinction, and *liang* as an appraisal of the rape victim's sexual history to the judgment of homosexual rape. Each case closely parallels one or more cases examined in the last two chapters, demonstrating the remarkable precision with which previously heterosexual standards were extended to cover this new terrain.

Consummating Homosexual Rape

The 1734 substatute distinguished between homosexual rapes that were consummated (*cheng*) and those that were not (*wei cheng*), borrowing terminology long used to evaluate the rape of a woman (see Appendix B.1). Consummation of homosexual rape required phallic penetration of the anus. The penal consequences were identical to those in heterosexual rape: death for the offender, as opposed to a beating and exile if the act were not consummated. There was no ritual consequence for the victim of a consummated homosexual rape that corresponded to a female victim's loss of chastity (made official by her disqualification as a chastity martyr if she died). Nevertheless, the stigma attached to being penetrated by another man appears to have been powerful and pervasive.

Given such serious consequences, Qing judicial officials made an intense effort to determine whether acts of coercive sodomy had been consummated. This process closely paralleled (and no doubt was based on) the investigation of consummation in heterosexual rapes. Young males who alleged they had been raped would be inspected by the forensic examiner, in counterpart to the midwife who examined young female rape victims. We find the process mentioned in many central cases from the eighteenth and nineteenth centuries. It is illustrated in great detail in a Beijing case referred to the Board of Punishment for "immediate examination" in 1904 (when the 1734 sodomy substatute was still in force). The widow Chen Hu Shi accused bannerman De Shan of raping her fourteen-*sui* son, Chen Qishier (De Shan fled and was not apprehended). A rough draft of the boy's testimony (his answers to questions that are not recorded) found in the case file shows the board trying to establish exactly what had been done to him:

De Shan pulled down my pants and sexually polluted (*jian wu*) me; the rape was consummated; I wanted to scream but De Shan held my mouth tight . . . with his left hand and didn't let me cry out. . . . With his right hand, he pulled my pants down, and forcing me to bend at the waist, he also bent at the waist, and pushed towards inside (*wang li nong*). . . . He moved wildly (*luan nong*) with his penis and made water (*liu shui*) on my thighs; De Shan tore my pants; De Shan consummated sodomy with me; De Shan scratched me with his hand.

The board ordered a forensic physician to examine the boy. He reported that "just below the anus there is a scratch made by a fingernail; it is now completely healed. Close examination reveals that the crease of the anus is tight, and the anus has not been opened. In fact the sodomy was not consummated." Therefore, in the official version of the boy's testimony recorded by the board, the incident is described as follows: ". . . On that evening, I was seized by De Shan, who used coercion to sodomize me but did not consummate the act (*qiang xing ji jian wei cheng*), and used his hand to scratch and injure my anus."

It appears that the rapist had scratched the boy in his attempt to achieve penetration and had even ejaculated. But since his penis never penetrated the boy's anus, "sexual pollution" did not occur.

This logic resembles the Qing policy that manual penetration of the vagina did not consummate heterosexual rape (XB, SC/19959).

Sodomy Between Masters and Servants

No law addressed the issue of homosexual relations between masters and their servants, slaves, or hired laborers. Unlike the sexual use of servile females, which had long been explicitly tolerated but was increasingly ruled out by Qing jurists, there was never any specific exemption or prohibition of the sexual use of servile males. Seventeenth-century novels like *Plum in the Golden Vase* and *The Carnal Prayer Mat* (*Rou pu tuan*) suggest that such activity was not uncommon (master penetrating servant); like sex with female servants, it was unlikely to be prosecuted, regardless of the degree of coercion involved.[15]

But the *Conspectus of Legal Cases* reports an unusual test case from 1798 that addresses coercive sodomy between master and servile laborer. The governor of Shandong had asked for advice about this case because he felt unsure about how to reconcile two conflicting legal principles. The facts were not in dispute: a landlord named Pan Junting had attempted to rape his worker-serf (*gugong-ren*), a man named Shao Xing; resisting, Shao had kicked his master in the testicles with such violence that the man died. As we know, Qing law treated homosexual rape as a heinous offense, and no explicit exception was made for masters raping servile males. The judiciary even considered self-defense against homosexual rape a mitigating factor for homicide, as long as there was proof of the rape attempt. In this case, had the men been status equals, Shao's most likely sentence would have been strangulation after the assizes for the "unauthorized killing of a criminal," with the certainty of eventual reprieve (see Appendix B.2). But they were not status equals. By the late eighteenth century, most hired laborers were being treated as their employers' equals for purposes of law, but there remained exceptions, depending on precise terms of employment. Evidently, Shao was considered a worker-serf in the classic sense as his master's status inferior, and as a consequence, the old Ming statute on a worker-serf killing his employer-master (*guzhu*) still applied: if the homicide resulted from fighting, then even if it were unintentional, the penalty would be immediate beheading (DC, 314-00).

The question, then, was how to balance status distinction against leniency for self-defense against rape. The governor recommended leniency and the Board of Punishment severity, so the emperor struck a balance. The final judgment confirmed that homosexual rape was an abomination; nevertheless: "For a worker-serf (*gugongren*) to kick his master to death holds the gravest implications for the principle of status difference. . . . It is inappropriate to judge this case according to the substatute on 'committing homicide while resisting rape,' which applies to status equals (*chang ren*), so that the offender would be sentenced [merely] to strangulation after the assizes; such a sentence would show reckless indulgence." Therefore, Shao received the more severe sentence of beheading, but with the qualification "after the assizes," which kept open the option of a reprieve (XA, 53/16a–17a). Shao's sentence was more severe than it would have been had the two men been social equals, but much lighter than if his master had not been trying to rape him. This judgment parallels that of a 1738 case from Zhili, discussed in Chapter 2, in which a male servant used violence to defend his sister-in-law against rape by their master. Like that earlier case, its most remarkable feature is the extent to which senior jurists showed sympathy for a servile laborer's defense against rape by mitigating his punishment.

Sodomy as a Pollution of Status

In the last chapter, we examined an unusual test case of gang rape, in which the victim was a chaste woman of debased occupation—that is, she was *liang* in the new sense of sexual virtue but not in the traditional sense of legal status. *Conspectus of Legal Cases* reports a parallel example of homosexual rape, at least as unusual as the other, memorialized in 1824 by the governor of Shaanxi. A pair of thugs, armed with knives and clubs, had waylaid and raped two men on a road, each attacker raping one victim. The case was complicated by the fact that the victims were both actors who performed female *xiao dan* roles in opera, and therefore, the governor argued, "they cannot be treated as 'sons or younger brothers of a commoner' (*liang ren zi di*)," as would be required for the rapists to receive the full penalty for coercive sodomy (strangulation after the assizes). But such a vicious crime could not go unpunished. The solution, approved by imperial rescript, was to reduce the full penalty one degree, to 100 blows of the heavy bamboo and life exile at a distance of 3,000 *li*.

The victims were not prostitutes, and there was no evidence that either had previously been penetrated by another man, and thus they could be considered *liang* in terms of sexual history. But because their profession clearly debased their legal status, they could not be considered *liang* in the sense of being commoners. Moreover, as female impersonators, these men already embodied the gender inversion suffered by a victim of anal penetration. The judgment, therefore, balanced the principle of status hierarchy against that of punishing rape—exactly mirroring the sort of compromise made when a chaste (*liang*) woman of mean status (not *liang*) was raped by a commoner.

Sodomy as a Pollution of Masculine Purity

Previous experience of being penetrated disqualified a male from being considered *liang* in the sense of sexual history. Therefore, like status subordination or debasement, such experience also was judged to lessen the harm caused by rape, justifying a reduced penalty for the rapist. This logic was the same used to evaluate a female rape victim known to be unchaste. But it is awkward to translate *liang* as applied to male sexual history—it makes no sense to refer to "chaste" *males*. Female chastity was a form of loyalty, and women penetrated in the context of marriage were considered just as chaste as unmarried virgins. But Qing law recognized no legitimate context for homosexual intercourse that corresponded to marriage. In short, a *liang* male was a euphemism for an *unpenetrated* male. (To maintain that euphemistic nuance, I translate *liang* in this context as "of good character.")[16]

The *Conspectus of Legal Cases* contains many examples of such judgments. In a case reported by the governor of Shanxi in 1815, Guo Zhengqi had been raped by Li Lengsan but admitted that earlier he had already consented to being "sexually polluted" (*jian wu*) by another man. As the governor reasoned, "There is a difference between Guo Zhengqi and 'a man of good character' (*yu liang ren you jian*). Therefore, Li Lengsan should be sentenced to 100 blows of the heavy bamboo and life exile at a distance of 3,000 *li*, a reduction by one degree from the penalty of strangulation after the assizes that is prescribed by the substatute for committing coercive sodomy without injuring the victim." In other words, if a man were shameless enough to consent to being penetrated, the harm he might suffer by being raped could not be great enough to warrant the death penalty for the rapist. Moreover, for his earlier consensual penetration, Guo himself received 100 blows of the heavy bamboo and one month in the cangue, according to the provision against "consenting to be sodomized" (*he tong ji jian*) (XA, 52/7b–8a).[17]

A similar approach was followed in a Beijing case of gang rape judged in 1819. The principals were all Manchu bannermen. Because of a personal grudge, Jilin'a had filed false charges of theft against Zhabuzhan. Zhabuzhan was aware that Jilin'a had an ongoing sexual relationship with another man named Guangning (who took the penetrated role). To get revenge on Jilin'a, Zhabuzhan enlisted two friends to help him abduct and gang-rape Guangning. Because Guangning had previously been penetrated by his lover, his attackers would not receive the death penalty. Instead, they were punished with military slavery and exile by analogy to the substatute against the gang rape of "a woman who has previously committed offenses of illicit sex" (DC, 366-12). Both Jilin'a and Guangning were sentenced to 100 blows of the heavy bamboo (converted to whipping, since they were Manchus) and one month in the cangue under the provision against consensual sodomy. Also, in a mark of the stigma specific to the penetrated male, Guangning was expelled from his banner registry. None of the others had been penetrated, so none were expelled (XA, 52/8a–b).

Previous experience of penetration could affect homicide judgments, too, as seen in a central case from Ci Department, Zhili, memorialized in 1762. In 1751, the widow Ma Shi had hired an unmarried, landless peasant, Lin Ermengdong (twenty *sui*), to help her orphaned grandson, Li Changzuo (ten *sui*), work their land in exchange for 60 percent of the harvest. During crop-watching, Lin and Li shared a hut in the fields, and Lin began penetrating the boy, in a friendly relationship that lasted several years. In 1758, when Lin and Li were twenty-seven *sui* and seventeen *sui* respectively, they became the subject of village gossip, and the younger man broke off both the sexual and work relationships. However, one evening in 1761, Lin encountered Li and propositioned him. As Lin later confessed, Li rejected him, saying, "Before, we were seen screwing around together (*zan liangge gan de goudang*) . . . and the whole village talked until it was unbearable. Who would want to do that shameful thing (*mei lian de shi*) with you again?" A quarrel ensued, and Lin beat his former lover to death.

In evaluating this homicide, the magistrate first considered this clause of the 1734 sodomy substatute, "Whoever murders a young man of good character (*liang ren zi di*) in the course of an attempt at illicit sex . . . shall also be immediately beheaded according to the substatute on 'ringleaders of rootless rascals'" (Appendix B.1). Upon reflection, he rejected this measure, reasoning that "Li Changzuo had previously submitted to illicit sex with Lin Ermengdong, so Lin

Ermengdong cannot be compared to someone who schemes to sodomize and murders 'a young man of good character'." Accordingly, he sentenced Lin to the lesser penalty of beheading after the assizes, which kept open the possibility of reprieve (XT, 173/QL 27.3.18).[18]

Judicial Stereotypes of Vulnerable and Dangerous Males

In judicial discourse, being penetrated involved a stigmatized loss of status for males; this loss to a certain extent corresponded to a woman's loss of chastity, and its effects were measured in similar ways by the penal system. Males of debased status and males who had already been penetrated did not suffer the full degree of harm when raped. It followed that their rapists did not deserve the full penalties mandated by law.

But there remained fundamental differences between the loss suffered by a penetrated male and a female's loss of chastity. By definition, a woman was legitimately penetrable—however, she had to reserve that penetrability for her husband. An adulteress offended against her husband; thus, the burden on the female rape victim was to prove that she had not committed a betrayal. This fact was reflected in the Ming-Qing penalty for consensual intercourse, identical for heterosexual and homosexual couples except that a wife convicted of adultery could be sold in marriage by her husband. No comparable measure applied to the male who engaged in illicit intercourse with a female or played either sexual role with another male—a penetrated male could not be sold off by his wife, if he had one! Nor did the Qing state orchestrate a cult of virtuous males who died guarding their penetrability to correspond to the female chastity martyrs canonized on a regular basis.

Here we see an essential difference in the way jurists imagined male and female gender. Males were not expected to be weak, fatalistic, or suicidal; theirs was not to reserve themselves as vessels for one legitimate master. They were not supposed to be penetrable at all, but rather penetrators, subjects rather than objects of action.

Even so, Qing law acknowledged that males could be raped, and that they might consent to sodomy. But for this penetrability to make sense, the male had to be somehow less than male. To grasp this unstable masculinity, let us examine more closely the standard of evidence for coercion applied to sodomy cases. What sort of male did the judiciary imagine as a credible rape victim?

Coercion, Youth, and Powerlessness

Unlike the Qing code's original statute on illicit sex (Appendix A.2), the sodomy substatutes do not spell out an exact standard of evidence for coercion. Case records show that the standard long established for the rape of a female generally applied: they cite injuries and torn and bloodstained clothing, judges asked if victims had cried out and struggled, confession was required for conviction, and it was best to have witnesses. Even so, the male rape victim was imagined as fundamentally different. The issue of domestic space, for example, never comes up in cases of homosexual rape. It was perfectly proper for men and even young boys to be outside the home for a wide variety of reasons, and the most common site of homosexual rape in cases I have seen is on a road or path out in the fields between villages. Indeed, case records show that it was routine for unrelated men to share beds at night—a practice that did not necessarily imply sexual activity but certainly provided such opportunity.

The crucial distinction in the prosecution of heterosexual versus homosexual rape is that judges saw men as fundamentally empowered, whereas they assumed women to be weak. Of course, a woman should resist, but her strongest evidence of coercion was that she had been killed or had committed suicide; barring death, serious injury was the best defense. These were decidedly weapons of the weak. In contrast, the judiciary was highly skeptical that a man could be raped at all: if sodomy had been consummated with an adult male, then it must have been consensual. Only a powerless male could be penetrated against his will—and the most unambiguous form of male powerlessness was youth. The statutory language specifies the male rape victim as a "son or younger brother (*zi di*) of a commoner," or "of commoner family." Such phrasing implies that the male rape victim was a young, junior member of a family unit. The corresponding phrase for the female rape victim is "a wife or daughter (*qi nü* or *fu nü*) of commoner family." "Daughter" implies youth, to be sure, but "wife" does not; the emphasis here is gender subordination within the family, not youth. Sodomy legislation says nothing about husbands to correspond to the "wife" envisioned as a potential rape victim.

Indeed, the victim's youth and family seem to have been crucial factors in the prosecution of homosexual rape. I have collected 39 central cases involving homosexual rape (including thirteen cases of homicide in self-defense against rape, where judges credited such claims). The youth of the victim (and relative maturity of the rapist) is the most consistent and striking feature of the sample: *in every case*, the rapist is older than his victim, by an average of fifteen *sui* in the rape cases, and twenty *sui* in the self-defense homicides. The average age of homosexual rapists is thirty-three *sui*, while that of victims (including killers in the homicide cases) is only sixteen *sui*.

These data confirm that the Qing judiciary imagined the male rape victim as a young boy who was attacked by a much older man. In cases that involved homicide (of either rapist or rape victim), that homicide itself became the main focus of judicial inquiry and guaranteed prosecution; thus, if we exclude all such cases, we come even closer to the judiciary's ideal homosexual rape, in which rape alone was the focus of concern. In these "pure" cases, the average age of victims falls to thirteen *sui*, strongly reinforcing the stereotype of the credible male rape victim as a young boy. All these cases were reported to authorities by a parent or other senior relative of the victim, suggesting that, as in heterosexual rape, this crime was envisioned as an assault on the family as much as on the person of the victim.

We should not conclude that older males were never in fact raped, but rather that there existed a strong judicial bias against accepting an older male as a rape victim. Even with an adolescent, judges might exhibit great skepticism about whether coercion had truly been used to consummate sodomy. In an 1851 case from Baodi County, Zhili, the victim was Chen Shang'er (fourteen *sui*), a peasant who worked on the village watch with three older men. One of the other men, Han Yunrui (fifty-two *sui*), was an ex-convict recently released after several years of penal servitude. The men worked in pairs in alternate shifts, and the pair off duty would sleep in the watch-shed. One night when the others were out on duty, Han raped Chen Shang'er. The boy's father reported the rape, and forensic examination established that Shang'er's anus had been penetrated. Arrested, Han confessed. The magistrate recommended strangulation after the assizes for "forcibly sodomizing a young man of good character, without injury." However, the provincial judge of Zhili overturned the judgment for the following reasons:

In cases of consummated rape, if violent coercion has truly been employed, the rape victim should exhibit physical injuries from the struggle. . . . In this case, *Chen Shang'er is already fourteen sui, and absolutely cannot be considered a child . . . it should not have been difficult for him to escape immediately; why is it that all he could do was weep and cry out?* When he was forced down on the *kang*,[19] *he did not struggle vigorously, and thereby allowed himself to be sexually polluted.* Moreover, [the other watchmen] must have been in the vicinity; how is it that they heard nothing when Chen Shang'er was being sodomized and cried out? In addition . . . his body exhibited not even the slightest injury. [Emphasis added]

Here, the provincial judge cited the standard of evidence for rape applied to women in Ming-Qing law—but note his emphasis of the boy's age, an element that did not figure in this way when the victim was female. He ordered the case retried in Baoding Prefecture to establish beyond doubt whether coercion had been used. The Baoding prefect evaluated the facts as follows:

Just as [Han] was about to penetrate Chen Shang'er, [the boy] was startled awake; refusing to cooperate, the boy got up and shouted and cursed. But Han Yunrui's lust had not been satisfied, so, deciding to rape the boy, he grabbed Chen Shang'er and forced him face down on the *kang*. Using his hands to pin down Chen Shang'er's upper body and arms, he pressed down on Chen Shang'er's lower body with his own body. Not being strong at all, Chen Shang'er was unable to struggle free. He wept and yelled loudly, but since there were no neighbors close by, no one heard him. Therefore, he ended up being sexually polluted by Han Yunrui.

Persuaded, the provincial judge accepted the original sentence (SF, 167/XF 1.2.6).

Homicide in Defense Against Homosexual Rape

The clearest expression of judicial skepticism came in the prosecution of men who committed homicide in self-defense, they claimed, against rape. Most cases involved the use of a knife or other edged weapon to kill the alleged rapist. Qing judges deemed it unlikely that even a teenage male would have to resort to such a weapon to prevent rape, and they treated any such claim with great suspicion, assuming it was a lie that obscured the true motive for murder.

Still, Qing law sometimes granted leniency to males who committed homicide while resisting rape. Until the late eighteenth century, the procedure was for the provincial governor reporting the case to recommend formally that the prisoner be executed according to the relevant homicide statute, but to add an explanation of the mitigating circumstances, with a suggestion that the sentence be commuted. The final decision would be made at the Palace (Wu Tan 1992, 785).

But the age of the killer (that is, the alleged victim of sexual assault) was key to whether leniency would be granted. In a 1744 case from the Four Banners region of Zhili, a man named Ma Zhongxiao used an axe to kill one Wu Guodong, with whom he was sharing a bed, and who he claimed was trying to rape him. The governor-general recommended leniency, but the Palace refused: "If Ma Zhongxiao was already twenty *sui*, then he was a strong man in the prime of life. How could Wu Guodong possibly coerce him into sodomy?" The case was sent back to the local magistrate for retrial. When pressed about his age and strength, Ma testified, "I was only nineteen *sui*, and I have always been weak. He was a very strong man, and when I was held tightly by him, there was no way I could struggle free." The magistrate reported:

According to the offender, he was only nineteen *sui* at the time, and although that is not so young, the offender is not really very strong either. This humble official personally examined the offender in court, and it was obvious that his constitution is not tough or strong at all. Moreover, Wu Guodong was more than twice the offender's age, and it seems credible that he could have sought to use coercion to sodomize him, taking advantage of his youthful weakness.

The governor-general then personally inspected the prisoner, drew the same conclusion, and confirmed his original recommendation to the Palace (MQ, 133-99).

A degree of leniency toward males who committed homicide while resisting rape was codified in the late eighteenth century; however, in addition to unimpeachable evidence of a rape attempt, any offender to be granted leniency had to meet strict qualifications based on age. A substatute of 1783 specified that for a reduction of penalty to be considered, it was necessary for "the dead man to be at least ten *sui* older than his killer." Furthermore, "if the dead man and his killer are of the same age, or if the dead man is only a few *sui* older" (literally, "three or five *sui* older"), then the case should be judged according to the basic homicide statutes without any reduction of penalty. Twelve years later, an amendment granted that even if the dead man were "not quite ten *sui* older than his killer," but strict evidential requirements were met, then a reduced sentence could apply. In 1823, a final measure absolved boys of fifteen *sui* or under of any penalty for killing men at least ten *sui* older who tried to rape them, as long as strict evidential requirements could be met. If the evidence did not quite meet the strict standard of the substatute, but authorities were persuaded the boy was resisting rape, then he would receive a nominal sentence to be commuted to a fine (Appendix B.2; QHS, 801/769).

The intent of this legislation was to prevent murderers from escaping with penalties lighter than they deserved (Wu Tan 1992, 785; Meijer 1985, 124–26). However, by spelling out the narrow circumstances that partly excused such homicide, the judiciary also articulated its image of a plausibly rapable male. Only a boy or a young, weak man attacked by someone older and more powerful might be successfully raped—and therefore might be excused for resorting to an equalizing weapon like a knife in self-defense.

No such equation of youth with powerlessness appears in the elaborate judicial discourse on heterosexual rape. Any woman who immediately killed a man attempting to rape her was excused punishment; the code mentions no qualification based on age (DC, 285-20). Among males, only those fifteen *sui* and under could be granted such complete clemency, and only if they were at least ten *sui* younger than their attackers and could meet an unusually strict standard of evidence (including confession of the rapist before witnesses prior to death). The implication was to associate the powerlessness and penetrability of being very young with being female: the weakness (and consequent need for an equalizing weapon) of *any* woman was on a par with that of a young boy.

We find confirmation of this thinking in two edicts of 1765 that imposed administrative sanctions on local magistrates who failed to apprehend "rootless rascals" who had raped "young girls, young boys, or women" (*you nü, you tong, funü*). These edicts make clear by omission that any male other than a "young boy" was not considered a possible rape victim (QHS, 128/658–59).

Unlikely as it may seem, laws promulgated by the millenarian Taiping rebels in the mid-nineteenth century reveal the same assumptions about rape. One statute mandates that "in cases of sodomy of a younger brother among the faithful (*lao di*), if that younger brother is at least thirteen *sui*, then both shall be beheaded. If the younger brother is under thirteen *sui*, then only the penetrator (*xing jian zhe*) shall be beheaded; but if the sodomy is consensual (*he jian*), then both shall be beheaded [in spite of the younger brother's youth]." In other words, *any* male over thirteen *sui* who had been penetrated was assumed to have consented; but no such age qualification applied to females (Qiu Yuanyou 1991, 50). That rebel and dynastic law would agree on this principle suggests that it derived from basic assumptions about gender performance that were very widespread.

Adult males were seen as powerful and nonpenetrable; therefore, penetration of a male could be explained only in terms of youthful powerlessness or shameful consent. Females of all ages were seen as powerless and penetrable, but they were expected to safeguard that penetrability by whatever means necessary, the classic scenario being chaste martyrdom rather than homicide in self-defense. The Qing judiciary imagined the male rape victim as juvenile, therefore powerless; powerless, therefore penetrable; and, being both powerless and penetrable, therefore approximating the condition of being female. It was such a condition that made it possible to conceive of males as rapable. The discourse of *liang* never included men who penetrated other males, any more than it included men who engaged in illicit sex with women; *liang* applied only to males and females positioned in the "female" sexual role. Feminists argue that to be rapable is to be socially female, regardless of biological sex (e.g., MacKinnon 1989, 178). The Qing judiciary seems to have shared this view.

Profile of the Ideal Homosexual Rapist

As with heterosexual rape, the evidence in cases of homosexual rape tends to confirm the statutory stereotype of the rapist as a "rootless rascal." My sample of 39 central cases includes 42 rapists (two cases involved gang rape). Their average age was thirty-three *sui*. We know the occupations of 37 men: two are described as having no proper occupation, and another seventeen did work that can be considered disreputable or marginal: they include five soldiers, four itinerant porters/peddlers, three clergy, two beggars, two casual laborers, a night watchman, and a barber. Twelve of those engaged in more respectable work were peasants. Among the rest, we find an innkeeper, a tavern keeper, an apprentice, a student, and one man who was "in trade." Almost all are described as very poor.

We know for sure the marital status of 28 men in the sample: 24 were single (57 percent of the total of 42 rapists), four married. For the other fourteen rapists we have no explicit information, but I believe it is reasonable to assume that most of these men were single as well (for reasons explained in the last chapter). Their unmarried status should not be mistaken for a voluntary lifestyle choice. In Qing China, as in many contemporary societies, the decision of whether and whom to marry usually depended very little on the personal preferences of individuals.

Most of the rapists knew their victims at least slightly, but in nine instances they were complete strangers, and in twelve they were outsiders (from a different village or county). Four were ex-convicts, and another four were characterized by witnesses as "evil rascals" (*e gun*), and so on. At least ten were drunk when they attempted rape.

Once again, we recognize the rogue male who lacks property or family and who, though still young, is old enough perhaps to resent his lack of prospects. It is no accident that this profile closely resembles that of the heterosexual rapist outlined in the last chapter. Qing jurists imagined the same rootless rascal to be a sexual threat to the wives and daughters of upright householders, and to their "sons and younger brothers" as well.

The Bisexual Object Choice of the Rootless Rascal

What can we say about the sexuality of this rogue male, who is stereotyped as a rapist of both chaste women and young boys? Several cases portray a single rapist as bisexual in object choice: he pursues both male and female objects, but consistently plays the role of aggressive penetrator.[20] But this bisexual targeting of lust in and of itself does not seem problematic; jurists do not single it out for special explanation or commentary. Rather, it is the rootless rascal's incontinence, his lack of respect for *all* boundaries, that threatens social order.

One example is a 1745 case from Suining County, Hunan, in which Long Xiuwen (twenty-two *sui*) attempted to rape and then strangled his neighbor's son, Hu Yanbao (thirteen *sui*). Long was a poor peasant, single and without prospects, who secretly engaged in sexual relations with a neighbor girl. She was betrothed, but Long planned to elope with her before she could be taken in marriage. One day, however, Long saw Hu Yanbao working in a field and felt aroused by the boy's youth and by the way "he looked so white and clean" (*sheng de bai jing*); he then lured Yanbao to a remote place and tried to rape him. When the boy resisted, Long strangled him—and conceived the idea of dismembering the boy's corpse sufficiently that he would appear to have been killed by animals. He also hoped that after he and the neighbor girl had eloped, her parents might mistake the mutilated corpse for *her*, and not think to pursue them. After being caught with incriminating evidence, Long was sentenced to immediate beheading for the rape and murder of "a son or younger brother of commoner family."

The memorial on this case stresses Long Xiuwen's abominable defiance of all convention. Fornication, elopement, rape, murder, and dismemberment—he seems willing to violate every conceivable taboo in order to indulge his criminal impulses. But there is no particular emphasis on the fact that he happened to desire both males and females (XT, 119/QL 10.12.3).

A second example is a 1752 case from Nanzheng County, Shaanxi, involving one Li Shishou (mid-thirties), an unmarried, impoverished barber from another county. Li befriended a neighbor boy named He Tingzhu (seventeen *sui* at the time); one day, he pinned Tingzhu down and "forcibly sodomized" him. Tingzhu was too ashamed to tell anyone what had happened; but perhaps he did not mind so much, since he continued to visit Li, and was "frequently" sodomized by him. But Tingzhu eventually contracted a case of "syphilitic sores," so that his father found out what had been going on and ordered him to stop seeing the barber (Tingzhu no longer submitted to sodomy, but secretly continued to spend time with Li). Later, when Tingzhu married, Li began pressuring him to share his wife. Tingzhu refused; however, one night, Li jumped over the wall of the He family compound, confronted Tingzhu with a knife, and tried to rape his wife. Tingzhu finally rescued his wife by stabbing Li to death.[21]

Li Shishou represents as well as anyone the Qing judiciary's quintessential rootless rascal: he is an outsider without family or property who seems bent on destroying an upright family, violating multiple sacrosanct boundaries in the process. The case report concludes by observing that the magistrate's men discovered among Li's effects a pair of woman's bound-foot shoes, ultimate proof of his dangerous, transgressive sexuality (he must have stolen the shoes—and what did he want them for, anyway?[22]) (XT, 144/QL 17.7.4).

In the depiction of these rootless rascals, bisexual object choice seems almost taken for granted. The focus is on their aggressive penetrant role and utter disregard for convention. Homoerotic desire is singled out for no greater or lesser censure than heteroerotic desire (both being described with the same vocabulary); apparently jurists did not find such appetites particularly noteworthy or hard to comprehend.

In vernacular fiction from the late Ming and Qing, we find a counterpart to this aggressive penetrator, in the role of the libertine. In object choice, the libertine is bisexual, too, although his primary obsession is women. Like the rootless rascal, the danger that the libertine represents is his insatiable pursuit of sexual objects, not his eclecticism. Thus, when Ximen Qing (hero of *Plum in the Golden Vase*) penetrates his page boy Shutong, the episode serves to underscore the protagonist's indiscriminate self-indulgence; Ximen's more dangerous behavior consists of his promiscuous seduction of other men's wives, leaving a series of wrecked households in his wake. Again, when Vesperus (hero of Li Yu's *The Carnal Prayer Mat*) finds no female vessel at hand, he substitutes the "south gate" of one of his male pages; but his energies, too, are spent primarily in the pursuit of other men's wives. These novels present their heroes' transgressive overindulgence as harmful to health. But more important, it ruptures the boundaries that frame familial and social order.[23]

The fictional libertine differs from the stereotypical rootless rascal represented in rape cases by being a member of the privileged elite who enjoys material and social resources, and therefore rarely falls afoul of the law. But he shares with the rootless rascal the aggressive penetrant role, bisexual in object choice, which represents a specifically phallic threat to social order.

Eroticization of the Young Male

The judicial stereotype of the rogue male as a threat to sons or younger brothers of commoner families resonates with widespread evidence that in late imperial China, the young male was eroticized as an object of possessive desire. For the aggressive penetrator, in Qing legal cases as well as in Ming-Qing fiction, the young male is cast in the "female" role as a penetrated object, and the penetrator seems attracted to the same kinds of feminized features regardless of the sex of the individual who possesses them.

It is routine for the memorials that report homosexual rape cases to note that a rapist's lust was aroused when he saw that his victim was "young" (*nian you*) or "young and beautiful" (*shao ai*). The latter term carries a strong connotation of femininity, and frequently appears in the same context in reports of *heterosexual* rape as well. The confessions of homosexual rapists are sometimes more specific. For example, in a 1729 case from Guangdong, Yu Zidai (fifty-seven *sui*) explains that his victim (sixteen *sui*) "was young and lovely" (*nian shao mei hao*) (MQ, 41-7). In a 1739 case from Shaanxi, Wang Chongye (twenty-two *sui*) says of his victim (nine *sui*): "Sanbaoer's face looked clean and attractive (*mian mu sheng de gan jing*), so I had wanted to sodomize him for some time" (XT, 70/QL 4.9.5). In a 1745 case from Hunan, Long Xiuwen (twenty-two *sui*) explains that because his victim (thirteen *sui*) "looked so white and clean (*sheng de bai jing*), I suddenly had the impulse to sodomize him" (XT, 119/ QL 10.12.3). These sentiments were not limited to rapists—we find such language also in cases of consensual sodomy.

Just as the bisexual object choice of rapists warranted no particular judicial analysis, this sort of testimony is transcribed without comment. Clearly, then, the memorialists assumed that no special explanation was necessary to make the rapists' comments understandable to the senior officials who would review them. The reason they could make this assumption is that the eroticization of the young male as a penetrated, feminized object was by no means peculiar to a subculture of marginalized sexual predators.

In *Plum in the Golden Vase*, males who play the penetrated role are uniformly eroticized for their youth and feminine refinement. For example, an encounter between Ximen Qing and his adolescent page Shutong begins thus: "Shutong had been drinking wine, so his fair face was glowing; his lips were red and fragrant, and his teeth were as white as grains of glutinous rice—how could one not be enchanted (*ru he bu ai*)? At once, Ximen Qing's lust was aroused (*yin xin che qi*)." While they engage in intercourse, Ximen Qing addresses the boy as "my child" (*wo de er*), and Shutong calls him "Daddy" (*die*—a term also used by Ximen's concubines) (34/11b–12a). Later in the novel, we find the following account of the Daoist priest Jin Zongming's attraction to the males he penetrates:

Under his supervision he had two novices who were fresh, clean, and young (*qing jie nian xiao*), and who shared his bed; but this had gone on for some time, and he was getting bored of them. He saw that Jingji had white teeth and red lips, and his face was as white as if it had been powdered; Jingji looked fresh, refined, and charming (*qing jun guai jue*) . . . so the priest arranged for Jingji to stay in the same room with him.

The novel notes in passing that Jin Zongming also patronizes female prostitutes (93/10a).

In *The Carnal Prayer Mat*, Li Yu explains the hero's sexual attraction to his pages ("Satchel" and "Sheath"—appropriate nicknames for the penetrated!) in similar terms: "Both boys were attractive; indeed, apart from their big feet, they were on a par with the most beautiful women." The hero prefers Satchel, because he is the more "artful" and "coquettish" of the two, and can manipulate his buttocks "like a woman" (Li Yu 1996, 120–22). In his story "A Male Mencius' Mother," Li Yu presents the young male as a third gender, possessing a femininity more "natural" and alluring than that of a genuine woman. The willow-waisted boy Ruiliang is described as "a woman of peerless attraction"; when he begins to develop masculine attributes (his genitals are growing and he feels an insatiable penetrative lust), however, he castrates himself, so as to retain the characteristics that make him attractive to his "husband" (Volpp 1994).[24]

In all these texts, both legal and fictional, the male sex object appears attractive to the extent that he possesses a certain feminized standard of beauty. Youth, whiteness and cleanliness, clarity of complexion, red lips and white teeth, a willowy physique—all these features are conflated and eroticized. (Ming-Qing pornography depicts both women and penetrated males with lighter skin and less facial and body hair than their masculine partners.[25]) The aggressive penetrator depicted in these sources seems attracted to the object of his desire more by these gendered features than by the object's biological sex.

This evidence helps us to understand the threat from which, jurists believed, the "sons and younger brothers" of good families had to be protected. The legal discourse of the vulnerable male is pervaded by anxiety over the ambiguous gender of the adolescent boy, whose adult masculinity has not yet been confirmed by the social and sexual roles taken up with marriage. Jurisprudence was guided by the assumption that to be penetrated feminized a person in a profound and important way: it gendered a biological female as a *woman* (that is, as wife and mother), just as to penetrate gendered a biological male as a *man* (as husband and father). For a young male to be penetrated threatened to derail his delicate journey to adult masculinity, by degrading or inverting his gender.

Popular Perceptions of Hierarchy and Stigma

But how widespread, really, were such views? So far, we have examined legislation and central cases involving homosexual rape in order to identify judicial stereotypes of the rootless rascal and of the male who was vulnerable to his sexual predation. We have seen that some of the basic assumptions behind these stereotypes are reflected in contemporary vernacular fiction. But what about ordinary people, who were neither officials nor novelists? What does the evidence in Qing case records tell us about their views of sodomy? And what about *consensual* same-sex union—can we learn anything of the circumstances in which such union actually occurred? How did the partners in such relationships perceive themselves, and how were they perceived by others?

Parallel Hierarchies

The evidence in case records shows a clear coherence between basic judicial thinking and very widespread practices and perceptions. Most obviously, the penetrated male was younger than his penetrator, and thus the gendered hierarchy of sexual roles coincided with that of age. This is true in rape cases, as we have seen. But it is also true in all examples I have seen that the judiciary treated as consensual, with only two exceptions. Both exceptions (examined below) can be seen to prove the rule that the hierarchy of sexual roles was seen properly to conform to age hierarchy. Not only was the penetrated male younger, but in the great majority of cases he was unmarried. In relations deemed consensual by the judiciary, hierarchies of age and of sexual role often parallel others: seniority or status (for example, Buddhist or Daoist clergy penetrating novices), economic means (with the penetrator supplying money or other resources to his partner), and sometimes class (employers penetrating employees). The effect is to reinforce the gendered power relations already inherent in the hierarchy of sexual roles.

In the consensual same-sex unions reported in legal cases, we also notice signs apparently gendering the penetrated male as feminine. Some involve division of labor: in one example, the penetrated male wove cloth at home, which his partner sold at market. In many cases, two or more penetrators fought over a penetrated male, but I have yet to see the opposite; the penetrated male appears as an object of possessive desire.[26] Sometimes, the relative authority of partners mimicked that of heterosexual couples. In a 1762 example from Raoping County, Guangdong, Pan Asan (eighteen *sui*) lived with and was informally apprenticed to a barber, Miao Aliu (twenty-six *sui*), who penetrated him. Pan ran away for several days, staying with another man, whom he allowed to penetrate him. Finally, Miao tracked him down, took him home, and scolded him. After that, Pan often defied and cursed his partner. One evening, he refused to sharpen razors in preparation for the next day's work, so Miao beat him. Later that night, Pan refused to be penetrated, and Miao strangled him (XT, 170/QL 27.4.18). This scenario closely fits the pattern of wife-killings recorded in Qing legal archives, in which a wife's failure in gender duty (adultery, leaving home without permission, refusing sexual intercourse, and other defiance) provokes her husband to homicidal rage.

The Adult Male as Penetrator

Case records suggest that a male's sexual role could change, depending on his stage in life (cf. Hinsch 1990, 136). Most basic is the sense that an adult male should be a married householder, whose role was to penetrate (his wife), not to be penetrated. Marriage represented the key rite of passage: with consummation both male and female took up their respective roles in the division of sexual and social labor, as husband (penetrator) and wife (penetrated).

Several cases reveal a change in perceived role on the part of a male who had in his youth consented more or less willingly to being penetrated by an older man. Sometimes the younger man, having matured, rejects the advances of his former lover: "I'm grown up now, and I'm not going to do that" (XT, 177/QL 27.3.30). Sometimes this change in attitude coincides with taking a wife. In a 1739 case from Luojiang County, Sichuan, the peasant Zhou Jiu (nineteen *sui*) killed an older monk named Qing Yue. According to Zhou's confession, he lived not far from Qing's temple; in 1736, Zhou had gone there to play, whereupon Qing Yue persuaded Zhou to let him penetrate him in exchange for some walnuts. They had sexual intercourse once, after which Zhou did not return to the temple. One day in 1738, Qing Yue tried to repeat their sexual encounter by force, and Zhou killed the monk with a knife. When arrested, he claimed self-defense, but the magistrate was skeptical: "Since Qing Yue had already sodomized you, why did you reject him on this one occasion? . . . Obviously there was some other reason why you wished to stab him to death." Zhou's response: "Before, I was still young, and was sodomized by him because I was greedy to eat walnuts. When I later recalled this, I was deeply ashamed (*hao bu xiu kui*). Now, I've already grown up, and have also taken a wife. How could I still be willing to do this shameful thing (*mei lianmian de shi*)?" The magistrate accepted this explanation, as did his superiors (XT, 71/QL 4.7.12).

A male's changing sexual role figured too in a 1739 case from Wendeng County, Shandong, in which the peasant Dong Er (twenty-eight *sui*) killed an older monk surnamed Sun. According to Dong,

When I was a boy, I often went to the temple to play, and was seduced by monk Sun, who gave me sweets to eat, and sodomized me (*ba xiaode ji jian le*). Later, monk Sun moved to Fengshan Temple, a little over four *li* from [our village]. He often came to our village to collect alms, and when it got late he would spend the night at our house, and would have illicit sex with me.

At the age of twenty-one *sui*, Dong Er took a wife, Xiang Shi. As Dong recounted,

Monk Sun told me many times that he wanted to sleep with my wife, but I didn't let him. But in 1736, I was too poor to get by, and I often asked monk Sun to lend me a hundred cash or so to buy rice; then I let him have sex with my wife. After that, he often came and went, and I spent several hundred cash of his.

Poverty finally forced the couple to move in with Xiang Shi's natal family, which hampered Sun's sexual access to her. Shortly thereafter, Dong went to Sun's temple to ask for another loan to get through the winter. Sun refused to pay unless Dong brought his wife to live nearby. Dong then revealed his plan to travel to the east in search of employment. Sun got into a huff and went to bed (it was evening); Dong (who was spending the night at the temple) climbed onto the *kang* with him and went to sleep. Later, however, Sun woke him up and again pressed him to move nearby so they could continue their arrangement of trading sex for money. A quarrel ensued, in which the monk cursed Dong, who then beat him to death.

In six years, then, Dong went from being Sun's willing penetrated partner to taking a wife and becoming a penetrator in his own right. At this point, Sun's sexual interest shifted from Dong to his new wife, and, in exchange for money, Dong began sharing Xiang Shi so that both men could penetrate her. The focus of Sun's lust had shifted so completely that on his last, fatal night, he evinced no interest whatever in having sex with Dong himself—even though the two men were in bed together (XT, 69/QL 4.6.20).

A 1739 case from Gaoling County, Shaanxi, illustrates attitudes toward changing sexual roles in the male life cycle from a different angle. Zhao Quanfu (fifty-three *sui*), a Daoist mendicant from Henan, had taken a disciple, Miao Zhenglai (thirteen *sui*), at the behest of Miao's father, a peasant who could not provide for him. Zhao began penetrating the boy on the morning after he took him as his disciple. When the boy tried to resist, Zhao threatened him with a beating. After that, the two wandered from place to place, begging alms in exchange for ritual services. Miao always slept with Zhao, who penetrated him at will. After four months, they fell in with another Daoist mendicant, Yang Zhangming (thirty-nine *sui*), whom Zhao engaged to teach scripture to Miao. Shortly thereafter, Yang also began penetrating Miao. When Miao first refused, Yang told him he had not memorized his lesson properly, and threatened to beat him and to tell his master; so Miao submitted.

Not long thereafter, Yang tried to persuade Miao to abandon Zhao and go off with him. "Why should you leave family life to join the clergy (*chu jia*)? If you follow me and return to secular life (*huan su*), I will arrange for you to take a wife." Zhao overheard this, and later accused Yang of plotting to abduct the boy. Zhao also suspected that Yang was having sex with his disciple, and was jealous. In the fight that ensued, Yang was killed.

The most interesting detail is the promise Yang made, no doubt insincerely, to persuade Miao to leave with him. Miao was both a Daoist novice and a homeless beggar (in a year or so, he and his master wandered through much of northern Henan and central Shaanxi). Returning to secular life and taking a wife implied leaving behind both sorts of marginalized status in exchange for the rooted life of a married householder, a life to which most landless peasants probably aspired. It also held out the promise of a clear transition to male adulthood, both in age and in sexual role, from dominated, penetrated boy to adult penetrator in his own right, with his own wife to subordinate and use sexually. The offer seems to have been attractive; Zhao jealously noted that Yang and the boy were getting along famously (XT, 75/QL 4.5.11).

So many sodomy cases show an older monk (or Daoist priest) penetrating an adolescent novice, as a sort of initiation, that we can speculate that many of these older men themselves had been penetrated as boys by older clergy. It seems plausible that a division of sexual labor existed, with the boys serving the older men in an unofficial *quid pro quo* for their training and care, later growing up and themselves penetrating newer, younger novices. This speculation is strengthened by the parodic representation of sodomy among male clergy in vernacular fiction.

What stands out in the case evidence is not simply that hierarchy of age reinforced hierarchy of sexual role, but that fully socialized adult males should act as penetrators only, and that a transition to that role was extremely desirable. Such a transition might involve several elements: age (growing up); marriage (taking up the social role as husband, reinforced by the sexual role as penetrator); and avoidance of being penetrated (if it had happened before, preventing it from happening again).

The Stigma of Being Penetrated

Cases from various regions reveal a pervasive, powerful stigma attached to the penetrated male, a stigma that did not touch his partner. Some men who wanted to penetrate others violently refused to be penetrated themselves. In a 1738 case, Wang Si (twenty *sui*), a poor man from Gu'an County, Zhili, was looking for work in Beijing as a casual laborer. One winter evening, without money to pay for space in a heated public room at an inn, he squatted at the base of the city wall by Chongwen Gate to get through the night. In the middle of the night, Wang was accosted by another man who planned to sleep by the wall as well. He was later identified as Dong Kui (mid-twenties), an impoverished bannerman who beat a drum in funeral processions. As Wang later testified,

[Dong] said, "If the two of us sleep together, we'll be warmer." I said, "I'm not sleeping next to you," and he said, "If you don't sleep with me I'll beat you up." I saw he was big and strong, and that I couldn't win a fight with him, so I [agreed to] sleep next to him.

Then he felt my pants, . . . saying, "If you let me sodomize you, I'll buy you a pair of cotton pants to wear." I said, "If you let *me* sodomize *you*, I'll give *you* a pair of cotton pants." He cursed me, saying, "If you don't let me sodomize you, I'll beat you to death!"

It was the middle of a dark night, and no one was around, . . . so I was afraid; I tricked him, saying, "Now it's still early, and someone might walk by and see us—that would be embarrassing. Why don't you sleep for a while and then we'll talk about it?" So he went to sleep.

After Dong fell asleep, Wang Si murdered him. Even if his retort about reversing roles may have been facetious, Wang seems to have felt that penetrating Dong would be better than being penetrated *by* him—and Dong took the retort as an insult, growing belligerent in response (XT, 74/QL 4.3.2).

Sometimes, the shame felt by the penetrated male contrasts sharply with the bravado of the man who has penetrated him—as illustrated by a case from Bagou Sub-prefecture, Zhili, memorialized in 1739. One night, Li Xuan (twenty-nine *sui*), a casual laborer from Wenshui County, Shanxi, was sleeping at the home of two friends, Niu Yongtai and Chi Tingguang. These two lived and farmed together (one wonders about their relationship). The three men were sharing the same *kang*. As Li later testified: "I was already sound asleep, when that Niu Yongtai started to sodomize me. I was awakened by his sodomizing me (*bei ta jian xing le*), but at the time, since Chi Tingguang was also on the *kang*, and since this kind of shameful thing is not easy to speak of, all I could do was bear it and keep silent." Some days later, Li met an acquaintance, Wei Minghou, in a wineshop: "He said to me, 'You men from Wenshui County are all born to be rabbits (*tuzi*).' I thought of Niu Yongtai sodomizing me, and suspected that Niu Yongtai hadn't kept his mouth shut and had told people about it, so that Wei Minghou had that in mind when he made this comment; because of this, I felt ashamed (*lian shang haixiu*)." Li went to Niu's home to confront him. It was night, and Niu was already in bed:

I said, "You sodomized me, but I bore it without saying anything, but now you've gone and told other people about it—what is this supposed to mean? Get up, so we can settle this!" He said, "But I'm not going to get up. What are you going to do about it?" I saw there was a rock sitting on the stove, so I picked it up to threaten him, saying, "If you don't get up, I'm going to beat you!" Niu Yongtai said, "I'll bet a rabbit like you wouldn't dare (*liao ni tuzi ye bu gan*)!"

Li Xuan took the dare, and beat him to death. After confessing, he summarized his motive: "In truth, because Niu Yongtai sodomized me, and then I was ridiculed by others, and then, when I went to confront Niu, he cursed me as a 'rabbit'—because of all this, I became so extremely angry that I wanted to beat him to death."

Clearly, Niu Yongtai was not ashamed of his lust for another man; he did not consider himself a "rabbit" (slang for a male prostitute[27]). Li, in contrast, felt deeply shamed by having been penetrated and especially by publicity of the fact. It seems that his role in the act was far more shameful than any sense of having been taken advantage of or coerced. It was more important to Li that Chi Tingguang, asleep beside them, not find out that he was being penetrated than it was to stop the intercourse itself—so he suffered the act to continue. Equally, it was public loss of face, more than the fact of having been penetrated, that provoked Li to confront and kill Niu (XT, 76/QL 4.3.23).

Penetration Stigma and Family Shame

The stigma of being penetrated attached not only to the individual himself. A number of cases suggest that the family of a penetrated male suffered an acute loss of face, too, especially if that penetration were made public. For example, in a 1742 case from Baoji County, Shaanxi, Li Chuanjia (twenty-six *sui*) raped a boy from the next village, Yang Sijia (sixteen *sui*), after getting him drunk. The boy was too ashamed to tell anyone what had happened. About a month later, however, he encountered Li on the street with a group of friends; in front of the others, Li demanded to sodomize him again. As the boy recounted, "I refused, and he hit me and cursed me. Crying, I went home, and my father asked me again and again what had happened, so I told father how Li had sodomized me." The boy's father, Yang Guihe, was particularly enraged by this public aspect of his son's humiliation, and he confronted Li at a teahouse in the nearby market town. As Yang Guihe later testified, Li retorted (again, in public), "So I fucked your son—do you have the nerve to do anything about it (*wo jian ni erzi, ni gan ba wo zenyang*)?" Then, Yang Guihe killed him with a cleaver.

Once again, the bravado of the penetrator contrasts sharply with the humiliation felt by the penetrated male, which was intensified by Li Chuanjia's publicity of the rape. This public shame became unbearable for the boy's father, who felt he must face down the bully or else suffer even greater shame (XT, 184/QL 27.2.20).

Sometimes, such shame provoked family members to violent acts against the penetrated male himself. A case memorialized by the governor of Henan[28] in 1739 involved the agricultural laborer Song Chaohan and his younger brother, Song Wu. Their parents had died long before, and Chaohan had raised his younger brother to adulthood. They were very poor, and both were unmarried. According to Chaohan, Song Wu had been "stupid and silly" since childhood; he spent his time "hanging out with beggars," and "did not work at any honest occupation." One day, according to the summary, Chaohan noticed that his brother was walking with difficulty:

Questioning him, [Chaohan] learned that [his brother] had an ulcerous sore on his anus, which had been caused by other men sodomizing him. Song Chaohan considered this a disgrace to the family's reputation (*you dian jia sheng*), and ordered his brother not to go outside anymore. Then Song Chaohan went out to work, but when he came home in the evening, he saw Song Wu lying outside in the gateway. Song Chaohan ordered him to go inside, but Song Wu did not obey.

Chaohan became so incensed that he strangled his brother (XT, 74/ QL 4.4.25).

Sometimes, Qing magistrates took a family's loss of face into account as a mitigating factor when judging such violence. *Conspectus of Legal Cases* reports an 1822 case, also from Henan, in which a man named Su Yongmu attempted to rape a boy aged nine *sui*. The boy's father, Su Fengjia, complained to Yongmu's father, who scolded Yongmu severely. Because of this, Yongmu went to Fengjia's gateway and loudly insulted and taunted the family, referring openly to what he had done to the boy. Su Fengjia became so upset at the public loss of face that he strangled *his own son*, the victim of the attempted rape. The magistrate who judged this homicide decided that the boy's death "was caused, in fact, by [Su Yongmu's] attempt to sodomize the boy." He found Yongmu guilty of coercive sodomy of a young boy (not consummated), but to reflect Yongmu's responsibility for the boy's death, the judge changed his penalty from ordinary life exile (*liu*) to the much harsher one of military slavery in Xinjiang. It appears that Su Fengjia was not punished at all (XA, 52/6b).

These examples reinforce our sense that to be penetrated was perceived not just as a matter of individual shame, but also as a humiliating assault on the family as a whole. They suggest that the judiciary's image of the vulnerable male as "a son or younger brother of commoner *family*" reflected widespread assumptions about the damage inflicted by such an assault.

Stigma and Secrecy in Consensual Relationships

Many men who were penetrated in affectionate relationships feared public exposure as well. This seems especially clear when the sexual partners inhabited a larger community of peasant households. (In contrast, same-sex unions in all-male contexts outside mainstream communities—for example, among soldiers, sailors, or clergy—appear to have been less secretive, though equally hierarchical; case records show that such relationships were often well known to couples' associates.) In a number of previous examples, public knowledge that one had been penetrated was described as a powerful loss of face: the phrases most commonly used are "to have no face" (*mei lianmian*); "to lose face" (*diu lian*); and "to be unable to face people" (*jian bu de ren*). In fact, the force of humiliation through village gossip is a major factor in a large proportion of cases involving the gamut of sex offenses, both heterosexual and homosexual. It is repeatedly cited as a motive for desperate acts, including homicide (to avoid or avenge exposure of rape, adultery, or homosexual relations), suicide (by women despairing over the stigma caused by rape or sexual proposition), and crude attempts at abortion (most often by widows, to avoid the exposure of an affair).

A case from Ding Department, Zhili, illustrates the pressure of stigma on an affectionate sexual relationship between two young men. Zhang Qibao and Huang Niuer were hired as long-term laborers by peasant Bai Chengwen in 1727, when they were twenty-four and nineteen *sui*, respectively. Neither was married, so they shared a bed at Bai's house and soon began having sex. Early on, the men may have alternated roles—Zhang confessed that he and Huang had "sodomized each other" (*bici ji jian*)—although later, Zhang played the penetrated role, in spite of being older than Huang. (Perhaps in a loving relationship, stereotypical role-playing mattered less.[29]) As Zhang recalled, "At that time we swore not to tell anyone else," and then "had a good relationship for these four or five years." In 1731, the two began working for separate employers, and since they no longer lived together, they met at the local temple to have sex. One time, a villager happened upon them and asked what they were doing—and, to Zhang's horror, Huang told him that he had been sodomizing Zhang. As Zhang later confessed, "I couldn't believe it. . . . I thought to myself, I'm a man of almost thirty *sui*, but here he goes telling other people about this; everyone in the village will find out—how will I be able to face them? (*hai you shenme lianmian qu jian ren*) I felt incredibly angry. . . . To my surprise, he wouldn't admit he was wrong, but instead argued and began to curse me. I became even angrier. . . . " Zhang later used an axe to kill Huang while he was taking a nap.

In the first hearing on this case, Zhang made no effort to deny the murder, but in an apparent attempt to protect his reputation, he did not confess the sexual relationship—instead asserting that Huang had "defamed" (*wu mie*) him by *claiming* to have penetrated him. He did not reveal the truth until a second hearing (the record does not say why he confessed, but no one in the community had suspected that the men were more than friends). As an unmarried, poor laborer, Zhang had few claims to status in his community. The only ones, perhaps, were his maturity and masculinity, yet even these meager enough claims would be severely undermined by public knowledge that he had been penetrated, and by a younger man to boot. Huang Niuer obviously did not share Zhang's concern: Huang told Bai that *he* had penetrated Zhang, bragging about an act that apparently enhanced his own masculinity (MQ, 50-4).

Similar pressures were at work in a 1762 case from Hubei, in which three men from Xiaogan County worked as hired laborers in Zaoyang County (about 200 kilometers to the northwest). Wu Damou (thirty *sui*) had been sexually involved with his sworn older brother, Shi Shikong (thirty-one *sui*), for six years; as their relative ages would suggest, Shi penetrated Wu. Wu actually had a wife and daughter back in Xiaogan. Because of poverty, he had left them in 1761 to accompany Shi to Zaoyang, where they were employed by Zhu Fengqi working ten *mu* of land, and lived in a room of Zhu's house. Wu supplemented their income by weaving cloth, which Shi sold at market (note the apparent gendering of household roles). According to Wu, the couple "got along extremely well."

After six months, they met another immigrant laborer from Xiaogan, Liu Huaizhi (twenty-four *sui*); he moved in with the couple and swore brotherhood with them. Within three days of moving in, however, Liu had discovered the couple's sexual relationship *and* the division of roles within it; on the third day he caught Wu alone and gave him an ultimatum: if Wu would not let Liu penetrate him as well, Liu would expose Wu as Shi's penetrated sexual partner. Wu submitted. Shortly thereafter, an outraged Shi Shikong discovered their liaison. Wu then moved out with Liu, but two weeks later, jealousy provoked Shi to murder Liu.

Shi Shikong and Wu Damou were arrested, and at trial the magistrate pressed Wu to explain his behavior: "You had had sodomy with Shi Shikong for several years, so your affection (*qing yi*) for him must have been greater. Why did you stop living with Shi Shikong, and instead move in with Liu Huaizhi, with whom you had been having sodomy for only a short time? Furthermore, Liu Huaizhi is younger than you; how could you let yourself be sodomized by him?" Wu answered:

At first my affection with Shi Shikong was stronger. But our illicit relationship had been discovered by Liu Huaizhi, so that one day when he saw Shi Shikong was not at home, he trapped me [with his knowledge] and demanded to sodomize me (*xia zhu yao jian*); even though he's younger than I am, I had no choice but to submit.

Afterwards, we were discovered by Shi Shikong, and he made a big scene. . . . I feared that outsiders would find out and I would lose face. At that point, Liu Huaizhi told me that all three of us living together in a single room made things inconvenient, so he rented another place and asked me to move there with him. I thought to myself that if I moved out with him . . . at least we could avoid quarrels and the risk of being overheard and ridiculed by outsiders. So I moved out with him.

At a second hearing, pressed again by the magistrate, Wu added: "As far as me being somewhat older than Liu Huaizhi—I had done this vulgar (*xia liu*) thing with Shi Shikong, and because this had been found out by Liu Huaizhi, I was trapped and extorted by him so that I had no choice but to let him do as he wished."

Everyone seems to have found it strange that an older male would be penetrated by a younger one. Even so, the magistrate finally accepted Wu's explanation that fear of public exposure as a penetrated male forced him to submit to the private humiliation of submitting to a younger man. Wu's fear was so great that it induced him finally to abandon the partner for whom he had had such affection and to move in with his blackmailer. It was Liu's awareness of the stigma of being penetrated that enabled him to manipulate Wu in this way (XT, 185/QL 27.9.24).

The interrogation of Wu underscores the coherence between judicial standards and popular perceptions in this area. (This is the only case I have seen of a magistrate commenting on the relative ages of sexual partners.) It seems that stigma would attach to any male who was penetrated, but that penetration might be more comprehensible if it conformed to the sexual partners' respective positions in other hierarchies: age, class, wealth, and the like. Only a violation of the "natural" congruence of these hierarchies required special explanation.[30]

Homosexual relationships obviously could be more complex, both physically and emotionally, than an exclusive focus on anal intercourse would imply. Case records show magistrates developing evidence about particular acts to be prosecuted as crimes: the judicial fixation with sodomy was what gave that act much of its prominence. We cannot hope to learn from these sources the entire meaning of such relationships to the participants. Nevertheless, legal cases do provide enough information on the symbolic meaning of sodomy to demonstrate that the judicial construction of that act conformed to a more pervasive pattern of understanding. The judicial analogy between sodomy and heterosexual illicit sex codified the contemporary common sense of what phallic penetration meant for both penetrator and penetrated.

Stratification and Male Sexualities

One senses that opportunities for marriage, reproduction, and erotic expression depended far more on material and social resources than on any individual, personal inclination. The knowledge that males outnumbered females, especially among the poor, only strengthens this impression. From this perspective, we can map a tentative hierarchy of male "sexualities"—here I simply mean typical patterns of sexual practice—against the hierarchy of social stratification. At very least, we can speculate about how the extreme ends of that hierarchy might look—a picture quite different from the dichotomy of sexual orientation familiar today.

Marginalized Males: Sex as Survival Strategy

As must be obvious by now, it was not only the stereotypical *rapist* who existed on the margins of society, outside the settled family order. Indeed, the overwhelming majority of cases I have seen of homosexual relations deemed consensual by the Qing judiciary also involve marginalized males—that is, men excluded from mainstream patterns of marriage and household by some combination of poverty, status, and occupation. Here, I am talking about both sexual partners, penetrator and penetrated. They are agricultural laborers, beggars, Buddhist and Daoist clergy, soldiers, sailors, pirates, barbers, peddlers, and so on. A fair number are impoverished immigrants; almost all are unmarried and without family ties. In short, these are the marginalized individual males left out of the mainstream of Qing society.

That is not to say that elite men never engaged in sex with other males—far from it. The fictional libertine is only the most familiar example. But it went without saying that men of means would be expected to marry and to beget sons to ensure the continuity of descent and property transmission. Such men might penetrate servants, or patronize actors and male prostitutes (more marginalized males), but these diversions would not likely be allowed to interfere with filial duty. A paradigmatic example might be the Qianlong Emperor, who managed to sire 27 children in spite of his reputed taste for men (Hummel, ed., 1970, 372).

To the extent that there existed a social identity linked to sodomy, or a sexual practice based exclusively on same-sex union, it was probably associated with the marginalized males who for whatever reason could not buy into the valorized pattern of marriage and household. In case records, we find marginalized males bonding with each other as a way to satisfy a range of human needs. These relationships are a subset of the larger pattern of "unorthodox households" found in Qing legal cases: in such relationships, sex coincides with different forms of resource pooling, coresidence, and fictive kinship (sworn brotherhood, master-novice ties, and the like). Of course, we sometimes also see evidence of strong affection (and jealousy) between sexual partners. But in this milieu, sexual bonding seems to play an instrumental role, as one element of multifaceted alliances in a world hostile to individuals on their own.[31]

The late Ming literatus Shen Defu took for granted the existence of same-sex unions among men isolated from sexual contact with women:

Sometimes, males are taken as sexual objects (*nan se*) because there is no alternative. For example, men who live in monasteries must take leave of the female quarters, and the statutes binding on Buddhist priests prohibit illicit sex [with females]. It is the same with those private tutors who live as guests in dormitories. These men must all "adapt to circumstances" (*jian jing sheng qing*) and "settle for second best" (*tuo wu bi xing*)[32]—the situation cannot be avoided. In addition, there are criminals in prison for a long time who, if given the chance, will inevitably seek out a man to serve as a mate. . . . Also, in the northwest, the soldiers of the frontier garrison are too poor to pay to sleep with prostitutes, so they always pair up with fellow members of their ranks. . . . It is lonely, bitter, and distasteful, but such men do these things because they have no choice. . . . It is laughable, but also inspires pity.

Shen contrasted this normal pattern with what he saw as a new, decadent fashion among "gentlemen of ambition who install young catamites (*luan tong*) among their servants" or who pursued actors (*luan tong* means a young effeminate male who serves as a penetrated sexual partner). What made this fashion decadent, Shen implied, is that elite men enjoyed more than adequate outlet for sexual energies within marriage (and concubinage). For such men, sodomy would be a wanton indulgence of lechery (Shen Defu 1976, 24/26a–b; Furth 1988, 13–16).

The Case of the Manchu Libertine: Sex as Personal Indulgence

We see an example of what provoked Shen Defu's disapproval in a highly exceptional case from 1764 in which a Manchu nobleman was prosecuted for sodomy. This is the only example I have seen in the archives of an obvious member of the elite being punished for any sex offense. (Unfortunately the only document I have on this case is a brief memorial summarizing the judgment for imperial approval; it contains no record of testimony, so many details are unavailable.) Wudang'a was a baron of the third degree who belonged to the red-bordered banner and lived in Beijing. His age is not given, but he is described as "a foolish young man." Together with his friend Funing'a (who held the same rank in the same banner), Wudang'a had served in the retinue of the Qianlong Emperor during the southern tour of 1762. In Hangzhou the two barons had patronized one Wang Erguan, a young Han Chinese who worked as a barber and as a homosexual prostitute.[33] Subsequently, Wang Erguan had come to Beijing to seek employment as a servant in Funing'a's household. After several months, however, Funing'a was sent into exile for "engaging the sexual services of actors, drinking, and committing offenses" (*xia you*[34] *yin jiu fan shi*). (Unfortunately, the details of this scandal are not provided.) With Funing'a out of the picture, Wudang'a tried to persuade Wang Erguan to come work for him, but the barber declined, finding employment in a Beijing barbershop-brothel, where he was on call to serve clients at their homes. Wudang'a paid to sodomize him several times, and then paid off the barber's debt to the barbershop owner (thereby buying him out of service). Wang finally agreed to move in with the baron. Over the next five months, Wudang'a bought fancy clothes for Wang, supplied him with cash, and had intercourse with him many times; even so, Wang felt underpaid, and he left. Nine days later, Wudang'a persuaded him to come back, but after two months, Wang left once again. Hoping to frighten the barber into submission, the baron reported him to the police as a runaway slave. Wang Erguan was arrested, but the police commander who interviewed the men found the situation suspicious, and held both of them in custody overnight. The next day, Wudang'a admitted that his accusations were false; however, a well-connected uncle of his (a former county magistrate) pulled strings to get both men released.

Still the besotted baron could not master his passion. Over the next month, he continued to pursue the barber, trying to force him to return. More than once, the two men got into public altercations. Desperate, Wudang'a finally returned to the police and again accused Wang of being a runaway slave and a thief. This time, the matter was referred to the Board of Punishment, the truth of their relationship was exposed, and now the baron's connections proved useless. The board saw this as no ordinary case of sodomy:

Baron Wudang'a, who has been stripped of his rank, is a Manchu who held a responsible position as a military officer, but he did not remain content and obey the law. Instead, he invited the vulgar, debased barber Wang Erguan (*ti tou xia jian*) into his home and retained him there, consensually sodomizing him; also, when Wang Erguan ran away on several occasions, the offender searched for him, and twice went to the authorities to file false petitions against him. Such behavior is unusually shameless!

Like Funing'a before him, Wudang'a was exiled to Yili to serve as a runner (an extra-statutory penalty warranted by his multiple offenses). Wang Erguan's sentence was the standard month in the cangue and 100 blows of the heavy bamboo for "consensual sodomy" (preceded by deportation back home to Hangzhou). The fact that the barber had been briefly employed as a servant in Wudang'a's household, and was characterized in the record as "debased," in no way excused their sodomy. (By 1764, the judiciary had sharply narrowed its tolerance of sex with female servants; it seems to have allowed no room at all for sex with male servants.) The well-connected uncle and the police commander who had released the pair at his behest were punished as well, and an imperial rescript approved the judgment (XB, ZL/1112).

The brief memorial on this case mentions no female sexual partners, and it is certainly possible that the Manchu barons' interest focused exclusively on males. Still, it is safe to assume that men of their station had wives, whether they desired women or not—just as the marginal males more typically prosecuted for sodomy did *not* have wives, whether they desired women or not. Following Shen Defu, we can conclude that Wudang'a and Funing'a pursued male sex objects entirely as a matter of personal pleasure and fulfillment. On the other hand, the prostitute Wang Erguan seems more typical of the men found in sodomy cases; for him, sex was a way to get by, a precarious business at best.

Another point stands out. The judgment of Wudang'a emphasizes the scandalous lengths he had gone to in order to consort with a person of such vulgar status and occupation, thereby disgracing his position as a Manchu nobleman. Nevertheless, his reckless behavior had continued for at least two years before he finally ended up being prosecuted, and he came to the attention of the police only because he brought himself to their attention by twice filing false charges. In other words, a man of Wudang'a's status had many sexual options, and with even the slightest discretion he could have indulged his taste for men without any trouble at all.

The Decline of Chen Jingji

We conclude with Chen Jingji, Ximen Qing's son-in-law in *Plum in the Golden Vase*: the story of Jingji's declining fortunes in the latter part of the novel maps the hierarchy of sexual roles and opportunities against social stratification in a way that pulls together the many themes of this chapter. Shortly after Ximen Qing's death, Jingji begins an affair with Ximen's notorious concubine Pan Jinlian. This is the consummate penetrant role: a great deal of attention is paid to Jingji's penis, by Pan Jinlian (and her chambermaid Chun Mei) and by the novel's narrative voice (see Figure 1). Some chapters later, however, Jingji loses both fortune and wife and becomes homeless; he takes refuge with a gang of beggars who sleep in a nightwatch shed, and their leader sodomizes him. (At night, he dreams of the good old days with Pan Jinlian, and bursts into tears when he awakes and finds himself surrounded by beggars.) Next, Jingji takes refuge as a novice in a Daoist temple, where he shares a bed with the priest Jin Zongming:

That evening, the priest drank wine with Jingji until midnight and got him very drunk, and then they laid down to sleep on the same bed. At first they slept headed in opposite directions, head to toe, but the priest complained that Jingji's feet stank, and had him turn around and share a pillow with him. Then, after a while, he complained that Jingji's breath stank, and had him turn to face away, so that Jingji's buttocks pressed against the priest's belly. Jingji just pretended to sleep and ignored him.

The priest manipulated his penis until it was very hard, a stick standing straight up; he smeared some spittle on its head, and then thrust it right into Jingji's anus. Now it happens that Jingji had already been fucked (*nong guo*) by the beggar boss Flying Demon Hou Lin at the nightwatch shed, and his anus was already stretched out; so the priest's penis slipped right in, without any difficulty.

Jingji said nothing, but thought to himself, "This rascal is certainly taking advantage of me—I don't know who he thinks I am, treating me like this." (93/10a–b)

Chen Jingji's fate epitomizes the ironic logic of *Plum in the Golden Vase*. A major theme of the novel is karmic retribution, which visits each of its villains in turn (in the penultimate chapter, Jingji is murdered by one of the husbands he has cuckolded). Jingji's descent down the hierarchy of sexual roles symbolizes the karmic decline of his fortunes: this rich, arrogant penetrator of other men's wives ends up playing the female role himself, in ignominious service to beggars and clergy. Jingji's descent into this Hobbesian world of marginal males requires him to submit in order to make the best of a bad situation. In each instance of sodomy, there is a *quid pro quo*: the beggars give Jingji shelter and sustenance to survive the winter, while the Daoist becomes his patron and protector within the temple.

陳敬濟美一得雙

Figure 1. Chen Jingji as penetrator (in *ménage à trois* with Pan Jinlian and her chambermaid, Chun Mei), frontispiece to chapter 82 of *Plum in the Golden Vase*. The caption reads: "Chen Jingji fucks one and ends up with two." (Chongzhen-era print)

金道士變淫少弟

Figure 2. Chen Jingji penetrated by Jin Zongming, frontispiece to chapter 93 of *Plum in the Golden Vase*. The caption reads: "Daoist Jin debauches the young disciple." (Chongzhen-era print)

Moreover, Jingji—a man of twenty-four *sui*—is caricatured in this new sexual role as a feminized youth. Jin Zongming's lust is aroused when he notices that "Jingji had white teeth and red lips, and his face was as white as if it had been powdered" (93/10a). The original woodblock illustration of this scene depicts the penetrated Jingji as a beardless youth, in contrast with the full-bearded priest. The caption reads "Daoist Jin debauches the youthful disciple (*shao di*)" (see Figure 2). Jingji's reversal of sexual roles is a direct consequence of his loss of wealth, status, and power, and it is confirmed by a corresponding loss of masculine maturity. His fate sums up the contemporary common sense of what phallic penetration meant, a common sense that informed judicial thinking.[35]

The Meaning of Penetration

Penetration implied a gendered hierarchy of domination. In this respect, China resembled the Greco-Roman world, where "surrendering to penetration was a symbolic abrogation of power and authority—but in a way which posed a polarity of domination-subjection rather than of homosexual-heterosexual" (Boswell 1990, 155). In late imperial China, the model for the judicial construction of sex between males was heterosexual intercourse in conditions of gender inequality, in which the roles of penetrator and penetrated were perceived as fixed to the male and female, respectively. Male subject acted upon female object. In such circumstances, the act became inextricably bound up with the unequal distribution of power in the gender hierarchy and constituted both an expression of that unequal power and a means of inscribing it on the bodies and psyches of partners. Penetration became both the metaphor and physical expression of gender domination.

In the proper order of things, as seen by High Qing jurists, this act took place only within marriage. The husband and master penetrated his wife: by doing so, he reproduced the patriarchal household and reinforced the axis of gender hierarchy at its heart. In late imperial China, males and females came of age socially with marriage; a key transition point was its sexual consummation. Without consummation, a bride might be rejected, as sometimes occurred when she refused intercourse or when some anomaly of her anatomy prevented the groom from achieving penetration (XT, 74/QL 4.3.27). With consummation, male and female took up their respective social roles as husband and wife, embodied in their sexual roles as penetrator and penetrated. Penetration represented an initiation into gendered and hierarchized roles: the division of *sexual* labor reflected and defined the division of *social* labor. In Bourdieu's terms, these symbolic connections represent a homology between sexual and sociopolitical domains (1990, 71).

During the Ming and Qing dynasties, both chastity cults and criminal penalties codified this vision of penetration. If a woman were penetrated outside of legitimate marital context (by illicit sex, widow remarriage, or rape), she suffered a pollution of her chastity, an objective degradation that imperial chastity cults symbolized by disqualifying her from canonization (if she were a victim of rape-murder or rape-suicide). Such pollution corresponded to that of debased status; therefore, the rape or abduction of a woman polluted by illicit sex or by debased status caused less harm than that of a chaste commoner woman, and it would be punished less severely. This vision of penetration as initiation, possession, or pollution informed both the popular perception and the judicial construction of anal intercourse between males. For males, too, penetration positioned both roles on a hierarchy; the penetrated suffered a loss interpreted as an inversion or degradation of masculinity. The penetrator suffered no such loss, as he played the definitively masculine role.

We begin to understand why no Qing or earlier legal text even refers to, let alone bans, female homosexual activity. The lack of legal references does not, of course, imply that women never formed erotic relationships with each other—there are plenty of references in *non*-legal sources.[36] Nor does it mean that lawmakers were necessarily ignorant of such matters. Sex between women was simply not constructed as a crime. This interpretation makes sense, given the phallocentrism of both law and social norms: if gender and power were keyed to a hierarchy of phallic penetration, then sex without a phallus would seem to undermine neither.[37]

This chapter has told a story of both continuity and change. The continuity was profound: that is why anecdotes from Ming fiction can help us make sense of eighteenth-century legislation. The prosecution of illicit sexual intercourse (*jian*) originally aimed to control access to women; therefore, the earliest laws against intercourse between males did not call that act *jian*. Nevertheless, even Song and Ming legislation against homosexual acts shared with *jian* a fixation with the polluting danger of penetration out of place. This shared fixation informed the Qing innovation of reconstructing sodomy as a variant of *jian*: hence, the logic of equal penalties for "parallel" homosexual and heterosexual offenses. Eighteenth-century concern about sodomy, like the contemporary obsession with female chastity, did not appear *ex nihilo*; heightened anxiety about gender performance prompted Qing jurists to scrutinize sodomy more closely, but their construction of that crime reveals a basic continuity with what came before.

What changed in the Qing dynasty? The Ming sodomy statute could hardly be more explicit about the sexual act itself, yet it makes no reference to coercion, to the age of the penetrated male, or to the character or social background of either sexual partner, and the penalty it imposes is still on the low end of the scale. In the Qing, we see the emergence of the rootless rascal, and fear of homosexual rape comes to parallel fear of heterosexual rape. For both females and males, as the concept of *liang* lost its nuance of legal status, it took on the meaning of normative gender roles. The Yongzheng legislation, in particular, shows a new, intensive focus on fixing male gender in self-conscious analogy to female gender, in an effort to defend chaste wives and daughters *and* young boys of upright households against the predatory rootless rascal.

It stands to reason that the growing numbers of surplus males would have raised the profile of same-sex union and of homosexual rape in both peasant society and judicial caseloads. Perhaps this helps explain the new perception of a threat to masculinity. In his 1780 commentary, jurist Wu Tan notes that in the past there had been no explicit policy on "males committing homicide in self-defense against rape"; but in the Qianlong era such cases were common enough that it had become necessary to issue a substatute to guide magistrates (1992, 785). In addition, the new judicial attention to the penetrated male in Ming and Qing law may be another sign of the "peasantization" we have already considered in heterosexual rape law. The intense stigma of the penetrated male in settled peasant society may reflect in part the profound anxiety of a poor peasantry about downward mobility: if homosexual union was associated with desperate, marginal males, then the penetrated role was the lowest a male could possibly sink. It seems plausible that to a peasant eking out a bare subsistence, the penetrated male might represent the distilled essence of his greatest fears: the risk of falling into the most desperate poverty and marginalization, losing livelihood, family, and even masculinity.

The conflation of eroticized youth, femininity, and penetrability implies an instability in the gender of young males, especially prior to transition with marriage to adult masculinity. It seems that young males were perceived as vulnerable to penetration, and, in that sense, as potentially female. (Some of our cases show adolescent males being relatively open to penetration, an attitude some abandoned with maturity.) Thus, in the statutory language, it is the unpenetrated (*liang*) "sons and younger brothers" of commoner (*liang*) status who must be protected—vulnerable junior males who have not yet emerged from ambiguous youth into masculine adulthood.[38] Moreover, they must be protected from the rogue male threatening the household from without.

Qing jurists aimed to channel behavior into accepted gender roles—an ever greater priority as other social boundaries blurred. The spate of new laws against sodomy betrayed increasing fear of the threat to vulnerable males, but also, perhaps, of their possible enjoyment of roles that conflicted radically with the demands of order. Pollution of female chastity threatened the gendered hierarchy of the household—but the degradation of masculinity did so, too.

CHAPTER FIVE

Widows in the Qing Chastity Cult:
The Nexus of Sex and Property
in Law and in Women's Lives

Introduction

For widows in late imperial China, sex and property were linked in multiple ways. This statement applies to both official discourse and social practice, which influenced each other to such a degree that it is difficult (and perhaps inappropriate) to separate them completely. Qing legal cases involving widows allow us to explore this zone of interplay: between interest and emotion, between official priorities and popular strategies, and between outward representations and closeted lives.

To imperial authorities, the widow constituted an ideologically vital point of intersection between property relations and sexual relations. The "chaste widow" played a signal role in propaganda that tied sexual loyalty (of wife to husband) to political loyalty (of subject to ruler).[1] Ming-Qing law granted widows the strongest rights of any women with regard to property and independence. However, these rights depended on chastity, a status violated by either remarriage or adultery: for this purpose, the two acts were simply variations on a theme. This nexus of sex and property provided the fodder for a huge amount of civil and criminal adjudication, which was the most direct means by which the Qing state sought to enforce moral standards. The surviving records open a new window on both the imperial effort to promote female chastity and the impact that effort had on the lives of ordinary people.

This chapter begins with the official discourse of widow sexuality and property. But the basic question it tries to answer is what difference such discourse made for the kind of people who appear in case records: peasants, petty urbanites, and others of modest means and humble ambition. How were sex and property connected in their lives, and what relationship, if any, linked the practical logic of ordinary life to the priorities and pretensions of the state?

The most basic link between property and sexual norms is well known: it took a certain amount of property to make chaste widowhood a viable option. Therefore, widow chastity served as a status symbol for the elite, while remarriage prevailed among the very poor.[2] The evidence in legal cases gets us further, revealing the logic of sexual contract that framed the survival strategies of impoverished widows. We grasp more clearly what it meant in individual women's lives for official standards of virtue to lie beyond reach.

But most of the legal action in this area focused on the young widow who had just enough property to get by, without resorting to remarriage, charity, or prostitution. As long as she maintained her claim to chastity, such a widow might enjoy a degree of independence unusual for women at any level of society. But two factors threatened that independence. First, there was the possibility of tension with in-laws (if a widow had any). Even though orthodoxy and law demanded the preservation of every male line of descent,[3] the surviving brothers of a dead man might have other priorities—especially if they were peasants with little surplus above subsistence. The equal shares brothers received in household division might be small indeed. Thus, while surviving brothers may not have begrudged the dead man his share, they might have felt differently about his widow. We need not ascribe any great evil to in-laws who eyed a young widow's property; they simply wished she would begin a new life elsewhere, so that their brother's assets could improve their own standard of living, however marginally. Some, perhaps, believed this best for the woman herself: young widows seem to have found new husbands easily (given the high male / female ratio), whereas a single woman might encounter difficulty.[4]

Second, a widow with property was subject to a minimum of direct supervision: *she* was the authority in her dead husband's household, backed by custom and legal guarantees. This practical autonomy created a space for personal freedom that sometimes produced highly unorthodox results. The independence justified by chastity provided the opportunity for adultery—which, in turn, might jeopardize the very independence that had made it possible.

These factors interacted in various scenarios of conflict between widows and their in-laws. The sexual basis of a widow's rights to property and independence may have derived from official discourse, but it was well understood by the people (mostly peasants) who appear in legal cases. Whether ordinary people shared official values remains an open and complex question—surely, some did to some degree.[5] But even if they did not, they knew perfectly well that power and property could be secured by *invoking* such values: usually, the authorities became involved because some party to the dispute sought their intervention as a strategy of empowerment. Conflicts over the status of a widow were fought out in court in terms of the official discourse of chastity and property, with both sides mobilizing official categories and stereotypes in their own interest—facilitated, no doubt, by the "pettifoggers" (*song gun*) who helped litigants package their stories in the form of persuasive written plaints (Karasawa 1993; P. Huang 1996, 152–68). Here, we see a practical process by which different levels of patriarchy legitimated and reinforced each other: the state's pretension as defender of family values was strengthened when humble people recited official standards of virtue in seeking judicial support. At the same time, those who could convincingly pose as defenders of those standards received the backing of state power.

One risk of reading legal cases is that they may convey the impression that conflict and crisis were the norm. The crises they highlight did occur. More important, however, the lines of cleavage and the practical logic exposed by such crises shaped the lives of far more people than that small number found in court cases. In their unmobilized, potential form, these same forces exerted a practical influence in mundane, unobtrusive ways—an influence reinforced by the occasional public crisis which provided the opportunity for explicit, overt enforcement of the sexual order. We must try to imagine how the forces that such crises reveal would frame the choices of the many people who never ended up in court.

The Official Assessment of Chastity

Chastity Heroines: The Ritual Dimension of Law

A woman's chastity—understood as absolute sexual loyalty to her husband—was evaluated by the Qing state according to her response to challenges such as the death of her husband, a rape attempt, or a sexual proposition. How high a standard of chastity did she set for herself? How far was she willing to go to defend her husband's sexual monopoly?

The Qing state evaluated chastity in two formal ways, representing the ritual (*li*) and penal (*fa*) dimensions of imperial law, respectively: the canonization (*jing biao*) of chastity heroines and martyrs by imperial edict,[6] and the evaluation of crimes against chastity according to the conduct of the victim. The classic chastity heroine was the chaste widow or *jie fu* (literally, "chaste wife")—that is, the widow who neither remarried nor engaged in sexual intercourse following the death of her husband. Honoring of chaste widows dated from at least the Han dynasty, which first institutionalized Confucian morality as imperial dogma. The Qing system derived directly from precedents in the Yuan and Ming dynasties (Liu Jihua 1991; Elvin 1984). In 1304, the Yuan Board of Rites established qualifications for a chaste widow to receive official recognition: she should spend at least the twenty years from age thirty to fifty *sui* as a widow without remarrying or engaging in adultery, and her "purity" (*zhen*) should be well known in her community. Upon nomination by neighbors, qualified widows were reported to the capital by local officials to receive imperial testimonials of merit (*jing biao*) (YD, 33/17a).

In 1368, the new Ming regime confirmed these qualifications, and added the reward of forgiving the labor service owed by a chaste widow's household. Also, by 1511, the Ming began to honor "chaste martyred women who have avoided pollution by criminals" (*bu shou zei wu zhen lie funü*)—in other words, women who died by assault or suicide in the course of a rape attempt without being penetrated by the rapist. Such women were to be commemorated with official monuments and their burial expenses paid by the state (MH, 79/457).

Both the chaste widow and the chastely martyred rape victim were represented as going to extraordinary lengths to avoid being penetrated by any man other than their husbands, whether through remarriage, adultery, or rape. Remaining unmarried was assumed to involve both economic and emotional hardship (often referred to in legal documents as *ku shou*, "suffering hardship to maintain chastity"). Choosing death over surrender of the husband's sexual monopoly was raised to the level of martyrdom (like the death of an official during loyal service to his ruler). In theory, each type of martyr consciously chose a supremely difficult but virtuous path over an easy but shameful alternative.[7]

The Qing state awarded silver to the households of chastity heroines to finance memorial arches, and it also established local "temples of chastity and filial piety" where canonized martyrs would have
tablets erected for sacrifices in their honor. The Yongzheng Emperor
also initiated a major push to extend chastity honors to ordinary
commoners; he idealized the *poor* chaste widow as the pinnacle of
female virtue (Elvin 1984). During the Yongzheng and Qianlong
reigns, Qing authorities greatly expanded the range of qualifications
for official celebration, by elaborating the principle of absolute sexual loyalty which defined the original two paradigms. The result
was an unprecedented proliferation of memorial arches—as Elvin
observes, "the system had become an assembly line" (1984, 135).

Chaste widowhood came to include a woman whose betrothed
died prior to the consummation of marriage but who moved in with
her parents-in-law to serve them and refused to marry any other
man. Also, over the course of the mid-Qing, a sort of inflation gradually shortened the time required to qualify as a chaste widow. Candidates for chaste martyrdom came to include a widow who killed
herself to follow her husband to the grave; a woman who committed suicide to follow her betrothed to the grave; and "a widow who
has resolved to raise her sons and preserve her chastity, but then
hangs herself because relatives are forcing her to remarry" (QHS,
403/503).[8] These additions combined the two heroic paradigms of
widowhood and martyrdom. Then, beginning in 1759, women who
committed suicide in response to noncoercive sexual propositions
were canonized as chastity martyrs (QHS, 403/510–11). This measure extended the logic of avoiding pollution by adultery or rape,
with absolute sexual loyalty coming to imply a mortal repugnance
at even the suggestion of sex with a man other than one's legitimate
husband (Meijer 1981).

But not just any woman could qualify as a chastity martyr, even
if she had performed these heroic deeds. As in the Ming, a dead rape
victim was disqualified from canonization if she had been penetrated by her attacker.[9] The same was true if she had a prior record
of sex outside marriage. A remarried widow could not qualify either,
even if she had *not* been penetrated by a rapist: by remarrying, she
had already failed the most basic test of chastity (QH, 30/254).[10]
Only a woman who held herself to the highest standard—death,
without penetration by any man other than her husband—might be
honored as a chastity martyr.

Crimes Against Chastity: The Penal Dimension of Law

Some challenges to chastity involved male acts defined by Qing law as crimes. But the definition of the crime and the fixing of penalties depended on the woman's reaction: the higher the standard of chastity she upheld in meeting the challenge, the more severe the offender's penalty would be. We have already seen this principle at work in the adjudication of rape cases. The most dramatic example, however, may be the crime of "sexual proposition" (*tiao xi* or *tiao jian*). If a man proposed a sexual liaison to a woman and she simply complained, he might receive a beating and/or a term in the cangue, depending on the circumstances (DC, 366-13). But if she committed suicide, she qualified as a chastity martyr, and (beginning in the Yongzheng reign) the offender would be sentenced to strangulation after the assizes (DC, 299-14 and 18). What defined the man's crime and fixed his penalty was how the woman reacted, rather than his act itself.

Another example is the crime of forcing a widow to remarry. For this crime, an elaborate scale of penalties was keyed to the degree of kinship between offender and victim (see Appendix C). For each degree, the most severe penalties applied if the widow committed suicide to prevent the new marriage from being consummated. This martyrdom defined the coercion as a grave offense (even her own parents might receive a beating and penal servitude for the crime); the dead widow would be canonized. If the new marriage had been consummated, but the woman chose to stay alive, considerably lighter penalties applied. But penalties were lightest if the widow could eventually be induced to submit to the forced remarriage, for, as with rape, submission after the fact amounted to consent. In fact, during the Yongzheng and early Qianlong reigns, a widow whose forced remarriage was consummated, but who failed to commit suicide, did not even retain the option of separating from her new husband; he would not be punished at all. As a 1725 memorial opined, such a widow "has already lost her virtue ('lost her body': *shi shen*), and has no chastity left to maintain (*wu zhi ke shou*), so there is no need to recover her and return her" to her former husband's household (Wu Tan 1992, 446). Finally, if a widow forfeited her chastity through adultery, then her in-laws gained the legal right to sell her in marriage, regardless of her wishes (DC, 366-00). Clearly, the crime of forced remarriage applied only to chaste widows, and it was based on their objective status as such, rather than on the violation of their wishes.

Each category of crime required a prior judgment of the victim that determined the weight of the penalty meted out to the offender. The highest standard of chastity was death without penetration, to be rewarded with both canonization for the martyr and the severest penalties for the offender.

The Widow as Sexual Being

Chastity and a Widow's Contingent Legal Rights

Qing jurists imagined the widow as a sexual being, either chaste or unchaste,[11] with a series of legal consequences following each alternative. A widow who could claim chastity enjoyed legal rights unique among women. They should not be confused, however, with the modern Western concept of inalienable human rights: if a widow remarried or committed adultery, her status in her husband's household and the rights contingent on that status would be forfeit.[12]

In both law and custom, the property rights of women in late imperial China depended on marital status.[13] The fundamental factor underlying marital status was chastity. The property rights of widows (main wives or *qi*, not concubines or *qie*) were defined by a Ming edict later adopted as a substatute in the Qing code:

> If a wife without sons maintains her chastity (*shou zhi*) after her husband dies, then she should receive her husband's share of property, and lineage elders should select an appropriate male from the correct family branch and generation to be appointed as successor and heir (*ji si*) [to her husband]. If she remarries, then her first husband's family shall determine the disposition of both his household property and her original dowry.   (DC, 078-02)

A chaste widow had the right to independent control of her husband's share of his father's household property. If her husband had no sons, then an heir should be appointed (to carry on her husband's line of descent and to care for her in old age). These mandated rights made a widow uniquely independent among women, so long as her husband had left enough property to secure her living. But if she remarried, she left her husband's lineage and lost all claim to property, including any dowry she had brought into the marriage. What goes without explicit statement in the law is the assumption that children remained within the patrilineal descent group: a widow who remarried lost her claim to them as well.

Both Ming and Qing codes prohibited a widow (whether wife or concubine) from remarrying during the official three-year mourning period, the penalty being 100 blows of the heavy bamboo and nullification of the new marriage. The widow of a senior official (*ming fu*) could *never* remarry. One who did so would be stripped of any title or honor (*chi gao*) she had received through her dead husband's status and would suffer the same penalties due a commoner widow who remarried during mourning (DC, 105-00). The latter measure underscores the association between sexual and political virtue: loyalty of wife to husband gained in importance when the husband was an honored official of the imperial state.

Apart from these conditions, widows could legally remarry, even if the practice was stigmatized. In fact, most remarriages probably occurred within three years (since they were motivated by poverty) and hence violated the law. Magistrates sometimes waived the ban on remarriage during the mourning period for poor widows who had no other means of support. In such cases, remarriage was treated as a lesser evil by a judiciary that sought to place every woman in a household, even as it promoted an absolute standard of chastity (MQ, 57-121). In judicial practice, a remarried widow lost her rights *vis-à-vis* her first husband's household, but seems to have acquired the same rights *vis-à-vis* that of her new husband. In other words, if the *second* husband of a remarried widow died, she had the right to manage his property and care for her children by him, as long as she refrained from remarrying again (or other unchaste conduct). This rule appears nowhere in the Ming or Qing codes, but can be inferred from the adjudication of various cases (for example, SF, 162/DG 25.3.8; and Wang Huizu 1970, 360–63).

The other form of unchaste behavior was adultery—that is, consensual illicit sex (*he jian*). In addition to corporal penalties, the basic Ming-Qing statute on this crime provided that "a wife who engages in illicit sex (*jian fu*) may be sold in marriage by her husband (*cong fu jia mai*); if he is willing to keep her, then he shall be allowed to do so" (Appendix A.2). Far from retaining any rights to property or children, an adulteress herself was an object to be sold. A wife who ran away from home, too, could be "sold in marriage by her husband" (DC, 116-00). The Ming and Qing codes do not single out the adultery of widows, but in practice the same provisions applied (a widow being treated as a wife whose husband happened to be dead), and her in-laws could sell her in marriage. For example, in a 1762 case from Fengjie County, Sichuan, the widow Zhou Cai Shi was convicted of adultery with a hired laborer. After she was beaten, the magistrate ordered her sold in marriage and turned her over to her father-in-law for that purpose. Through a matchmaker, her father-in-law found a new husband, who paid a bride-price of 65 taels (XT, 187/QL 27.12.11).

It seems to have been common, however, for a magistrate simply to order an adulterous widow "returned to her natal lineage" (*gui zong*). She would become the responsibility of her natal family, to support or to marry off a second time.

Many cases show that widows expelled in either way retained no claim to property or children (although some in-laws showed mercy in this regard). In 1831, when Wei Yang Shi of Ninghe County, Zhili, was expelled for adultery, she had to obtain the permission of her husband's appointed heir (*ji zi*) to keep even her own "coarse clothes"; he brought them to court to be handed over in the magistrate's presence (SF, 169/DG 11.3.?). In 1799, when the magistrate of Ba County ordered Gong Li Shi expelled, she was forcibly separated from her children, in spite of repeated petitions for mercy (BX, 2-4148, 4152, 4154).

A widow convicted of adultery would not necessarily be expelled, but a reprieve depended on the attitude of her husband's relatives, in an extension of the provision that "if her husband is willing to keep her, then he shall be allowed to do so" (DC, 366-00). We find an example of such leniency in a 1762 case from Poyang County, Jiangxi. Wu Shi (thirty-six *sui*), the widow of Wang Guangman, confessed to adultery with a distant relative of her dead husband but added this plea: "I beg only the mercy that I not be sold in marriage. I am willing to reform and devote myself to raising my son. I will be so grateful for the mercy of the court, if only my son and I are not separated." Her in-laws supported her plea: "Our uncle Wang Guangman left behind only this one son, and he really cannot be taken away from Wu Shi and cared for separately. Now, since Wu Shi is willing to reform, we beg that she be released into the custody of the lineage so that she can return and care for our young cousin." Wu Shi was beaten and ordered "released into the custody of her lineage elders, so that she may raise her son into adulthood, in order to continue Wang Guangman's line of descent."

Here, the support of in-laws played a crucial role: leniency was justified by Wu Shi's promise to serve her dead husband, caring for his son so as to secure his line of descent. It may be significant that Wu Shi's husband had no brothers and his parents were dead. Thus, she had no immediate in-laws to interfere or to covet her property. Her husband's cousins knew of her illicit affair, and although they had not exactly tolerated it—her lover had been warned off—neither had they taken legal action. Her conduct came to official attention only after her lover was killed in the night by her hired laborer, who mistook him for a thief (XT, 185/QL 27.4.20).

With regard to property and children, the legal status of an adulterous widow was the same as that of one who remarried. A widow's status in her husband's household—including the rights to manage his property and to reside with and raise her own children—depended entirely on maintaining her claim to chastity.

The Right Not to Remarry

A chaste widow enjoyed the unique legal right *not to marry*. Anyone who forced her to do so, including her own parents or parents-in-law, risked serious penalties. No other woman had the right to refuse to marry (with the exception of female clergy, who as a rule acquired such status either with parental approval or after being widowed)—certainly no unmarried daughter could go to court to defy her parents on this matter (or on any other!). Also, as we have seen, once a widow committed adultery, her in-laws could sell her off in marriage, regardless of her wishes.

The basic Qing substatute banning the "marrying out by coercion" (*qiang jia*) of a widow "willing to maintain her chastity" (*zi yuan shou zhi*) reached final form in 1801, but its essential features were in place by 1740 (see Appendix C.1). The premise of this law was that the widow in question was chaste and wished to remain so. Therefore, as we have seen, the crime was defined as an offense against her chastity. It was understood as being committed by the widow's own relatives. Outsiders (for example, matchmakers and prospective husband) were considered secondary to the ringleaders related to the widow. The crime, therefore, also violated the moral bond between family members. The substatute posits a hierarchy of levels of seriousness for the crime, determined by what was done to the widow and the standard of chastity she upheld in her reaction. Then, at each level, a scale of penalties is mandated for offenders, depending on their relation to the widow. Specific penalties are determined in the same manner as for violent crimes between relatives. Thus, if the offender is a senior relative, then the closer his relation to the widow, the lighter his penalty; if he is a junior relative, then the closer his relation, the heavier his penalty. This system reflects the principle that close senior relatives have legitimate authority over their juniors, who owe them deference and obedience (seniority being measured in terms of relative age and generation). For a close senior relative to coerce a widow was *less* of an offense, and for a close junior relative to coerce a widow *more* of an offense, than for distant relatives or unrelated persons to do so. The penalties of prospective husband and matchmakers were lower than those of the ringleaders.

A complementary substatute singled out the motive of *pecuniary gain* for forcing a widow to remarry (Appendix C.2). The culprits envisioned by this measure are relatives of the second or more distant degrees—that is, anyone but the widow's own parents or parents-in-law. The penalties are far more severe than those in the basic substatute on forced remarriage: thus, a junior relative who committed the offense could be sentenced to strangulation or beheading after the assizes, if the marriage was consummated or the widow committed suicide. (Autumn Assizes rules issued in the Qianlong reign prescribed that in such cases the death penalties be enforced without exception or delay—Gang Yi 1968, 259). As in the case of rape and sexual proposition, the penalties for both kinds of forced remarriage became far more severe in the Qing dynasty, with death penalties first being imposed during the Yongzheng and Qianlong reigns.[14]

The substatute cites two ways to gain by forcing remarriage: "plotting to usurp property" (*mou zhan zicai*) and "scheming for bride-price" (*tan tu pinli*). In the first, the culprits are imagined forcing the widow to remarry so that she forfeits her claim to her husband's property—which then becomes vulnerable to seizure. The second is more straightforward: selling the woman for profit. Case records show that this scenario occurred among the very poor, for whom the bride-price would exceed the value of any possessions the widow left behind.[15]

The intended purpose of these legal guarantees was not to empower the widow for her own sake, but rather to secure her husband's household unit and line of descent, of which she became the chief guardian. Lawmakers imagined the chaste widow as vulnerable to abuse by her closest relatives, particularly her in-laws, who were stereotyped as seeking to thwart her sacred resolve out of greed. The means to their profit was the pollution of her chastity and the dismemberment of her husband's household. In the final analysis, however, a truly chaste widow held the trump card, since she would choose death rather than submit to such base schemes.

If the widow were unchaste, however, roles reversed: she would lose all claim to property and children, which would be entrusted to her in-laws, now cast as the guardians of family values. Inasmuch as the whole rationale for a widow's veto over remarriage was to remain chaste, her adultery eliminated that veto, and expelling or selling off an adulteress became a legitimate act of lineage self-defense.

Forced Remarriage, Suicide, and Standards of Chastity

One Widow's Suicide: Chastity Martyr or Slut?

The legal secretary Wang Huizu recounts an excellent example of how the judiciary evaluated widows based on the alternative premises that they were chaste or unchaste. The case concerned the suicide of the widow Ye Shi, which took place in Zhejiang in 1782. Ye Shi's first husband had died after a seventeen-year marriage; soon thereafter, she had remarried to a man named Sun, who in turn died after less than one year. She was left at age thirty-four *sui* a widow for the second time. Her household included Sun's son (four *sui*) by a previous wife, and a hired laborer named Qin, who helped work Sun's twenty-plus *mu* of land.

After a short time, an in-law named Sun Lejia tried to persuade Ye Shi to dismiss Qin in order to avoid gossip. She agreed but never acted on the promise—so Sun Lejia confronted Qin, who claimed he could not quit because his mistress owed him back wages. After this, Sun Lejia and other family members began to pressure the widow to remarry. Ye Shi put them off by claiming that it would take time to find an appropriate match. Then, when they found her a prospective husband in a neighboring village, she filed charges accusing the Suns of trying to force her to remarry. Her laborer acted as the male guarantor for her plaint (required, since she was female). In response, the lineage head and Sun Lejia searched for Qin to reprimand him for supporting the lawsuit, but he ran away. Then they scolded Ye Shi, who hanged herself later the same night.

The magistrate and his superiors agreed that this suicide had been provoked by the in-laws' pressure on the widow to remarry, but controversy ensued over which law should apply. If the Suns had been trying to seize her husband's land, they should suffer the more severe penalties mandated by the law on pecuniary gain. The sub-prefect of Huzhou asked Wang Huizu for his opinion.

The version of events accepted by the judiciary up to this point assumed that the widow had been chaste. Her reluctance to remarry, then, had stemmed from devotion to her dead husband Sun, which had motivated her delaying tactics, her lawsuit, and finally her suicide. But in reviewing the case record, Wang Huizu learned that at the time of suicide,

Ye Shi's face was smeared with make-up; on her upper body were a red outer garment and colorful underclothes; on her lower body were a green skirt, red underclothes, brightly patterned leggings, and red embroidered shoes. Her sleeping quarters consisted of a single room, the inner part of which was Ye Shi's bedroom; the room was divided by planks but no door, and in the outer part was Qin's bed.

To Wang, these details strongly implied that Ye Shi had been illicitly involved with her hired laborer. Anyway, because the widow had remarried after the death of her *first* husband, it made no sense to credit her now with a high standard of chastity:

Ye Shi's death occurred less than a year after that of [her husband] Sun, but she was made-up and dressed in fancy clothes. Could these possibly be the circumstances of a widow guarding her chastity (*ci qi shou gua qingxing*)? Having discarded her gratitude toward her first husband of seventeen years, would she then remain faithful to a second husband of only eleven months? Such a scenario simply could not occur! Her supposedly chaste death represents nothing more than her reluctance to lose Qin. . . . Ye Shi's suicidal impulse was caused by Qin running away, and Qin alone should be punished for it.

The laborer was tracked down, and, as expected, he confessed to adultery. The final judgment declared that no criminal attempt at forced remarriage had taken place.

The case hinged on whether Ye Shi was chaste or unchaste; each premise produced a chain of legal and symbolic consequences. If she were chaste, her death became a paradigmatic gesture of wifely virtue; the in-laws who had provoked it, perhaps to seize her husband's land, should be severely punished. But if she were not chaste, then her death was just the end result of wanton lust, and only the lover complicit in that lust would be culpable—indeed, her in-laws' conduct could be seen as an effort to secure the integrity of their lineage. By failing to uncover Ye Shi's adultery, Wang Huizu observed, "the earlier investigations had all overlooked the root of the matter" (1970, 360–63).

The Representation of Heroic Martyrdom

A 1739 case from Xuancheng County, Anhui, provides a classic example of the morality play of covetous in-laws versus the chaste widow. Such cases represent the most direct interaction between the ritual and penal aspects of imperial chastity policy. As the judicial summary explains:

In 1728, [Wu Shi's husband] Chen Lai died of illness. [Her parents-in-law] wanted to make Wu Shi remarry, but she cut off her hair to make clear her resolve to remain chaste. Later, after [her parents-in-law] had died, poverty forced the widow to take her son out begging. Her son was still a small child, and became lost and disappeared. Thus, [by the time she was martyred,] she had already endured the hardship of maintaining her chastity for ten years, alone.

Chen Zhiwan was Wu Shi's closest surviving in-law. He had "often urged her to remarry, but she refused. Finally, he decided to wrest her chastity from her by force (*qiang duo qi jie*)"—in other words, force her to remarry—to relieve his family of her constant begging for support; he also coveted the bride-price he could get for her. But when the widow was abducted and delivered to her new husband, Miao Zitong,

she wept and cursed and refused to consummate the marriage. Zitong . . . learned that she had been coerced into remarriage, so he did not dare force her to submit; he had his son Miao Zhaoer, still a small child, spend the night with her, and he absolutely did not consummate the marriage (*cheng hun*). The next day, Zitong went searching for [the matchmakers] to demand that they refund the bride-price, but they evaded him and he did not find them. Finally, on the fourteenth, he told his son to accompany Wu Shi back [to Chen Zhiwan's] home. [She begged Chen to let her live with him and maintain her chastity] but he cursed and scolded her. Angry, and unwilling to accept this insult, she hanged herself and died that very night inside Chen Zhiwan's house.

After sentencing her abusers, the magistrate ordered the widow's meager possessions recovered (from in-laws who had divided them) and entrusted to her brother, who was charged with finding her long-lost son. As to the widow herself,

Wu Shi . . . cut off her hair to make clear her resolve, remaining chaste for ten years, and then, when Chen Zhiwan and the others forcibly remarried her, she refused to submit, and was provoked into the martyrdom of hanging herself (*ji lie zi yi*). Such chastity, maintained through such suffering, is truly worthy of praise! It is meet to request that she be canonized, so as to promote the public morality.   (XT, 75/QL 4.5.30)[16]

To prove a martyr's chastity beyond doubt, judges would scrutinize what had happened once she had been delivered to her new husband, extracting a detailed account from that man. The following confession (from Liuan Department, Anhui, memorialized in 1817) highlights the heroic struggle against coercion. Elicited in the form of answers to discrete questions, the confession appears as a monologue recording the widow's reactions to a series of challenges. The voice is that of Lin Dairong (thirty-nine *sui*), prospective husband of the widow Yu Shi (thirty-four *sui*). Lin did not realize the widow was being coerced until he arrived to pick her up, but he accepted the deal all the same ("I just assumed that once I had taken her home in marriage, I could persuade her to submit"):

By the time we reached my home, it was already the middle of the night. Yu Shi cried and made a fuss and refused to consummate the marriage (*cheng qin*), so my mother spent the night with her and calmed her down.

On the afternoon of the fifteenth, I urged Yu Shi to eat, but she smashed the dishes and cut off her hair, and cursed and insulted me. I got angry, and punched her. . . . Yu Shi made a shrewish fuss (*po nao*), so I grabbed hold of her, picked up a piece of kindling, and beat her. . . . Yu Shi rolled around violently on the floor, and never stopped cursing me, so I struck her again. . . . My father rushed in and shouted to stop, and he scolded me and told me to find the matchmakers and make them help take Yu Shi home, so as to avoid trouble. That night, he told my mother to spend the night with Yu Shi again.

On the morning of the sixteenth, I went to look for [the matchmakers] to make them return the bride-price so Yu Shi could be sent home. But unexpectedly, Yu Shi waited until my mother was in the kitchen . . . and then hanged herself. . . . In truth, I beat her out of anger, because she made such a scene and cursed and insulted me. I absolutely did not beat her into consummating the marriage.

As in the previous case, we find female defiance in its proper place, defending chastity. After being forcibly delivered to her new "husband"'s home, the widow refused to eat: eating might have implied willingness to join the new household. Moreover, like the widow in the previous case, she cut off her hair, a classic gesture to renounce sexual life, specifically associated with becoming a nun.[17] When beaten, she cursed and fought, and finally hanged herself, to avoid further contact with the usurper of her husband's place (XT, 138/JQ 22.6.26).

A crucial point of the interrogation of the prospective husband was to establish whether he had consummated the marriage. If he had sexually polluted the widow, then he might deserve harsher penalties. But also, if the widow had "allowed" herself to be penetrated, she would not be eligible for canonization as a chastity martyr. The issue was important enough that provincial officials singled it out in their orders to magistrates on how to handle such cases: "Sternly interrogate the witnesses and accurately establish all the facts about the initiation of the plot to seize the [widow's] property, the recruitment of the gang, and the forced remarriage which caused [the widow] to hang herself; furthermore, verify *whether or not she was sexually polluted (you wu jian wu)* [emphasis added]." This passage comes from the 1762 case of the widow Xie Shi, from Sui Department, Hubei, who committed suicide after being forcibly remarried out by a cousin-in-law who coveted her property. Upon receiving these instructions, the magistrate pressed the "groom" (Wang Huazhang, thirty *sui*) specifically on the question of consummation, resulting in the following confession:

Xie Shi refused to consummate the marriage; she said she had been married out by force . . . and told me to take her back to her home. . . . I asked the neighbor woman Zhang Shi to keep Xie Shi company and calm her down; but Xie Shi said that if she were not taken home, she would kill herself.

When my father heard what she had said, he got scared, and told me to go quickly and find the matchmakers to clear this up so we could send Xie Shi back. I went looking for [the matchmakers], but they avoided me, and I couldn't find them, so in the evening I came back home. My father said, "It's already late, today, so go again tomorrow to look for them." Then father told Zhang Shi and Xie Shi and her daughter to sleep together in the south room; father also told me to sleep in the same bed with him.

But then, early the [next] morning, Zhang Shi screamed that Xie Shi had hanged herself and was dead. I hurried with my father to their room and undid Xie Shi from the bed frame and brought her down, but it was already too late. . . . I did not sexually pollute Xie Shi by forcing her to consummate the marriage (*qiang bi cheng hun jian wu*)—Zhang Shi is here, you can ask her.

The neighbor woman Zhang Shi and Wang's father both confirmed that Wang had spent the night in a separate room, with no opportunity to force himself on the widow. In fact, Wang's father had been so nervous about the situation that he had purposely slept in the same bed as Wang to make sure that no consummation would take place (XT, 182/QL 27.7.29).

The next priority was to secure the interests of the dead husband, for whom the widow had ostensibly sacrificed her life. In the first case cited in this section, the magistrate ordered that the widow's possessions, however humble, be restored as a unit and entrusted to her brother until her son could be found to inherit them (XT, 75/QL 4.5.30). In the last case cited, Xie Shi's husband had had more property, but no sons. His land, cows, and daughter were turned over to the widow's brother, pending the adoption of an appropriate male as her husband's son and heir. That heir would receive the property and become responsible for raising the widow's daughter and arranging her marriage; he would also take on the ritual duties of a son toward his deceased adoptive parents (XT, 182/QL 27.7.29). In each case, the magistrate attempted to reconstitute the material and human components of the dead husband's household as an independent unit, so that the widow would not have died in vain.

Such memorials conclude with a request for an edict of canonization, couched in language heavy with political overtones. We saw one example in the first case cited. A second follows, from the case of the widow Xie Shi: "Huang Zhengji and his cohort forced Xie Shi to remarry, but she maintained her rectitude and was not polluted, sacrificing her life to prove her chaste resolve. This was truly a chaste martyrdom worthy of praise! It is meet, therefore, to request that she be canonized, so as to promote public morals and solace her lonely soul (*yi wei fenghua, yi wei you hun*)." In such passages, the logographs *jing biao* (to canonize) are raised two spaces into the margin above the rest of the text, an honor reserved for direct references to the emperor: with canonization, the emperor personally recognized the martyr's heroism. The cliché used for "sacrifice her life," *juan qu* (literally, "to sacrifice/contribute one's body") was most often employed to describe the heroic death of a soldier or loyal minister. Such wording—as well as references to "rectitude" (*zheng*), "martyrdom" (*lie*), and "public morals (*fenghua*)"—epitomize the analogy drawn between chastity and political loyalty (XT, 182/QL 27.7.29; XT, 176/QL 27.10.14).

In these memorials, the chastity martyr is portrayed as self-conscious and assertive, but all her energy goes into self-abnegation, ending in the logical extreme of suicide. To the state, self-abnegation epitomized appropriate female assertiveness; such virtuous subjecthood found ultimate expression in the woman's erasure of herself from the scene, leaving a blank to be filled in by judges with paeans to her righteousness. The chastity martyr is presented as a subject with choices, but what ennobled her in official discourse was the assumption that she was an actor more in her husband's life than in her own—the only point of her own life (and death) being absolute commitment to him.

The women elevated as chastity martyrs are perhaps the most inaccessible figures in Qing legal records. Judicial summaries of their cases recall the formulaic language of gazetteer hagiography, and the widows' own motives remain obscure. It seems plausible that their defiance and despair did not necessarily derive from the official agenda; some may have valued independence for its own sake.[18]

"Pretending to Submit"

A 1769 case from Ba County, Sichuan, offers a more down-to-earth look at a widow who resisted forced remarriage. Instead of achieving heroic martyrdom, this one escaped to complain about the experience. He Liu Shi (thirty-six *sui*) was the widow of He Ruixiang, who had left her the means to live independently with their young son and adopted daughter-in-law. According to her petition,

> I encountered the misfortune of being constantly pressured to remarry by my husband's younger brother, He Ruilin, who plotted to usurp the property left by my husband. . . . On the twenty-sixth day of the third [lunar] month of this year, Ruilin and his gang swarmed into my home, seized me, bound my hands and feet, and took me by force . . . to marry a man from Hunan named Huang. I wanted to kill myself, but I could not bear to leave behind my son, who is only nine *sui*, as an orphan, so I preserved my life by the ignoble means of pretending to submit (*tou sheng jia shun*) to Huang. Then, on the eighth of this month, I was finally able to escape. . . . Weeping, I sought sanctuary with my neighbors . . . and we discovered that my husband's silver from land sales and even my clothes, grain, and furniture had all been stolen by Ruilin.

Her story was backed by an affidavit from eight neighbors, but the magistrate's cynical reaction focused on the widow's own conduct: "This woman was abducted on the twenty-sixth day of the third month, and she returned home finally on the eighth day of the fourth month. That means her marriage with Huang had been consummated for nearly half a month—can she still call this 'pretending to submit' (*shang de wei zhi jia shun hu*)?" Even so, he found her abductors guilty and ordered them to return her property. He canceled the marriage and authorized the widow's brother to report any future abuse by her in-laws. But the culprits got off remarkably lightly, considering the severity of penalties mandated for relatives who forced a widow to remarry so as to seize her property. He Ruilin and the others were beaten and released on pledge of good behavior; but as a junior relative of the fourth degree whose motive had been gain, He Ruilin could conceivably have been beheaded (see Appendix C.2, item B). It appears that the "groom" was not punished at all, but treated, rather, as a victim of fraud.

Clearly, the magistrate found this widow's reaction to the challenge of forced remarriage far from ideal. She tried to justify herself:

naturally, she would have *preferred* to die, but her primary duty was her son—the surrogate for her husband—so she did what was necessary to stay alive. But the magistrate thought little of her idea of sacrifice, hence his leniency toward her abusers (BX, 1-1673, 1674, 1677).

Widows Without Property

Poverty and the Limits of Official Virtue

The chastity so celebrated by the Qing state was literally unaffordable for many widows. It is not unusual to learn from case records that a widow remarried quickly in order to raise enough money to liquidate the debts of her first husband, or even to finance his burial. In effect, she sold herself to her new husband, using the bride-price to settle outstanding debts before joining him in marriage.[19] We find a concise summary of the issues in a contract from Ba County:

Mrs. Sun née Yu Shi (Sun *men* Yu *shi*) establishes this contract authorizing her own marriage out [of the Sun lineage]: Now that her husband has died, leaving a son Sun Wenbang, who is still only a small child, and since she is poor and has no means of support, it is difficult for her to endure the suffering of maintaining a chaste widowhood (*nan yi ku shou*). In the city, there is the trader Wang Zhao, who has invited mediators to arrange with those surnamed Sun and Yu that Yu Shi shall promise herself (*zi xing zhu xu*) to Wang Zhao as wife. The son Wenbang and daughter Ergu left [by her first husband] shall follow their mother and be taken to the Wang household to be educated, raised, and married; he of the Sun surname (i.e., Wenbang) upon reaching adulthood shall return to his own lineage, and [the Wangs] may not hinder him. On this day, relatives, friends, and neighbors have been invited to discuss the bride-price and have settled on exactly 26,000 cash, which shall be used to repay the funeral (*chu ling*) and coffin expenses [of her first husband]; today that amount has been handed over in full and used to repay these various debts. Wang may choose a date for her to join him in marriage (*wanju*). From this day on, no brother-in-law or other relative from the Sun lineage may say anything to the contrary, this being the voluntary decision of both families, and there being absolutely no coercion involved; fearing that there will otherwise be no evidence of this, [Yu Shi] hereby establishes this marriage contract as proof.

TO SERVE AS PROOF FOREVER (*yongyuan wei zhao*)[20]

Mediators: Brothers-in-law (*qinshu*) Sun Fangju, writing for [Yu Shi] (*daibi*), and Sun Guofu, presiding over the marriage (*zhuhun*).

Done, on the twenty-second day of the third month of Qianlong 25 (1760), by the person establishing this marriage contract, Mrs. Sun née Yu Shi.

This text places great emphasis on the widow's active, voluntary consent, in particular by representing her as the party "establishing" (*li*) the contract. In this respect, it differs from ordinary marriage contracts of the period, which are never written in the voice of the bride. This feature of the contract implies an awareness that widows had the customary and legally protected right not to remarry.

It seems to have been common for propertyless widows to take children into a second marriage, as stipulated here, because in-laws were too poor to feed extra mouths. In the examples I have seen in Qing archives, widows sought guarantees that sons of a first husband would not be forced to take the second husband's surname.[21]

One purpose of this contract is to record the terms so as to enable their enforcement in court if necessary. Another, perhaps, is to justify the widow's decision to remarry. The contract depicts her abandonment of chaste widowhood as reluctant but necessary, given her poverty and the youth of her son. But an effort has been made to portray the widow as loyal to her dead husband: she is using the bride-price from the second marriage to pay the debts incurred by his funeral, and though she herself leaves his lineage, she has ensured that his son will not, thereby securing his line of descent. In other words, this woman has done her best to be a chaste widow, given her material circumstances. There is no way to know how much this document represents her own feelings—at most, it may record her "voice" filtered through several intervening layers (conventional written style, contractual format, male scribe, and so on). Even so, it reminds us that people often feel guilt over hegemonic values they cannot hope to realize in their own lives (BX, 1-1623).

The hollowness of official virtue stands out in a 1733 case from Zunyi County, Guizhou. After Zheng Shi's husband, the peasant Yuan Yu, died late in 1732, she and her four young sons were able to survive only on loans from a maternal aunt. Her brothers-in-law tried to help, but they could hardly feed their own families. The widow was able to secure a coffin for her husband only by promising to pay for it with the bride-price she would receive by remarrying.

Having resigned herself to remarriage, however, Zheng Shi found herself much sought after because of her proven ability to bear sons. For this reason (and because her in-laws, who handled the negotiations, took her interests into account), she was able to hold out for a good deal. One offer came from a cousin, Lei Dong (thirty-five *sui*), whose wife "had not been able to have children, and seeing that Zheng Shi could bear many sons, he wanted to take her as his concubine." Through an intermediary, Lei offered two taels of silver for the widow. But Zheng Shi did not want to be a concubine, and it was not clear what would become of her children if she married Lei. A more attractive offer came from Zhou Dengchao (thirty-seven *sui*), whose wife had died, leaving him without a son; so if Zheng Shi married him, she would have the full status of wife. Zhou offered *five* taels, enough to pay her debts. He also agreed to raise her sons, while letting them keep their father's name. Zheng Shi accepted, and became Zhou's wife some six months after her first husband had died.

The timing of Zheng Shi's second marriage came to the attention of the magistrate when Zhou was later prosecuted for homicide (the frustrated suitor Lei Dong attacked Zhou, who killed him in self-defense). As we know, the code prohibited a widow from remarrying for three years. When the magistrate confronted Zheng Shi with that fact, she attempted to justify herself:

My husband left behind four sons who are all still very small. They were so hungry, and were crying day and night. I was starting to feel hunger, too, but even if I starved to death, I couldn't really be pitied (*shuo bu de ke lian*). But if these four sons starved to death, that would completely cut off my husband's line of descent (*ba zhangfu de hou dai dou jue le*)! I had no choice but to remarry in order to preserve these four sons.

She seems to have been referring to the famous Neo-Confucian polemic against widow remarriage: "It is a small matter to starve to death, but a large matter to lose one's chastity" (*e si shi xiao, shi jie shi da*) (Liu Jihua 1991, 526; Ebrey 1993, 199). Like the widow who "pretended to submit," Zheng Shi had denied herself escape for the sake of her husband's long-term interests.

The magistrate also interrogated the matchmaker for the widow's illegal remarriage, who was also liable for punishment. But this man offered a frank appraisal, devoid of moralistic rationalization:

When Zheng Shi's husband died, they didn't even have a coffin, and were able to buy one on credit only by promising to pay for it after Zheng Shi remarried! Her four sons were crying day and night because they had nothing to eat. How could she wait until the mourning period was over? The whole family would have starved to death (*nali deng de sangfu man, zhe xie ren dou hao e si le*)! . . . By acting as matchmaker, I just thought I was doing a good deed (*zhi suan zuo le yi jian hao shi*).

In the end, the magistrate acted leniently: "Although Zheng Shi was poor and had no means of support, she still should have completed the mourning period. . . . But since she was motivated by a desire to preserve her sons in order to continue her husband's line of descent, her behavior can be forgiven. . . . Under the circumstances, it seems appropriate to request that she be pardoned and not ordered punished or divorced." Both widow and magistrate felt compelled to rationalize her early remarriage in terms of a profound level of devotion to her first husband. One cannot avoid the sense, though, that the magistrate simply bowed to the economic reality that made remarriage nearly universal among propertyless widows. In fact, I have not seen a single case record in the archives in which the ban on early remarriage is enforced (MQ, 57-121).

During the nineteenth century, a measure of lenience in such cases gained central endorsement. In 1816, the Board of Punishment ruled that widows who remarried during mourning could be allowed to remain with their new husbands after punishment unless adultery had preceded remarriage (Yao Yuxiang et al., eds., 1987, 9/5b). The commentary in an 1878 edition of the code states that a widow who remarried in order to finance her first husband's burial should receive only the lighter penalty (80 blows of the heavy bamboo, versus 100 blows) for "doing inappropriate things," and should be left with her new husband. By the early nineteenth century, the same approach was being taken in cases of wives who were sold in marriage by their husbands because of poverty (Yao Run et al., eds., 10/14b). Behind such lenience lay a growing sense of the futility of imposing chastity on the poor (Sommer 1994, 387–90).

Voiding the Sexual Contract

Not every poor widow had in-laws who protected her interests when they negotiated her remarriage. As a result, some widows suffered a rude shock upon realizing, too late, what circumstances they had been contracted into. Widows seem to have felt especially dismayed if the new husband turned out to be very poor: they had decided to remarry above all to escape poverty, and were horrified to realize they had married back into it. Some tried to get out of such marriages by refusing to consummate them.

In a 1739 case from Laifeng County, Hubei, the widow Zhang Shi (forty-five *sui*) was killed by her new second husband, Jiang Changyi (forty-three *sui*), when she refused to consummate her marriage with him. Zhang Shi was Miao; the other protagonists were all Han Chinese. Jiang Changyi's confession reads as follows:

I'm a poor man. I struggled with blood and sweat to save up twenty-some taels of silver, and spent it all on the fourteen taels of bride-price, plus sedan chair, wine, and so on, in order to marry Zhang Shi. At first, I hoped she would be of the same mind, and would devote herself to helping me set up a household (*tong xin xie li bang xiaode zuo ren jia*). I didn't expect her to be so unhappy when she saw that I was poor and learned that I had no land.

The first night, she slept until dawn with her clothes on. The second night . . . after her relatives had been sent off and our guests had gone to sleep, I told her to come to bed. But she just sat by the stove and ignored me. So I [tried to] pull her into the bedroom. She said that her only reason to remarry at her age was to secure food and warmth. "Now I've come to your home and you turn out to be this poor—what should I marry you for? But you still dare to come and harass me (*dao le ni jia ni zheyang qiongku, wo jia ni zuo shenme, ni hai lai chan wo*)!" So I picked up a knife that was on the stove and threatened her. She pulled open her blouse and stuck out her stomach, saying "If you want to kill me, go ahead! I'd rather die than let you have your way (*ni yao sha jiu sha, ning si ye bu cong de*)!"

Then he stabbed her to death.

In the adjudication of this homicide, we again see the weighing of alternative premises of chaste and unchaste, here necessary to evaluate the man's sexual advance, the widow's defiance, and the homicide. If the widow had consented to the marriage, then her new husband was justified in demanding sexual intercourse, and in becoming angry and to some extent violent when it was refused. But if she had not, then he might be a rapist and she a chastity martyr.

The judicial summary documents in detail the legality of the widow's remarriage to Jiang Changyi:

In 1739, Changyi had, through the go-between Ran Wenmei, taken [Zhang Shi] as his wife. . . . Her father-in-law, Liang Wu, had authorized the marriage, receiving a bride-price of fourteen taels of silver. On the first day of the fourth month, the go-between, together with the woman's cousin Zhang Xiangrong, her former husband's cousin Liang Wenchen, her former husband's younger brothers Liang Er, Liang Yaozi, and Liang Shibao, and her son-in-law Zhang Tiande, had escorted her to the Jiang household to join [Changyi] in marriage.

Proper form had been observed in the use of a go-between, the payment of bride-price, and the transfer of the woman by relatives in a procession. An appropriate authority had authorized the marriage. And, since her own parents were dead and she had no siblings, her natal family had been represented by a cousin. In addition, a valid marriage contract was presented as evidence.

Moreover, all witnesses testified that the widow had agreed to remarry. Jiang's neighbors affirmed that "Zhang Shi came properly (*shi hao hao lai de*), and we have heard nothing about her being forced to remarry." Her brothers-in-law (by her first husband) testified: "Our sister-in-law was willing to remarry in order to repay the debts which our brother incurred while he was alive, so as to avoid causing problems for her son in the future. . . . Ran Wenmei acted as go-between on behalf of the Jiang household and agreed to a bride-price of fourteen taels; we received this money and gave it to our father, who repaid our brother's debts." This account was confirmed by the woman's cousin, Zhang Xiangrong: "First, she married Liang Junzheng, and gave birth to a son and a daughter. In 1736, Junzheng died. Zhang Shi gave her daughter to me as daughter-in-law, and then followed her to stay in my home. Since her first husband had owed people money, Zhang Shi decided to remarry in order to pay off his debts, and also to secure her own clothing and food." Since she had entered the new marriage voluntarily, her defiance was entirely inappropriate, stemming as it did from resentment of her new husband's poverty and (according to the magistrate) from her violent "Miao temper" (*Miao qi*).[22] Jiang was sentenced to strangulation after the assizes—but his wife's defiance guaranteed a commutation of that sentence when it came up for review at the Autumn Assizes. Indeed, the memorial on the case is written to stress both the legality of the widow's remarriage and the degree to which she had provoked her husband.

For evidence on the survival strategies of poor widows, the case is equally rich. Zhang Shi's in-laws had agreed to care for her son. But to provide for her daughter, she had to pledge her in marriage to her cousin's son; as part of the deal, Zhang Shi received temporary shelter from this cousin. Her husband's debts remained, however, and she herself had no long-term means of support. To solve both problems, she saw no choice but remarriage. The bride-price cleared her debts, but she seems to have known nothing concrete about Jiang Changyi until she arrived at his home and saw that she had exchanged one life of insecurity for another.

Zhang Shi's refusal to sleep with Jiang underscores the degree to which she considered this marriage a *sexual contract*, in which she exchanged sexual and other gender-defined labor for economic security from a man she had never seen before. Upon arriving at his home, she decided that she had been cheated, and if she could not expect economic security from the man, then she would not sleep with him. She may have hoped that he would send her back and demand a refund, as sometimes happened when a bride refused to consummate her marriage. Zhang Shi was not the only one who saw the marriage in such starkly contractual terms. Jiang's complaint of how hard he had worked to save enough money to get married makes it clear that *he* felt cheated, too, when Zhang Shi refused to consummate the marriage (XT, 68/QL 4.9.28).

Zhang Shi's predicament was not unique. An 1861 case from Baodi County, Zhili, involved the widow Zhang Zheng Shi, who "would not maintain her chastity as a widow because her husband had died and her household was poor." Her brother-in-law, Zhang Xiong, arranged for her to marry Feng Zhongli, who paid a "body price" (*shen jia*) of 200 strings of cash. But when she arrived at Feng's home, "Zhang Zheng Shi saw that the Feng household was bitterly poor, and so she refused to consummate the marriage with Feng Zhongli. She wept, caused a scene, and threatened suicide, and the Fengs did not dare force her to stay." The next morning, Feng Zhongli and his brothers returned the widow to her brother-in-law and demanded a refund. Zhang Xiong refused, and a fight broke out, in which one of the Fengs was killed (SF, 166/XF 11.3.6).

For these widows, economic security was the minimum qualification for an acceptable second husband. Both they and their new husbands understood sexual submission to be a minimum requirement for a wife. The fact that these women (and other unhappy brides) refused sex suggests a widespread understanding that refusal was a woman's best (and perhaps only) strategy to annul a marriage she did not want.

The strategy of refusing consummation underscores the limits on a widow's control over her decision to remarry. Once she had agreed in principle to remarry, the judiciary washed its hands of the matter. She had no right, apparently, to back out if her wishes had not been taken into account by the matchmakers. Once she had arrived at the man's house, she was his wife, and thenceforth, *that* legal status defined her duties and his rights. The only way to get out of the deal was to provoke him into sending her back.

Widows with Property and Their In-laws

Autonomy and Adultery

Chaste widowhood required property. In rich lineages, poorer widows might be supported by charitable estates, and they would not feel compelled to remarry. In this way, a lineage bought sym-bolic capital, enhancing its ability to recruit the daughters of other elite families in marriage (Dennerline 1986).

Here, we focus not on the rich, but rather on young widows with just enough to get by without remarrying.[23] These women's chas-tity depended on precise calculations. As the brother of one chaste widow explained, "While he was alive, my sister's husband had ac-quired over a *shi* of paddy land and three cows, so my sister decided to maintain her chastity (*shou jie*)" (XT, 182/QL 27.7.29). In most cases I have seen, the widow's husband had already divided his par-ents' property with his brothers and established his own household; upon his death, the widow became the head of this independent household. Holmgren suggests that "where division of the parental property had occurred before the husband's death, a 'faithful' widow with sons could achieve a considerable degree of economic inde-pendence, respect and power in the community" (1985, 11). Never-theless, as cases of forced remarriage show, the very property which enabled that independence could be a source of vulnerability, if it provoked the envy of in-laws—and a son was no guarantee of im-munity. To complicate matters further (in Susan Mann's words), "the still-fecund widow in the Chinese family became an instant source of ambiguity and anxiety . . . her presence in the household was bound to produce sexual attraction and tension" (1987, 44).

The legal discourse of chastity had little practical relevance for propertyless widows, but for a widow living on her husband's estate, the claim to chastity was the vital prerequisite for independence and livelihood. A widow could not legally be deprived of these as long as she maintained that claim. But in-laws understood that if she could be induced to remarry, then she could be eliminated as an obstacle to their control of property (Spence 1978, 70–72; Fuma 1993). The same was true if she could be branded an adulteress. We see this logic in the confession of an in-law who forced a widow to remarry:

I wanted to get her property, so I got the idea to sell her in marriage. . . . I went to Xie Shi's home and urged her to remarry, but, as expected, she re-fused, and we had a big quarrel. But I was still determined to marry her off [so] I decided to marry her off by force. . . . I forced her to remarry so I could occupy her land. I planned to wait until she had arrived at the Wang house-hold and had consummated the marriage with Wang Huazhang—only then would I have dared to take her property. (XT, 182/QL 27.7.29)

When such disputes ended up in court, both widow and in-laws would be judged in terms of her chastity: the law would back whichever side could convincingly claim to be defending the interests of the dead husband.

Many of these widows were quite young—in their twenties or early thirties—and had small children. Since they needed help working their land, they would hire a laborer, often some poor shirt-tail relative of the dead husband. Not uncommonly, this man would move in with the widow and her children, especially during the busy seasons, trading his labor for the simplest forms of compensation: board and room, clothes, or a bit of the harvest. The widow would wash and mend his clothes. He would eat at her table, play with her children, and might become her confidant, especially if she felt at odds with her more immediate in-laws. In this way, the basic elements of a nuclear family fell into place, albeit in decidedly un-orthodox fashion.

Some widows became sexually involved with their laborers. There is no way to know how often this happened, but the pattern I describe appears repeatedly in legal cases (as seen in examples already cited above). In many cases, it was the widow who initiated sexual relations with her laborer—who was probably too poor to risk offending his mistress and losing his job. There were exceptions, but the inversion of the accepted power relations of the household—with the "man of the house" subordinate to the woman and dependent on her for his livelihood—meant that such women enjoyed a possibly unparalleled degree of control over their relationships with their male companions.

In this way, the need to remain chaste (to claim independence, property, and children) contradicted other needs. Such a relationship was a high-risk gamble: even a false accusation might jeopardize a widow's status. Legal archives show that the main action with regard to chastity took place not on the rarefied level of official heroine worship, but on this mundane level, where widows of modest means struggled to protect their autonomy from in-laws bent on expelling them, whether out of righteous indignation, shameless avarice, or some more complex mix of motives. Each side posed as defender of patriarchal values, arguing in terms of the legal paradigm of widow sexuality. The rest of this chapter explores that struggle and the strategies that went into it.

Material Calculations and Practical Compromises

To be sure, not every widow was always at odds with her in-laws. Some widows achieved practical accommodations that may not have fit neatly into official categories but balanced their own needs with those of their husbands' families.

A 1762 case from Zhaocheng County, Shanxi, shows one situation in which in-laws might tolerate adultery. Zhang Shi (thirty-three *sui*) was the widow of Yan Siqi, who had died eight years before without a son. In 1758, the widow's nephew Yan Lagen—the second son of her husband's older brother—was appointed her husband's heir and successor. But, as she later recounted, "since Lagen was still too young to look after our household affairs, in 1759, I hired lineage nephew Yan Guofu to do our farm work. He didn't ask for any wages from me, and instead I made clothes, shoes, and socks for him." According to Yan Guofu (thirty-seven *sui*), "I saw that Zhang Shi was a young widow, so I often flirted (*tiao xi*) with her. In 1760, Zhang Shi and I started having illicit sex, and after that we had illicit sex whenever we got the chance." The judicial summary reports that the widow's affair was "discovered by her husband's nephew, Yan Miwa, but since it would make the family look bad, no one was willing to make the information public." Thus, the affair continued unhindered for well over a year. Then Zhang Shi decided to sell a piece of land to settle a debt, but before she could act, her in-laws found out. Yan Nianwa, older brother of the widow's adopted heir, sought out her lover for a confrontation. Yan Guofu recalled: "As soon as he caught sight of me, he stripped off his clothing so that his [upper] body was naked (that is, indicating readiness to fight), and started cursing me, saying that I had violated his aunt and now I was selling his family's land (*jian le ta shenmu yo mai ta jia de changdi*), and he threw himself at me." In the fight that followed, Nianwa suffered mortal injury.

In Nianwa's accusation, sexual encroachment on the woman parallels economic encroachment on the land, and he seems to see both as violations of *his* family's assets. The widow's in-laws had tolerated her affair as long as it did not threaten the household property—which, after all, would be inherited by one of their own. When word spread that the widow was planning to sell land, suspicion immediately fell on the hired laborer: he must be using his illicit connection to milk the household of its property. A similar crisis might have been provoked if she had become pregnant (XT, 188/QL 27.9.20).

A strategy open to some widows was uxorilocal marriage: a widow with enough property to get by could marry a poor man, bringing him in to live with her. By not taking his surname, she could technically remain part of her dead husband's household. But this option seems to have been possible only if in-laws did not object. Then again, quite a few widows had no immediate in-laws to interfere in their lives. Susan Mann points out that among the peasantry, small families of three generations were common (in 1929–31, average family size nationwide was 5.2 persons), and thus a high proportion of widows must have had no brothers-in-law at all. Mann argues that a widow whose husband had been his parents' sole heir would find herself relatively autonomous and empowered, because her parents-in-law and young children depended on her for survival. Uxorilocal marriage was most likely to be considered by a widow who enjoyed such autonomy, because she would probably not face the threat of forced remarriage, regardless of how she behaved.[24]

An 1876 case from Pengze County, Jiangxi, shows that a widow not under the scrutiny of in-laws might carry on an affair and marry uxorilocally with relative impunity. The widow Wu Luo Shi lived alone with her son, Wu Leixia; in 1872, she hired a landless immigrant, Zhang Chunxing, to help with the farm. After a few months, the widow and her laborer became sexually involved and began sleeping together in the widow's bedroom. When Wu Leixia—already in his twenties—tried to intervene, she kicked him out of the house. In spite of this treatment, Leixia's fear of Zhang Chunxing and his reluctance to face the consequences of exposing his mother's adultery prevented him from taking action. Rumors spread, however, and Zhang began to fear that the village head might expel him from the village. He then proposed that the widow take him as her uxorilocal husband. When she demurred, he threatened to expose their affair, and she gave in. Again, her son—the only member of her husband's family both on the scene and qualified to object—did not interfere.

Several years passed before the matter attracted official attention. That happened only when Zhang Chunxing tried to sell off the Wu family's land, and the widow's son acted, finally, to protect his inheritance. (He and several friends killed Zhang. He received a relatively light sentence, and his claim to his father's estate was enforced.) Here, too, the threat to property was what provoked intervention (cited in Sweeten 1978, 52–58).

What gave this couple such leeway was the absence of anyone from the dead husband's lineage willing or able to intervene. The Qing code specified that only a woman's husband or immediate relatives were permitted to "seize her in adultery" (*zhuo jian*) and turn her and her partner in for punishment (DC, 285-10 and 25). In all cases I know of adultery being used against a widow, the accuser is an immediate in-law, a stepson, or an adopted heir. Only such persons were qualified to act and also stood to gain from an unchaste widow's exposure.

A 1762 case from Suiping County, Henan, illustrates the power of in-laws to veto a uxorilocal match and the possible consequences of defiance. The peasant Xiao Song died in 1759, leaving behind his widow, Xiao Chen Shi, and their three small sons. A year later, just after the New Year, Xiao Song's older brother Xiao Fengchun and younger brother Xiao Si divided their father's property between themselves and the widow, awarding her the full third that was her husband's rightful share. Fengchun also arranged for a hired laborer, Wang Hu, to handle the widow's farm work. With Wang's help, Xiao Chen Shi maintained an independent household, although she continued to live in her deceased father-in-law's dwelling (in the division, she had received the central rooms and her brothers-in-law the front and rear, respectively). The judicial summary reports what happened next:

Wang Hu and Chen Shi never avoided encountering each other, and Chen Shi . . . told Wang Hu that she wanted to take him as her uxorilocal husband. Wang Hu agreed, urging Chen Shi to discuss the matter with Xiao Fengchun. But Xiao Fengchun refused. That night, however, Chen Shi secretly went to the barn where Wang Hu was sleeping and engaged in adultery with him. After that, they often spent the night together. . . .

Chen Shi became pregnant and gave illegitimate birth to a girl, who immediately died. Wang Hu feared [what would happen] when Xiao Fengchun found out and wanted to flee, but Chen Shi told him to wait. That evening, Xiao Fengchun came home and heard what had happened, and he and Xiao Si interrogated Chen Shi. She openly acknowledged her adultery with Wang Hu, and again asked to take Wang Hu as her uxorilocal husband.

When Xiao Fengchun heard this, he became enraged and scolded and insulted her; he decided to summon her father, Chen Zhixiang, so that together they could deliver her to the authorities for punishment. But since it was evening, it was too late to summon him. The next day, Xiao Fengchun . . . sent Xiao Si twice to fetch Chen Zhixiang, but he did not come. [Two days later,] since Chen Zhixiang still had not arrived, Xiao Fengchun became even angrier, and scolded and cursed his nephew Xiao La, telling him that the next day they would go into town together to turn her in to the authorities. Xiao La told this to his mother Chen Shi.

That night, Chen Shi drowned herself and her three sons in a nearby river. The final judgment blamed the deaths on the widow's lover, sentencing him to beheading after the assizes for causing the disaster with his "licentiousness." Fengchun was beaten for failing to kick out the laborer in time to prevent the affair.

Chen Shi initiated her sexual affair with Wang the very night Xiao Fengchun had refused her permission to marry him uxorilocally. This defiant act may have been part of a conscious strategy to force her in-laws' acquiescence to her wishes: hence, when she was exposed, her open admission of the affair and her renewed proposal to take Wang as uxorilocal husband. Many in-laws might have accepted the *fait accompli*.

Chen Shi's brothers-in-law had behaved perfectly decently, by contemporary standards. When their brother died, they made a fair settlement on his widow and did their best to help set up her household. Fengchun's outrage at his sister-in-law's affair seems genuine enough. He was not grasping after her property, and may well have preserved it for his nephews even after expelling their mother. But her expulsion was imminent, as shown by the priority placed on summoning her father—who would help deliver her to the authorities, and then take her back to her natal home. The widow understood: rather than lose her children, she took them with her into death (XT, 188/QL 27.8.6).

The picture of widow chastity seen in Qing legal cases differs markedly from that drawn by anthropologist Arthur Wolf in his landmark studies of marriage practices based on data collected in Taiwan by Japanese colonial authorities in the early twentieth century (1975 and 1981; Wolf and Huang 1980). Wolf shows that adultery and uxorilocal marriage were common among widows in rural northern Taiwan, implying that widows were free to engage in such practices with impunity. In one article, he even asserts that "the ideal of the virtuous widow exerted no influence whatsoever" on the behavior of ordinary people in "pre-modern China" (1981, 146).

Legal cases may exaggerate the importance of state power—after all, they are government records. But we should not assume that Wolf's generalization can be applied to all widows, or to other regions or historical periods. Perhaps the high rate of unchaste behavior detected by Wolf simply reflects the high incidence of widows who had no brothers-in-law to interfere with them. If so, it may tell us what many women would do *if they could get away with it*, but says nothing about the real risks that others would face if they did such things.[25] Another possibility is that Wolf's image of widows in "pre-modern China" is colored by the political peculiarities of Taiwan. What is entirely missing from his data is the enforcement of orthodox values by the Qing judiciary—which, after all, played no role in Taiwan after Japanese annexation in 1895. It is not clear how the change in regime (and the departure of much of the traditional elite, who opted to remain under Qing rule) affected the enforcement of moral standards and property rights.

In all the cases I cite, the actors evinced a clear awareness that the force of law might be brought to bear on one side or the other in a dispute. In most cases, magistrates became involved only because some party to a dispute chose to involve them. To be sure, not every unchaste widow was hunted down by the authorities or expelled by her in-laws. If a widow's parents-in-law depended on her for survival, or better yet, if she had no in-laws at all, then she might very well behave as she liked, without risk. But the discourse of chastity and property could be invoked to empower either a widow who could claim to be chaste, or in-laws who could show she was not. Adultery and uxorilocal marriage were tolerated sometimes, but not always—and people clearly understood that the force of law would back in-laws who rejected such behavior.[26]

Scenarios of Struggle

A time-honored strategy for expelling a widow was "to seize her in adultery" (*zhuo jian*). The act had a ritual quality: there seems to have been a well-known, established way of doing things. In-laws who suspected a widow of adultery might lie in wait to catch her *in flagrante delicto*; often a large group would be organized for the seizure, so that there would be plenty of witnesses to the widow's disgrace. They would interrupt the couple in bed, beat them thoroughly, tie them up as found (naked was best), and take them straight to the yamen.[27] Sometimes, in-laws staged the event to frame a widow, their goal being the same as that in forced remarriage. Magistrates were well aware of the possibility, and often gave a widow the benefit of the doubt, unless there was decisive evidence against her.

Righteous Indignation or a Setup?

In 1821, Xu Shi, the widowed concubine of Wang Huixian, was caught in bed with her husband's maternal cousin. The widow was living in Chongqing with her brother-in-law, Wang Rongxian, who had suspected her for some time; finally, he burst into the widow's room one night and caught the couple naked. Next morning he filed charges, but he had made the mistake of acting alone. The widow and her lover managed to organize ten friends and neighbors to testify that her brother-in-law was trying to "frame her for adultery" (wu jian) in order to expel her and seize her husband's assets. The magistrate believed the widow, and he ordered Rongxian beaten and confined in the cangue for a month (it later came out that Xu Shi hosted a victory party for her witnesses). Some months later, however, the widow suddenly remarried, and word spread that she had done so to legitimize a pregnancy. Shortly thereafter, she gave birth to a son. Rongxian's mother appealed to the prefect, and the widow and her partisans were punished (BX, 3-8633).

An 1850 case, also from Ba County, involves a failed attempt by in-laws to seize a widow in adultery—but the matter is ambiguous, and they may have been trying to set her up. The widow, Wang Zhao Shi (thirty sui), lived with her two young sons on her husband's land, which was farmed by a tenant. One day, she appeared at the county yamen, covered with bruises and a black eye, and filed a complaint against her brothers-in-law:

My husband Wang Chaoci and his older brothers Chaoqing, Chaoshun, and Chaobao divided their household property; after that, my husband took me as his wife, and I gave birth to two sons, both of whom are still little children. In 1843, my husband fell ill and died. I vowed to serve my mother-in-law and endure the suffering of maintaining my chastity (feng gu shi shou ku ji). My greedy brothers-in-law plotted to usurp my husband's property, but there was nothing they could do to achieve this goal.

Finally, she claimed, they tried to set her up, by paying two men to visit her one evening and ask for a drink:

I did not feel it appropriate to disturb the night by rebuking them—but just then a dog barked, so I called for my tenant Liu Hongcai to take a look outside. Then Chaoqing and the rest . . . violently burst into my home, carrying weapons. They used disgraceful and evil language to accuse me falsely of adultery (zha wu jian dian e yu), and beat me with wooden clubs. . . . They tied me up, releasing me only after they forced me to promise to surrender my property to their absolute control. . . . How cruel, for a chaste widow to suffer such a disgraceful and false accusation . . . !

The widow's story was corroborated by her tenant, who had been beaten and slashed with a knife (their injuries were duly recorded by the forensic examiner). He asserted that her brothers-in-law had framed her, and had attacked him, too, when he tried to defend her.

Wang Zhao Shi's ire focused on her brothers-in-law, the classic culprits in the discourse of widow victimization. But it was the widow's *mother*-in-law who responded, accusing this "rebellious daughter-in-law" (*ni xi*) of "not maintaining the way of a wife" (*bu shou fu dao*), causing a scandal by "illicit dalliance" (*gou yin*) with the tenant and other men, and now filing false charges against her innocent sons. It was the mother-in-law who had ordered her sons to seize the widow and her tenant and deliver them to the yamen for punishment, and only the widow's plea for mercy and the mediation of neighbors had softened her resolve.

The magistrate held a hearing, and decided that the widow had indeed entertained her tenant and another man on the night in question, but that a neighbor woman had been present the whole time. Overhearing sounds of revelry, brother-in-law Chaoqing had summoned his mother and brothers, who burst through the door expecting some sort of orgy. But no adultery was discovered; all the same, the in-laws had beat up the widow and her guests and were planning to deliver them to the yamen, when the neighbors, aroused by the commotion, had intervened and persuaded them to stop. On the basis of these findings, the magistrate had the widow and her guests slapped (*zhang ze*), and ordered her to "return home and submit to your mother-in-law's supervision."

It is impossible to know the exact truth of these events. Yet, the hostility between this widow and her in-laws is obvious, as is the discourse of chastity and property that framed the way their conflict unfolded. Whatever their motive, the in-laws clearly hoped to catch the widow in an infidelity that would allow them to expel her; whatever the truth of her behavior, the widow struck back by portraying herself as a chaste widow oppressed by greedy in-laws. Also, without proof of adultery, the magistrate was not about to expel the widow, even if he felt that she deserved the black eye her brothers-in-law had given her (BX, 4-4910).

Successful Seizure of Adulterers

An 1831 case from Ninghe County, Zhili, gives an example of *zhuo jian* that succeeded. In this case, the principal contradiction opposed a widowed concubine and her dead husband's adopted heir, whose conflict went through several stages over a number of years, even as they continued to live together. As a concubine, this woman's authority in her dead husband's household was far less absolute than that of a widowed main wife; still, chastity guaranteed her respect and support. (The only other concubine mentioned in this chapter is Xu Shi from Ba County, in the previous section; all other widows were main wives.)

Wei Yang Shi (forty-one *sui*) was the widowed concubine of shopkeeper Wei Jingwen, who had purchased her because his main wife bore no children. The concubine produced only a daughter, and thus her husband adopted nephew Wei Shiyi, who moved into his uncle's home. When Wei Jingwen and his main wife both died in 1827, Wei Shiyi presided over the funerals, formalizing his status as son and heir.[28] From then on, the widowed concubine and the heir lived together as the household of the deceased Wei Jingwen, but trouble began almost immediately. In a lawsuit, Wei Yang Shi tried to reject Shiyi as heir on the grounds that he was still too young to manage the household (he was about seventeen *sui* at the time). But the lineage elders backed him, and the magistrate confirmed Shiyi as Wei Jingwen's heir, ordering that a list of the household property be prepared to secure his inheritance.

Some time later, however, Wei Shiyi visited his mother, taking money and grain with him from his adoptive home. This incident incensed the widow, but the young man's uncles took his side; she finally sued both heir and in-laws, accusing them of stealing her property, abusing her, and pressuring her to remarry. The magistrate rejected her charges but declined to punish her, "in light of the ignorance of women" (*gu nian funü wuzhi*). Instead, he tried to impose peace by clarifying the statuses and duties of all parties:

Wei Yang Shi is the concubine of Wei Jingwen. Since her husband and master died, she has resolved to maintain her chastity, in spite of her youth, and so truly deserves praise. Wei Shiyi is the adopted heir of Wei Jingwen, and therefore should carefully serve and nurture her; but also, she should not presume upon her status as his father's concubine to bully him. In addition, the elders of the lineage . . . should take care to see that this widow and young son do not lose their household property.

A couple of years later, however, Wei Yang Shi became sexually involved with a distant relative of her husband's, Wei Hongzheng (thirty-seven *sui*). Although they tried to keep the affair secret, rumors abounded, and finally heir Wei Shiyi and four of his relatives decided to trap them. As Wei Shiyi later testified,

I waited until two strokes of the watch, heard that they were sound asleep, and then opened the street door to let the others in. I grabbed two handfuls of quicklime, and pushed open the bedroom door. . . . Wei Hongzheng and Auntie heard us and got up, but I threw quicklime into their eyes. . . . My brother got on the *kang* and grabbed hold of Wei Hongzheng, and I also climbed onto the *kang* and grabbed hold of Auntie. Wei Hongzheng and Auntie struggled and cursed, but Wei Shixiong and the others picked up wooden clubs . . . and beat them more than ten strokes, until Bai Yufeng stopped them. . . . Then everyone helped tie them up. . . . We picked the two of them up stark naked, and together with their clothes hauled them in a cart to the yamen to turn them in.

The forensic examiner recorded that both of Wei Hongzheng's eyes and one of the widow's were swollen shut by the caustic quicklime; both adulterers were covered with bruises, and part of the woman's hair had been torn out.

Upon her arrest, the widow filed a petition depicting herself as the classic victimized widow:

My husband lacked an heir; there are three other branches in his family, and they struggled with each other for control of this branch's household property. Finally, there was a lawsuit, and I received the merciful judgment of Magistrate Tang that Wei Shiyi, a son of the fourth branch, should become my husband's heir; the magistrate also ordered him to treat me as his main-wife mother (*dimu*; that is, as his father's main wife). Our relative status (*mingfen*) was established in this manner. . . .

Later on, though, Wei Shiyi did not submit to my authority, indulging in gambling without restraint. [Also,] since the property of my household is somewhat plentiful, there were many in the lineage who borrowed money without repaying it, and when I asked for payment they bore a grudge.

On the third of this month, I told Wei Shiyi to invite his lineage uncle Wei Hongzheng over to discuss the planting of the fields with me. . . . But then Wei Shiyi demanded 2,000 cash in order to play at dice, but I did not give it to him. Who would think that Wei Shiyi would lead . . . a gang of some 25 men, all carrying fearsome weapons, to force their way into my room.

She concluded by accusing her attackers of looting her home: "If they charge that they caught me in the act of adultery, then why were . . . money, grain, and other things stolen? Obviously, this is a scheme to steal my household property." Of particular note is the widow's false claim that the previous magistrate had ordered Wei Shiyi to treat her as his *dimu*, or "main-wife mother," the formal term used by a son for his father's main wife, even if his own birth mother had been a concubine. The corresponding term for one's father's concubine was *shumu*, "concubine mother." Such an order would have represented a major promotion in status, bolstering her proprietary claim over her dead husband's household.

But Wei Shiyi again received the support of his lineage, whose representatives asserted that "Yang Shi has never peacefully kept to her station (*an fen*)," that her adultery with Wei Hongzheng was a public scandal, and that Shiyi's actions had been provoked by "righteous anger" (*yi fen*). When the case came to trial, Hongzheng confessed to adultery, and the widow finally did so as well. The last documents in the file are damaged, but the basic outcome is clear: the widow's expulsion. Her confession ends with: "I am willing to leave the Wei household. I only beg the court to show mercy by having Wei Shiyi give me back my coarse clothes (*cu chuan yifu*)." The magistrate approved the arrangement: "We find that since Wei Shiyi is willing to give Yang Shi the clothing she has requested, he shall bring it to court to be delivered to her, and an affidavit of receipt shall be taken from her." (By this point neither lineage elders nor magistrate referred to her any longer by her married surname.) Once the widow had been expelled, even her own clothing was no longer her property: she needed Shiyi's permission to remove even that from her dead husband's household (SF, 169/DG 11.3.?).

This case is an excellent example of kinship as what Bourdieu (1976) calls "strategic practice," rather than the automatic result of bloodlines. It centers on a household missing all of its natural elements: there remained only the purchased concubine and the adopted heir foisted on her by in-laws and court order. The two loathed each other, yet they endured the unpleasant ritual of coresidence in order to secure the respective statuses (chaste widow versus filial son) from which their rival claims derived. After the widow failed in two attempts to expel him, the tables were turned by the heir, whose resentment found outlet in the violence of his attack. The Wei lineage's outrage at the widow was no doubt genuine, but their mutual hostility long predated her affair. If Wei Yang Shi had not created a scandal, she probably would have remained secure. Sincerely or not, the battle had to be fought in terms of the legally sanctioned chastity/property discourse: as the magistrate had made clear in the earlier lawsuit, as long as Wei Yang Shi remained chaste, her interests would be protected. That is why she clung so desperately to her claim of chastity, even after being seized naked in bed with her lover.

Pregnancy and Desperate Measures

Pregnancy might expose the most clandestine liaisons, and fear of the consequences sometimes pushed pregnant widows to extremes. One scenario found in legal records is the amateur abortion: in a 1739 example from Haining County, Zhejiang, the widow Xu Zhu

Shi died of hemorrhage after taking a drug called "lady-bird musk" (*hong niangzi she xiang shan*). She had discovered that she was pregnant and had asked her lover, a monk, to procure an abortifacient (XT, 74/QL 4.2.18). This sort of disaster was common enough to prompt the following 1740 substatute:

> If a woman becomes pregnant because of illicit sex and, fearing discovery, discusses this with the man with whom she has had illicit sex, and then uses a drug to induce abortion, with the result that she miscarries and dies, then the man shall be sentenced to 100 blows of the heavy bamboo and life exile at 3,000 *li*, in analogy to the statute on "knowingly selling poison to another for the purpose of committing homicide."[29] (DC, 299-11)

A 1762 case from Renqiu County, Zhili, gives more dramatic testimony to the desperation of some widows. Ma Shi (twenty-seven *sui*) maintained an independent household with her son and daughter. She had some land and rooms of her own, since her husband had divided his parents' household with his brother prior to his own death in 1755. She lived in the front part of a larger complex that had belonged to her parents-in-law; her brother-in-law, Gao Wei, lived with his wife Wang Shi in the rear. Ma Shi and her in-laws did not get along. A signal point of tension was her control of her husband's full half of the property that had been divided.

Ma Shi also rented a room to an immigrant laborer, Li An (twenty-five *sui*), who did farm work for her and for other families nearby. As Li later confessed:

> [One day in] 1761, I saw Ma Shi was alone in her room. . . . A few days before, I had left a worn-out pair of pants in her wash basin for her to wash for me; she held them up and asked, "What's this stuff on these pants I washed for you?" So, since these words were obviously meant as a proposition (*ming shi you yi gouyin*), I made a pass at her (*tiao xi*), and then we had illicit sex there on the straw. After that, we had sex whenever there was a chance. . . .
>
> One morning [late in 1761], after breakfast, I went into Ma Shi's room, and she said, "We're in trouble—I'm pregnant. Now don't worry about me, just come quickly and step on my stomach." Then she lay down on her back on the *kang*, and I got on top and stepped on her two or three times—but just then Gao Wei's wife Wang Shi walked in and saw us. She asked, "What are you two doing? This doesn't look quite honest to me!" I answered, "She said there's something wrong with her and she told me to step on her," and Ma Shi also said, "I told him to step on me." Wang Shi said, "On top of this, you want to tell lies (*hai yao nong chou zui ma*)? Just wait till I tell your brother-in-law!" So Ma Shi got down on her knees, and I kowtowed in front of Wang Shi, too, begging her not to tell, but Wang Shi just ignored us. . . .

[Later,] Ma Shi said, "What can I do? She's going to tell my brother-in-law, and make it impossible for me to face people. I'm better off dead (*jiao wo zenme jian ren, bu ru si le ba*)!" I said, "If you die, then I'll die too." She said, "Do it for me quickly, okay? It looks like Wang Shi won't [keep our secret] for us, and I'll bet it's because if I'm dead, they can get my rooms and land! After I'm dead, you take revenge for me. And also let my daughter follow me, so that she won't be left behind to be tormented by these people." I said, "All right, that's enough. Go call the bitch in here, and I'll take care of her (*qu jiao ta niangrmen lai, wo gei ta yi ge ganjing ba*)!"

I went out to a wine shop and drank four ounces of wine. When I came back, I saw that Wang Shi and her two daughters were sitting on the *kang* in Ma Shi's room. So Ma Shi and I begged her again, but all Wang Shi would say was, "I don't know." I hated her so much—I saw there was a hay-chopper in Ma Shi's outer room, so I took it down . . . and aimed a blow at Wang Shi's neck: I cut her head right off.

Then, Li An killed his lover and the three young daughters of the two women. After that, he tried to kill himself but failed—surviving to confess, and to be executed by slicing, for the crime of "murdering three or more persons of a single household" (XT, 177/QL 27.3.26).

What stands out is the utter desperation of the couple: life after exposure would be worse than death. Ma Shi had her daughter killed in what she apparently saw as an act of mercy, given the girl's uncertain status after the widow's own disgrace and death (though she expressed no such concern for her son, who survived the slaughter). This fear of stigma may reflect conformist pressure more than internalization of dominant values, but there is no denying the material effect of those values on this couple.

Li An's retelling of Ma Shi's comments provides further evidence of the close linkage between chastity and property, in popular perception as well as in formal legal discourse. For a widow, the property issue seems always to have lurked in the background. As soon as she realized that her sister-in-law intended to expose her pregnancy, Ma Shi attributed this intent to a desire to seize her property. This linkage makes sense, since the widow would likely have been expelled if she did not commit suicide. One way or another, she would be removed from the scene, and her property would become vulnerable. She feared humiliation, but at the same time she immediately thought of the more material loss that was imminent.

Immaculate Conception?

Not every pregnant widow met such a ghastly end. As long as a widow maintained her claim to chastity, she could not be deprived of her rights—even in the most unlikely circumstances. An example is Hu Shi, the widowed second wife (*ji qi*—not a concubine) of the prosperous peasant Zhang Yu, of Baodi County, Zhili. Zhang's first wife had given birth to two sons before she died. He had then married Hu Shi, who gave birth to three more sons. Therefore, when Zhang Yu died in 1842, Hu Shi was left a widow at age forty-three *sui* with two stepsons, both married adults, and three natural sons, the oldest of whom was in his mid-teens. When the events in the case occurred, because Zhang Yu's household had not yet been divided, Hu Shi retained considerable authority over both property and all five sons.

The crisis was precipitated in 1845, when Hu Shi gave birth to a baby girl. Because she had denied being pregnant, her stepsons and brother-in-law, Zhang Mo, waited until they actually saw the infant before acting. Hu Shi killed the infant immediately, but Zhang Mo had already summoned her brother and ordered him to take her home and "marry her off." She was allowed to take nothing with her; her sons were put in the care of their stepsisters-in-law.

Some women might have yielded to fate—but not Hu Shi. A couple of months after being expelled, she returned to the Zhang household and demanded to move back in. Her pregnancy was a mystery, she insisted, because *she had never engaged in adultery*. Since she was a chaste widow, the Zhangs had no right to kick her out.

Her stepsons and Zhang Mo refused to let her move back in, whereupon she threatened to commit suicide in front of the house. At this point, the neighbors stepped in to mediate. Given Hu Shi's absolute denial of adultery, and the fact that the Zhangs had no idea who had gotten her pregnant, the mediators suggested setting aside the question of chastity. As they saw it, the essential problem was that the stepsons and Hu Shi could no longer get along (the tension between them seems to have predated Hu Shi's pregnancy; one can guess how the older stepsons felt, watching their own shares of the estate shrink as she gave birth to one son after another).[30] The solution was to divide Zhang Yu's property into six equal shares, one for each son and one for Hu Shi; that way, the stepsons could establish separate households, with Hu Shi retaining her own means of support. She agreed, but her stepsons and brother-in-law refused, insisting that her obvious adultery disqualified her from receiving her husband's property or enjoying access to his children. Instead, she should be expelled—and prosecuted, if necessary. If the property was divided, there should be only five shares, one for each son.

The village authorities feared trouble and reported the dispute to the county magistrate. But when there was a delay, Zhang Mo went over the magistrate's head, petitioning the prefect that the widow had been impregnated by Tian Youkui, a neighbor who had provoked Zhang's ire by attempting to mediate. Zhang also accused Tian of bribing a yamen clerk to influence the case on his behalf. The prefect delegated the case to the Donglu sub-prefect, who held a hearing. Hu Shi stuck to her story: "I felt my belly gradually getting bigger, and it seemed like I was pregnant, but since I hadn't engaged in adultery, I paid no attention. Then, on the third day of the first month of this year, my belly started to hurt, and after that I gave birth to a baby girl. . . . I really can't say how I got pregnant." The sub-prefect's skepticism at this story was offset by his anger at Zhang Mo, who had lied about Tian Youkui and had failed to cooperate with the county magistrate. The sub-prefect also seems to have shared the judicial preference for solving family disputes when possible by community mediation instead of litigation and prosecution. To persuade Zhang Mo and the stepsons to settle, he gave them an ultimatum. If they refused the original mediated settlement, then Zhang Mo would be punished along with Hu Shi. Zhang Mo backed down: "Hu Shi cannot say how she got pregnant, and I do not dare persist in my false accusations. I request that she be spared prosecution." The sub-prefect reported to the prefect:

The mediators' suggestion that the property be divided and each party live separately is designed to end the dispute and seems appropriate enough. Therefore, I have ordered that the property left by Zhang Yu be divided into six equal shares, the five brothers each receiving one share, and Hu Shi receiving one share to pay for her support and for her burial expenses after death. She shall be allowed to live separately with her own sons. . . . Both sides have submitted to this settlement and have no more to say on the matter. . . .

As to the question of Hu Shi giving birth out of wedlock, she absolutely insists under strict interrogation that she has never engaged in adultery with anyone, and that she does not know how she became pregnant. This is hard to believe. . . . Nevertheless, the event occurred before an Imperial Amnesty, and her accuser is willing to drop all charges. Therefore, it is appropriate to request that the matter not be pursued, so as to avoid further complication.

Hu Shi retained her property and children only through the stubborn assertion that she remained chaste in spite of the pregnancy. Her chutzpah induced first the mediators, and then the sub-prefect, to drop the question of chastity and opt for compromise. The sub-prefect could have pressed the widow further, but he probably would have had to resort to torture—an unappealing option, given Hu Shi's strength of personality. Successful prosecution required confession; if a judge used torture but failed to obtain one, he risked trouble (SF, 162/DG 25.3.8).[31]

It was not unheard of for chaste widows to give birth, as an 1803 legal handbook cautions. It cites a 1749 case from Zhejiang, in which the widow Ma Shi gave birth four years after her husband's death. Her father-in-law accused her of adultery, but she denied it, and there was no evidence apart from the pregnancy itself. Stymied, the presiding officials consulted medical texts and learned that extreme emotional disturbance could cause a fetus to "dry up," delaying its birth for three or four years. On this basis, they decided that the timing of the birth must have been caused by Ma Shi's inordinate grief over the death of her husband. The child was proclaimed legitimate and the widow's reputation for chastity even *enhanced*, since it had been devotion to her husband, rather than betrayal, which caused the unusual timing of the birth (Lü Zhitian 1893, xia/10b–11a). We can speculate that this was a face-saving solution with the primary purpose of clearing the magistrate's desk. Nevertheless the widow had to be defined in terms of moral absolutes: if a decision were necessary, there was no room for ambiguity between chaste and unchaste.[32]

Both of these pregnant widows escaped punishment and expulsion. But they won their cases *not*, for example, by claiming the right to sleep with whomever they chose. Instead, they insisted that they had not slept with anyone at all. Arthur Wolf argues that his data on widows point to "the active pursuit of their own best interests [rather than] their passive acceptance of a cultural ideal" (1981, 146). The evidence in legal cases suggests the same thing. But even widows who did fairly well within the constraints of the legally sanctioned sexual regime could not escape or defy that regime outright. Not every widow was a tragic victim of chastity. Nevertheless, chastity defined the legal standing of all widows, and even those who asserted themselves had to do so on its terms. This practical linkage between chastity and women's claims to independence, property, and children was one of the most impressive achievements of the Qing judiciary, and it goes a long way toward explaining the proliferation of memorial arches across the landscape of eighteenth- and nineteenth-century China.

Conclusion

The intent of chastity law was to guard the interests of husbands, defending each patriarchal unit against encroachment by avaricious relatives and subversion by unchaste wives and widows. Legal policy complemented the propaganda effort on behalf of chastity, and it formed a vital part of the sanctification of family relationships that legitimated imperial authority.

The evidence in legal cases gets us beyond the top-down, functionalist perspective of imperial ideologues, and shows how ordinary people incorporated the courts and official discourse into their own strategies. People involved the authorities and invoked official standards of virtue for their own purposes, to shore up their own positions within particular families and communities. The result was a process of mutual reinforcement. Magistrates empowered litigants who could convincingly claim to be defenders of patriarchal values. Usurpers were disciplined, and in this way, legitimate gender and sexual relations were enforced on the most intimate level. At the same time, the fact that humble people went to court and invoked official discourse to protect their own positions in the local patriarchal scheme reinforced the state's pretension as defender and embodiment of patriarchal values writ large. In this way, the authority of fathers, husbands, and chaste widows achieved concrete linkage with political authority, and the defense of legitimate hierarchy in the most personal contexts helped underpin the imperial order as a whole. Widows and their rivals may have gone to court in fact for reasons having little to do with imperial priorities, but one likely effect of their engagement with the law was to reinforce state claims and state power.

Dorothy Ko's research on elite women of the seventeenth century demonstrates the role of female agency in sustaining the normative gender system (1992 and 1994). Indeed, she argues that the "complicity" of literate, well-connected women was indispensable to the success of imperial propaganda. "Without the active promotion of these women—as mothers, writers and editors—the cult of domesticity and chastity would not have taken root in the hearts and minds of so many Ming-Qing women" (1992, 452). Certainly, the evidence in legal cases highlights the importance of female agency; even the very poorest women described in this chapter do not appear to have been utterly passive objects of economic exigency or family manipulation. But should we consider the representational strategies of ordinary widows to be "complicity" in the imperial chastity cult, like that seen by Ko in the writings of elite women?

Some women certainly used the discourse of chastity to their own advantage, to defend their independence and property. When accused of impropriety, a widow's best defense was that her accusers were simply trying to usurp her husband's property—a defense taken seriously by magistrates and, if persuasive, backed by their full authority. Occasionally, a widow could even persuade a magistrate to order in-laws to provide financial support, as long as she remained chaste (BX, 1-1638). Some women used chastity discourse to attack other women—for example, when a widowed main wife sued her husband's concubine (BX, 3-87647). Ideally, such widows would live together, joined in devotion to their husband's memory. In fact, conflicts between such women centered on the control of property and the efforts of concubines to gain independence. The best way for a wife to undermine a concubine's status was to impugn her chastity.

Official standards of virtue could empower individual women, to the extent that they could claim to uphold the state's patriarchal values. Thus, the empowerment of chaste widows promoted a value integral to imperial legitimacy and elite pride.[33] But ironically, the contingent rights of widows created space for some to achieve unparalleled freedom in their personal lives. Their closeted lives had to be shielded by representations of chaste self-denial, of dedication to their dead husbands. In a sense, then, the exigencies of a double life reinforced official values, by making public performance the condition for private freedom. At the same time, however, the double life must have provoked a continual demystification, an exposure of misrecognized contradictions, by confronting hegemonic values with lived experience ("I am chaste!" insists the pregnant widow). The logic of sexual contract that framed the choices of impoverished widows may have provoked a similar process.

We can discern a continual dissemination and reinforcement of official values, in which litigation played a vital role. But also, we begin to detect an irritant, a subversive force acting against the internalization of these values among people for whom they contradicted lived experience—even if those same people found it necessary to mouth those values as part of the daily game of getting by. This mundane, everyday subversion appears to have been an inherent byproduct of the enforcement of official virtue, and it was one reason why a sexual order represented as fixed and natural had to be defended as contested ground.

Sexual Behavior as Status Performance: The Regulation of Prostitution Before 1723

A Deceptively Simple Question

Did Qing law prohibit prostitution? The question seems straightforward, but to answer it is not.

One source of complexity is that with regard to prostitution, the Qing founders adopted Ming-dynasty law wholesale. The Ming statutes, which date to the fourteenth century, were modeled closely on specific Yuan-dynasty precedents. When eighteenth-century lawmakers finally modified judicial policy, they left the old laws on the books, implementing change mainly by reinterpreting them in ways that cannot be traced except through their application in practice to actual criminal cases.[1]

The more fundamental source of confusion is that we never find in these legal codes a clear statement of whether "prostitution"—the sale of sexual services—was legal or illegal. The matter was more complex than that. As we have seen, sexual intercourse, like many other kinds of conduct, simply could not be abstracted from a context of status and gender relations: the legal significance of an act depended on who did it to whom. Prostitution was no exception.

During a long period of fundamental continuity up to 1723, prostitution was one factor used by the imperial state to support the legal fiction of a fixed hierarchy of status groups to which distinct moral standards applied.[2] For certain legally debased (jian) groups, sex work constituted an essential stigma that defined their social and legal status. In this context, judicial authorities found sex work perfectly acceptable. But for free commoner (liang) women, any sexual intercourse outside marriage constituted criminal activity, regardless of whether money changed hands. The salient issue, then, was not the legality of a certain kind of conduct, but rather the fixing of clear boundaries between different status strata, and making sure that individuals behaved in a manner appropriate to their station.

Until the Yongzheng period, then, the purpose of law was not to ban the sale of sexual services per se, but rather to maintain the fiction of a fixed boundary between a debased stratum tainted by sexual promiscuity and the free common people (*liang min*), whose moral quality was implied by the double meaning of the term used for their legal status, *liang* ("good"/"commoner"). *Liang min* were simultaneously the "common people" and the "good people."[3] The organizing principle was that sexual mores and behavior constituted *status performance*. Just as prostitution acted out the debased status of *yue* households and their ilk, the moral status of commoners found definition in their supposed adherence to the norms of marriage, female chastity, and other official family values.

Such a system suggests comparison with imperial Rome, which honored a sacred cult of vestal virgins, and made the adultery of a freeborn woman a grievous offense. Nevertheless, it had no trouble accepting and regulating the public existence of prostitute guilds. In Rome, as in China, the central issue was to organize sexual behavior in such a way as to confirm and reinforce the normative basis of social and political hierarchy (Clarke 1998).

The year 1723 brought dramatic change. The Yongzheng Emperor expunged the debased status of the key groups associated with prostitution and, in effect, extended a commoner standard of morality and criminal liability to all.[4] The result was the complete prohibition of prostitution. But the post-1723 story will be told in the next chapter. First, we shall explore here the longstanding legal fiction that tied sexual mores to status difference, the juridical effort to support that legal fiction, and some of the contradictions and tensions that foreshadowed its demise.

The Imperial State's Connection with Sex Work

For centuries, the imperial state played a critical role in the production and management of sex workers. In his classic history of Chinese prostitution, Wang Shunu goes so far as to characterize the era lasting from the Tang dynasty until the end of the Ming as "the grand age of official prostitution" (*guan ji ding sheng shidai*).[5] During this long era, the paradigm for legally tolerated prostitution was penal servitude performed under official supervision by individuals formally registered with debased status. Actually, "prostitution" is a misnomer for much of this period, since it implies paid work in a commercial sex market, and at least the possibility of female agency and choice. The sexual servitude described here was really a form of slavery, not unlike the use of sexual slaves ("comfort women") by the Japanese army during World War II. It is only in the late Ming and Qing dynasties that we see the emergence of a pervasive, private commercial sex market.

As far back as the Han dynasty, the wives and daughters of some male criminals had been sentenced to servitude in military brothels. Legal codes from as early as the Northern Wei (A.D. 386–532) show that the penal system was an important source of the debased-status group most closely associated with official prostitution, the *yue hu*—literally, "music households" (*Wei shu*, 2888). (Legal texts also refer to *yue ren*, "music people," and *yue gong*, "music workers.") In that and subsequent dynasties, the punishment for a number of violent and political crimes included execution of the male offender (and his adult male family members), confiscation of his estate, and enslavement of his wives and daughters into sexual and other entertainment services under official supervision. These women (and any young sons spared execution) would be registered as *yue hu*, a status passed on to their descendants. In some periods, prisoners of war and their families met the same fate.[6]

The punishment of men's political crimes with the legal debasement and sexual exploitation of their women continued at least into the Ming dynasty. The most notorious example occurred in 1402, when the Jianwen Emperor was overthrown and murdered by his uncle, Zhu Di (who became the Yongle Emperor). In the aftermath of this *coup d'état*, loyal ministers who refused to accept Zhu Di's version of events were slaughtered, along with hundreds of male relatives. Their female dependents were registered as *yue hu* and forced to serve in various humiliating capacities under official supervision. At least some were forced into sexual servitude.[7] The founders of the Qing dynasty preserved a number of Ming laws mandating that the dependents of rebels and other political offenders be "confiscated by the state to become slaves" (*ru guan wei nu*), and in the first few decades of the Qing, some of these unfortunates too may have ended up as "official prostitutes" (*guan ji*).[8]

No doubt, such measures had the practical aim of eliminating a politically suspect family that otherwise might become a threat in the future. But the specifically sexual nature of the penalty seems to reflect the specifically political nature of the crime. If chastity was the female counterpart to the male political virtue of loyalty, then a man's disloyalty might logically be punished by violating his wife's chastity—that is, by having his wife betray him in turn. Challenges to chastity supposedly presented women with a *choice*: a truly chaste wife would choose suicide over submission to any man other than her husband. If such women "chose" to submit to violation, they would *reveal* themselves as unchaste, by failing the ultimate test of wifely virtue. Their lack of chastity symbolically confirmed their husbands' lack of loyalty.[9]

In the Yuan, Ming, and early Qing dynasties, the office with jurisdiction over enslaved *yue* households and over official prostitution was the Bureau of Instruction (*jiao fang si*). Under the aegis of the Board of Rites, this bureau's principal duty was to supply musicians, dancers, and other personnel for court entertainment and ritual.[10] The Ming dynasty established branches of the Bureau of Instruction in both Nanjing and Beijing that, among other things, supervised and taxed government prostitutes. According to Xie Zhaozhe (writing in the early seventeenth century), this tax was known by the euphemism "rouge and face powder cash" (*zhi fen qian*). Government prostitutes outside the two capitals, also labeled "*yue* households," were subject to supervision by local authorities, who usually did not tax them, but could summon them to serve at banquets and perform in festivals (Xie Zhaozhe 1959, 225; Appendix D).[11] Within the Bureau of Instruction, *yue* workers were supervised by the "Master of Actors" (*pai zhang*) and "Master of Colors" (*se zhang*). Their specific duties are not entirely clear, but "color" may be a reference to prostitution, since that word can denote an object of sexual attraction, albeit with a pejorative connotation. Ming law punished these supervisors if prostitutes under their management committed offenses, and they seem to have been responsible for keeping sex work within acceptable boundaries. For example, if *yue* prostitutes slept with senior military officers, the master of colors with jurisdiction would be dismissed from his post.[12] The founders of the Qing dynasty preserved the Beijing branch of the Bureau of Instruction and its various traditional functions (QHS, 523/1043; Wang Shunu 1988, 198, 261).

To be sure, not all prostitutes in late imperial China could claim ancestors as illustrious as the 1402 martyrs. Nor, it seems, were all subject to such direct registration and control by the state (especially in the large commercial sex market that emerged by the end of the Ming). Nevertheless, in late imperial law, officially enslaved *yue hu* served as the paradigm of prostitutes as a distinct social stratum, and of sex work as a hallmark of debased status. This hereditary status group was identified with prostitution, as well as musical performance, dance, and other despised entertainment occupations, but *yue* status attached both to the individuals directly involved in such work, and to immediate family members and descendants (both male and female) who may not have been. By the early Qing, many *yue* households lived as ordinary peasants, far from the capital (especially in Shanxi and Shaanxi), but suffered the stigma of their hereditary label all the same. In addition, during the early Qing dynasty, several regional subethnic groups were similarly registered with hereditary mean status: for example, the "beggar households" (*gai hu*), "lazy people" (*duo min*), and "nine surnames fishing households" (*jiu xing yu hu*) of the Yangzi delta, and the "*dan* households" (*dan hu*) who lived on the river estuaries of Guangdong and other parts of southeast China. Generally speaking, the stigma attached to these groups derived from their failure to conform to the traditional valorized division of labor whereby men farmed while women spun and wove. That some of their women sold sexual services (or engaged in other polluted activities, such as barbering and assisting in funerals) only added to their moral taint. These regional subethnic groups were not slaves, and the fact that Qing lawmakers attached the status label *jian* (mean, debased) to them illustrates how the meaning of that term had shifted, with the nuance of moral stigma or pollution coming to outweigh that of servitude.[13]

The people to whom such labels attached by no means all worked in prostitution. At the same time, in Ming and early Qing case records we encounter many people involved in sex work who do *not* appear to belong to any specific hereditary group or to be working under official supervision, but nevertheless are treated by magistrates as members of the same debased-status stratum, separate and distinct from ordinary commoners. In fact, legal discourse generally lumped sex work together with mean status: prostitution as an occupation debased those who practiced it, while people of mean status in general (including domestic slaves, cross-dressing actors, and the like) were not expected to conform to the norms of marriage, female chastity, and occupation that supposedly went along with commoner (*liang*) status.

The *legal fiction* framing this thinking was that fixed status boundaries separated stable populations who were fundamentally different from one another in terms of ancestry, occupation, and morality. It derived from the old (and increasingly anachronistic) aristocratic ideal of a caste society in which function matched status in a way that was transparent to all. This legal fiction probably *never* represented with perfect accuracy the complexity of social practice (either of sex work or of the social structure as a whole). We should interpret it not as a description of empirical reality, but rather as an ideological program by which the judiciary sought to impose a certain vision of moral order.

The Problem of Terminology

One problem of studying this subject is that historical sources use a variety of terms for prostitutes and related persons. Yuan, Ming, and early Qing legal texts use the term *yue hu* in conjunction with other words for prostitutes, the most common being *chang* and *ji*, but such usage is far from consistent, and the sources that do offer precise definitions tend to contradict each other. This confusion derives at least in part from socioeconomic change that undermined the legal fiction of fixed status categories.

Take, for example, the term *yue hu* itself. Some texts draw a distinction between *yue*, on the one hand, and *chang* and *ji*, on the other. In such instances, *yue* (and its derivatives *yue ren*, *yue gong*, *yue fu*, *yue ji*, and *yue yi*) appears to refer to the specific hereditary status group working under government supervision, not all of whom necessarily engaged in *sex* work, whose origins we have described above. In contrast, *chang* and *ji* (and their derivatives *chang ji*, *chang fu*, *chang nü*, and *ji nü*) refer generally to persons engaged in sex work, regardless of whether they possessed *yue* household registration or were managed by the state. For example, a commentary on one Ming law notes that "the term '*yue* persons' in the statute refers to prostitutes (*ji*) of the Bureau of Instruction (*yue ren nai jiao fang si ji zhe*)." The same text goes on to distinguish such persons from *liu chang*—"itinerant" or "unregistered" (literally, "flowing" or "circulating") prostitutes. The latter, presumably, were sex workers operating outside direct government supervision (TM, 14/8b). The late Ming writer Xie Zhaozhe makes a similar distinction: he defines "*yue* households" as "those who work under official supervision" (*li yu guan zhe*), in contrast to *tu ji* ("local prostitutes"), "who do not work under official supervision" (*bu li yu guan*) (1959, 226).

Another commentary on the Ming code, however, makes a different distinction: "*'chang'* means [prostitutes of] the Bureau of Instruction; *'yue'* means women of *yue* [household] (*chang shi jiao fang, yue shi yue fu*)" (XF, 13/14b). The implication here is that not all women of *yue* status were necessarily prostitutes or under the direct supervision of the Bureau of Instruction—perhaps reflecting the breakdown over time of a close match between fixed status categories and actual occupation.

But these terms are not consistently distinguished from each other at all; most often, they simply appear as synonyms. One Qing legal commentary defines *chang* simply as "women of *yue* household registration" (*chang zhe yue ji funü ye*) (Yao Run et al., eds., 1878, 33/14b, commentary). Many texts use the terms *chang hu* and *chang jia* ("*chang* household") interchangeably with *yue hu*; when the suffixes *hu* or *jia* ("household") are used, the compound refers either to a husband who pimps his wife or to an entire household involved in sex work. Ming and early Qing texts also use the term *shui hu* (literally, "water household") as a synonym for *yue hu* and *chang hu*. Xie Zhaozhe states that "[prostitutes] who work under official supervision are known as *'yue hu'*; they are also known as *'shui hu'*" (*li yu guan zhe wei yue hu, you wei shui hu*) (1959, 226). By one account, the latter were *yue* households outside the capital that fell under the looser supervision of local government officials instead of the direct control of the central Bureau of Instruction (cited in Jing Junjian 1993, 229). ("Water," *shui*, may have carried the same nuance as the "flowing," *liu*, in "*liu chang*," indicating a lack of tight regulation or fixed residence.) But early Qing case records also refer to pimps and prostitute households in the imperial capital of Beijing as *shui hu* (for example, XT, 939/SZ 12.2.17).

As a practical matter, magistrates did not need to draw fine distinctions among these terms. In a criminal case report, when the persons involved are identified by these labels (*yue hu, shui hu, chang, ji,* and so on), we can be certain that they would *not* be prosecuted for the commoner offense of "illicit sexual intercourse" (*jian*). Such language served the important purpose of signaling a jurist's *a priori* assumption that since the individuals in question were of debased status, their sex work should be tolerated. That is what really mattered for legal purposes, and those who drafted such documents clearly did not think that anything else needed to be said.[14]

Distinction Between Status Groups: Legislation

The homicide chapter of *Collected Statutes of the Yuan* reports two cases from the year 1268 in which men murdered women whom they had slept with. The first case record, found in the section headed "Homicide of domestic slaves, prostitutes, or bonded laborers," states briefly that one Zhizhen killed "a prostitute who had previously served him" (*yuan zuo ban chang nü*) named Haitang ("flowering crabapple"). For this crime, he was sentenced to 107 blows of the heavy bamboo, in application of the statute against "killing a domestic slave who belongs to another" (YD, 42/25a).

The second case record, found in the section headed "Homicide because of illicit sex," tells of one Sun Ban'ge, who killed A-Yin, the wife of Liu Sun'er. A-Yin had "repeatedly engaged in illicit sexual intercourse (*tong jian*)" with Sun Ban'ge, but one night she refused his advances, so he struck her with an axe. The judgment found that "leaving aside his lesser crime of 'engaging in illicit sexual intercourse,'" Sun Ban'ge should be executed for A-Yin's murder, and that 50 taels of silver should be confiscated from his estate to finance her burial (YD, 42/30b).[15]

The disparity in penalties, as well as the strikingly different terms used to narrate these two parallel cases, makes sense only when we realize that Yuan law defined the two murdered women as belonging to fundamentally unequal status categories, and that it construed sexual intercourse between a commoner male and each category of woman as utterly different phenomena. In fact, from a contemporary judicial perspective, the two cases were not "parallel" at all—and jurists of the Ming and early Qing dynasties would have found little reason to disagree. A violent crime that crossed status lines downward generally deserved a lesser penalty than an offense against a status equal, even an adulteress.[16] Moreover, the engagement of a prostitute's services bore no comparison to adultery with the wife of another commoner: the lawful, if despised, livelihood of a prostitute household constituted criminal "illicit sexual intercourse" (*jian*) if practiced by commoners.

Until 1723, the purpose of laws related to prostitution was to preserve and reinforce the differences that are highlighted by a comparison of these two examples. Relevant legislation concentrated on marking prostitutes as different from commoners, fixing status boundaries, preventing the transfer of commoners to debased households, and banning sexual behavior among commoners that violated the assumed moral basis of their status. The purpose was not to prohibit a certain conduct, but rather to channel conduct in ways that reinforced the *status quo*.[17]

Sumptuary Laws

Sumptuary legislation of the Yuan, Ming, and early Qing dynasties included dress codes for people associated with sex work.[18] Yuan edicts complained that members of "prostitute households" (*chang ji zhi jia*) had been wearing the same sorts of clothing as "officials, gentry, and commoners" (*guan yuan shi shu*) so that "no distinction is made between the honored and the debased" (*gui jian bu fen*). These edicts forbade members of prostitute households from riding on horseback or wearing certain kinds of elegant clothing, and required the heads of prostitute households and their male relatives "to wrap their heads in green cloth" (*guo qing bu*) (YD, 29/8b–9a; Shen Jiaben 1976, 8/24b).

Ming-dynasty law mandated specific uniforms for the "*yue* musicians" (*yue yi*) and "*yue* prostitutes" (*yue ji*) under the Bureau of Instruction, with the intent that "they be prohibited from [dressing] in the same manner as the wives of commoners" (*bu xu yu shu min qi tong*) (MH, 61/394). Green headgear was required for government prostitutes; as the late Ming writer Xie Zhaozhe explains, "the regulations set down at the beginning of our dynasty ordered that their head cloths be made green to exhibit their shame (*lü qi jin yi shi ru*)" (1959, 226). Qing edicts of 1652 and 1672 confirmed green headgear for actors (*you ren*) and members of *yue* households (QHS, 328/886–88). To such rules, we owe the Chinese slang for being cuckolded, "to wear a green hat" (*dai lü maozi*), since that was the visible mark of a prostitute's husband.[19]

Prohibition of Intermarriage

A second set of measures banned intermarriage between prostitutes and males of higher-status groups. Late imperial legal codes designated degree-holding government officials a distinct status level above ordinary commoners,[20] and an explicit part of such distinction was prohibiting such officials from marrying prostitutes. But ordinary commoners were generally forbidden to marry prostitutes as well.

At least one Song-dynasty magistrate was scandalized by the thought of a man of the official class (*shi ren*) marrying an "official prostitute" (*guan ji*): "It is not permitted! It is not permitted! It is absolutely not permitted!" (QM, 344). The Yuan code included the following statute: "Any official who marries a prostitute (*chang*) as his main wife (*qi*) shall receive 57 blows of the light bamboo and shall be dismissed from office; they shall be divorced" (TM, 14/8b). A separate edict of 1311 prohibited commoner males from marrying *yue* prostitutes under the jurisdiction of the Bureau of Instruction: "Henceforth, females of *yue* households shall be given in marriage only to other *yue* households" (YD, 18/46a–b).

The Ming code included the following statute: "Any official who marries a *yue* person (*yue ren*) as wife or concubine shall receive 60 blows of the heavy bamboo, and [the couple] shall be divorced. If the son or grandson of an official marries one, his penalty shall be the same" (ML, 6/30b). A commentary expanded the scope of this Ming statute to include all prostitutes, not just those with specifically *yue* household registration: "The term '*yue* person' in the statute refers to prostitutes (*ji*) of the Bureau of Instruction; but cases involving unregistered prostitutes (*liu chang*) should also be judged according to this provision" (TM, 14/8b; ML, 6/32a). This statute was preserved in the Qing code (DC, 113-00).

The Ming statute fails to mention ordinary commoners, but two other commentaries fill the gap. The first recommends that "If a commoner (*min ren*) marries a *yue* woman as his main wife (*qi*), then he should be punished according to the statute on 'doing inappropriate things'; if he takes a prostitute as his concubine (*qie*), then he need not be punished" (TM, 14/8b; ML, 6/32a). The logic here is that marriage to a main wife should match social equals; banning the marriage of persons of unequal status aimed at reinforcing horizontal social boundaries. Hence, the greater the social gap violated by intermarriage, the worse the offense. A concubine ranked higher than a bondservant or slave but lower than her husband or his main wife. In addition, the gap between a prostitute and an ordinary commoner was not as great as that between a prostitute and an official. Therefore, according to this commentator, it was less problematic for a commoner to take a prostitute as wife than for an official to do so; thus, he recommends a lighter penalty for a commoner offender (the basic penalty for "doing inappropriate things" being 40 blows of the light bamboo; DC, 386-00). If a commoner took a prostitute as a mere concubine, then the offense would not be serious enough to warrant any punishment.

The second commentary confirms this basic logic: "The statute does not mention commoners (*chang ren*); today, it is generally not allowed for them to take women of *yue* registration (*yue ji*) in marriage. Even if a prostitute (*chang fu*) is not a *yue* person, all such people engage in offensive conduct. [If a commoner marries a prostitute], the penalty should be reduced [from that for an official] by only one degree" (XF, 3/11b). In other words, marriage between a commoner and any sort of prostitute should be punished, but the penalty should not be as severe as that for an official who married a prostitute.

Officials Prohibited from Sleeping with Prostitutes

Marriage aside, it was illegal for imperial officials even to sleep with prostitutes. The Yuan code provided that "any official who habituates tea houses, wine shops, or brothels (*chang you zhi jia*) shall be tried and dismissed from his post" (*Yuan shi*, 2614). In addition, *Collected Statutes of the Yuan* cites a 1319 case from Fujian in which two county defenders (*xian wei*) were punished for partying and spending the night with a pair of *yue* prostitutes. These women were the daughter and daughter-in-law of one Zhang Cheng, whose *yue* household functioned under the Bureau of Instruction. The two officers were sentenced to 47 blows of the light bamboo for debasing themselves and ignoring their duties; the fees Zhang Cheng had collected were confiscated. It also appears that Zhang Cheng's household was dismissed from doing government-managed work as a result of the affair: they are referred to in the case record as "dismissed *yue* [prostitutes]" (*san yue*). But this dismissal did not remove their hereditary *yue* status; nor, apparently, did they suffer any criminal penalties (YD, xin ji, xing bu/51a–b).

The Ming code included the following statute against "officials sleeping with prostitutes" (*guan li su chang*): "Any official who sleeps with prostitutes shall receive 60 blows of the heavy bamboo; the go-between shall receive a penalty one degree lower. If the son or grandson of an official sleeps with prostitutes, then he shall receive the same penalty" (ML, 25/12a). A commentary adds that officials should "redeem their penalties with cash fines" and "be dismissed from office" (ML, 25/12b). This statute also appeared in the Qing code (DC, 374-00).

As in the law on intermarriage, the gap between officials and prostitutes was too great to brook such intimate contact. But Yuan, Ming, and early Qing law do not mention *commoner* males sleeping with prostitutes, which was normal and legal, even if the women who engaged in the business were stigmatized for it. The offense in this Ming statute was not the sale of sex per se, but rather its purchase by men of high rank. The point is underscored by another commentary on the statute:

In this measure, "officials sleeping with prostitutes" is not the same as the crime of "engaging in illicit sexual intercourse" (*fan jian*). Therefore, a *yue* prostitute who knowingly [sleeps with an official] shall be sentenced for the same crime [as the official], but she may have the penalty carried out while wearing a robe (*dan yi di jue*); those who are able may also pay a cash fine [in lieu of a beating]. (ML, 25/12a–b)

In other words, a prostitute who slept with an official should *not* be treated like a commoner woman who engaged in "illicit sexual intercourse," since the prostitute's only offense was to take the wrong sort of person as customer in an otherwise tolerated business. The Ming code mandated that adulteresses of commoner status (*jian fu*) undergo the added humiliation of being "stripped naked to receive punishment" (*qu yi shou xing*); this commentary, however, allowed prostitutes who had slept with officials to remain clothed. Ordinary adulteresses could not redeem their beatings with fines, either; nor could prostitutes who committed other offenses. But this commentary permitted prostitutes who had slept with officials to do so (ML, 1/46b, 51a).

In the Yuan and early Ming dynasties, the Bureau of Instruction supplied "official prostitutes" (*guan ji*) to entertain guests at official banquets; no doubt, these women were highly refined courtesans rather than ordinary sex workers. As the Ming writer Jiang Mingshu explains, officials were strictly prohibited from "entering brothels and sleeping with prostitutes" (*ru yuan su chang*), but they could still "summon prostitutes to serve them wine" (*zhao ji you shang*). But an edict of the Xuande reign (1426–35) prohibited this sort of intimacy, too; thenceforth, official prostitutes were excluded from state entertainments. Nevertheless, according to Xie Zhaozhe, this prohibition "did not apply to the attendance [of prostitutes at private banquets] at officials' own residences" (*jin shen jia ju zhe bu lun*), and that practice remained common for the rest of the dynasty.[21]

Transfer of Commoners to Prostitute Households

A further set of measures prohibited the transfer of commoners to prostitute households. The Yuan code provided that

Whenever a commoner (*liang ren*) is sold or bought to become a prostitute (*wei chang*), the seller and buyer shall receive the same penalty,[22] and the woman shall be returned to commoner status (*huan wei liang*); one-half the price paid shall be confiscated by the state and the other half awarded to whoever reports the offense; if the woman herself reports the offense, or it is discovered without being reported, then the entire sum shall be confiscated. (TM, 26/25a; *Yuan shi*, 2644)

Clearly, being sold into prostitution caused a degradation of status. The victim was to be "returned to commoner status," which implied simultaneous rescue from sexual slavery and recrossing of the boundary violated by the transaction. A separate edict aimed to strengthen enforcement by keeping authorities up-to-date on the official prostitute population, and by imposing sanctions on those with jurisdiction (presumably the Bureau of Instruction) who failed to guard against such transactions:

All prostitute households (*chang ji zhi jia*) shall report the birth of male or female children no later than the tenth day of the following month, and each quarter the total number of births shall be tallied and reported to the Secretariat; it is prohibited to abort unborn fetuses or heedlessly to take the lives of those already born. It is strictly prohibited for any prostitute household presumptuously to buy a commoner to become a prostitute; it is further prohibited for the bureau with jurisdiction carelessly to issue official certification for such transactions without investigating them and uncovering malfeasance (*bu shen lan gei gong ju*). . . . All offenders shall be severely punished.   (*Yuan shi*, 2687)

Ideally, by maintaining an accurate record of all children born into prostitute households, it would be a simple matter to identify any commoner youth who had been illegally purchased.

Ming lawmakers drew on Yuan precedent, according to Xue Yunsheng (TM, 26/25a), in drafting the following measure against "buying commoners to become prostitutes" (*mai liang wei chang*):

Any prostitute (*chang*), actor (*you*), or *yue* person (*yue ren*) who buys the son or daughter of a commoner (*liang ren zi nü*) to become a prostitute or actor (*wei chang you*), or takes [the daughter of a commoner] as wife or concubine, or adopts [the son or daughter of a commoner] as son or daughter, shall receive 100 blows of the heavy bamboo. Anyone who knowingly marries off or sells [a commoner to a prostitute, actor, or *yue* person] shall receive the same penalty. The go-between shall receive a penalty reduced by one degree. The amount paid shall be confiscated, and the son or daughter shall be returned to his or her natal lineage (*gui zong*).   (ML, 25/13a)

A substatute of the Jiajing reign (1522–66) added one month in the cangue for any *"yue* worker" who committed this offense (WX, xing li/24a).

The catch-all phrase "prostitute, actor, or *yue* person" (*chang you yue ren*) seems designed to cover every category touched by prostitution stigma (actors being associated with male homosexual prostitution, as well as female impersonation on stage).[23] The statute expands on its Yuan precedent by prohibiting the degradation of commoner status by marriage or adoption, even if the individual in question was not necessarily forced into sex work. As a handbook for magistrates from the Wanli reign (1573–1619) explains, "the abominable thing about this crime is that it presses commoners into mean status" (*wu qi ya liang wei jian*). Returning the victim to his or her natal lineage would correct that wrong (XF, 13/24b). The first edition of the Qing code preserved this Ming statute, and subsequent editions incorporated the Jiajing amendment as well (DC, 375-00).

The Commoner Crime of "Abetting Illicit Sexual Intercourse"

As we have seen, it was perfectly legal for a commoner male to sleep with prostitutes, and he might even get away with taking one as a concubine. But what of commoner women who sold sexual services? A commentary on the Ming statute against "officials sleeping with prostitutes" answers the question: "The term 'prostitute' (*chang*) in the statute refers to *yue* households of the Bureau of Instruction and of the various prefectures and districts. Among the common people, those who privately sell illicit sex (*min jian si zi mai jian zhe*) should be prosecuted according to the ordinary statutes on 'offenses of illicit sex' (*dang yi fan jian zhi lü lun zhi*)" (ML, 25/12a–b). Here, we find a distinction between legal prostitution among the debased-status group under government supervision—*chang* or *yue* households—and illegal prostitution among commoners. The distinction is underscored by word choice: only the latter sort of sex work is referred to with the legal term "illicit sexual intercourse" (*jian*), automatically defining it as criminal, so that citation of the "statutes on 'offenses of illicit sex'" seems almost redundant. Also, the adverb translated as "privately" (*si zi*) carries a strong connotation of illicitness: it might be better translated as "illicitly" or "without authorization."

Similarly, the late Ming writer Xie Zhaozhe distinguishes *"yue hu"*—"those who work under official supervision" (*li yu guan zhe*)—from *"tu ji"* ("local prostitutes")—that is, "those who do not work under official supervision, but sell illicit sex at their homes" (*bu li yu guan, jia ju er mai jian zhe*). By characterizing the latter business as "selling illicit sex" (*mai jian*), Xie strongly suggests that such private prostitution was criminal—in other words, that the prostitutes involved were commoners, rather than people of officially registered debased status. He adds that these private brothels are colloquially known as *si kezi; kezi* means "nest" or "burrow," and once again, the meaning of *si* in this context is closer to "illicit" or "contraband" than to "private" (1959, 226).

In theory, then, there existed two models of prostitution: (1) the sex work of people officially registered with hereditary debased status, conducted under official supervision and tolerated by the judiciary, and (2) private, unauthorized sex work performed by ordinary commoners, which could be prosecuted as "illicit sexual intercourse" under criminal law.

The equation of commoner prostitution with illicit sexual intercourse can be clearly seen in a Southern Song edict: "Any wife who on her own accord goes and . . . acts as a prostitute (*wei chang*) shall be punished for 'illicit sexual intercourse' (*yi jian lun*). . . . The male [who engages her services] shall not be punished for illicit sexual intercourse" (QY, 80/23b). Presumably, the customer would not be punished because he might not have been aware that the "prostitute" he had hired was a commoner; only in that detail did the wife's crime differ from ordinary adultery. A second Song edict prohibited a commoner male from pimping the women of his household:

If a man has (*ling*)[24] his own wife, the wife of his son or grandson, or his female servant (*nü shi*) act as a prostitute (*wei chang*), or if he arranges for her to engage in illicit sexual intercourse (*jian*) with another man, then even if the act has not been consummated, the woman shall be divorced; even if he has not arranged the act, as long as he knows of it and has accepted money, then this law shall apply; a female servant so treated shall be released to do as she wishes (*fang cong bian*).   (QY, 80/24b)

These edicts are included with others pertaining to *jian*, and they clearly were meant to apply to commoner wives. The key penalty here is divorce (it is not clear whether other penalties would apply during the Song): sexual promiscuity was incompatible with the marital norms binding on commoners, and a marriage so tainted could not be allowed to stand. Compulsory divorce would be part of the penalty for this crime in Yuan, Ming, and Qing law as well.

We have more information about Yuan judicial policy on this matter. In 1303, the grand councilor for Jiangxi province reported to the Board of Punishment that cases of "husbands abetting their wives to act as prostitutes" (*zong qi wei chang*) had become very common, with "urban and rural people of all jurisdictions competing to imitate the fashion." One reason for this trend, he believed, was that both the prevention and successful prosecution of adultery depended on husbands to take responsibility for their wives' conduct: "The law mandates that a wife who commits illicit sexual intercourse may be seized only by her husband (*jian cong fu bu*)—this is probably the reason that a husband who abets his wife [to act as a prostitute] can do so without fear." Only if neighbors and officials were empowered to act on their own initiative would there be any hope of deterring the trend of "commoners debasing themselves" (*liang wei jian*) in this way. The latter comment indicates that commoner prostitution threatened to blur the sacrosanct boundaries of status distinction.

The Board of Punishment agreed, and issued the following proclamation:

The bond between husband and wife is vital to the moral foundation of human relations, and a husband who abets his wife to act as a prostitute gravely injures the public morality (*da shang feng hua*). . . . If a husband accepts money to have his wife engage in illicit sexual intercourse with other men, then the bond of moral duty between them has already been broken (*yi jue*).

For this reason, let the word be spread that *anyone* may report such offenders and deliver them to the authorities, who shall make a clear investigation of guilt. [In such cases] the husband (*ben fu*), the wife who engages in illicit sexual intercourse (*jian fu*), and the man who engages in illicit sexual intercourse (*jian fu*), shall all [be punished] in the same manner as ordinary offenders who engage in illicit sexual intercourse, and the couple shall be divorced.   (YD, 45/9a–b)

On this basis, the following statute was promulgated:

If a husband accepts money to abet his wife or concubine to act as a prostitute, then the husband, the wife who has engaged in illicit sexual intercourse, and the man who has engaged in illicit sexual intercourse shall each receive 87 blows of the heavy bamboo, and the couple shall be divorced. If the wife or concubine herself reports the crime, then she shall not be punished; but if a long period of time has passed before she finally reports it, than she shall not be excused.   (*Yuan shi*, 2644; TM, 26/17b–18a, 25a)

The woman would be returned to her natal family to be married off to someone else (see, for example, YD, 45/8a–9b).

The term in the Yuan statute translated as "to abet" (*zong*) implies active complicity on the part of both husband and wife. The literal meaning of the logograph is "to release" or "give rein" (for instance, to a horse); it can also mean "to indulge." In the Confucian scheme, a husband has legitimate authority over his wife, as a father has over his children: it is up to him to discipline her, to set limits on her behavior. The image of the statutory language, then, is of a husband failing in the duty conferred by his position, when he lets his wife indulge in sexual promiscuity. It is this failure on the husband's part that prompted the Yuan judiciary to make proactive vigilance against such offenses a community and official responsibility.

The Yuan statute employs the phrase "to act as a prostitute" (*wei chang*), but the woman and her sexual partner are distinguished from a tolerated, debased-status prostitute and her customer by the statement that they have "engaged in illicit sexual intercourse (*jian*)." They are labeled with the same homophonous terms used elsewhere in Yuan law for an adulteress and her partner: *jian fu* and *jian fu*, respectively (see Character List). (In general Song, Yuan, Ming, and Qing legal texts use the term *jian* only when referring to criminal acts of commoners.) The identification of this conduct as adultery is reinforced by the penalty of 87 blows of the heavy bamboo, the same penalty mandated by Yuan law for partners in "consensual illicit sex" (*he jian*) if the woman were married (YD, 45/1a). In other words, the commercial element did not warrant any extra penalty: it was the sexual promiscuity that was being punished, not the use of money to facilitate it.

The basic principle here is that prostitution, like all female promiscuity, contradicted the norms of marriage and female chastity binding on commoners, and thus constituted a form of "illicit sexual intercourse." As the grand councilor for Jiangxi put it, such conduct amounted to "commoners debasing themselves" (*liang wei jian*)—in essence, acting like persons of debased or mean status (*jian min*). Since such conduct "broke the bond of moral duty" between husband and wife, an offending couple should be divorced. The difference with ordinary adultery was that the husband had colluded in the crime. Therefore, he suffered exactly the same punishment as the sexual partners themselves, and lost his wife to boot. Compulsory divorce was no trivial penalty, especially for the husband. The typical man punished for this crime was probably very poor, and having lost one wife, he was unlikely ever to get another.

Ming law reasserted these principles with a statute that closely resembled the Yuan measure, except for one significant difference:

> If someone abets or tolerates (*zong rong*) his wife or concubine to engage in illicit sexual intercourse (*tong jian*) with another, then the husband, the man who engaged in illicit sex, and the wife who engaged in illicit sex shall each receive 90 blows of the heavy bamboo. . . . [25] In all cases, the woman shall be divorced and returned to her natal lineage. If someone abets . . . his own daughter, or the wife or concubine of his son or grandson, to engage in illicit sex with another, then the penalty shall be the same.   (ML, 25/3a–b)

Here, the Yuan statute's phrase "to act as a prostitute" (*wei chang*) has been replaced by an explicit reference to the crime of "illicit sexual intercourse." The direct reference to the husband's pecuniary motive has disappeared as well, underscoring the point already seen in Yuan law: it was not the money that mattered. In this way, Ming lawmakers broadened the commoner crime of "abetting or tolerating" illicit sexual intercourse to include both a husband's active pimping of his wife and more passive toleration of an extramarital affair without money changing hands at all. As in the Yuan dynasty, the penalty exactly equaled that mandated for partners in "consensual illicit sexual intercourse" if the woman were married; the commercial element in prostitution warranted no increase of penalty (ML, 25/1a). The Qing code included this statute unchanged (DC, 367-00).

Yuan law also prohibited commoner males from "forcing" (*le*) a wife, concubine, or adopted daughter "to act as a prostitute" or "to sing and dance to entertain others," or forcing a domestic slave (*nu bi*) "to act as a prostitute." In each case, the same basic principles applied, with the wife, concubine, or adopted daughter being returned to her natal lineage, and the slave being "freed to become a commoner" (*fang cong liang*). A wife forced to act as a prostitute might or might not be punished, "depending on the circumstances of the case" (TM, 26/18a, 25a; YD, 45/9a–b; *Yuan shi*, 2644). Ming lawmakers drafted similar provisions (also preserved in the Qing code), but again they dropped all direct references to money or to "acting as a prostitute"; also, Ming law exempted females "forced (*yi le*) to engage in illicit sexual intercourse" from any punishment (ML, 25/3a–b; DC, 367-00). These laws, like those on "abetting" illicit sex, underscore the Confucian principle that authority derives legitimacy from its moral basis. The contractual family relationships of marriage and adoption (and in Yuan law, slavery) might be canceled if that moral basis were violated (*yi jue*). It was the expectation to conform to such norms that distinguished commoners from the debased-status groups to whom such rules did not apply: the performance of different standards of sexual and familial morality was the essence of the legal fiction that distinguished debased from commoner status.

Commoner males, however, were not polluted by intercourse with prostitutes; as long as they penetrated persons of debased status, there was no problem. As we have seen, because phallic penetration implied hierarchy, with the person penetrated thereby subordinated, only the penetrated person suffered pollution from sexual intercourse out of place. This thinking applied to prostitution as much as to rape, adultery, and sodomy.

A Ming substatute (of the Jiajing reign, 1522–66) highlights the difference between commoners and debased-status prostitutes by using separate clauses to prohibit the two groups from committing what seems like essentially the same crime. This measure was intended as an amendment to the old statute against "buying a commoner to be a prostitute," but in addition to adding extra penalties, it spelled out separate scenarios for commoner and debased-status offenders:

If [a commoner] buys a child of commoner family (*liang jia zi nü*) as a concubine, adopted daughter, or other such status, and abets or forces that person to engage in illicit sexual intercourse with someone else, then he shall be liable for punishment under the law; [in addition to the penalties already prescribed in the code,] the husband or adoptive father, as well as the man who has engaged in illicit sex, shall each be sentenced to spend one month in the cangue before the doorway of his own home (*ben jia men shou*).

If a *yue* worker (*yue gong*) illicitly (*si*) buys a child of commoner family to become a prostitute, then, too, the buyer, seller, and go-between shall all be liable for punishment; [in addition to the penalties already prescribed in the code,] they shall be sentenced to spend one month in the cangue before the courtyard gate (*yuan men shou*).

The necessity to spell out two distinct scenarios underscores how the same conduct was defined differently depending on the legal status of the offender—even when, as in this instance, it was to be punished in more or less the same way. The first clause applies to ordinary commoners, and the key element is the commoner crime of "illicit sexual intercourse"; pecuniary motivation is not mentioned.

The point of exposing the commoner offender in the cangue at the doorway of *his own home* was to humiliate him before family and neighbors, thereby mobilizing community pressure to deter such offenses. The assumption was that every commoner existed within an extended network of family and community whose values would be offended by the prohibited conduct.

In contrast, the *yue* worker's crime is to make a commoner "become a prostitute"—not simply forcing that person to perform sexual services, but also degrading his or her status irrevocably by transfer to a household whose legal debasement was linked to that occupation. Moreover, exposure in the cangue before "the courtyard gate" suggests not a context of outraged family and community but rather some sort of official compound or brothel; according to an eighteenth-century Japanese commentary, "courtyard" (*yuan*) in this context refers to the "three courtyards" (*san yuan*) where *yue* personnel resided (Ogyû 1989, 835). In the final, third clause of the substatute, this contrast becomes clearer still:

[In cases of commoner offenders,] any rural agent, decimal unit leader (*huo jia*), or neighbor who allows such conduct and fails to report it shall be punished; so, too, [in cases of *yue* worker offenders,] any supervising official, master of actors, or master of colors who allows such conduct and fails to report it shall be punished.   (WX, xing li/24a)[26]

Lawmakers imagined the commoner offender as living under the watchful eyes of neighbors and community authorities, whereas the *yue* offender was the responsibility of his overseers in the Bureau of Instruction.

Yuan law allowed an interesting exception to the ban on commoner prostitution and the crossing of status boundaries: "If a wife of commoner household (*liang jia fu*) who has been discarded by her husband because she committed illicit sex wishes to become a prostitute, or if the relative of a prostitute or an actor wishes to become a prostitute or an actor, then they shall be allowed to do so" (TM, 26/25a; Yuan shi, 2644). This exception truly confirmed the rule of status distinction: only a commoner already tainted by adultery or by relation to prostitutes might be allowed to become a prostitute herself without compromising the larger mission of the judiciary. At the same time, however, it points to a gray area of the law. How would this have worked in practice? Would a commoner adulteress who "wishes to become a prostitute" be allowed to operate privately, on her own? Or would she be officially registered with

debased status and turned over to the Bureau of Instruction for supervision? The Yuan code is silent. We see here a hint at the complexity of social reality, which (even as early as the Yuan) surely included a great deal of private sex work performed by women who
started out as commoners but ended up being treated, for all practical purposes, in the same way as debased-status prostitutes.

Status Enforcement: Ming and Early Qing Practice

How did the juridical project of status distinction work in practice? In this section, we examine the practical efforts of Ming and
early Qing magistrates to safeguard the boundary that separated
commoner from debased. How was that boundary transgressed or
crossed, in the context of sex work? How did magistrates deal with
such transgression in practice? These scenarios illustrate the application of some of the laws cited above, as well as some of the tensions and ambiguities that bedeviled the effort to organize sexual
behavior according to status-based norms.

Lü Kun's "Prohibitions Issued to Yue Households"

One of the best pieces of evidence we have of how local officials
dealt with debased-status prostitution is a set of "prohibitions" issued to *yue* households by the Ming official Lü Kun in the 1590s,
while he was serving as governor of Shanxi (see translation in Appendix D).[27] One can infer from Lü Kun's rules that the category *yue*
households included a number of separate occupations: prostitutes
(*chang fu*), actors (*you*), and musicians (*yue gong*). Lü distinguishes
yue households from "commoners of established households" (*lao
hu liang min*), to whom they are clearly inferior and must defer;
therefore cursing or striking such a commoner is punished with extra severity. *Yue* households are also excluded from the community
covenants organized at the subcounty level;[28] they must conform to
sumptuary rules that distinguish them from commoners; they are
prohibited from recruiting commoner females; prostitutes and actors
are barred from participating in solemn ritual occasions; prostitutes
are not allowed to provide services at commoners' homes (that is,
patrons must visit the brothel for that purpose); and so on. All these
rules aim to set *yue* persons apart and to mark them with stigma.

But it is equally clear from Governor Lü's rules that *yue* households have a proper, accepted place in the social order. They are to
be governed by specially designated *Yue* headmen (*yue shou*)—"two

individuals with a reputation for justice and fairness" nominated collectively by the *yue* households and confirmed by the local magistrate. Each jurisdiction is to maintain an official register of its *yue* status population. They are to pay taxes if they own land, and *yue* musicians are required to perform on official occasions according to an annual quota of labor service. Most significant, Lü Kun takes pains to differentiate "officially registered *yue* households" (*guan yue hu*) from two other groups that are involved in *illegal* prostitution.

The first is "vagrant prostitute households that migrate in from elsewhere (*liu lai shui hu*) and seduce or lead astray local people from commoner families"—here, the contrast is between the law-abiding local *yue* households who keep in their proper place, and unregistered migrants of uncertain origin who wander about causing trouble and threatening to blur status lines. Governor Lü also distinguishes *yue* households from "a husband and wife originally registered with commoner status (*yuan ji liang min fu fu*) who, being stupid and untalented, willingly sell illicit sex (*mai jian*) to make a living." This passage is one of the most revealing in the text; according to Lü Kun, such people "insult their ancestors and dishonor their relatives, and are shameless to the extreme." To manifest their disgrace, he prescribes that they be subordinated to the properly registered *yue* households:

When they encounter members of officially registered *yue* households (*guan yue hu*), they should kowtow and sit to one side, and if ridiculed or cursed, they should not be allowed to reply—the purpose of this policy is to provoke them to reform their conduct. If they come before a magistrate because of any offense, they should be punished more severely than members of officially registered *yue* households would be for the same offense.

The idea that sexual mores constitute status performance could hardly be expressed more clearly. The *yue* households who practice prostitution are behaving as they should: such conduct suits their station, a fact that lends them a certain respectability. But commoners who "sell illicit sex" (and the word choice underscores the illegality of such conduct) violate the family morality binding on their status and are beneath contempt. For this reason, they should even be treated as inferior to the *yue* households, who at least know their proper place.

The Prosecution of "Buying a Commoner to Be a Prostitute"

The Ming jurist Zhang Kentang reports two cases of commoner women sold into prostitution that he judged in the 1620s while serving as magistrate of Jun County (then located in the Northern Metropolitan Province, now in present-day Henan).[29] The first case concerns He Shi, of nearby Anyang County, whose husband took her to Changtan County and sold her to a madam known as "Prostitute Li" (*Li Chang*). Prostitute Li later resold her for a body price of 40 taels of silver to a Jun County pimp (*shui hu*) named Zhang Youcai. He Shi worked as a prostitute under Zhang for two years, until her father, He Shangcang, finally tracked her down and filed suit at the prefectural yamen to rescue her.

The case was first judged by the magistrate of Wei County,[30] and once He Shangcang had proven that he was the woman's father, "there was no doubt that He Shi should be returned to him." But the magistrate also ordered Shangcang to refund the entire 40 taels that the pimp had paid for his daughter. Because Shangcang could not afford such a large sum, the pimp sued him at Jun County, where Zhang Kentang was magistrate. In reviewing the financial settlement, Magistrate Zhang reasoned that, "He Shi has already been with Zhang Youcai for two years; since she is young, he must have made a lot of money by hiring her out as a prostitute. Even though her body cost him a certain amount, he has no right to expect a full refund." He ordered her father to pay the pimp only ten taels. Magistrate Zhang concluded by noting, "Youcai lost some of his investment; but given the circumstances of the case, I preferred to be stingy with him and generous to Shangcang" (Zhang Kentang 1969, 7/6b–7a).[31]

The second case concerns Yin Shi, who was sold into prostitution during a famine (the exact circumstances are not detailed) and worked under pimp Wang Sansheng for several years. Her closest living relative, it seems, was a first cousin named Yin Shuangbing; he had fled the famine, but when he finally returned home he found out what had happened to her. "He could not bear to have his family's reputation degraded in this way" (*bu ren zhui qi jia sheng*); therefore, he filed suit, and the magistrate ordered the pimp to let Yin Shi quit prostitution and return to commoner status (*cong liang*). Her cousin then arranged a proper marriage for her. But the pimp Wang Sansheng was not happy with this outcome and wanted to contest it. He realized that "there was no way he could succeed if, with his debased status, he tried to dispute over a commoner woman (*yi jian zheng liang shi bi bu de*); but a suit represented as *a husband trying to recover his wife* would look absolutely correct (*yi fu huan fu tuo ming gu shen zheng ye*)." Thus, he enlisted a confed-

erate to file a false suit alleging that Yin Shi was in fact the confederate's wife and had been kidnapped.

Magistrate Zhang uncovered this fraud, and he ordered both pimp
and confederate beaten; still, he felt a certain sympathy for Wang
Sansheng: "Since Sansheng is a scoundrel, he may be punished, and
may [even] be driven out [of this jurisdiction]. But to make him lose
both the woman and the money he invested in her (*ren cai liang
wang*), so that he is left utterly without recourse, should be more
than a kind-hearted person can bear (*yi yi ren ren zhi suo yin yi*)."
Therefore, he ordered the woman's new husband to pay the pimp
ten taels of silver in partial compensation for his loss (Zhang Kentang 1969, 8/8a–9a).

In these two cases, it is absolutely clear that the women had to be
rescued from prostitution and restored to commoner status via their
natal families. But it is equally obvious that there was nothing illegal about prostitution per se, if practiced by the right people, and
that both pimps even enjoyed a certain recognized standing in
court. Neither pimp was punished for the crime of "buying a commoner to be a prostitute," perhaps because they had not known the
women were commoners. Indeed, by ordering financial compensation for the pimps, Magistrate Zhang treated them as victims of
fraud.

A case from Beijing judged by the Board of Punishment in 1655
illustrates how the early Qing judiciary treated the problem of commoner women being sold into prostitution. Cai Shi was the concubine of Zhu Xiu, a Han bannerman. Since Zhu had fallen ill and
needed money, he passed his concubine off as a prostitute and sold
her to a pimp (*shui hu*) named Bao Huizi for 75 taels of silver. The
transaction was documented in a written contract. After some
twenty days, Bao Huizi discovered the truth—that Cai Shi was a
commoner—and sought to cancel the deal, but Zhu Xiu had already
died. For this reason, Bao turned Cai Shi over to her brother-in-law,
Zhu San, without pressing for a refund ("the situation frightened
me, so I didn't ask for my money back").

But instead of taking Cai Shi back into the family, Zhu San
placed her in the brothel of another pimp (*shui hu*), Liu Jiu, who
paid him a share of what she earned. What is more, during the two
weeks that Cai Shi worked in Liu Jiu's brothel, Zhu San himself
slept with her seven times (for free). Later, Zhu San sold her outright
to a third pimp (*shui hu*), He Wu, for another 75 taels of silver (also
documented in a written contract). But before the money could be

paid, Cai Shi's uncle learned what had happened to her and filed charges. At first, Zhu San denied everything, but when confronted with the testimony of Cai Shi and of the pimps and go-betweens who had dealt with him, he finally confessed.

Since Zhu San had slept with Cai Shi, the judges first considered whether he was guilty of incest. They decided that criminal category did not apply, however. "Since Cai Shi had already been sold out of the family by Zhu Xiu to be a prostitute, [Zhu San's sleeping with her] cannot be compared to the crime of 'engaging in illicit sexual intercourse with the concubine of one's elder brother' (*fei jian xiong qie zhe bi*)"—which would have been a capital offense.[32] (The question of rape never comes up in the case record.) Instead, Zhu San was sentenced to 100 blows of the heavy bamboo and a month in the cangue, according to the statute on "buying or selling a commoner to be a prostitute."

The Board of Punishment acknowledged that the first pimp, Bao Huizi, "had believed Cai Shi to be a prostitute, since she could play music and sing, and so had sought to purchase her (*yi Cai Shi tan chang ren chang tao mai*)," and that he had returned her as soon as he learned the truth. Nevertheless, "he failed to investigate Cai Shi's background before buying her, nor did he pay the requisite tax on buying persons," and thus he too was sentenced to 100 blows of the heavy bamboo and a month in the cangue, for "buying a commoner to be a prostitute." The pimp He Wu received the same sentence, and the go-betweens for both sales were sentenced to 90 blows of the heavy bamboo under the same statute. Because pimp Liu Jiu had not actually purchased Cai Shi, he was sentenced to only 80 blows of the heavy bamboo, for "doing inappropriate things—severe cases."[33] A customer of Cai Shi's (who had slept with her more than twenty times) testified as a witness but was released without sentence, since he had not known she was a commoner sold into prostitution at the time he engaged her services. Cai Shi herself was ordered returned to her family.

As in the Ming examples reported by Zhang Kentang, no one in the present case was punished for pimping, prostitution, or sleeping with a prostitute. The only problem of law was that Cai Shi as a commoner could not legally be sold into prostitution: everyone who participated in that crime was sentenced accordingly. Here, the Qing Board of Punishment treated the pimps more harshly than Ming magistrate Zhang Kentang probably would have; in the present case, they were sentenced for buying the woman even though they did not know she was a commoner, and there was no question of compensating them for "damages."

As in the Ming cases, the main purpose of judicial intervention was to restore the woman to her proper place. Cai Shi's standing had been affected to some extent, however, since her husband had sold her to be a prostitute. Although criminal, this act nevertheless resulted in her leaving the Zhu family and becoming, for a time, a prostitute. Hence, when her brother-in-law slept with her, it did not even count as the crime of "illicit sexual intercourse," let alone as the capital offense of incest or rape. In the initial questions put to Zhu San, he was asked if he had "engaged in illicit sexual intercourse" with Cai Shi; but the rest of the memorial uses the neutral, nonlegal term "to sleep with" (*shui* or *shui jiao*) in reference to their sexual relations. Questions put to Cai Shi's customer used the equally neutral verb *piao*—"to engage a prostitute's services"—and as we have seen, he was charged with no crime. Here we detect a tacit recognition by the early Qing judiciary of the fictive and permeable nature of legal status boundaries, of the real possibility that a commoner wife might become a prostitute (XT, 939/SZ 12.2.17).

These case records contain a certain ambiguity: the unspoken premise in each is that these pimps' enterprises were legal, as long as they operated on the basis of debased status. Perhaps they were taxed; the records do not say. Yet clearly, these were *private* enterprises, a far cry from the old paradigm of legal prostitution being a kind of penal servitude performed under imperial supervision. It seems that by the early seventeenth century, at latest, debased-status prostitution had detached from direct state supervision and control, to be accepted as private business. This development represented a blurring of what had once been, in theory anyway, a clear-cut distinction between different status levels, between imperial prerogative and private criminality, between penal servitude and commercial profit.

Escaping Prostitute Status

What about a prostitute crossing status lines *upward*—that is, quitting sex work and acquiring commoner legal status? Perhaps the most common term for such promotion, when legally authorized, was *cong liang* (literally, "to follow the good"). By the late eighteenth century, this term had come to be used almost exclusively to refer to women who quit prostitution, and it had lost all but its moral connotation. For this reason, *cong liang* has occasion-

ally been translated into English as the intransitive verb "to reform," suggesting some kind of individual, self-determined effort
to improve the morality of one's own conduct (like "to turn over a
new leaf").[34]

But for centuries, *cong liang* applied not just to prostitutes; nor
did it refer just to the moral dimension of change. As Niida Noboru
has shown, the original distinction in early imperial law between
the legal concepts of *liang* (good, commoner) and *jian* (mean, debased) was between the *free* and the *unfree*, in an aristocratic society marked by an elaborate hierarchy of legally distinct status
groups. As late as the early Qing, *cong liang* denoted any formal promotion from unfree (debased) to free (commoner) legal status, the
typical scenario being the manumission of slaves and bonded laborers. For example, when a master freed a slave, that act was known as
fang cong liang or *fang liang* ("to release for promotion to commoner status"), and would be documented with a *fang shu* ("manumission certificate"), *liang shu* ("certificate of commoner status"),
or *cong liang shu* ("certificate of promotion to commoner status").
By presenting this certificate to a magistrate, the freed person could
have his or her registration changed to that of a commoner, thereby
becoming eligible for labor service taxation (a longtime mark of free
commoner status). The opposite term, *cong jian* ("to follow the debased"), referred to the legal imposition of mean status on the offspring of some sexual unions between commoners and their status
inferiors. In this instance, the child would "follow" (*cong*) the status
of the debased parent.[35]

Of course, *yue* households and other prostitutes and their families were considered a subset of the larger category of unfree, mean
persons (those under the Bureau of Instruction, in fact, were slaves
of the imperial state), so this terminology could apply to them, too.
As Niida notes, *cong liang* could certainly refer to a prostitute
"shedding her status" (*tuo ji*), but such usage represented just one
instance of the term's broader application (1943, 694).

In this broader usage, the moral dimension of the word *liang*
(which literally means "good") clearly took second place to that of
formal status distinction. But since becoming a commoner meant
conforming to commoner standards of sexual and familial morality,
status promotion for prostitutes naturally implied abandoning the
debased occupation of sex work. For example, Yuan law mandated
that if a prostitute (*chang nü*) became pregnant, and someone "forced
her to abort the fetus" (*le ling duo tai*), then "the offender shall be

punished," and the prostitute shall be "freed to become a commoner" (*fang wei liang*) (*Yuan shi*, 2644). The Yuan statute against selling commoners into prostitution provided that victims be "returned to commoner status" (*huan wei liang*); the statute prohibiting a master from forcing a female slave into prostitution mandated that any slave who was abused in this way be "freed to become a commoner" (*fang cong liang*). In these instances, promotion to commoner status obviously included an end to sex work (TM, 26/25a). By the same logic, *cong liang* usually implied that a prostitute would marry a commoner; a woman's legal status "followed" (*cong*) that of her husband, but also, the definitive social role for a commoner female was that of wife.[36]

Ming sources provide many examples of *cong liang* as a formal status promotion that required official action. For example, in the case of Yin Shi reported above, Magistrate Zhang Kentang "ordered that she be allowed to *cong liang*" (*duan ling cong liang*), whereupon she left her pimp, rejoined her natal lineage (in the person of her cousin), and was promptly married off to a commoner; the marriage both confirmed and implemented the magistrate's order (Zhang Kentang 1969, 8/8a–9a). In a second Ming example, from Le'an County, a prostitute (*chang fu*) named Feng Meilan petitioned the magistrate for a "license to *cong liang*" (*cong liang zhi zhao*), which he duly granted. Here, too, *cong liang* implied marrying a commoner male as much as quitting sex work; the prostitute's petition contrasts her disgust at having to service multiple partners with her aspiration to a marriage in which "one wife and one husband" (*yi fu yi fu*) can live out their lives together. (Perhaps it was this convincing articulation of "commoner values" that swayed the magistrate.) But it was not enough for Feng Meilan to do these things on her own: instead, she found it necessary to petition for official license to change her status, much as a freed slave would have presented a certificate of *cong liang* to a magistrate to obtain a change in household registration (*Ke fa lin zhao*, 4/1a–b).[37]

Ming literati writings that address prostitution, such as Feng Menglong's *Anatomy of Love* (*Qing shi*) and Mei Dingzuo's *Lotus in Dark Mud* (*Hui tu qing ni lian hua ji*), offer a great deal of relevant evidence. The writers of these collections of anecdotes were interested mostly in "famous courtesans of the Bureau of Instruction" (*jiao fang ming ji*) and other sophisticated women who, legal debasement notwithstanding, occupied an elite position in the sex trade hierarchy and served patrons of correspondingly high status.

From what I have seen, elite courtesans never appear in criminal case records. Nevertheless, these literati collections supply a sample of the contemporary discourse of prostitution that nicely complements that in legal sources.

Their chief dramatic scenario involves the discovery of a tragic yet alluring young woman of good family who has somehow "fallen" into prostitution through no fault of her own.[38] A variation is the prostitute who in her loyalty to a patron demonstrates a moral standard far superior to her debased status: *yi*, the Confucian virtue of "morality" or "righteousness" that late imperial jurists used to characterize the mutual bond between spouses.[39] Resolution comes when the hero (a young exam candidate, or an official of some sort) manages to rescue the woman from her squalid life of sex work and debased status. The tragedy, these tales imply, is that the wrong kind of woman might languish in a debased condition (hence Mei Dingzuo's title, *Lotus in Dark Mud*, an old Buddhist metaphor for purity in the midst of pollution). The tragedy is *not* prostitution itself, which seems appropriate enough in its own place—after all, how do the heroes happen to meet these women? The heroines who manage to *cong liang* are exceptions who prove the rule that moral standards and status distinctions properly coincide. In that sense, these stories confirm the legal paradigm of fixed status strata, in spite of the boundary crossing that they portray.

Feng Menglong and Mei Dingzuo depict the process of *cong liang* as necessitating official intervention to change a woman's formal status registration (*ji*); this often involves the Bureau of Instruction. In addition to *cong liang*, they use a number of terms that make explicit reference to this change: *tuo ji* ("to shed status registration"), *luo ji* ("to drop status registration"), *qu ji* and *chu ji* ("to expunge status registration"), *xiao ji* ("to eliminate status registration"), and *chu ming* ("to remove her name [from the register]"). Thus, "Prostitute Yang" (*Yang chang*) was able to *cong liang* when a general fell in love with her and "secretly paid a large bribe to have her prostitute status registration eliminated (*xiao qu chang zhi ji*)." Zhen Shi (who had been born into a commoner family) attracted the pity of a senior official, who "eliminated her status registration and returned her to her former lineage (*xiao ji gui jiu zong*)." Another prostitute encountered a sympathetic magistrate who "issued a judgment ordering that she be allowed to *cong liang*," whereupon she became a concubine in an elite household. In another instance, an official requested that a senior minister intervene to "drop the status registration" (*luo ji*) of a prostitute who, it turned out, had been born into an elite family that had fallen on hard times; the minister "ordered the Bureau of Instruction to investigate her registration and eliminate it" (*ling jiao fang jian ji chu zhi*). In these stories, once a woman's prostitute status had been officially expunged, she became eligible to "remarry as the wife of a commoner" (*gai jia wei liang ren qi*); sometimes a powerful patron would "choose a commoner gentleman and give her to him in marriage" (*ze liang shi jia yan*).[40]

We find a similar example in Xu Fuzuo's early seventeenth-century play, *The Red Pear Blossom* (*Hong li ji*). A young exam candidate and a courtesan have fallen in love; fortunately, a sympathetic County Magistrate offers to help them. As his servant tells the courtesan, "His Honor will get rid of your *yue* status registration (*chu le yue ji ming zi*) and draw up a certificate of promotion to commoner status (*cong liang wen juan*) for you. Then Jieyuan can marry you, after his successful return from the exams." At the end of the play, things work out just as planned (Xu Fuzuo 1970, 4270).

These examples from Ming literature reveal the same assumptions about the relationship between sex work, legal status, and the imperial state that we find in contemporary legal texts. We can conclude that the imperial project to perpetuate a specific paradigm of prostitution informed perceptions not only within the judiciary, but among the much wider circle of literati who wrote such works, as well as the mass audience that consumed them.[41]

A gray area was how to evaluate the chastity of a former prostitute who had managed to *cong liang*; this was a potentially serious issue, since in Ming-Qing judicial practice, the penalty for rape depended on the chastity of the victim. Huang Liuhong raises this question (in his 1694 handbook for magistrates) after observing that a man who rapes an *adulteress* should not suffer the full penalty mandated by statute:

To extend this logic, if a prostitute can *cong liang* and become someone's wife or concubine, and she happens to be raped, then in my opinion the full penalty prescribed by the statute on rape should apply [in spite of her former status]. Why? Once she enters her husband's household, she has acquired the legitimate status of wife or concubine (*yi zheng qi qie zhi ming*); therefore, it is a man's wife or concubine who is being raped. This seems different from the rape of a woman who has previously committed illicit sex (*fan jian zhi fu*), in which the full sentence for coercion cannot apply. (Huang Liuhong 1973, 19/19a)

Huang assumes that the sex work of a debased-status prostitute cannot be equated with the "illicit sexual intercourse" of a commoner wife. Therefore, he argues, a former prostitute who had become a commoner wife could not be equated with a commoner wife who had committed adultery in the past. In other words, status promotion and marriage implied a clean slate. (By the same token, he implies that there would be no penalty at all for raping a prostitute who had *not* managed to *cong liang*: rape violated female chastity and polluted descent lines, both of which were attributes of commoner status.) But Huang stresses that this represents his personal opinion about a hypothetical situation.

Status promotion sometimes took place on a grand scale. On five occasions at least, Ming emperors ordered that large numbers of enslaved *yue* personnel be freed as commoners. One reason for such amnesties was that, as Benjamin Elman has written, the memory of Zhu Di's 1402 usurpation "weighed heavily on the conscience of the Ming." A particularly sore point was the treatment of the descendants of executed loyalists. The Yongle Emperor himself, once securely in power, had relaxed the persecution of some relatives of the martyrs. For example, after executing the loyalist Tie Xuan, the emperor had "sent his dependents to the Bureau of Instruction to be *yue fu*"; Tie's wife died almost immediately, but his two daughters managed "for several months to succeed in resisting violation (*bu shou ru*)." Their militant chastity so impressed the emperor that he finally freed them and restored their status by marrying them to civil officials.[42] But it was Zhu Di's successors who gradually reversed the verdict on 1402 with a series of amnesties that released the loyalists' descendants from *yue* slavery and expunged their legal debasement. In 1424, immediately after Zhu Di's death, his successor, the Hongxi Emperor, ordered the Bureau of Instruction to free thousands of relatives of loyalist Fang Xiaoru and to restore their commoner status. When the Xuande Emperor acceded to the throne in 1425, he emancipated the surviving relatives of loyalist Lian Zining. Over the decades that followed, a series of imperial gestures gradually effected the posthumous rehabilitation of the Jianwen martyrs (Jiao Hong 1991, 20/55b–56a; Elman 1993, 63–64).

The dynasty's bad conscience seems to have extended to enslaved *yue* personnel in general. In 1435, at the accession of the Emperor Yingzong, the Bureau of Instruction released more than 3,800 *yue* workers from servitude; this amnesty bore no overt connection to the Jianwen loyalists, but one suspects that it included many of their relatives (*Ming shi*, 127). In 1456, when Yingzong recovered his throne (after a period of captivity by the Mongols), he issued an edict to the Bureau of Instruction that reiterated the ban on "buying commoners to be prostitutes" and concluded with the following order:

> If it is found that there be any [personnel under the bureau's jurisdiction] who originally came from commoner households (*yuan xi min hu*), but are now classified as *yue* households (*jin wei yue hu*), then they shall now be permitted to correct their status (*xu jin gai zheng*). Any member of a *yue* household who is willing to become a commoner (*yuan cong liang zhe*) shall be allowed to report this, and shall be registered for labor service as an ordinary commoner (*yu min yi ti dang chai*). (MH, 105/571)

This edict, presumably, would have allowed any descendants of the 1402 martyrs (or anyone else) still languishing in official prostitution to *cong liang*. But apparently enough *yue* personnel remained that in 1521, upon the death of the Zhengde Emperor, his successor could order the "release" (*fang*) of an unknown number of "*yue* persons of the Bureau of Instruction," along with convicted criminals and "women who had been submitted in tribute from different regions of the realm" (*Ming shi*, 212). Indeed, the Bureau of Instruction continued to function well into the Qing dynasty, and I know of no evidence that the Ming dynasty ever considered ending official sponsorship of prostitution, let alone prohibiting that practice altogether.[43]

Prostitutes Not Allowed to Escape Their Status

We should not assume that the opportunity to *cong liang* was unconditionally available to all. A Ming statute (preserved in the Qing code) required all households to register according to correct status background; it was a crime punishable by 80 blows of the heavy bamboo to represent one's status falsely, in an attempt "to substitute better for worse" (*bi zhong jiu qing*). The same penalty applied to any official who carelessly approved such a fraudulent change of status. This law clearly applied to prostitutes: it specifically mentions *yue* households (Huang Zhangjian, ed., 1979, 456; DC, 76-00).

Zhang Kentang recounts a case of marriage fraud that involved an attempt to pass off a prostitute as a commoner. A *yue* pimp (*yue hu*) named Zhu Yigui owned a prostitute (*ji*) named Cheng Shi. She was "plain and simple, not like a daughter from a prostitute household (*bu si chang jia nü*)," so he decided to sell her off. But "he was concerned that people would look down on her as a debased prostitute, and be unwilling to pay a high price for her" (*ju ren zhi yi chang jian ye*); therefore, he moved her out of his brothel to the home of a friend and, after some time, moved her once again to the home of another friend. "After she had been moved to the third location, nobody knew her background anymore" (*san yi qi chu ze wu ren zhi qi lai li yi*)—which enabled Zhu Yigui to pass her off as a commoner. (One is reminded of the way criminal organizations "launder" money to conceal its origins.) Staying in the background, the pimp arranged through matchmakers to marry her as a concubine to a man from a different county, Zheng Zixin, for a bride-price of 16,000 cash. As Zhang Kentang comments, the pimp's "ambition to substitute a debased woman for a commoner (*yi jian zuo liang*) had succeeded."

But the pimp was too greedy. Once the money was in his pocket, he sued Zheng Zixin for *kidnapping* the woman. Apparently, he thought that Zheng would pay him off rather than let such an embarrassing case go to trial, but that calculation proved wrong, and Magistrate Zhang uncovered the fraud. Zhu Yigui, the matchmakers, and the men who had hosted the prostitute on the pimp's behalf all received beatings with the heavy bamboo. There is no word on the fate of prostitute Cheng Shi, but she certainly lost her chance to *cong liang* by marrying Zheng Zixin (Zhang Kentang 1969, 11/5a–b).

A 1655 case from Beijing confirms that the opportunity to *cong liang* was not available to all in the early Qing any more than in the Ming. In this case, a man named Yang Wu was arrested for creating a disturbance at the Gate of Heavenly Peace; he had tried to appeal a lawsuit directly to the emperor, but was prevented by guards from entering the Forbidden City. It is Yang's lawsuit that concerns us.

In 1648, he had borrowed 200 taels of silver from a Manchu of the Red Banner named Mengwoerdai, in order to buy a prostitute named Guige; he paid a "body price" (*shen jia*) of 180 taels. Yang was not a pimp but a commoner, and he apparently intended to marry Guige (in his testimony, he refers to her as his "wife"—*furen*—but elsewhere, the case record simply calls her his "prostitute"—*ji nü* or *chang fu*). Yang could neither repay the loan nor keep up with interest payments, however, and finally, in 1651, Mengwoerdai sued him at the court of the Northern City Administrator (*beicheng lishiguan*). This official ordered that the interest be forgiven but the principal repaid, and that the prostitute be handed over to Mengwoerdai until Yang Wu could repay him. But Yang never came up with the money, and finally, in 1655, Mengwoerdai sued him a second time. It was at this point that Yang Wu made his rash attempt to appeal and, when turned away, smashed a sculpted lion on one of the stone pillars in front of the Gate of Heavenly Peace.

The Board of Punishment sentenced Yang to strangulation for creating a disturbance at a palace gate. In addition, it settled the lawsuit by permanently awarding the prostitute Guige to his creditor—offsetting 180 taels of the debt with her body price—and ordering Yang's family to pay the remaining twenty taels. An imperial edict approved the judgment (but commuted Yang's penalty to exile).

In this case, since the woman in question was a debased-status prostitute, the judiciary itself treated her as a commodity to be bought, sold, and used as collateral for a loan. The Northern City Administrator's judgment even provided that her sexual labor should stand in lieu of interest payments as long as the loan remained unpaid—why else turn her over to the creditor? In no other way did the Board of Punishment concern itself with Guige; no testimony of hers appears in the record. Yang Wu had bought her out of prostitution to make her his wife, and his dangerously rash behavior at the palace gate tells us something of his despair. Nevertheless, in the board's recorded deliberations, the possibility that Guige might *cong liang* simply never comes up (XT, 1180/SZ 12.10.17; XT, 1197/ SZ 12.10.28).

This case provides instructive contrast with our other Beijing example from the same year, cited in the previous section, in which Zhu Xiu sold his concubine Cai Shi into prostitution (several of the same ministers helped judge both cases and appear as signatories on memorials related to both). An explicit double standard guided the judiciary: a prostitute's body and sexual labor were commodities, but a commoner wife's were supposed to be something else. The priority in such adjudication was not to suppress prostitution, let alone the commodification of women, but rather to maintain clear status boundaries and to channel behavior in order to reinforce them.

The Prosecution of "Abetting Illicit Sexual Intercourse"

Another form of boundary transgression was the "commoner" crime of "abetting illicit sexual intercourse." The Yuan lawmakers who first conceptualized this crime defined it, as we have seen, as "commoners debasing themselves" (*liang wei jian*) by acting in a manner appropriate to debased-status prostitutes rather than commoners. Four cases from the early Qing dynasty illustrate roughly the range of scenarios that were prosecuted under this rubric.

In a 1655 case from Qimen County, Anhui, a man named Ye Qin

"abetted" (*zong rong*) his wife Zhang Shi to engage in "consensual illicit sex" for some four years with one Wang Xiao (the case report also characterizes their crime as "selling illicit sex," *mai jian*). Wang even moved in with the couple. In return, he supplied Ye Qin with food and wine, and eventually lent him sufficient money to travel to Jiangxi and go into the grain business (Zhang Shi stayed behind with Wang Xiao). While in Jiangxi, Ye Qin "obsessively patronized prostitutes" (*lian piao*) and contracted syphilis (*yang mei du*), which manifested itself in painful running sores. Having failed in business, spent all his money, and fallen seriously ill, Ye Qin finally returned home. After living with his wife and Wang Xiao for a couple of months more, and quarreling with both of them, he hanged himself.

At first, the county magistrate supposed that Ye Qin might have committed suicide in reaction to his wife's "illicit sexual intercourse"—in which case, she and her partner, Wang Xiao, could have been liable for severe penalties under the statute against "causing the death of another person because of illicit sex" (*yin jian wei bi ren zhi si*). But everyone in the community had known that Ye was pimping his wife, and the magistrate's superiors, upon reviewing the case, decided that Ye Qin probably had killed himself in despair over his own illness and lack of prospects. Therefore, Zhang Shi and Wang Xiao should be punished with a beating only, for the crime of "illicit sexual intercourse." (The case record does not say whether the woman was ordered returned to her natal lineage, but the point may have been moot, since her husband was dead already.)

In this case, the husband's pecuniary interest could hardly have been more explicit, but his wife's extramarital relations were treated very differently from the tolerated prostitution of debased persons. Had the couple been legitimate prostitutes, Zhang Shi and Wang Xiao would have been released without punishment, once they were cleared of blame for Ye Qin's death (as we shall see in a later section of this chapter). Indeed, the case record draws an implied contrast between Ye Qin's sexual escapades in Jiangxi—characterized with the legally neutral term "patronizing prostitutes" (*piao*)—and the criminal "illicit sexual intercourse" of his wife, which he had "abetted" for profit (XT, 1371/SZ 13.8.5).

A 1645 homicide in Linqing Department, Shandong, involved a peasant named Zheng Er, who "abetted his wife to act as a prostitute" (*zong qi wei chang*):

In 1641 there was famine, and Zheng Er (who has already been punished, and is now in custody, *yi fa luo jin zai guan*) fell into poverty and had a hard time getting by. His wife, Li Shi (who has already been punished, and is now in custody), was young and attractive, so Wu Daode supplied Zheng Er with several taels of silver to buy grain for survival, and then privately engaged in consensual illicit sexual intercourse (*si tong he jian*) with Li Shi.

Here, the pejorative adverb "privately" (*si*) reinforces the criminality of the verb that follows, "to engage in illicit sexual intercourse" (*tong jian*). Indeed, despite the phrase "to act as a prostitute" (*wei chang*) appearing once in this case report, there is no question that Zheng Er and Li Shi were commoners, and that their sale of sexual services constituted criminal activity. (Nowhere in the record are they called *chang hu*, *shui hu*, or *yue hu*, as is the rule in discussions of tolerated prostitution.)

Having survived the famine, the couple apparently continued to depend on sex work as their primary source of income. Wu Daode remained Li Shi's principal customer until 1645, when he was killed by another man who wanted to sleep with her. The investigation of that homicide exposed the "illicit sexual intercourse" that had occurred, and both husband and wife received beatings (XT, 1607/ SZ ?).[44]

A 1650 homicide in Gan Department, Gansu, involved a slightly different scenario: "Huang Yu abetted his wife Yang Shi to engage in illicit sexual intercourse with Liang Mingkun," in exchange for interest-free loans of money and cloth. Huang had assumed that he need not repay the "loans," because he understood them to be payment for Yang Shi's sexual services. But Liang thought that having agreed to make the loans was itself compensation enough—perhaps he saw Yang Shi's sexual services as "interest"—and he demanded repayment of the principal. Such stinginess enraged Huang Yu, and he and a friend beat Liang Mingkun to death. For this homicide, Huang was sentenced to strangulation. Yang Shi was sentenced to a beating with the heavy bamboo, for her "illicit sexual intercourse" with Liang Mingkun, but in the end she avoided punishment because of an amnesty.

Huang and Liang's misunderstanding over the terms of compensation highlights the informal nature of much of the "commoner" prostitution found in Qing legal records. But such ambiguities mattered not at all to the judiciary, which would have punished this "illicit sexual intercourse" in exactly the same way, since the woman in question was a commoner wife, regardless of compensation or motive (XT, 1444/SZ 13.10.18).

The point is underscored by a fourth example, in which no money changed hands at all. This 1654 case from Bao'an Department, Shanxi, concerned a peasant named Fu Rong. One day, he entered the home of neighbor Yang Youde, found that Yang was away, and demanded that Yang's wife, Shi Shi, sleep with him. "Since Rong was strong and violent she could not struggle free, and so was sexually polluted by him. Thereafter, whenever Rong saw that Yang Youde was away, he would go to Shi Shi's home and engage in illicit sexual intercourse with her." Yang Youde found out what was going on, but "he feared that Fu Rong would use his strength to harm him, so he tolerated it (*rong ren*)."

Later, Fu Rong murdered another woman while attempting to rape her, and upon prosecution, his sexual relations with Shi Shi came out in court. As we have seen, when judging sex offenses the Ming-Qing judiciary interpreted subsequent consent as negating initial coercion; therefore, Fu Rong's intercourse with Shi Shi legally counted as "consensual." Moreover, Yang Youde's failure to intervene amounted to "abetting" (*zong*) his wife's "consensual illicit sexual intercourse." As the judgment summarized, "Yang Youde abetted his wife to engage in illicit sexual intercourse, and Shi Shi's lasciviousness knew no bounds of propriety. Therefore, it is appropriate under the law that they be beaten with the heavy bamboo." Each was sentenced to 90 blows, according to the statute on a husband "abetting or tolerating" (*zong rong*) his wife's illicit sex.[45]

These four early Qing cases display a range of scenarios in which husbands knew of their wives' extramarital sexual activity. In the first two examples, husbands received money and goods in explicit exchange for their wives' sexual services. In the third case, both the husband and his wife's sexual partner understood there to be some sort of *quid pro quo* involved, but they disagreed on exactly what the terms had been. In the last case, a bully forced himself on a woman, and she and her husband submitted out of fear, without receiving any compensation. But such differences did not matter to the judiciary, which defined and punished all four scenarios as cases of husbands "abetting" their wives to engage in "illicit sexual intercourse."

The available evidence suggests that Yuan dynasty law had defined this commoner crime in terms of the exchange of money for sex; nevertheless, cash payment had warranted no extra penalties, even in the Yuan. Ming-Qing law simply broadened the crime's definition to include *any* toleration of a wife's extramarital sexual activity, regardless of motive.

The prosecution of extramarital sexual intercourse in these particular contexts underscores what we have already seen in legislation from the Yuan through the early Qing: that the purpose of law during this long period was not to ban a certain kind of conduct per se, but rather to regulate that conduct in such a way as to make the performance of distinct moral standards a definitive mark of different levels of status. Laws against "abetting illicit sex" aimed to enforce among commoners a commoner standard of wifely chastity and husbandly responsibility.

The Lenient Criminal Standard Applied to Prostitutes

The legal status of prostitutes involved a paradox: like other debased groups, they were despised and discriminated against in various ways by the law. At the same time, however, the very basis for despising them—the assumption that they could not conform to commoner standards of sexual and familial morality—meant that sometimes they received treatment far more *lenient* than that accorded to commoners. In effect, they could get away with behavior considered criminal for commoners.

Of course, the obvious example of such excused behavior was sexual intercourse outside marriage: what was criminal for commoners served as the tolerated livelihood of prostitute households. But the logic of this exemption extended to some other situations as well, as we see in the following cases from the first reign period of the Qing dynasty.[46]

Rival Customers Fight Over a Prostitute: Is She to Blame?

A homicide that occurred in 1650 in Weinan County, Shaanxi, involved rivals for the attention of a prostitute (she is identified as *yue fu* and *chang ji*) named Wang Yuwa ("Jade Girl Wang"). A pair of brothers, Li Jiuwei and Li Jiuren, who had patronized the prostitute for years, felt intense jealousy toward another of her longtime customers, their cousin Li Bu. In the sixth lunar month of the year, the village held a festival at the local Guan Gong temple to celebrate the god's birthday, and *yue* entertainers, including the prostitute Wang Yuwa, were hired to perform as part of the festival. After the ceremony, Wang Yuwa was sitting and drinking wine with Li Bu out in the open. Jiuwei and Jiuren saw them together, were overcome by jealous rage, and beat Li Bu to death.

The brothers were sentenced to strangulation. More pertinent to us is the judicial treatment of Wang Yuwa. There was nothing illegal about her prostitution; this case involved no crimes of "illicit sex." But since it was her public drinking with Li Bu that had provoked the violence, the county magistrate sentenced her to a beating with the heavy bamboo, according to the statute against "doing inappropriate things." As he reasoned in his report on the case, "although she did not play a role in the beating, it was Yuwa who engendered this disaster, and she should be punished for it."

When the judicial commissioner of Shaanxi reviewed the case, he accepted the entire judgment *except for this detail*. "For Wang Yuwa to drink wine with Li Bu was utterly normal conduct for a *yue* prostitute (*yue fu chang tai*); what crime did she commit? Her sentence of the heavy bamboo should be corrected immediately; this is appropriate in terms of both common sense and the law (*qing fa yun xie*)." The judicial commissioner's opinion received imperial approval, and Wang Yuwa was released without punishment.

In short, Wang Yuwa avoided punishment *precisely because she was a prostitute*. The Qing judiciary would have treated a commoner wife who placed herself in the same position far more harshly.[47]

Judicial Tolerance of Marital Prostitution

Paradoxically, the legislation related to prostitution generally envisioned that activity as taking place within a context of marriage and household. This view was as true for the legally tolerated prostitution associated with debased status as it was for the illegal promiscuity of commoners. As we have seen, from the Yuan dynasty through the Qing, the basic approach to commoner husbands pimping their wives was to sentence both sexual partners and the husband to the same beating suffered by ordinary adulterers, and also to order the couple divorced. Such conduct broke the moral bond that defined legitimate marriage, making divorce necessary.

But what about the marriages of debased-status prostitutes? Most early Qing case records of tolerated prostitution that I have seen involve husband and wife teams in which the husband pimped his wife and they lived together off her earnings. On the basis of my small sample, it is hard to say just how common this arrangement might have been, although the lack of particular comment in these documents suggests that it was common enough. But for our purposes, the interesting point is that the Qing judiciary *accepted* such marriages.

This marital context of tolerated prostitution is illustrated by a homicide case, memorialized in 1660, which occurred in a market town in Wei Department, Shanxi. A resident of the town named Guo Liu ran a brothel (*yin dian*) where he employed three husband and wife teams. The memorial refers to these couples variously as *shui hu*, *chang fu*, and *ji*. As the memorial explains, they "had moved into Guo Liu's brothel, each couple renting a room and receiving customers to earn a living. If any prostitutes moved out, they had to settle the room bill with Guo Liu before they would be allowed to leave the brothel." A man named Jia Yizhao had opened a butcher shop in a neighboring village; he wanted to expand his business by moving in prostitutes and serving meat and wine to customers. Jia knew of Guo Liu's prostitutes, and through a mutual friend, Guo Ziqu, he tried, without success, to persuade Guo Liu to let one of the couples leave the brothel and set up at his shop. "Then, without notifying brothel-keeper Guo Liu, [Guo Ziqu and Jia Yizhao] improperly talked things over with [one of the couples], and agreed that they would go with Jia Yizhao and move to his village." When Guo Liu realized the couple was gone, he attacked Guo Ziqu with a knife, and he ended up killing a nephew of Ziqu's who intervened.

Guo Liu was sentenced to strangulation after the assizes for "homicide in a fight." The memorial makes no mention of "illicit sexual intercourse." Nor does it hint at any illegality in the prostitution, pimping, and brothel-keeping; the prostitute couples appear only as witnesses. In fact, the memorial suggests that the brothel-keeper's anger was justified: Jia Yizhao and Guo Ziqu were sentenced to a beating with the heavy bamboo under the statute on "doing inappropriate things—severe cases," since they had "started the quarrel" by "removing a prostitute from Guo Liu's brothel" (MQ, 36-116).

A second example is a 1653 case from Beijing, in which a prostitute went to court to seek justice for her murdered husband. The prostitute (*chang fu*) Zhang Yi and her husband-pimp (*shui hu*) Liu Er worked in a brothel run by another pimp (*shui hu*). One night, a man named Wang Lu came in drunk with a group of friends and demanded to sleep with a young prostitute (*chang ji*) named Qiang'er, who was managed by Liu Er and Zhang Yi. But Qiang'er was already busy with another customer. The men would not accept this, and they grabbed Zhang Yi to press their demand. She dodged away, and Liu Er demanded that they leave. Instead of leaving, they dragged him into the street and beat him to death. The next day, the brothel-keeper and Zhang Yi reported her husband's killing to the local *bao-jia* head, who reported it in turn to his superior, the censor in charge of security for central Beijing. The culprits were quickly arrested; Wang Lu was sentenced to strangulation, and his accomplices to beatings and exile, for "homicide in a fight."

Everything about the case record suggests that the brothel was well known to local authorities, and that the marital prostitution it hosted was perfectly acceptable to them. The memorial on this case begins by quoting prostitute Zhang Yi's plaint reporting her husband's murder:

> My husband Liu Er depended on my body to make a living (*ling shen chen du*). On the evening of the twenty-second of this month, Wang Lu and two other evil rogues caused a disturbance at our brothel (*chao wo*) and grabbed at me. My husband reasoned with them, explaining that there are rules prohibiting such conduct; how could they dare to behave in this manner? His words angered them, so they savagely beat him to death. . . . Violent rogues perpetrated this evil! The taking of human life concerns Heaven itself!

The memorial presents Zhang Yi's indignation at face value, despite her announcement in the petition's very first line that she was a prostitute pimped by her husband. Indeed, the basic thrust of the memorial is that the denizens of this brothel were law-abiding, responsible people, mean status and disgusting occupation notwithstanding. If this seems like a contradiction, we must bear in mind that debased-status prostitutes *in their place* constituted an essential part of the imagined social order. Their stigmatized occupation served the important purpose of defining, by contrast, the standard to which the great majority of subjects were expected to conform.

On the other hand, a gang of drunken rogues who would beat a man to death in public represented a threat that had to be ruthlessly suppressed. The memorial characterizes Liu Er's killers as "vulgar thugs" (*xia liu ba gun*) and "riffraff of the marketplace" (*shi jing wu lai zhi tu*). It mattered not at all that these dangerous criminals were commoners (XT, 579/SZ 10.4.25).

The Moral Content of a Prostitute Couple's Marriage

We can conclude that the judiciary did not consider marriage to be incompatible with the sex work of debased-status prostitutes.

Apparently, then, marriage meant something different for these people than it did for commoners, at least from a judicial standpoint. Three other homicide cases (also from the early Qing) tell us something of this difference because their circumstances forced judges to address more explicitly the paradox of a wife pimped legally by her husband. In each case, a pimp-husband was murdered by customers who had slept with his prostitute-wife. These cases raised fundamental questions, given the centrality of sex to the ideology of wifely fidelity. What duty, if any, did a wife owe her husband if he were also her pimp? To what extent could she be blamed for her husband's death?

In a case from Datong County, Shanxi, memorialized in 1660 by the regional inspector for that province,[48] a mill-worker named Liu Qi murdered one Zhang Er, who was the husband and pimp of the prostitute Hou Shi. (The memorial refers to the couple variously as *"yue* workers," *"shui hu,"* and *"chang"*; in testimony, Hou Shi refers to herself as *"chang fu"* ["this prostitute"] instead of the term usually employed by commoner women, *xiao fu ren* ["this humble wife"].) According to the inspector's summary: "[Liu Qi had been] sleeping with Hou Shi as her customer, becoming so passionately infatuated that he could not give her up. Later, because Qi owed 600 cash for sleeping with her, Zhang Er and his wife pressed him to pay, and Qi began to harbor hatred in his heart." One night Zhang Er stayed at the mill where Liu Qi worked because Hou Shi was occupied at home with a customer; Liu took advantage of the occasion to strangle him. Next day, Hou Shi came to the mill looking for her husband. Liu Qi presented her with a handkerchief, and "proposed marriage" *(jiang jia qu)*: "Why don't you *cong liang* and leave with me, and we'll become a married couple *(cong liang qu cheng liang kouzi ba)*?"[49] Hou Shi did not reject the proposal out of hand but continued searching for her husband; that night she again slept with Liu Qi. The next day, Zhang Er's corpse was discovered and Liu Qi and Hou Shi were arrested—the conversation about marriage had been overheard, casting suspicion on them both.

Liu Qi was sentenced to beheading after the assizes for "purposeful homicide." At first, the county magistrate assumed that Hou Shi had been in on the murder, and sentenced her to death by slicing *(ling chi chu si)*. That decision was overturned, however, and a new investigation cleared her of direct complicity. Nevertheless, she was condemned according to the old Ming statute (preserved in the Qing code) that mandated

When a wife or concubine engages in illicit sexual intercourse with another man . . . if the man who has engaged in illicit sex with her (*jian fu*) murders her husband on his own, then the wife who has engaged in illicit sex (*jian fu*) shall still be sentenced to strangulation after the assizes, even if she did not know [in advance of his plan to murder her husband] (*sui bu zhi qing*). (DC, 285-00)

However, this judgment was rejected by the regional inspector. The statute quoted above was designed to protect a righteous *commoner* husband against the consequences of betrayal—*jian*—by his wife. If her lover murdered her husband, then she should be punished for providing the *motive* for that murder. In rejecting the statute's applicability, the regional inspector noted the fundamental difference between Hou Shi and a commoner wife:

If Hou Shi knew of the murder in advance, then her penalty should not be as light as strangulation; if she did *not* know, then it seems that only the murder itself should be punished. There is a difference between a prostitute and a commoner (*chang fu yu liang ren you jian*)—would it really be appropriate to apply a statute on "illicit sexual intercourse" to this case (*lü yi jian tiao yi yi yun xie fou hu*)?

He sent the case back to the county for reconsideration, and the magistrate agreed that since she had not participated in the murder, "Hou Shi should be released." The decision was approved at all levels of review, including the Three High Courts of Judicature, which reported: "It has been determined that Hou Shi knew nothing of the murder, and, moreover, she is not the same as a commoner wife (*qie yu liang fu bu tong*); therefore, she need not be punished." Imperial rescript confirmed the judgment (MQ, 36-117).

The same issue complicated a homicide case reviewed in 1658 by the regional inspector for Jiangsu. This case, from Fengyang Prefecture, centered on a prostitute household made up of the husband-pimp Huang Jing and his wife-prostitute Zhang Shi. They lived and received customers on a boat, as was common among debased-status groups in the Yangzi and Pearl River deltas (the memorial refers to them simply as *tu chang*, "local prostitutes," but they may well have been *dan hu*). Two customers, Li Baisuo and Yang Gunzi, owed the couple money for having slept with Zhang Shi many times. One night, Huang demanded payment, and cursed them when they refused. Enraged, the two customers gouged out his eyes and stabbed him to death. Zhang Shi witnessed the killing but played no part in it; still, she was initially sentenced to strangulation after the assizes according to the "even if she did not know . . . " clause cited in the last example. Later, however, the regional inspector reviewed the case, and he too decided that the statute did not apply, given the couple's status as husband-pimp and wife-prostitute:

With regard to Zhang Shi's relationship to Huang Jing: although in *name* they were husband and wife, in *fact* they were disordered prostitutes (*ming sui fu fu, shi xi luan chang*). Li Baisuo and Yang Gunzi had long been infatuated with Zhang Shi's body, but were reluctant to pay the debt they owed for sleeping with her. Huang Jing demanded the money and cursed them, and for this reason he ended up being stabbed to death.

Key here is the rhetorical juxtaposition of "husband and wife" (*fu fu*) with "disordered prostitutes" (*luan chang*); as explained in Chapter 2, the word *luan* implies the complete disruption of moral order. In short, the moral standard of marriage binding on commoners could not be applied to the debased category to which the couple belonged; Zhang Shi's relationship to Huang Jing could be considered marriage only in the most superficial sense. Therefore, the facts of the case contradicted the purpose of the statute, which was to punish a wife whose betrayal of her husband provoked his murder.

But there was a catch: the regional inspector believed that Zhang Shi had to answer for her conduct *after* the murder:

It is abominable that, being on the scene, she did not cry out for help; nor, later on, did she report the murder to the authorities. Instead, she followed the criminals in flight, acting entirely without conscience (*sang xin wang gu*). It is on this point that Zhang Shi is to be judged; [when confronted with this conduct in court,] she became tongue-tied, and offered no excuse for herself (*jie she wu ci yi*).

Therefore, the inspector reasoned, although the "illicit sex" statute did not fit, the recommended sentence of strangulation "can be considered a proper balance of the facts with the law" (*yun cheng qing fa zhi ping*). Therefore, he approved the penalty, but found no specific law to justify it. This balancing effort highlights the difficulty of applying legal categories to a prostitute who was a wife. After explaining that the couple could not properly be considered husband and wife, the inspector condemned the woman, in effect, for not showing the loyalty proper to a wife. Her betrayal was not sexual promiscuity, he argued, but rather joining her husband's murderers in flight. This awkward conclusion implies that even for central judicial officials, the complexity of social practice might undermine the legal fiction of fixed status boundaries. (It is not known, however, whether this judgment received final approval from the inspector's superiors—MQ, 33-63.)

A third example is a homicide that took place in Pingyuan County, Shandong, in 1645. A yamen runner named Li Qifu was the principal customer of prostitute (*chang fu*) Li Shi, and had become infatuated with her. This situation had continued for "many years," until late 1644, when Qifu ran out of money, and the prostitute's husband-pimp Li Wenming cut off his access to her. At this point, Qifu persuaded Li Shi to run away with him, but Wenming filed charges against him at the county court, where the magistrate ordered Li Shi returned to her husband-pimp, and strictly forbade her and Qifu from seeing each other again. But Qifu defied this restraining order: in early 1645 he murdered Wenming, and once again absconded with the prostitute. The couple made it to nearby En County and remained at large for about a year, passing themselves off as an ordinary married couple, until finally being apprehended.

Li Qifu was sentenced to beheading for "purposeful homicide"; as the magistrate opined, "even though the victim was inferior and debased, the offender cannot avoid being beheaded to requite his murder (*sui xi xia jian, nan mian zhan di*)." Li Shi, it was judged, "did not know of the murder in advance"; nevertheless, as in the two previous examples, she was first sentenced to strangulation, according to the "even if she did not know . . ." provision. Upon review, however, Li Shi's sentence was overturned, according to the same logic cited in the other cases. As one of the reviewing judges explained: "A prostitute-wife cannot be punished on the basis of the moral bond between husband and wife (*zhi ruo chang fu bu ze yi yi*)." Running away with the murderer of her husband had been egregious—indeed, in our last example, the regional inspector of Jiangsu had sentenced Zhang Shi to strangulation on that basis alone, though we do not know whether his decision received final approval. But in the present case, Li Shi suffered only a beating; this judgment was confirmed by the imperial vermillion.[50]

This decision follows the pattern of the other two, in that the prostitute-wife was not held to the putative standard of "morality" (*yi*) that legally bound commoner couples. But this case adds an extra dimension to our understanding of the legal treatment of prostitute couples—namely, that an early Qing county magistrate would actually issue a restraining order to protect a pimp-husband's control over his prostitute-wife. Now if the magistrate of Pingyuan County had applied the law that governed commoners, he would

have found Li Wenming guilty of "abetting" his wife Li Shi to "engage in illicit sexual intercourse" with Li Qifu, and he would have
ordered them beaten and *divorced*. But instead, he returned the
prostitute-wife to her pimp-husband and prohibited her from contact with the customer who threatened to steal her away.

This remarkable episode suggests that a husband who was a pimp
enjoyed a "sexual monopoly" over his wife much purer than that
possessed by a commoner husband. It was a sexual monopoly that
he could legally rent out to other men. It was less conditional, having no basis in a mutual bond of moral obligation that might be broken, and closer perhaps to the naked property right of a slave owner.
"Official prostitutes" (*guan ji*) were traditionally slaves of the imperial state, but it seems from this example that a "private" prostitute-wife was something like the slave of her husband-pimp as well.
The law accepted that women of this status were commodities, pure
and simple, even as it demanded that commoner wives be treated
differently (XT, 482/SZ 9.11.24 and 1565/SZ ?).

To conclude, different expectations about the moral performance
of status groups implied different standards of criminal liability. In
some situations, the result was stricter treatment of commoners
than of debased-status prostitutes. The central judiciaries of Yuan
through early Qing saw marriage and other norms binding on commoners as fundamentally incompatible with prostitution. The commoner crime of illicit intercourse was banned precisely because it
was seen as a betrayal of marriage. But such norms could not be applied to the debased social stratum characterized by prostitution. To
say their conduct was *legal* does not quite grasp the point; more accurately, they were considered beneath the law.[51] Their essence was
moral disorder, and thus it made no sense to hold them accountable
for conduct that violated moral standards. At the same time, every
effort was made to mark such people as different, and to safeguard
the boundaries that separated them from decent society.

Legal Fiction Versus Social Fact

The evidence surveyed in this chapter testifies to the enormous
effort that went into regulating prostitution as a means to status
distinction. But the same evidence highlights the obstacles encountered by that effort. A basic tension characterized the entire pre-
1723 discourse of prostitution and debased status: the tension between an ideal social order that fixed people in place and a social

reality of growing complexity and fluidity. The imperial project to construct clear-cut status strata characterized by distinct standards of sexual morality was increasingly undermined by the reality of movement across all boundaries, both geographic and socioeconomic.

Everything we know about the big secular changes over the last thousand years of the imperial era suggests that movement across boundaries steadily increased, in conjunction with the expansion of population, cultivated acreage, urbanization, and commercialization; the decline of aristocracy and bonded labor; and the rise of the gentry and a free peasantry. These long-term processes were occasionally punctuated by the radical dislocation of dynastic collapse. To be sure, this long era witnessed much change of a cyclical nature, and many moments of "retreat," with the founders of each new dynasty trying once again to fix people in place, both geographically and socially. But by the High Qing, China's social structure had become far more fluid, and its population far more mobile, than they had been a few centuries before. It is no surprise that by the end of the seventeenth century, a legal fiction that linked morality to fixed, heritable status distinctions would have become a tenuous anachronism.

The earlier our sources, the stronger our impression of tight state control over sex work. By the mid-seventeenth century, criminal case records give the impression of what Wang Shunu calls "private enterprise prostitution" flourishing on a wide scale, and we find little evidence of direct supervision by the Bureau of Instruction or other imperial agencies. Nevertheless, even as early as the Yuan dynasty, the edicts that imposed sumptuary distinctions between status strata complained that members of prostitute households could not be distinguished from commoners or even members of the elite. The founders of the Yuan, Ming, and Qing dynasties each in turn felt compelled to impose such sumptuary rules, which were reiterated many times by their successors. Obviously, status distinction could not be taken for granted, even as far back as the Yuan: there was nothing self-evident or self-perpetuating about it.

The contradiction embodied by the elite courtesan posed a similar problem. Susan Mann describes how elite males of the High Qing resisted acknowledging the vulgar origins of such cultured, alluring women (1997, 138). We have seen, too, how the literati of the late Ming fantasized about rescuing women who did not "deserve" to be prostitutes. The cognitive dissonance suffered by such men came from their confrontation with a *status performance* (sophistication, literacy, skilled familiarity with high culture, "righteousness") that contradicted the fact of these women's legal debasement—all the more so in an era when female literacy and cultural achievement increasingly served as marks of elite pride (Ko 1994; Mann 1997).

On a more mundane level, we have the simple fact of geographic mobility. The legal fiction of status distinction assumed a society in which everyone's place—in family, community, social hierarchy, and geographic space—was fixed and transparent to all. Against that assumption, consider Magistrate Zhang Kentang's case of the pimp "laundering" a prostitute by moving her from place to place, so that eventually he could pass her off as a commoner woman eligible for proper marriage. As Magistrate Zhang wondered, "in a situation like this, how might a respectable commoner possibly evade such a trap (*zhi yu ru ci, liang min qi he dao yi tuo ci jing ye*)?" (1969, 11/5a–b). Or consider the situation seen in more than one early Qing case: if a prostitute absconded with a customer and they made it across the county line, no one would have any way to distinguish them from an ordinary commoner couple. By the early Qing, if not before, running away had become as effective a way to *cong liang* as any. As such examples suggest, movement and anonymity constituted a vital threat to the fiction of fixed, debased status.

Then again, consider the cases of commoner women being sold into prostitution narrated above. We know of these women only because they were rescued by their natal families, sometimes after the passage of years. It is safe to assume that if their own families had not tracked them down, then no one ever would have rescued them, literati fantasies notwithstanding. Moreover, as long as no one *claimed* these women as commoners, they had indeed become debased-status prostitutes, for legal as well as practical purposes. (Thus, the customers who had slept with them were not charged with "illicit sexual intercourse.") There must have been countless others sold into prostitution who were never rescued.

Finally, we have the imperial state's need to construct a criminal category of "abetting illicit intercourse," to cope with the fact that some commoners did sex work. The inclusion of such a crime in legal codes from Yuan through Qing makes it obvious that not all commoners were willing, for whatever reason, to live up to the putative "commoner" standard of morality they were charged with. The need to discipline such people, to rein their behavior back in within status bounds, shows more clearly than any other evidence the utter artificiality of the concept of status performance.

In practice, it appears that late imperial magistrates sometimes tacitly accepted the sort of self-debasement that, on paper, was so strictly prohibited. We find the evidence in two early Qing criminal cases that involve husband-wife teams engaged in sex work. The narration of these cases uses all the status-based terms for acceptable prostitution, and no one is prosecuted for "illicit sexual intercourse." But each record notes in passing how the couple *began* their career of sex work: "long before," the husband had taken his wife out and made her work as a prostitute, in one case because of poverty (XT, 1062/SZ 12.7.3), in the other because she had committed adultery (XT, 1335/SZ 13.r5.17 and 1644/SZ ?). It is clear that both couples began their marriages as ordinary commoners, but through a process of years of incorrigible self-debasement, they had effectively lost that status in the eyes of the jurists drafting these case reports. The only difference between such cases and those we have seen in which commoner couples were prosecuted for "abetting illicit sexual intercourse" is the sheer length of time the couples had been at it, and, perhaps, the number of customers the women had slept with over this longer period. It is as if jurists accepted that beyond some unspecified point, there was simply no use in trying to reimpose a commoner standard through punishment and divorce. Instead, they coped with such perverse couples by effectively demoting them to that stratum of people beneath the law. This demotion was reflected in the lack of prosecution for sex offenses, and in the vocabulary of tolerated debased-status prostitution used to describe them.

Regulating sexuality as a means of status distinction was a project fraught with ambiguity—and if anything, such ambiguity increased over time. The social reality of sex work was far messier than legal codes would have us believe, and the boundary between debased and commoner statuses, to the extent that it corresponded to real life at all, was far more permeable than late imperial dynasts would have liked. All the evidence points to the steady growth of a commercial sex market (what Wang Shunu terms "private enterprise prostitution") in which women circulated between marriage and prostitution on a widening scale. Such a market was anathema to imperial ideologues, who idealized the fiction of stable, self-reproducing populations fixed and distinguished in terms of legal status, occupation, moral standards, residence, and even dress. Even for debased-status prostitutes, whose commodification jurists accepted, the original paradigm had not been commerce, but rather penal servitude. But it was a paradigm that no longer made much sense by the seventeenth and eighteenth centuries.

The previous section included several cases that reveal a significant confusion about these issues within the early Qing judiciary. The key question was how to weigh a prostitute's moral responsibility for a homicide she had not herself committed—and in every case, a whole series of lower judges got it wrong, by condemning these women according to the standard appropriate to commoner wives. In the end, senior officials were able to put things right. But I suspect this confusion reflected a deeper paradigmatic crisis. If county magistrates and prefects did not understand how these principles should apply, then how many other people must have been confused?

There was no longer anything self-evident about the sexual dimension of status distinction, if there ever had been, even to many officials of the Qing judiciary. This growing gap, between an anachronistic legal fiction and the complexity of social practice, set the stage for the reforms of the eighteenth century.

The Extension of Commoner Standards: Yongzheng Reforms and the Criminalization of Prostitution

Previous Interpretations of the 1723 "Emancipation"

The last chapter began with a deceptively simple question: did Qing law prohibit prostitution? For eighty years after the founding of the dynasty, the answer was *both* "yes" and "no." As we have seen, imperial law long employed two distinct models of prostitution: (1) *criminal prostitution*, practiced by ordinary commoners and prosecuted, like ordinary adultery, as "illicit sexual intercourse"; and (2) *legally tolerated prostitution*, practiced by people of debased status under some degree of official supervision, supposedly as a form of penal servitude. Central case records from the early Qing provide ample evidence of this double standard operating in practice.

But during the Yongzheng reign (1723–35), the answer changed to an unequivocal "yes." Case records that postdate the Yongzheng reign reveal no sign of the second model: the legal space for tolerated sex work entirely disappeared. Every instance of prostitution that appears in these later cases was prosecuted simply as "illicit sexual intercourse." Much of the legal vocabulary of debased-status prostitution disappeared as well—I have never seen *yue hu* (or its derivatives) or *shui hu* mentioned in a post-Yongzheng case. The terms *chang* and *ji* survived, but their legal significance became the opposite of what it had been. They referred no longer to a category of people exempt from punishment, but instead to a category of *criminal*, like *zei* or *dao* ("robber"). In a conflation of long separate categories, any woman termed *chang* or *ji* was punished for "illicit sexual intercourse," along with her customers.

In effect, prostitution was completely prohibited, as the criminal category of illicit sexual intercourse expanded to cover this new territory. This innovation resulted from a series of well-known Yongzheng-era edicts that terminated official connections with sex work and eliminated the hereditary status labels associated with that activity, most notably *yue* status. But previous interpretations of the Yongzheng edicts have missed the prohibition of prostitution, concentrating instead on the question of whether the edicts should be considered an "emancipation" of the mean-status groups in question. Before getting into the evidence itself, we should consider these previous interpretations.

A Progressive Effort at Social Reform?

The most influential study by far is Terada Takanobu's seminal 1959 article, "The Yongzheng Emperor's Edicts of Emancipation for Debased-Status Groups." Terada addresses several aspects of the Yongzheng policy; for example, he suggests that it was in part an effort to take account of social change. By the late sixteenth century, many of the people registered with *yue* status no longer practiced the stigmatized entertainment professions; they owned and cultivated land, and could not easily be distinguished from commoners. In its last decades, the Ming dynasty began to treat these households more or less as ordinary peasants, at least for taxation purposes. From this standpoint, the edict on *yue* households updated the status regime by eliminating a category of household registration that no longer corresponded to social reality (1959, 126–27). This argument has great merit, complementing Wang Shunu's thesis that by the late Ming, "private enterprise prostitution" had begun to eclipse the age-old paradigm of "official prostitution" (1988); this is the aspect of Terada's article that has had the greatest influence on Susan Mann's work, although she focuses less on the motives behind the Yongzheng edicts than on their effect, in conjunction with socioeconomic change, of promoting the "slow erasure of old status barriers" (1997, 43). It also fits the evidence I have presented in Chapter 6, of a growing gap between the legal fiction of status performance and the social reality of boundary-crossing.

Terada also notes the role played by political propaganda. One of the arguments used to justify the Qing conquest was that Zhu Di's 1402 usurpation had rendered the subsequent transmission of the Ming throne illegitimate (Elman 1993, 66–67). In a variation on this theme, the Yongzheng Emperor and his successors represented his

elimination of *yue* status as the magnanimous rectification of an injustice committed by the former Ming—namely, Zhu Di's imposition of *yue* status on the dependents of his political enemies (Terada
1959, 124).[1] Qing propagandists of course found it convenient to ig-
nore the fact that *yue* status and sex work as a form of penal servitude had both been around for over a thousand years before 1402.[2]

But most important, Terada sees the edicts as a proactive effort to
achieve social reform. That is why he calls them edicts of "emancipation" (*kaihô*), a term not used at the time.[3] This emancipation
reflected the Yongzheng Emperor's "intense concern" for "social
problems" in his role as benevolent autocrat; he intended to eliminate "social discrimination" against most people of mean status.
The policy did "simplify status relations" (at least in legal terms),
and for this reason, Terada argues, its "progressive spirit" (*shinposei*) must be acknowledged (1959, 140). Nevertheless, he concedes,
"it cannot be denied" that the policy failed to achieve any practical
results commensurate with the emperor's goals. Emancipation took
place strictly "on the level of registered household status," without
any concrete measures being taken to liberate these people from
their debased occupations, and the groups in question continued to
suffer "social discrimination." Moreover, new laws of the Qianlong
era placed strict conditions on access to civil examinations for the
emancipated groups, including the requirement that at least three
generations pass before their descendants could take the exams. In
Terada's opinion, such conditions contradicted the Yongzheng policy: "In spite of being emancipated, those who could not satisfy
these conditions continued, as before, to find themselves locked out
of the route to becoming an official" (1959, 128). Therefore, although
the emancipation deserves to be considered "one of the Yongzheng
Emperor's excellent policies (*zensei*)," it failed to achieve any practical improvement in people's lives; in this respect, it "can only be
given a negative appraisal" (1959, 139–40).

A Less Positive Assessment?

If Terada reaches this conclusion on a note of regret, two eminent
Chinese historians are less positive in their assessment. T'ung-tsu
Ch'ü dismisses the Yongzheng edicts as insignificant, a position
necessary to sustain his thesis that Chinese law and social structure
remained essentially static for nearly two millennia: "After the law
had been crystallized by the Confucians, there were no funda-

mental changes in it up to the nineteenth century, as far as family and social classes are concerned. In spite of various changes in law, the fundamental characteristics of Chinese law remained the same" (1965, 283). Ch'ü blames the failure of China's legal tradition to "modernize" on its status- and family-based "particularism," which "prevented the development of universal law and abstract legal principles," and precluded attention to "such matters as individual rights." Specifically, there occurred "no significant change in the stratification system" (1965, 284). As to *yue* households and the other emancipated groups, "the removal of certain regionally defined groups from the 'mean' category should not be seen as the emancipation of the 'mean' people as a class." If anything, such adjustments "consolidated rather than weakened the stratification order." Like Terada, Ch'ü cites the Qianlong policy on examination access as proof of continuing discrimination that negated any emancipatory intent that the edicts may have had (1965, 132). Ch'ü further claims that "the category of the 'mean' people was extended in the Qing to include also prostitutes, entertainers and government runners; they were thus deprived of the right to take the civil service examinations" (1965, 282). This last assertion is a mystery: both Yuan and Ming dynasties had certainly imposed mean status on prostitutes and entertainers and barred them from the civil service (YD, 31/15b; MH, 77); moreover, *no* subject of the Qing empire enjoyed any "rights" that could be asserted against the imperial state.

Jing Junjian's thinking closely follows that of T'ung-tsu Ch'ü. Jing sees the Qing legal status system as "rigid" or "frozen" (*jiang hua*); he acknowledges that some change occurred, but only at an extremely slow pace, lagging far behind change in the economic and political realms (1993, 265). In his view, the Yongzheng elimination of *yue* status had little meaning, since it was not accompanied by a prohibition of prostitution (here he is mistaken), and since the business of prostitution was not stamped out (1993, 231–33). The edicts had no liberating effect on the lives of the relevant groups of people; nor did they touch domestic slavery, which Jing considers the heart of the debased-status system (1993, 265). Moreover, like Ch'ü, he argues that the "unreasonable" (*bu he li*) Qianlong policy on examination access proved emancipation to be a sham, by denying this portion of newly promoted commoners a basic "right" (*quanli*) of commoner status and giving other people renewed basis for prejudice against them (1993, 235).

Is "Emancipation" an Anachronism?

To summarize, Terada Takanobu sees the Yongzheng policy as a progressive attempt at social reform. T'ung-tsu Ch'ü and Jing Junjian dismiss the policy as insignificant, or even a sham. But all three scholars share the assumption that the important question is *emancipation*—by which they seem to mean liberation on the level of individual experience, with access to civil exams as the ultimate test of whether that was achieved. By that standard, they agree that the Yongzheng policy was a failure, at best. But behind this assumption, I suspect there lies a deeper disappointment in China's failure to modernize, a disappointment made most explicit by T'ung-tsu Ch'ü. In Ch'ü's words, "the emphasis on particularism . . . set a limit on the development in Chinese law," which finally began "modernization" only in response to "the impact of modern Western law" (1965, 284). The implied contrast, of course, is with the evolution of egalitarian individual rights seen in Western law since the eighteenth century. I would guess that Ch'ü and Terada in particular see the Yongzheng-Qianlong era as a missed opportunity to point Chinese history in a different direction, in the crucial century before the Opium War. The "emancipation" raises their hopes by *seeming* so modern and progressive (like Lincoln's Emancipation Proclamation)—as Philip Kuhn has astutely observed, "A free-wheeling labor market, the decline of personal dependency and servile status: these have great appeal to a twentieth-century Westerner, who associates them with Freedom and Progress" (1990, 35). But in the end these hopes are dashed.

This emphasis on emancipation, while not exactly wrong, may not be the most useful way to approach the problem. In particular, it would seem a strange anachronism to dismiss the Yongzheng edicts simply because they failed to liberate an oppressed people. We gain more insight, I believe, by considering the policy's implications for the regulation of sexuality. The Yongzheng Emperor certainly considered himself to be acting out of benevolence. However, he never intended to expand the *liberty* of the people whose legal status he changed; on the contrary, they were to be held to a far stricter standard of conduct than before. Rather, he sought (in his own words) "to extend the transformation of values" (*guang feng hua*), by expanding and making more uniform the application of moral standards and criminal penalties, and by intensifying surveillance by local officials.

"To Extend the Transformation of Values"

The 1723 Edict

Signs of change had appeared earlier in the Qing. Almost from the beginning of the dynasty, central authorities began widening the gap that separated imperial officials from prostitutes and courtesans. An edict of 1651 forbade "women of the Bureau of Instruction" from entering the palace and ordered that their court functions be taken over by eunuchs (QHS, 524/1043). According to Wang Shunu, this edict marked the end of "official prostitutes" (*guan ji*) within the Qing capital of Beijing, and began the systematic withdrawal of the imperial state from its traditional role in managing sex work (1988, 261). Moreover, as Susan Mann has explained, early Qing authorities succeeded in stamping out the widespread traditional custom whereby prostitutes and other *yue* personnel played a central role in local festivals—for example, the "welcoming of Spring" held annually in every county seat (1997, 26–27, 126–27).[4]

Decisive change came in 1723, upon the accession to the throne of the Yongzheng Emperor. According to ancient tradition, the death of an emperor and enthronement of his successor were accompanied by far-reaching amnesties. As the last chapter noted, several Ming emperors had marked the occasion by releasing some numbers of *yue* personnel of the Bureau of Instruction from slavery and status debasement. The Yongzheng Emperor opted for far more sweeping change: he eliminated the legal status category of *yue* households altogether, along with two other mean-status groups stigmatized in part by association with prostitution:

An exact investigation shall be made of people with *yue* household registration in the various provinces, and of the *duo* people and *gai* households of Zhejiang Province, and their [debased] registration shall be eliminated (*xiao ji*); they shall change their occupations to those proper to commoners (*gai ye wei liang*). If local bullies continue forcibly to shame them as before, or if any of them voluntarily pollute and debase themselves (*zi gan wu jian zhe*), then the offenders shall be punished according to law (*yi lü zhi zui*). Any magistrate who, upon receiving this order, does not exert himself to implement its provisions shall be reported by his Provincial Commander-in-Chief, and appropriate administrative sanctions shall be determined, as provided in the relevant substatute.   (DC, 076-06)

This edict elevated *yue* households and the other groups to commoner status. At the same time, by commanding that the affected households take up *liang* occupations, it prohibited the sex work that had marked their debased status. Entered into the Qing code as a substatute, this new law had the effect of eliminating the legal space for tolerating prostitution as a mark of debased status. At the same time, it imposed on local officials the burden of extirpating prostitution from their jurisdictions. Other edicts of the Yongzheng reign eliminated the mean legal status of groups such as *dan hu*, who were also associated with prostitution.[5]

What was the thinking behind the 1723 edict? The Yongzheng Emperor offered an explanation in a more personal statement issued in 1727, when he eliminated certain other debased statuses:

We take the reform of customs and mores (*yi feng yi su*) as a central concern. Those who have [bad] customs and mores that are long transmitted, and have not been able to shake them off, ought all be given a route toward self-renewal (*zi xin zhi lu*). Such was the case with the *yue* households of Shanxi and the *duo* people of Zhejiang, all of whom have had their mean status expunged (*chu qi jian ji*) and been made into commoners (*shi wei liang min*). This was in order to promote purity and a sense of shame (*li lian chi*), and to extend the transformation of values (*guang feng hua*).[6]

In the past, debased-status labels had long been understood as reflecting heritable moral taint; but here, the emperor implied that the labels themselves had become an obstacle to individual moral reform. For this reason, mass promotion to commoner status would serve as "a route toward self-renewal."

The emperor's reference to "self-renewal" (*zi xin*) had specific legal connotations. As early as the Han dynasty, this term was used to explain the purpose of imperial amnesties and other pardons: it signified the second chance granted to a criminal considered capable of reform. For example, a Yuan magistrate justified his decision to spare the lives of some robbers by arguing: "these people are all law-abiding commoners (*liang min*), who have been oppressed by hunger and cold, and who engaged in robbery because they simply had no choice; if we look upon them as robbers and inflict penalties accordingly, that will cut off their route toward self-renewal (*zi xin zhi lu*)" (*Yuan shi*, 4090).

Moreover, for centuries the standard argument against penalties of mutilation (like cutting off the ears or feet) was that they took away a criminal's "route toward self-renewal": even if he chose to reform, he could never escape the physical disfigurement or the socially crippling stigma of such a penalty (see, for example, *Song shu*, 1560). Jurists thought about tattooing in the same way. In the Liao dynasty, for example, criminals were tattooed with the name of their crime, for ready identification, but only on the shoulders (which were easily covered), not the face; a tenth-century edict explained that "some people who commit crimes later repent and renew themselves (*hui guo zi xin*), and good use can be made of them; but once their faces have been tattooed, the stigma stays with them for the rest of their lives (*zhong shen wei ru*)" (*Liao shi*, 943). Ming and Qing law mandated tattooing as part of the penalty for many crimes, on the face as well as the shoulders, but added that thieves and robbers who "can truly repent and reform" be allowed to remove their tattoos, after two or three years, and "once again become commoners" (*fu wei liang min*). The purpose was to give them "a route toward self-renewal" (DC, 281-18 and 20; *Qing shi gao*, 4196).[7]

Seen in this light, the Yongzheng Emperor's offer of "a route toward self-renewal" recalls the original paradigm of legal debasement and sex work as a form of punishment. Given their permanence and public stigma, these status labels, like the name of a crime tattooed on the face, prevented reintegration into commoner society, regardless of an individual's actual behavior or inner motivation. The elimination of these labels amounted to an amnesty that lifted a hereditary group punishment, giving the affected people an opportunity to rehabilitate themselves through good conduct.

But the emperor is referring not only to the ancestral crimes for which *yue* status had supposedly first been imposed. In addition, he appears to mean the sex work associated with debased status (that is, "bad customs and mores that are long transmitted"), that for commoners would always have been considered criminal conduct. Being "made into commoners" held debased people to the commoner standard of "purity and a sense of shame," thereby giving them an opportunity to reform their "customs and mores." But it also *required* them to do so: the imperial will aimed "to extend the transformation of values," whether people liked it or not. In other words, the emperor redefined the previously tolerated sex work itself as a crime that one might repent and move beyond, instead of a tolerated symptom of a fixed, debased condition. It followed that any future prostitution would be punished as a criminal offense.

The Reform of Imperial Music

In his 1727 explanation of the elimination of *yue* status (quoted above), the Yongzheng Emperor begins by saying, "We take the reform of customs and mores as a central concern." The phrase translated "the reform of customs and mores" (*yi feng yi su*; literally,

"move the wind and change the customs") is a standard trope for
the improvement of public morals. But it is also a specific allusion
to the classical Confucian discourse of the relationship between
music, morality, and good government—an allusion that any educated person in the eighteenth century would have recognized immediately. The specific allusion to music seems important, since after all, the emperor is talking about the "music (*yue*) households,"
including those who performed in state ceremonies and entertainments at the palace.

The phrase was traditionally attributed to Confucius, who is
quoted (in *The Classic of Filial Piety*) as saying: "For the reform of
customs and mores, there is nothing better than music (*yi feng yi su
mo shan yu yue*)" (*Xiao jing yi shu bu*, 100). The phrase also appears
in Xunzi's "Discourse on Music": "Hence, through the performance
of music the will is made pure, and through the practice of rites the
conduct is brought to perfection, the eyes and ears become keen, the
temper becomes harmonious and calm, and customs and mores are
easily reformed (*yi feng yi su*)" (B. Watson 1963, 116).[8]

According to Mark Edward Lewis, the classical discourse of music derived from the belief that wind (*feng*) existed in human physiology in the form of *qi*; hence "wind and the passions or impulses
that guided human action . . . had a direct, reciprocal influence"
(1990, 215). It followed that "men could consciously alter the behavior or nature of the winds in order to assure both improved public morals and bountiful harvests. The primary mechanism for such
alteration was music, a form of refined wind" (1990, 218). Music
both stimulated and gave form to basic human emotions. On the
positive side, this power of music to influence others could be harnessed as "a tool of the sage ruler who would guide lesser beings
through his mastery of true music" (1990, 221). In Xunzi's words,
"When correct sounds (*zheng sheng*) move a man, they cause a
spirit of obedience to rise, and when such a spirit has arisen, good
order results. As singers blend their voices with that of the leader,
so good or evil arise in response to the force that calls them forth"
(B. Watson 1963, 116). But the wrong kind of music could be dangerous, both morally and politically. In the *Analects*, Confucius warns
against the evil influence of music that was "licentious" (*yin*) (Waley 1938, 195–96), a warning echoed by Xunzi: "The gentleman does
not allow his ears to listen to licentious sounds (*yin sheng*), his eyes
to look at seductive beauty, or his mouth to speak evil words. . . .
When depraved sounds (*jian sheng*) move a man, they cause a spirit

of rebellion to rise in him, and when such a spirit has taken shape, then disorder (*luan*) results" (B. Watson 1963, 116). As this statement suggests, the potential danger of music was closely associated with the link between sexual and political disorder (note Xunzi's use of *yin*, *jian*, and *luan*). Lewis sums up this thinking as follows:

Just as correct music gave proper order to the winds and assured the state's prosperity and the people's obedience, so improper music would have the opposite effect. Through errors or innovations in musical performances the ruler could bring on drought . . . or pervert the people and bring ruin to the state. In one story in the *Guo yu*, the music master Shi Kuang prophesied the destruction of Jin's ruling lineage because the ruler delighted in the new music, the lascivious music of Zheng and Wei. . . . Music directly expressed the moral failings of those who produced it, and any who listened to corrupted music would be led to reproduce those failings.   (Lewis 1990, 220)

What does this classical discourse of music have to do with the Yongzheng reforms? The most important duty of the Bureau of Instruction, which had also traditionally supervised sex workers, was to supply musicians and dancers for court rituals and entertainments from among its *yue* personnel. Those who performed at the palace may have had no direct involvement with sex work, commercial or otherwise, but they bore the *yue* status label and its moral stigma all the same. From a classical perspective, the implications were irrefutable: music performed by debased people would reflect their moral debasement, with an inevitably corrupting effect on its listeners—in this case, the emperor, his family, and his most senior ministers. An emperor who allowed such corrupt musicians to perform in state ceremonies was courting disaster.

The Yongzheng Emperor apparently took his classics seriously, because in the same year that he "emancipated" the *yue* households he began a purge and reconstruction of the imperial music establishment. With the elimination of *yue* status, the hereditary musicians under the Bureau of Instruction were freed of their service obligations, and the emperor ordered the bureau to recruit new personnel strictly on the basis of musical training and skill, instead of *yue* status background (QHS, 524/1043). In 1725, he issued yet another edict mandating that "there be absolutely no officially supervised *yue* workers in any province" of the empire.[9] Then, in 1729, he eliminated the notorious Bureau of Instruction altogether, replacing it with a new "Office to Harmonize Sounds" (*he sheng shu*), which was incorporated into a new "Music Ministry" (*yue bu*) under the Board of Rites; at the same time, the positions of "master of actors" and "master of colors" were eliminated. The duties of the Office to Harmonize Sounds were strictly related to music (QHS, 524/1043; Ji Xu et al. 1989, 10/5b–6a; Hucker 1985, 598).

"To harmonize sounds" (*he sheng*) is another allusion to the classical discourse of music. *The Book of Rites* explains that using music to harmonize sounds is vital to good government, because music is one of the key "external things" that "stir" the human mind into movement (which "takes on form in sound"):

> Thus the former kings exercised caution in what might cause stirring. For this reason we have rites to guide what is intently on the mind; we have music to bring those sounds into harmony (*yi he qi sheng*); we have government to unify action; and we have punishment to prevent transgression (*jian*). Rites, music, government, and punishment are ultimately one and the same—a means to unify the people's minds and correctly execute the Way. (Owen 1992, 51)

In this way, the emperor replaced the "licentious music" of a morally debased caste with "harmonized sounds," to conform with the Confucian vision of music as a tool for moral order in the hands of a sage ruler. The reform of imperial music reflected the Neo-Confucian fundamentalism of the High Qing emperors, and went hand in hand with the "moral transformation" and the extension of penal law envisioned by the Yongzheng Emperor.

The Question of Access to Civil Examinations

Once *yue* households and related groups had been promoted to commoner status, there naturally arose the question of whether they would be permitted access to the civil examination system. In practical terms, the question mattered little to the great majority covered by the edicts; there is no evidence that large numbers were clamoring to sit for examinations. But defining the qualifications for entry into the civil service carried critical importance for the imperial state's conception of itself and of the social order it sought to uphold. Barring debased-status prostitutes and entertainers from the examination system had played a fundamental part in status distinction up to this time. Status promotion seemed to imply the elimination of such barriers, but the Yongzheng edicts did not explicitly address the question.

A policy on examination access was announced during the Qianlong reign. It represented a compromise between the continuing priority to exclude people tainted by association with debased or criminal conduct, and the Yongzheng mandate to offer the relevant groups "a route toward self-renewal." In 1771, the Board of Rites adopted the following proposal from the educational commissioner of Shaanxi (a province where many *yue* households had resided):

Members of the *yue* households and *gai* households that have had their debased status eliminated should be allowed to purchase degrees or sit for the civil service examinations, but only on condition that the close branches of their lineage have all maintained their purity and respectability (*qing bai zi shou*) for four generations; this time period should be calculated beginning from the day they officially reported that they would reform their occupations. Once the local official with jurisdiction has received affidavits from relatives and neighbors [testifying that the family has remained pure for four generations], then [the descendants of *yue* and *gai* households] should be allowed to do as they please [i.e., to purchase degrees or sit for the examinations]; unscrupulous rogues shall not be permitted to take advantage [of their ancestry] as a pretext to file charges or cause them trouble.

If an individual has himself shed debased status (*tuo ji*), or if only two generations have passed [since official report was made of reformed occupation], or if his own paternal uncles or aunts continue to practice such vulgar occupation (*wei ye*), then he shall absolutely not be permitted to join the ranks of officials or to try his luck at the examinations.

The *dan* households of Guangdong, the "nine surnames fishing households" of Zhejiang, and other similar groups in various provinces should all be handled in this way by the officials with jurisdiction. (Cited in DC, 76-06, commentary)

A substatute of 1788 reached beyond these specific status groups to cover people engaged in sex work generally: it prohibited "prostitutes and actors" (*chang you*), as well as their sons and grandsons, from sitting for the civil service examinations or purchasing degrees (DC, 76-19). In reference to this law, Xue Yunsheng notes that after three generations, the descendants of freed slaves were permitted to sit for examinations or to purchase degrees, and that the same rule would apply to the descendants of prostitutes and actors who had "changed their occupations to those proper to commoners" (DC, 76-19, commentary). Anders Hansson, however, cites evidence that only the descendants of musicians and actors would be permitted to sit for examinations, whereas descendants of prostitutes would be permanently barred. Even so, he argues that the "emancipation" of *yue* households "contributed to some marginal improvement in the status of entertainers generally or at least in that of their offspring" (1996, 72–73).

The Qianlong policy on examination access has been cited by Terada Takanobu, T'ung-tsu Ch'ü, and Jing Junjian as proof that the

Yongzheng initiative failed to achieve emancipation because it preserved and institutionalized discrimination against the very groups whose legal status had supposedly been changed. Certainly, this view has merit: during the required probationary period of three or four generations, an individual would be judged according to the standard of "purity and respectability" maintained by his entire extended family. On reflection, however, should we not read this policy as evidence of change, rather than as a cynical effort to preserve the past? Three or four generations may seem like a long time; however, by 1771, nearly fifty years had passed since the elimination of *yue* and *gai* status, and thus this legislation held out the possibility that half or more of the required period had already gone by. Imperial law had always richly favored degree-holding officials as a status level superior to ordinary commoners; a vast legal and symbolic gulf separated officials from prostitutes and other mean status persons. Yet, by specifying conditions for admission to the examinations, Qing authorities envisioned the possibility that descendants of debased entertainers might become degree-holding officials.

The practical impact of this policy appears to have been negligible (Hansson finds evidence of only a single individual of *yue* ancestry who tried to acquire a degree—1996, 75). Moreover, as I have said already, a narrow focus on emancipation strikes me as unproductive. Nevertheless, in terms of what we might call imperial constitutional theory, the Qianlong policy represented a significant break with the past. The civil examination system had originally been designed to break down hereditary distinction (specifically, aristocratic birthright to office) and was recognized as a powerful engine of social mobility. The Qianlong decision to open civil examinations to the descendants of *yue* households and other debased groups was the last nail in the coffin of an aristocratic vision of hereditary status and fixed social structure that had been on the decline ever since the Song dynasty.

Prostitution in Post-1723 Law

Extending the Reach of Existing Penal Law

Most concretely, the Yongzheng reforms represented an *extension of the reach of penal law*. This extension had far greater impact than any change in the policies on imperial music or access to civil examinations. The Yongzheng edicts do not state flat out that "prostitution" was prohibited; rather, they preserve the legal fiction that such activity had been tolerated only among the specific debased groups whose "customs and mores" were to be "reformed." But the practical result was the same: by extending commoner standards of sexual morality and criminal liability, the Yongzheng edicts eliminated the legal space for tolerated sex work (including the gray area of commercial prostitution, where the question of status background had not always been pursued with rigor). Hence, in 1780, the jurist Wu Tan could refer to a pre-Yongzheng law as having been drafted "in the period before prostitution had been prohibited (*zai wei jing jinzhi changji yiqian*)," and to add that "now, prostitution has already been strictly prohibited (*jin changji ye yi yan jin*)" (1992, 962).

In 1724, the year after the prohibition went into effect, the poet Wang Jingqi traveled through a region of Shanxi that had been well known for prostitution and other services provided by *yue* households. "In the past, there had been large concentrations of famous prostitutes (*ming chang*) in all of these counties. But recently, because of the strict prohibition of *yue* households (*yan jin yue hu*), they all have gone into hiding and refuse to come out [to receive customers]. . . . At every inn, not a single prostitute (*ji*) would dare go near the travelers' rooms" (1967, 20a). Only with great persistence did Wang manage to find women willing to serve him. He comments that some prostitutes were leaving the area altogether, "because of the great severity of the prohibition against *yue* households" (1967, 7b, 15b).[10]

The language of the 1723 edict had implied all of this: those who continued to "pollute and debase themselves" would be "punished according to the law"—that is, according to laws already on the books that banned "illicit sexual intercourse." Now that the previously exempt groups were held to *liang* standards, they became liable for *jian* crimes. Moreover, if all prostitution were "illicit sexual intercourse," then the male customers of prostitutes all became liable for prosecution as well.

In the years that followed, several new substatutes spelled out penalties for pimping and reinforced the requirement that magistrates (and rural agents, innkeepers, neighbors, and so on) take positive action against prostitution. But one searches the Qing code in vain for a new law defining prostitution as something different from noncommercial forms of "illicit sexual intercourse"; no law singled out the commercial aspect as deserving extra penalties.

Central case records (showing orthodox, "by the book" prosecution) from after 1723 enable us to outline how the reach of existing laws was extended in practice. A crucial factor was who, if anyone, had pimped the prostitute. If she had been pimped by her own husband, then judges employed the old Ming statute on "abetting or tolerating illicit sexual intercourse." As explained in the last chapter, the original intent of this statute had been to punish only commoners who debased themselves (that is, a husband either pimping his wife or tolerating her promiscuity); the practical effect of the 1723 edict was to extend this statute to include *all* cases in which a husband acted as pimp. The penalty for husband-pimp, wife-prostitute, and customer(s) was 90 blows of the heavy bamboo, and the wife would be divorced and returned to her natal lineage (DC, 367-00).

But if her husband did not abet her promiscuity, then it deserved a heavier penalty. If a prostitute was pimped by someone other than her husband, she and her customer(s) would be punished under the basic measure against "consensual illicit sexual intercourse" in force by the early eighteenth century: the substatute on "soldiers or civilians engaging in illicit sexual intercourse" (*jun min xiang jian*). The penalty was 100 blows of the heavy bamboo and one month in the cangue, and the woman would be returned to her natal lineage. If she were married, but had acted without her husband's collusion, then he could keep her or sell her off in marriage, just as in ordinary adultery cases (DC, 366-01). This penalty represented a significant increase over that for "consensual illicit sex" with a married woman in Ming and early Qing law, which had been 90 blows of the heavy bamboo (DC, 366-00; see Appendix A.3).

The same law was cited to prosecute women (and men) who engaged in prostitution on their own, as well as their customers. This judicial practice was eventually codified in a substatute of 1852:

If a female or male (*funü nanzi*) decides on her or his own to become a prostitute or an actor and to sell illicit sexual intercourse (*zi xing qi yi wei chang wei you mai jian zhe*), then that person shall receive one month in the cangue and 100 blows of the heavy bamboo, in application of the substatute on "soldiers or civilians engaging in illicit sexual intercourse." Whoever sleeps with prostitutes or engages the sexual services of actors (*su chang xia you*) shall also be sentenced to the cangue and the heavy bamboo in application of this substatute.   (QHS, 825/995; DC, 375-04)

This rather late measure formalized what had already been judicial practice since the Yongzheng reign, making explicit the equation of

prostitution with illicit sexual intercourse. (It also illustrates the
precise matching of penalties for parallel heterosexual and homosexual offenses that began in the Yongzheng reign, as well as the use
of "actor" as a euphemism for male prostitute.)

An unrelated pimp risked much harsher penalties than did a husband who pimped his own wife. A number of new provisions might
be applied, depending on the particular circumstances of a case. For
example, a substatute of 1740 increased the penalty for the old offense of "buying a commoner to become a prostitute" (*mai liang
wei chang*) to 100 blows of the heavy bamboo, three months in the
cangue, and three years of penal servitude (QHS, 825/995). This law
had originally been promulgated back in the Ming dynasty as a
means to enforce status distinction. After 1723, however, it was cited
to punish pimps who purchased *chaste* females (that is, ones who
had not previously engaged in illicit sexual intercourse). In this context, *liang* came to be interpreted strictly in terms of a woman's sexual history. When sentencing pimps, it was also common to cite the
new measures against "harboring prostitutes" (*wo chang*) that we
shall discuss below.

A further implication of the extension of commoner standards
was that all prostitution became incompatible with marriage. After
1723, if a husband had pimped his wife, the couple would invariably
be divorced and the woman returned to her natal lineage. The exemption that had previously existed for debased-status prostitute
couples disappeared. Nevertheless, as seen above, illicit sexual intercourse "abetted or tolerated" by a husband was now punished
less severely than prostitution managed either by the woman herself or by an unrelated pimp (that is, most brothel prostitution). The
worst offender was the pimp who rented out sexual labor that did
not properly belong to him even to enjoy, let alone to rent out to
other men. It was much less of an offense for a husband to share
with others his sexual monopoly over his own wife.

With the expanded application of the concept of "abetting or tolerating illicit sex," the law on homicide was amended to take it into
account. The following measure appeared in the Qing code as an official commentary in 1727, and was codified as a substatute in 1743:

If a husband abets or tolerates (*zong rong*) or forces (*yi le*) his wife or concubine to engage in illicit sexual intercourse with another man—and investigation establishes firm proof of this, and it is well known by other people—
then if . . . the man who engaged in illicit sexual intercourse himself
murders the husband, and the wife who engaged in illicit sexual intercourse

truly knew nothing [of the homicide in advance], then she shall still be sentenced only according to the basic provisions on "abetting, tolerating, or forcing [a wife or concubine to engage in illicit sexual intercourse]."[11]

Here we see a formal codification of the logic implied by the early Qing homicide judgments discussed at the end of the last chapter: if a husband had pimped his wife or otherwise tolerated her promiscuity, then his murder by her customer could not be blamed on her betrayal, and she should not be held accountable. The difference with the early Qing cases (in which debased-status prostitutes were released without punishment) is that the prostituted wife now had to answer for engaging in "illicit sexual intercourse."

Another old Ming law that expanded in its reach was the ban on a husband "forcing" (*yi le*) his wife or concubine to engage in illicit sexual intercourse with another man (DC, 367-00). The onus of this crime lay squarely with the husband (the wife received no penalty, as in rape law), but the logic of sexual monopoly applied here as well. The penalty for the husband (100 blows of the heavy bamboo) was marginally higher than that for "abetting or tolerating" (90 blows), but it was far lower than the penalty for rape (strangulation after the assizes). Such a husband seems to have fallen somewhere between a husband who raped his own wife (no crime, therefore no penalty) and a legally defined rapist (who had to be someone other than the victim's husband). In addition, the man who actually had intercourse with a wife forced by her husband to submit would receive a penalty (80 blows) that was lower, even, than that for "abetting or tolerating." Because rape was defined primarily as a violation of the husband's sexual monopoly, a rape that was authorized by the victim's husband constituted a relatively petty offense (and one that was never called by the legal term for rape, *qiang jian*).

As far as the judiciary was concerned, the crime of a husband "forcing" (*yi le*) his wife to engage in illicit sexual intercourse with another man appears to have been largely a matter of theory. My own survey of Qing cases suggests that the judiciary almost never applied this law in practice. Instead, when a husband prostituted his wife, the crime was invariably labeled "abetting or tolerating" (*zong rong*), and the woman would be punished along with the men, regardless of what she said about her experience (see, for example, XT, 186/QL 27.5.8). Proving the crime of forcing a wife to engage in illicit sexual intercourse would have been even more difficult than proving rape, because it would require similar proofs plus defiance of one's husband—and a wife could not file charges against her husband in a Qing-dynasty court. (For example, in 1852, a woman came to the yamen of Ba County, Sichuan, to accuse her husband of forcing her into prostitution; the magistrate had them both slapped and threw them out, ordering the husband to control his wife better in the future; BX, 4-4938). The law against "forcing" was occasionally cited to punish a father who pimped his daughter; evidently, Qing jurists saw a father's power to coerce his daughter as more absolute than a husband's power to coerce his wife. Even so, in the end the father would regain custody of his daughter—theirs was not a contractual relationship like marriage or adoption that could be nullified by improper acts (for example, XT, 194/DG 5.10.23).

Of course, a *truly* chaste wife who was pressured to engage in illicit sexual intercourse always retained the option of suicide, and in the wake of the Yongzheng reforms, the qualifications for canonization of chastity martyrs expanded to include wives who died to avoid prostituting themselves. A 1753 case from Jiangsu established the following precedent: "If a wife is forced (*bi le*) by her husband to sell illicit sex (*mai jian*), but she disobeys, resulting in her death, then canonization should be requested; her natal family should be ordered to accept the silver and to erect the memorial arch for her" (Yao Run et al., eds., 1878, 33/7b, commentary). The official rules on canonization of chastity martyrs were amended accordingly: "any wife who commits suicide to preserve her chastity while resisting her husband's effort to force her to sell illicit sex . . . shall have her memorial arch erected before her own parents' gate" (QH, 30/254).

We see an example of such canonization in an 1804 case. A man who could not repay a debt agreed to submit to sodomy with his creditor and later agreed to let the creditor sleep with his wife as well. She refused, however, and when they tried to force her, she killed herself by jumping into a well. The Jiaqing Emperor canonized her as a chastity martyr, and further honored her by imposing especially harsh extra-statutory penalties on both men: the creditor was beheaded immediately, and her husband was sentenced to slavery in the military forces stationed in western Xinjiang (QHS, 404/517).

The canonization of such a wife defined her husband's attempt to prostitute her as a challenge to her chastity that she had successfully met. In other such challenges, chastity required a wife to defy a rapist, or a man who proposed a sexual liaison, or (if she were a widow) relatives intent on forcing her to remarry. In each scenario, the martyr's alleged purpose was to safeguard her husband's interests—his sexual monopoly—even unto death. But in this scenario, chastity required a wife to defy *her own husband* to the point of suicide—an ironic result of the insistence on absolute sexual loyalty of wife to husband, taken to its logical, absurd extreme. Here, the focus of chastity shifted away from the real husband to the *ideal* of the husband, posing the problem of where a wife's loyalties should lie when her own husband did not conform to that standard. The contradiction was played out even in the manner of the martyr's commemoration: because it was her husband who had threatened her chastity, he and his family could not be allowed to erect her memorial arch at their home, as normally would be the case. Instead, that honor went to her natal family, which received the peculiar assignment of celebrating their daughter's suicidal devotion to the husband who had tried to pimp her. In effect, the martyr was "returned to her natal lineage" after death—a bizarre result, given the tradition that with marriage, a daughter left her natal family irrevocably, to be returned only if found unworthy.[12]

Throughout the eighteenth century, then, we can trace a series of judicial innovations that proceeded logically from the elimination of debased-status labels associated with prostitution. That initiative had eliminated the legal basis for tolerating some prostitution, and the criminal category "illicit sexual intercourse" expanded to fill the vacuum. Simultaneously, criminal liability extended to include the male customers of prostitutes. The penalties for pimps became quite severe, because now every female recruited into prostitution was seen as a commoner, and as having been chaste at one time. Finally, imperial exhortation to defend female chastity extended to wives pressured by their husbands to become prostitutes; in effect, the very women most likely to become prostitutes were appointed the first line of defense against that crime.

New Laws: "Harboring" and "Failing to Detect" Prostitutes

We have seen that the punishment of prostitution after 1723 involved the extension or reinterpretation of existing laws, rather than a promulgation of new laws defining a new crime of "prostitution." The new laws that *did* appear reflected a concern for security and administrative integrity, more than for sex work itself. In 1736, the newly enthroned Qianlong Emperor admonished his officials to honor the moral legacy of his father, the late Yongzheng Emperor, including the ban on prostitution:

We have heard that if villainy is not extirpated, then it is impossible for good and law-abiding people to have peace. If customs are not corrected, then there is no way to promote the transformation of values. There are four great abominations that afflict the villages. The first is called banditry. . . . The second is called gambling. . . . The third is called fighting. . . . The fourth is called prostitution (*chang ji*). . . . These four abominations rob the people of their wealth, destroy their lives, injure their bodies, wreck their households, and ruin their virtue.

Among things that harm the good and law-abiding, nothing is worse than these four abominations. For this reason, our father the late Emperor expressed his profound love and concern for the people by issuing strict prohibitions against them, and by warning the officials with local jurisdictions that they must enforce the law (*fa zai bi xing*). . . . [Over time, banditry, gambling, and fighting disappeared.] Prostitutes (*chang ji*) hid far away, and did not dare to linger at inns. For the thirteen years of his reign, our father the late Emperor concentrated his government, teachings, and spirit on this enterprise, and our subjects everywhere enjoyed the benefits that resulted.

After this preamble, the emperor gets to the point: since his father's death, law enforcement has slacked off, with the result that "the four abominations" are beginning to reappear; he threatens serious consequences for officials who fail to detect and prosecute these crimes (QHS, 399/449–50).

With regard to prostitution, the Qianlong Emperor backed up this rhetoric with the following substatute, also issued in 1736:

If any unlicensed individual[13] (*wu ji zhi tu*), first-degree licentiate, yamen runner, or soldier harbors (*wo liu*) itinerant prostitutes (*liu chang*) or local whores (*tu ji*), and engages in seduction and swindling, or if any such person accepts payment from a party harboring prostitutes, and acts to protect him, then he shall receive 100 blows of the heavy bamboo, according to the statute on "violating imperial edicts." If the offender is a first-degree licentiate, then he shall be stripped of his rank; if he is a yamen runner or a soldier, then he shall no longer be permitted to receive a stipend by filling that position.

If neighbors or local rural agents know of the situation and tolerate it, then they shall receive the more severe of the penalties provided by the statute on "doing inappropriate things"; anyone who has accepted payment may [also] be punished with the stricter of the penalties for "accepting a bribe for an illegal purpose" (*wang fa*), calculated according to the amount of the bribe. Any local magistrate who fails to detect prostitutes in his district (*shi cha*) shall be reported to the Board [of Personnel] for deliberation of appropriate administrative sanctions, as provided in the relevant substatute.[14]

A 1760 amendment added three years of penal servitude to the penalty for "harboring" prostitutes, if that activity had gone on for a

significant length of time (DC, 375-02; QHS, 826/995–96). In 1772
the Qianlong Emperor issued yet another edict, demanding renewed
vigilance against "local whores and itinerant prostitutes," as well as
wandering musicians and opera singers. Local magistrates were to
"drive out" such vagrants and send them back to their home jurisdictions, and to punish severely any "reprobate" who harbored such
women; officials who "fail to detect" such criminal activity would
have a year's salary withheld (QHS, 117/721). In 1811, a new substatute extended the bamboo and penal servitude to any landlord
who knowingly permitted his property to be used as a brothel; the
real estate itself would be confiscated (DC, 375-03).

   Most often, the laws against "harboring" prostitutes seem to have
been cited to punish pimps and brothel-keepers. But the purpose of
singling out licentiates, rural agents, yamen personnel, and magistrates was to reinforce the 1723 mandate that persons of authority
take positive action to root out all prostitution. The post-1723 measures also reflect the longstanding perception that brothels, like
gambling dens, were nests of criminal activity (the terms for "harboring" prostitutes, *wo liu* or *wo dun*, were the same as those used
elsewhere in the code for "harboring" robbers and fugitives); this
perception long predated the criminalization of all prostitution. In
his 1694 handbook for magistrates, retired official Huang Liuhong
had argued that prostitution should be seen as a security liability;
he urged magistrates to use the *baojia* system to identify prostitutes
and drive them out of their jurisdictions. His concern was not sex
work itself but rather the criminals who might find brothels convenient places to gather:

Those who engage in prostitution also harbor bandits and thieves. When a
gang of bandits or thieves plans to commit a crime, they need to assemble
their followers and spies. . . . Houses of ill repute are the best assembly
places because they are frequented by all sorts of people. After a robbery or
theft is committed, the criminals often hide there to wait for the hue and
cry to die down gradually. Therefore, to trace bandits and find their loot, it
is wise to search these houses first.

Huang also noted that "shameless rich men and unscrupulous licentiates" sometimes lent their protection to prostitutes, "hoping
to garner profits from sex (*jian zhen zhi li*)." Such men should be
punished and deprived of their degrees ("They are disgraceful and
vulgar! What difference is there between them and *yue* pimps?");[15]
prostitutes and pimps who associated with them should receive a
beating (Huang Liuhong 1973, 23/14a–15b). Huang's handbook was

widely influential, and some of his comments closely anticipate the language of the 1736 substatute and the 1772 edict cited above.[16]

The new measures also aimed to guard against new forms of corruption brought into being by the sudden criminalization of activity that was so widespread and that had been tolerated by the authorities for so long. Prior to the Yongzheng reign, the tolerated prostitution of debased-status groups outside the capital had often been regulated to some extent by local officials, and it probably constituted a semiformal source of income (just as regulated prostitution at the capital had once paid "rouge and powder" taxes to the Bureau of Instruction). (Huang Liuhong notes with disgust that some local magistrates made a great deal of money off entertainment by prostitutes and actors at officially sponsored festivals; 1973, 24/16a–17b.) The prohibition of prostitution would have converted such payments into graft, to the extent that they continued, having a corrupting effect perhaps similar to that of the prohibition of alcohol in the United States in the early twentieth century.

Prostitution was never eliminated from the Qing empire; indeed, the business seems to have flourished even in Beijing (Wang Shunu 1988). Yan Ming suggests that the end of official prostitution actually had the ironic effect of stimulating private, commercial prostitution, which expanded to fill the void (1992, 131). But even if it was ubiquitous, sex work remained illegal, and in the eighteenth and nineteenth centuries, one facet of the notoriety of local yamen personnel was a reputation for collecting protection money from pimps, or even running brothels themselves (Reed 1994). Post-reform case records (to be examined in detail later) reveal yamen runners extorting sexual services and cash payments from prostitutes and pimps, by threatening them with arrest and prosecution. This practice is not terribly surprising: county archives show that magistrates consistently prosecuted those cases of prostitution that actually came to their attention—but magistrates depended on their runners to investigate and report such crimes.

Another new substatute, of 1724, aimed to prevent women who were taken into official custody from being recruited or forced into prostitution:

Anyone who exploits his or her post as an official broker in persons (*jie chong ren ya*) by taking custody of a woman in order to sell her, and then forcing her to sell illicit sex (*mai jian*) for his profit, shall receive three months in the cangue and 100 blows of the heavy bamboo, and shall be deported to the "Three Surnames" region of Heilongjiang to serve as a slave for the armored troops. (QHS, 825/995)[17]

The "broker in persons" referred to here was more generally known as the "official matchmaker" (*guan mei*). This position, often held by a woman, appears to have been a standard fixture of every local yamen from at least the late Ming dynasty until the end of the Qing. Official matchmakers would hold in custody women who were awaiting trial, but the most important service they provided magistrates was to find husbands for any women ordered "sold off under official auspices" (*dang guan fa mai*). Most of the women sold in this way were convicted adulteresses (whose husbands had refused to take them back) and, after 1723, prostitutes. Magistrates dealt with such women by placing them with new husbands, who paid a "body price" (*shen jia*) that included a commission for the official matchmaker who negotiated the deal. It may be that before 1723, the recruitment of prostitutes by official matchmakers would have been tacitly tolerated, since most of their charges were considered unchaste already, and since other official connections with prostitution had been accepted. With the criminalization of prostitution, an increasing proportion of the women retained in custody would have been convicted prostitutes being sold in marriage. If the matchmakers themselves pimped these women or sold them back into prostitution, it would defeat the whole purpose of taking them into custody.[18]

The practical impact of such measures is hard to gauge; my main point here is that the new legislation after 1723 was prompted largely by interrelated concerns about security and administrative integrity. Nothing was added to the Qing code to define prostitution itself as a new category of crime, or to add extra penalties for the commercial element involved. Sex work was prosecuted by the extension of old laws to previously exempted groups; with the redefinition of such groups as commoners, they became liable for the commoner crime of "illicit sexual intercourse."

Post-Yongzheng Central Cases

Husband as Pimp: "Abetting Illicit Sexual Intercourse"

To highlight the changes in the judicial treatment of prostitution, I have chosen the following example, memorialized by the governor of Shandong in 1762, because it parallels several of the early Qing homicide cases examined in Chapter 6. This memorial, too, meticulously applies the orthodox standards of the code even to secondary offenses, because as a capital case, it would ostensibly be reviewed by the emperor himself. In this case, Yuan Liu, who had pimped his wife, Ming Shi, was murdered by two of their customers (the case record refers to Ming Shi with the old terms for "prostitute": *chang* and *chang fu*). The change in the law made the prostitution itself, as well as the homicide, a focus of prosecution; thus, this case provides far more detail than the early Qing ones. For example, where the early Qing cases included no particular inquiry into the background of prostitute households, taking them for granted as a distinct status group, the present memorial gives a detailed account of Ming Shi's entry into prostitution. As she confessed:

> My husband liked to eat but was too lazy to work, so he would not continue living with my older brother-in-law; instead, he sold the land he had received in household division and spent all the money he got for it. . . . Then he wanted me to leave home with him and do these shameful things (*jian bu de ren de shi*). There was nothing I could do but follow him. We stayed at Song Xianye's inn. My husband gave me the name "Charming Jade" (*qiao yu*), and made me receive customers and sell illicit sex (*mai jian*).

Nothing in Ming Shi's testimony or the rest of the case record implies that the couple possessed any fixed status different from other peasants. Yuan Liu is portrayed as a simple alcoholic who squandered his inheritance and then survived by renting out his sole remaining asset: his wife. He mitigated the stigma of this conduct by taking Ming Shi to the next county, where he could pimp her in relative anonymity. We do not know whether this social reality was any different from that behind the Shunzhi period cases; but the inclusion of this information in the memorial shows that the judiciary had abandoned the fiction of fixed status boundaries in order to focus on specific incidents of criminal conduct.

A frequent customer was Song Tiehan, a single man who ran a restaurant near the inn; Song also introduced Xu Liu, a single peasant from a nearby village, and the two men would visit the inn together and sleep with Ming Shi in turns. By her own account, Ming Shi got along well with the two—but the same could not be said of her husband-pimp, Yuan Liu. As Ming Shi recalled: "There were three or four times Song Tiehan didn't pay. My husband only wanted to get money and drink, and he always had a bad temper, so when Song Tiehan didn't pay, my husband would get drunk and curse him—this happened more than once. When Xu Liu reproached my husband for this, he wouldn't back down, but cursed Xu Liu, too. . . ." Finally, Yuan Liu cut off Song's credit, making him pay cash up front before letting him sleep with Ming Shi. Song Tiehan resented Yuan's greed. After all, it was Song who had introduced Xu Liu as a customer, bringing Yuan considerable extra income to finance his drinking. He then proposed to Xu Liu that they murder Yuan and take his wife for themselves. As Song later confessed,

I said, "After all, Ming Shi is Yuan Liu's wife. . . . What if he takes her somewhere far away? Then we won't be able to fool around with her anymore. Now, if you help me kill Yuan Liu and bring Ming Shi to stay at my restaurant, then the two of us can be with her forever; we can also take customers and sell sex to earn some money and divide it between ourselves. Wouldn't that kill two birds with one stone (*qi bu liang bian*)?" Xu asked, "Will Ming Shi be willing to go along with this?" I said, "We have to keep this from her for now. . . . Anyway, she's a woman, and the hearts of women are all fickle (*fu dao jia shui xing yang hua*). She gets along with us well enough, and besides, once her husband is dead, there will be nothing she can do about it."

Xu Liu agreed, and together they strangled Yuan Liu.

After their exposure and arrest, Song Tiehan and Xu Liu were sentenced to death for committing a "planned murder."[19] Ming Shi denied any role in her husband's murder, and the magistrate believed her. Since her husband had "abetted" her illicit intercourse, the magistrate cited the new homicide law drafted to take that crime into account:

Yuan Liu abetted his wife Ming Shi to go out in public as a prostitute (*chu wai wei chang*), giving her the name "Charming Jade." This fact has been confirmed by the innkeepers who harbored them, Song Xiange and Liu Dayong. Furthermore, the dead man's older brother Yuan Zhenjiang testifies that he too had heard about this. It was truly "well-known by other people" [as required by the relevant substatute]. . . . Interrogation has established that Yuan Ming Shi knew nothing of the homicide; therefore, she should receive only the 90 blows of the heavy bamboo mandated by the basic statute on "abetting a wife or concubine to engage in illicit sexual intercourse with another man. . . ."[20] As a "wife who has engaged in illicit sexual intercourse" she shall have the sentence carried out according to substatute, and shall be divorced and returned to her natal lineage.

If the couple had stayed at home, and if Ming Shi had slept with only one or two patrons in exchange for economic support, keeping the matter secret, then the prosecution would have ended at this point; the pimping and sex work would have constituted "abetting illicit sex" pure and simple (see, for example, XT, 75/QL 4.5.24). But because of the couple's occupational specialization (having left home to work out of an inn, the woman taking a pseudonym) and the extent of their promiscuity (servicing multiple customers, many of them anonymous), the presiding magistrate labeled Ming Shi a "prostitute"—using the old terms *chang* and *chang fu*—a legal category defined after 1723 not by fixed hereditary status, but by occupation/conduct: the open sale of sexual services to multiple customers. The label *chang* made no difference to the definition of Ming Shi's offense, or to the punishment she would receive; she was punished for "illicit sexual intercourse," and the commercial aspect of her promiscuity did not indicate any extra penalties. The legal significance of *chang* was to trigger a wider investigation of people who might have "harbored" the couple, or who had failed in their duty to detect their criminal enterprise. This second stage of the investigation stemmed from the new legislation that prioritized security and administrative integrity.

The magistrate pressed witnesses to determine exactly when Ming Shi had commenced selling sex, and which counties she had sold sex in—this information identified which magistrates to report as derelict in their duty. Ming Shi and her husband had sold sex at some of the inns they visited but not at others; the magistrate pressed for specific information on this point so as to identify which innkeepers to arrest for "harboring prostitutes." That information also helped identify the neighbors and rural agents to be summoned to find out if they had known of or been bribed to tolerate the criminal enterprise. The magistrate further pressed (unsuccessfully) for the names and addresses of other men (aside from the murderers) who had paid to sleep with Ming Shi; if identified, these men, too, would have been arrested and punished for "illicit sexual intercourse." Finally, he elicited an account of the prostitution fees so as to decide how much money to confiscate from whom.

The information gleaned from initial hearings was used to summon the innkeepers, rural agents, and neighbors for a separate hearing. First to be interrogated were the two rural agents for the market towns where the different inns were located; the magistrate found them innocent of knowingly tolerating the prostitution, but nevertheless sentenced each man to 40 blows of the light bamboo, according to the statue on "doing inappropriate things—petty cases," because they had "failed in their duty to detect" the illegal activity. Next, the magistrate interrogated the heads of households living on either side of Song Tiehan's restaurant and Song Xianye's inn, and found them innocent of wrongdoing. The neighbors of innkeeper

Liu Dayong testified: ". . . We saw that Liu Dayong was keeping a woman named Yuan Ming Shi and her husband Yuan Liu at his inn. She looked like an immoral woman (*bu zhengjing de nüren*), and we were afraid that they would involve us in trouble, so we demanded that he get rid of them. After a few days they left . . . so we didn't bother to notify the rural agent." None of the neighbors were punished. Innkeepers Song Xianye and Liu Dayong were interrogated at length; each had been paid 400 cash per week to let the couple stay at his inn, with the understanding that the room fee was owed regardless of whether any customers slept with Ming Shi. No customers had come to Liu Dayong's inn, where the couple stayed for only a week; nevertheless, Liu too had explicitly agreed that they could sell sex at his inn. Both men were sentenced to 100 blows of the heavy bamboo, according to the substatute on "harboring itinerant prostitutes" (*wo dun liu chang*).[21] Since they had been paid only room rent, the magistrate decided not to confiscate that money; nor did he try to confiscate the money paid for sex with Ming Shi, since Yuan Liu had spent it all.

The case report concludes by considering the magistrates of the counties in which these events had occurred:

> Yuan Ming Shi did not act as a prostitute in her home jurisdiction; only after going to Chengwu County did she begin to sell illicit sex (*mai jian*). The official who "failed in his duty to detect itinerant prostitutes" (*shi cha liu chang*) is Magistrate Wu Bingren of Chengwu County. . . . It is requested that he be reported to the Board [of Personnel] for deliberation on appropriate penalties. (XT, 184/QL 27.2.17)

Local magistrates who "failed to detect" prostitution forfeited a year's salary (XT, 125/QL 15.12.15). This was a common, largely symbolic penalty for administrative failure (most of a magistrate's actual income came from unofficial sources), and it seems unlikely that any official career would have been wrecked over a matter like prostitution. In some memorials on prostitution-related cases, if the prostitute had not been active for very long, the magistrate would request that the sanctions for "failing to detect" be waived, on the grounds that it was unreasonable to expect him to have detected the enterprise so quickly; such requests seem to have been honored by the central judiciary (see, for example, XT, 181/QL 27.5.16). I find no evidence that magistrates ever requested sanctions for themselves in *routine* cases of prostitution; sanctions seem to have been applied only in cases that reached the attention of the central authorities because capital offenses were involved. The Board of Punishment sometimes complained about the failure of local authorities to recommend penalties for officials who had had prostitution discovered in their jurisdictions, and ordered stricter adherence to the code in this matter (see, for example, a 1789 circular, XA, 53/20b–21a). There is no evidence that such complaints had any effect.[22]

Prostitution Outside Marriage

Two other central cases from the post-1723 era illustrate how the law applied when no husband acted as pimp. A 1758 case from Guangdong concerned a second captain of Green Standard Forces, Yang Jiade, who took advantage of his duty of river patrol to dally with prostitutes among local boat people. In 1756, Yang became infatuated with a particular prostitute, Luo Shi. He neglected his duties—at one point spending several days and nights on her boat without leaving—until he was finally reported to his superiors and arrested. Yang and Luo Shi were punished under the substatute on "soldiers or civilians engaging in illicit sexual intercourse" (DC, 366-01). According to the clause on "an official engaging in illicit sexual intercourse with the wife of a soldier or civilian," Yang was dismissed from office and sentenced to 100 blows of the heavy bamboo; according to the basic clause (used to punish ordinary adultery), Luo Shi was sentenced to 100 blows of the heavy bamboo and a month in the cangue. Her fees were confiscated. The memorialist did not recommend penalties for local officials who had "failed to detect" prostitution, perhaps because Yang Jiade himself bore such responsibility (XT, 175/QL 23.12.21). Interestingly, the obsolete statute against "officials sleeping with prostitutes" (*guan li su chang*) was not applied, although it remained on the books; that law focused on preserving status distinction rather than punishing intercourse outside marriage, and its penalty (60 blows, plus dismissal) was lighter than those mandated by the newer law applied here (DC, 374-00).

The second example is an "immediate examination" case from Beijing judged by the Board of Punishment in 1860. A pimp named Zhang Er had bought a teenage girl, Yin Li'er, from her desperately poor mother, who later died. Zhang claimed the girl to be his "concubine," but because he could produce no marriage contract or go-between, the Board of Punishment treated them as unrelated parties. In 1859, when Li'er was eighteen *sui*, Zhang Er agreed with a widow, Chen Su Shi, to rent a house and jointly operate a brothel. Zhang provided the sexual services of Li'er, and Chen Su Shi brought in two other women. The widow entered into a fictive kinship relation with Li'er (as she had with the other two), addressing her as "adopted daughter" (*yi nü*).[23] In two months, however, the venture had failed, and the pimps withdrew their prostitutes to operate separately. But while at the brothel, Li'er had agreed to elope with one of her customers, Zhang Zhengtai. Zhengtai persuaded Chen Su Shi to help him remove Li'er from Zhang Er's home behind his back. When Zhang Er discovered that Li'er was missing, he accused the widow of stealing her, and Chen Su Shi, frightened, went to the Beijing Gendarmerie (*tidu yamen*), where she charged Zhang Er with trying to abduct her "daughter." Everyone was arrested, and the police transferred the case to the Board of Punishment (routine treatment for incidents in the capital).

After establishing the facts, the board punished the two pimps as follows: "Zhang Er and Chen Su Shi . . . should both receive 100 blows of the heavy bamboo and three years of penal servitude, according to the substatute on 'harboring itinerant prostitutes or local whores for a considerable period of time. . . .'[24] As a woman, Chen Su Shi shall redeem her penalty as a fine." Yin Li'er and Zhang Zhengtai were punished in the same manner as adulterers:

Both shall receive one month in the cangue and 100 blows of the heavy bamboo, according to the substatute on "soldiers or civilians engaging in illicit sexual intercourse". . . . Since Li'er is a "woman who has committed illicit sex," she shall have her beating carried out, but shall redeem her term in the cangue as a cash fine. She shall be separated [from Zhang Er] and returned to her natal lineage; they may not marry her to Zhang Zhengtai. (XB, JS 09324)

The last detail stems from the law that an adulteress could not be married to her partner in adultery (DC, 366-00).

To sum up: post-1723 cases from central courts show prostitutes and their customers being punished in exactly the same way as persons who engaged in noncommercial "consensual illicit sexual intercourse." The principal factor in determining penalties for the illicit sex was whether the prostitute had a husband who had "abetted" her promiscuity. The commercial element played no role except in the last case, and there only in determining the penalties of the pimps.

Prosecution of Sex Work at the County Level

All the cases cited in this chapter so far have been from central court records, illustrating the treatment of prostitution "by the book," usually as an offshoot of homicide prosecution. But only a small percentage of cases at the county level were ever prepared for review by senior officials. What about ordinary cases of prostitution that involved no homicide or other capital offense, and thus never received the scrutiny of central courts? Did the ban on prostitution really have any effect on routine judgments and police work at the county level?

The earliest archival records from the county level that I know of—the Ba County archive—postdate the Yongzheng prohibition by some thirty-five years. Therefore, in our examination of the pre-1723 regulation of prostitution on the local level, we have been limited to the published writings of magistrates like Lü Kun, Zhang Kentang, and Huang Liuhong. But the Ba County archive provides a wealth of evidence showing how magistrates enforced the prohibition of prostitution in the late eighteenth and nineteenth centuries.

A sample of relevant cases from 1758 to 1852, representing the decisions of more than a dozen different magistrates, demonstrates three basic points. First, and most important, these decisions all share the assumption that prostitution was criminal activity that should be suppressed. I find no evidence that any magistrate would tolerate sex work in Ba County, if he learned of it. Second, rather than rigidly applying the exact prescriptions of the Qing code, magistrates opted for practical, expedient settlements that minimized complication and kept cases out of the review system. (For example, they apparently never sentenced pimps to penal servitude, as prescribed by the substatute on "harboring prostitutes"—this penalty would have required review up to the provincial level.) Third, there is little evidence of any proactive effort to extirpate all prostitution: in this domain as in many others, magistrates usually did not go looking for trouble but waited for it to come to them before acting.

Prostitutes' Relatives File Charges

How did prostitution come to the attention of Ba County magistrates? When they learned of it, what did they do about it?

One way magistrates learned of prostitution is that relatives of prostitutes sometimes filed charges against their pimps. Typically,

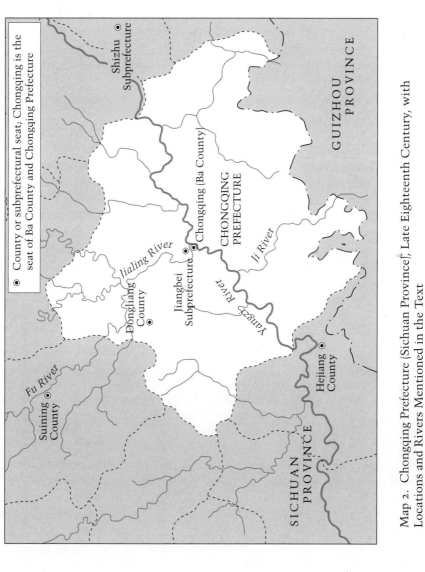

Map 2. Chongqing Prefecture (Sichuan Province), Late Eighteenth Century, with Locations and Rivers Mentioned in the Text

in these cases, the woman in question had been acquired by a pimp under false pretenses: her family thought she was being adopted or married, and later discovered that she had been forced into prostitution. These scenarios resemble the earlier cases of "buying a commoner to be a prostitute" (*mai liang wei chang*) examined in Chapter 5. Indeed, Ba County magistrates continued to use this old legal term, although after prohibition *liang* apparently referred to any female not already a prostitute or adulteress. The women in these cases were treated by magistrates as victims, rather than criminals, and thus were not punished. The pimps, however, received fairly severe treatment.

A standard example is an 1852 case involving a widow who lived in Longmenhao (just east of Chongqing, on the opposite bank of the Yangzi). Having fallen on hard times, the widow decided to adopt out her teenage daughter and for this purpose entrusted her to their landlady, one Zhao Chuichui, who moonlighted as a matchmaker. Zhao Chuichui advanced the widow 8,000 cash, and then took the girl across the river to Chongqing, where she sold her to a pimp named Chen Sanxi. After some months of forced prostitution, the girl was finally tracked down and rescued by her uncle, who filed charges against the matchmaker and the pimp at the Ba County yamen.

The magistrate approved the girl's return to her natal family and ordered that she be properly married. Chen Sanxi was slapped (*zhang ze*), exposed in the cangue for six weeks, and then released after pledging never again to engage in the sex trade. (This penalty, though fairly severe by Ba County standards, was far lighter than that prescribed by the substatute in force at that time: 100 blows of the heavy bamboo, three months in the cangue, and three years of penal servitude—DC, 375-04.) Matchmaker Zhao Chuichui was spared because of her advanced age and released on pledge of good behavior (BX, 4-4958).

An 1851 case unfolded somewhat differently. A man named Qin Guangdou petitioned that his younger sister, Qin Yingu (eighteen *sui*), had been sold to a Chongqing pimp named Gan Peide. Years before, Qin Guangdou had adopted the girl out to be the daughter-in-law of one Li Chaopin, but he had recently learned that Li had sold the girl to Gan Peide. Horrified at this news, the petitioner had come from their home in Shizhu Sub-prefecture (east of Chongqing, some 120 kilometers down the Yangzi) to search for his sister and had discovered her working in Gan's brothel. Gan had bought Qin

Yingu ostensibly as a wife for his son, Gan Dayou. But according to the girl's testimony, both father and son "used coercion to force me to engage in illicit sexual intercourse" (*qiang bi tong jian*), and to receive customers as a prostitute; they had made her use the name "Golden Phoenix," and were forcing her to learn to play music and sing as well. When arrested, the Gans admitted "earning a living by prostitution and singing" (*mai chang chang qu du ri*); but they denied that the girl's name was "Qin Yingu," and asserted that Qin Guangdou was an impostor (perhaps one of the girl's customers).

The magistrate ordered Gan Peide and Gan Dayou slapped, and he had Peide exposed in the cangue for an unspecified period. He did not punish the prostitute, but ordered runners to escort her back to Shizhu Sub-prefecture and deliver her to the local authorities for return to her natal family. Because he suspected that the girl's "brother" was indeed lying, he had him slapped, too, and held in custody until he received word that she had been safely delivered. He even left open the question of the girl's real name (the documents that accompanied her back to Shizhu list her as "Qin Yingu, a.k.a. Gan Jinfeng"). What really mattered was that she be taken away from the pimps and sent home to Shizhu Sub-prefecture—where pinning down her identity and finding her a place would be another magistrate's problem. This was a typically expedient settlement, which achieved with dispatch the basic priorities of punishing the pimps, disposing of the woman, and closing the case (BX, 4-4902).

Runaway Prostitutes Detained by Yamen Runners

The most frequent way prostitution came to the attention of Ba County magistrates was that yamen runners on patrol would arrest "suspicious" women found wandering in the city and bring them in for interrogation. These women often turned out to be prostitutes who had made their way to Chongqing after running away from brothels in Jiangbei (the seat of Jiangbei Sub-prefecture), just to the north across the Jialing River (the boundary of Ba County). A typical example is a woman aged twenty-one *sui* who was picked up on the waterfront in 1778. Her original surname was Ma, and she had grown up in Hejiang County (about 100 kilometers southwest of Chongqing on the Yangzi River). Her parents had both died when she was in her teens, and she had no brothers, and in 1774 she ended up being sold down the river to a Jiangbei pimp named Wang. He had made her use the name "Autumn Cassia." She ran away from the brothel, she testified, "because I could not stand the torture anymore." Her pimp had chased her down to the river, but two boatmen saved her by ferrying her over to Chongqing.

Magistrates treated these women, too, as victims rather than criminals, and did not punish them. This treatment seems to have been the rule in handling prostitutes who sought to quit sex work (including those whose families' petitioned for their rescue). In every case, magistrates dealt with runaways by turning them over to the official matchmaker to be sold in marriage. As a rule, they had been purchased a considerable distance from Chongqing, often as little girls, and it was judged a practical impossibility to return them to their families (if indeed they had any). The depositions of these women always end with a formulaic plea for mercy, and a statement that they are willing to *cong liang*—in a post-1723 context, the term simply meant to quit prostitution and marry. The official matchmaker would find a prospective husband, negotiate an appropriate "body price" (including a fee to cover the woman's room and board while in custody), and submit the contract to the magistrate for approval. In Autumn Cassia's case, within two weeks the matchmaker found a man willing to pay twenty strings of cash; the magistrate approved, and her new husband took her home after pledging not to resell her or force her back into prostitution (BX, 1-1718).

We should not overlook the coercive dimension of these settlements, despite the gloss of benevolent paternalism (the magistrate acting as a good father to find the women husbands). The prostitutes being "rescued" by sale in marriage had no say in the matter, in spite of their formulaic agreement to *cong liang*. Most probably did want to quit sex work; nevertheless, they had not sought rescue from the magistrate, but had been detained under duress. There is no evidence that they enjoyed the right to veto prospective husbands. Since the body prices paid for ex-prostitutes varied widely, and official matchmakers sometimes had trouble unloading older or "ugly" women, it is pretty clear that they were sold to the highest bidder on the basis of youth and looks (Sommer 1994, 404–6). Nor do I find any evidence that magistrates pursued such cases further—either to follow up on the women after they were sold, or to notify Jiangbei authorities about the pimps that they had run away from. Rather, their priority was to settle cases as simply and quickly as possible by marrying off the women.

Chongqing prostitutes sometimes ran away to Jiangbei—in either city, an effective escape seems to have required getting across the river (perhaps because local yamen runners in each jurisdiction were in cahoots with their local pimps). In 1851, two prostitutes who escaped from a Chongqing brothel were detained in Jiangbei by runners attached to the Sub-prefecture yamen. He Xigu, aged eighteen *sui*, had grown up in Suining County (150 kilometers up the Fu River, northwest of Chongqing). When she was a little girl, her parents had sold her as an adopted daughter-in-law to a widow, who in 1849 resold her to a Chongqing pimp named Chen Fu. The other prostitute was Wang Liu Shi, aged twenty *sui*, from Dongliang County (80 kilometers up the Fu River). She, too, had been sold in childhood as an adopted daughter-in-law, but in 1850 her husband had resold her to Chen Fu because of poverty. The women had become friends at the brothel and decided to run away together.

The Jiangbei magistrate decided that both were "chaste women who had been bought into prostitution," and since "neither has any natal lineage to which she can return," he turned them over to his official matchmaker. He then reported the case to the magistrate of Ba County, after learning that pimp Chen Fu was trying to get the women back, by using a surrogate to file charges at Ba County alleging that the women were daughters-in-law who had been seduced into running away from home.[25] Sure enough, such charges had been filed; upon receipt of the letter, the magistrate of Ba County ordered the pimp's arrest and asked the Jiangbei magistrate to send the women back to Chongqing under escort to serve as witnesses against him. (The record is incomplete, and thus we do not know the final outcome.) This is the only example I have found of inter-jurisdictional cooperation in prosecuting prostitution—for the most part, magistrates seem to have concerned themselves only with what happened within their own jurisdictions (BX, 4-4891).

Not every runaway prostitute sought to quit the trade altogether. In 1797, runners detained a woman who had her head shaved and was dressed in the manner of a Buddhist nun; the cause for suspicion was that she was observed coming and going from a lay residence. She turned out to be a prostitute who went by the name Yang Sannüzi ("Yang's Number Three Girl"); born in Dongliang County, she had been sold to a Jiangbei pimp at the age of thirteen *sui*. Now, eighteen years later, she had run away from the brothel with a favorite customer, one Xie Tianxi, and had accompanied him to Chongqing, where he lived with his older brother and sister-in-law. She continued working out of Xie's home as a prostitute. She even acquired a particular patron, a monk, who paid the family ten taels of silver in exchange for regularly sleeping with her (he had also slept with Xie Tianxi's sister-in-law, Xie Yue Shi). Yang Sannüzi had adopted the disguise of a nun in order to facilitate her free movement and her interaction with the monk.

Yang Sannüzi showed no interest at all in being "rescued"; nor did the magistrate treat her as a victim. Instead, he ordered her exposed in the cangue for a week (harsh treatment for a female offender; the code provided that women could redeem nominal sentences to the cangue with cash payment), and had her sold off in marriage by the official matchmaker. The sister-in-law, Xie Yue Shi, was slapped and released; both Xie brothers were exposed in the cangue for a week, given twenty blows of the bamboo, and released on pledge of good behavior; their offenses included "sleeping with prostitutes," "harboring prostitutes," and "abetting illicit sexual intercourse." The monk was put in the cangue for a month, beaten, and stripped of his clerical status. These penalties were fairly harsh by Ba County standards, but more lenient than those prescribed in the code (also, Xie Yue Shi was allowed to remain with her husband) (BX, 2-4129, 4132).

Prostitution Reported by Yamen Runners

The Ba County archives contain many examples of yamen runners turning in prostitutes who had escaped from Jiangbei brothels, but it is far less common to find runners reporting prostitution rackets that operated within Ba County itself. Detecting prostitution lay well within the scope of their duties, and we know from the many reports that came to magistrates from other sources that there was plenty of it in Chongqing (which, after all, was a major port); nevertheless, runners clearly found it convenient to overlook a great deal of local prostitution.

When runners did report prostitution within the city, magistrates sometimes responded cynically. In 1821, for example, runners reported that they had discovered a large brothel in their district run by a pimp named Sun Mao; they had tried to persuade him to leave or to reform his ways, but because he defied them, there was nothing for it but to turn him in. The magistrate ordered the pimp's arrest but added, "if I find that this is a spurious report based on some personal grudge or extortion attempt, you runners will be severely punished." Sun Mao was arrested, along with seven of his prostitutes. One of the prostitutes later remarked in testimony, "I don't know what kind of quarrel Sun Mao had with the yamen runners to make them arrest us." The magistrate let this remark pass without comment, but it would seem that the runners had known about Sun's brothel for some time before finally turning him in.

Upon interrogation, the pimp confessed to "harboring" the prostitutes in rented rooms, where he charged customers 140 to 200 cash per trick. Sun claimed that he would give each woman half of whatever she earned; the prostitutes corroborated his statement, but added that they had to pay for all their own food and other necessities themselves. The women had all started working for Sun out of desperation: "we have been polluted and insulted by him because we have no other means of support." Five women testified that their husbands had abandoned them to go off in search of work or to wander as vagrants; the other two were widows. Sun Mao slept with them whenever he liked, and would beat them cruelly if they refused to receive customers.

Despite this sad testimony, these seven prostitutes were not treated as victims, because they had not run away from their pimp. Instead, they were beaten and released on pledges of good behavior. Unusually, the magistrate did not turn them over to the official matchmaker (almost invariably the practice in other cases), perhaps because there were so many of them. (It seems a strange omission by the magistrate: since poverty had driven them to prostitution, it is hard to imagine they would have any better alternative once they had been turned back out on the street.) The magistrate also ordered Sun Mao beaten and exposed in the cangue. It was the hottest part of the summer, in one of the hottest and most humid places in China, and thus the cangue constituted especially severe treatment: in Ba County, it was not uncommon for prisoners serving a term in the cangue during the summer to die from typhoid or dysentery (conditions in the jail where they spent the night may have been more hazardous than the cangue itself). For this reason, punishment was often postponed until the weather had cooled. Sun Mao was finally released after a month, when his mother petitioned for mercy: with severe diarrhea and vomiting, he could consume neither food nor drink. Perhaps this was enough to teach him not to quarrel with yamen runners (BX, 3-8626, 8634)!

Citizens' Complaints

A final way prostitution came to official attention was through the complaints of local townspeople. In a typical 1851 example, a student preparing for the civil examinations petitioned that next to his school there lived two "itinerant prostitutes" (*liu chang*); their customers ("criminal elements from other jurisdictions") came and went at all times of day and night, disturbing the peace of the neighborhood. The prostitutes' landlord wanted to evict them, but he feared reprisal. The situation was "truly harmful to morality and ruinous to customs"—so would the magistrate please do something about it?

In cases of this kind, magistrates routinely ordered runners to investigate the reported location and "expel from the boundaries of the county" any pimps and prostitutes they discovered (*zhu ban chu jing*). The warrants issued in these cases specify that pimps and prostitutes were to be arrested only if they resisted; otherwise, they should simply be driven out. Magistrates showed no concern about what might happen once the culprits had crossed the county line: the guiding principle seems to have been "not in *my* county."[26]

A petition submitted to a newly installed magistrate in 1821 gives us some insight into how difficult it might be to get rid of prostitution in a jurisdiction as complex as Ba County. The four petitioners complained that the "evil pimp" Fu Xiazi ("Blind Man" Fu) had opened a brothel in their neighborhood some five years before. The petitioners had complained many times to their district head, Ou Chaogui, but he did nothing, because he was on the pimp's payroll. Finally, in 1818, they had appealed to the prefect, whose name was Lin, and got results.[27] At Prefect Lin's orders, Fu was arrested and exposed in the cangue; Ou Chaogui and unnamed others were beaten for "taking bribes and failing to expel the pimp and prostitutes"; and the house Fu had used as a brothel was confiscated.

But as Prefect Lin's term of office soon ended, he referred the case to the county yamen for follow-up. Continuity was further disrupted when new county magistrates took office in 1819 and again in 1821, and several temporary acting magistrates served in between. As a result, Ou Chaogui managed to hold on to his post as district head, and by 1820, the pimp Fu Xiazi had managed (with Ou's help) to get his house back and reopen the brothel. Now, the petitioners reported, the debauchery continued as flagrantly as before: "day and night, the prostitutes' customers arrive by sedan chair, causing great noise and disturbance." The petitioners begged the new magistrate to punish and expel the culprits.

In response to this petition, the magistrate ordered the runners responsible for that district to arrest the pimp and his prostitutes.

Unfortunately, the case file ends with a draft of their warrant, frustrating our curiosity about how this new effort fared. Nevertheless, this 1821 snapshot suggests how difficult it might be to enforce the ban on prostitution with consistent effect. The evidence from Ba County shows that degree-holding officials answerable to Beijing took seriously their mandate to suppress prostitution. But even in a city like Chongqing (top-heavy with agents of the imperial center, compared to most places), the most forthright attempts at enforcement might be stymied by the frequent rotation of centrally appointed officials, and by the indifference and downright corruption of local personnel (BX, 3-8634).[28]

Criminalized Prostitution and Yamen Corruption

Two central cases (not from Ba County) clarify the connections between the criminalization of prostitution and the corruption of yamen personnel. One effect of criminalization was to create new and lucrative opportunities for extortion.

In 1729, a yamen runner of Anyang County, Henan, named Li Delu (thirty-two *sui*) heard about a prostitute couple who were doing business in his district. The husband, Li Erbao (no age given), was pimping his wife, Zhang Shi (twenty-six *sui*)—the case record refers to them as *tu chang* ("local prostitutes"). Li Delu tracked them down and began extorting sexual services from Zhang Shi by threatening the couple with arrest and prosecution: "I went to arrest them, and saw that Zhang Shi was good-looking (*you xie zi se*). So on my own, I tied the two of them up, and threatened to take them to the magistrate to be punished. Li Erbao was afraid, so he agreed to hand Zhang Shi over to me so I could have sex with her. Then I let them go." Eventually, the three worked out an arrangement that modified outright extortion into something like patronage: Li Delu paid them an allowance and even rented quarters for them, in exchange for exclusive use of the prostitute. Later that year, however, Li Delu was dismissed from his post for drunkenness and dereliction of duty. Not long thereafter, the couple tried to sever their relationship with him, because he could no longer support them; for this reason, he beat Li Erbao senseless and abducted Zhang Shi, enforcing her cooperation by threatening to kill her. For the next few years, Li Delu passed Zhang Shi off as his own wife and pimped her to other men, until he was finally arrested in another county (for breaking the leg of a teenage boy who insulted him).

Now Li Delu may have been an unusually vicious man, even by

the stereotypical standard of yamen runners. But what made Zhang Shi and her husband vulnerable to his abuse in the first place was that he could threaten to arrest them for prostitution. It was the criminalization of prostitution that put them in his power (XT, 159/ QL 3.1.26).

The second case, from Shanyang County, Jiangsu, memorialized in 1738, illustrates what may have been a more typical relationship between pimps and yamen runners. The principal crime in the case was a homicide: a brothel-keeper named "Baldy" Zhang (Zhang Tuzi, thirty-seven *sui*) beat to death the husband of one of his prostitutes. According to his confession, Baldy Zhang began "harboring prostitutes" in 1735, when prostitute Wang Shi (twenty-five *sui*) and her husband Chen Jiu (twenty-nine *sui*) moved in with him and started working under his supervision. Wang Shi worked as a prostitute for some months, but then she "got in trouble with the law" (*zao le guan si*—the details are not provided), and refused to receive any more customers after that. Baldy himself enjoyed sleeping with her, however, and so he reserved her for his own use, paying her husband 4,000 cash per year in compensation. But because Baldy needed more income, in the spring of 1737 he told Chen Jiu "to find him a woman who would do business" (*xun ge nü ren zuo sheng yi*). Chen found a peasant named Wei Guochen who "was poor and having a hard time getting by," and had decided to have his wife, Sun Shi, "become a prostitute" (*wei chang*). In exchange for Sun Shi's sexual labor, Baldy agreed to provide the couple's food and drink and to pay Wei Guochen a daily allowance of 25 cash. The couple moved to his house, and that very night, Sun Shi slept with her first customer. Later, however, Baldy wanted to have sex with Sun Shi too, but Wei Guochen objected. A fight ensued, and Baldy beat Wei so severely that he died a couple of days later.

The pimp feared that he would be accused of murder, but fortunately he was on good terms with the yamen runners for his district: he had been paying them protection money for some time. He later testified: "At first, I never made any payments or presents to the yamen runners. But last year [i.e., 1736], Tong Tai was appointed the runner for this district, and he somehow found out [that I was harboring prostitutes]. Since then, I've had to give Tong Tai 30 big cash and treat him and [his assistant runner] Tian Mei to wine every time there is a festival." Baldy had begun paying off the runners even though Wang Shi had already stopped receiving customers. When asked why, he testified: "Tong Tai and Tian Mei knew that

Chen Jiu's wife [Wang Shi] was originally a prostitute, and they knew that I was paying to have her for myself; so they came to press me for payment. I could hardly refuse them, so I paid up." If Baldy had paid protection money to Tong Tai's predecessors, Wang Shi might not have gotten in trouble in the first place.

What did Baldy do after Wei Guochen died? According to his testimony:

I went to Tong Tai's assistant runner, Tian Mei, and lied to him, saying "Wei Guochen was sick for a few days, didn't respond to medicine, and finally died. His wife Sun Shi has no complaints to make about it. Now I'm willing to provide a few strings of cash for the group of you to divide among yourselves, as long as you don't report his death to the magistrate, so that we can just bury him." Tian Mei agreed, and had me go with him to talk it over with Tong Tai. Tong Tai said, "Well, since he died of illness, it's all right just to bury him." Then Tian Mei informed the rural agent, Li Rusheng.

Later, Tian Mei and Li Rusheng visited Baldy Zhang's house to collect the money; he gave them 480 cash to share with Tong Tai. The dead man's wife, Sun Shi, did not tell the men that her husband had been beaten, but she insisted on making an official report of the death (apparently hoping that an inquest would expose Zhang's guilt). But the runner and the rural agent discouraged her from pursuing the matter by threatening her with prosecution for prostitution. As Tian Mei later testified, "Li Rusheng and I knew that Sun Shi was a prostitute, and we told her, 'You've come out and done this illegal business (*fei shi*), so if you report the death you'll definitely be punished for your crime. You'd be better off just burying him.' After that, she said nothing."

But word somehow leaked, and an investigation exposed the runners' complicity. The magistrate found it hard to believe that the runners and rural agent had not demanded larger bribes, especially to cover up a homicide, and he threatened them with torture; however, all witnesses agreed on the amounts stated above. (Perhaps Baldy Zhang was not the only pimp paying these runners, and thus their total income from such sources may have been far more than these small sums would suggest.) The runners insisted that they had believed the pimp's story, and had assumed he wanted to avoid official attention simply because of his pimping. But the way Tian Mei and Li Rusheng intimidated Sun Shi into silence suggests that they knew there was more to hide than just prostitution. Of course, once they had taken bribes from the pimp, it was in their own interest to see that he avoided scrutiny.

In the end, the runners were ordered beaten and dismissed from their posts (the rural agent escaped). Baldy Zhang, his lesser offense of "harboring prostitutes" aside, was sentenced to strangulation after the assizes for the killing. Sun Shi was sentenced to 100 blows of the heavy bamboo and three years of penal servitude, as "a wife who reaches a private settlement with someone who murders her husband"; since she was "a wife who has engaged in illicit sexual intercourse," the magistrate ordered that her beating be carried out, though he commuted the penal servitude to a fine (standard practice for female offenders). Chen Jiu and his wife Wang Shi were both sentenced to 90 blows of the heavy bamboo, and Wang Shi was ordered divorced and returned to her natal lineage, according to the statute against "abetting one's wife or concubine to engage in illicit sexual intercourse." The magistrate technically responsible for "failing to detect" prostitution had himself prosecuted the case, so the penalty for that oversight was waived.

Everyone involved in this case knew that prostitution was illegal, and that Baldy Zhang and the couples he employed could be prosecuted (as, indeed, they eventually were). That is why Wang Shi had "gotten in trouble with the law" for prostitution before Baldy Zhang began paying off the local runners. That is why Tong Tai demanded protection money as soon as he discovered the brothel, and why Baldy complied. It also explains the threat used to silence Sun Shi when she sought to report her husband's death. As in the previous case, it was the criminalization of prostitution that made the people involved in that trade vulnerable to extortion and other hazards (XT, 159/QL 3.5.15).

The criminalization of prostitution had a real effect on judicial and police practice at the county level. The evidence from Ba County, in particular, persuades me that degree-holding representatives of the imperial center made a serious effort to enforce the ban on prostitution. But criminalization had a corrupting influence as well, by creating new sources of graft for the indispensable local personnel on whom magistrates depended to put policy into effect. Moreover, if the policy imposed a standard of sexual morality that could not be enforced with consistent effect, it may well have undermined respect for the moral and legal authority behind it. (Another Yongzheng initiative, the criminalization of opium trafficking, evidently had a similar corrupting effect.)[29]

At the end of the nineteenth century, Xue Yunsheng weighed the results of the Yongzheng policy on prostitution:

Successive reigns have found it impossible to stamp out prostitution, in spite of the strict laws established for that purpose; so it would seem that we can do without such laws. If we look at the facts, has it been possible to eliminate even one percent of prostitution? The only result [of prohibition] has been to create new opportunities for local thugs and yamen clerks and runners to collect protection money (*de gui bao bi*). Moreover, even when we punish prostitutes and actors [i.e., male homosexual prostitutes] with the bamboo and the cangue, can we really make them "change their occupations to those proper to commoners"? On the contrary, they just go on being prostitutes and actors, as before.

After 175 years, it seemed clear that the "transformation of values" envisioned by the Yongzheng Emperor had failed.[30]

Conclusion

Past scholarship has generally interpreted the Yongzheng elimination of certain debased-status labels as a project of "emancipation" that failed, at best. We gain more insight by considering the policy's implications for the regulation of sexuality. The premise of the 1723 edict was that prostitution had previously been tolerated only as a symptom of specific categories of debased status. The practical implication of being promoted to commoner status was that these groups would henceforth be held to commoner standards of morality and criminal liability. The Yongzheng vision of "self-renewal" began with the criminalization of the sex work that had provided a living for many of these people: it was less an offer of personal liberation than a sharp narrowing of the scope of acceptable activity, backed by intensified official surveillance and the threat of criminal prosecution.

But this initiative reached well beyond the specific groups mentioned by edict. The "emancipation" of these groups eliminated the legal basis for tolerating any sex work by anyone. The legal fiction of sex work as a hallmark of debased status had permitted, in practice, much commercial prostitution in a gray area where questions of status background were not always pursued with great rigor. But now this gray area vanished, as all sex work became equated with the commoner crime of "illicit sexual intercourse."

In practical terms, then, the Yongzheng policy meant a dramatic extension of the reach of penal law. The 1723 edict and subsequent measures effectively prohibited sex outside marriage to *all* women for the first time. But it was not just women who were held to a new standard—any husband who pimped his wife became liable for punishment, including mandated divorce, and the male customers of prostitutes all became criminals as well. Perhaps the most dramatic change affected the legal standing of pimps: before 1723, debased-status pimps had enjoyed a recognized social role and even, under some circumstances, a legitimate claim to legal protection. After 1723, pimps who managed unrelated prostitutes (that is, not their wives) came in for the harshest penalties associated with prohibition, both on paper and (as the Ba County cases show) in judicial practice as well. If all prostitutes and their customers were now defined as ordinary adulterers, a pimp was reconceptualized as something far more dangerous. Now that *all* potential recruits for prostitution were viewed as commoners, a pimp had to be considered a parasite who profited from the systematic pollution of chaste women.

The extension of commoner status to the previously debased groups did promote equality before the law; in that sense, at least, it certainly had a leveling effect. But was it *progressive,* to use Terada Takanobu's term? The answer depends on what we mean by progress. The history of centrally engineered social leveling in China is largely a record of maneuvers to concentrate power in imperial hands, by eliminating autonomous claims to status and authority (aristocratic birthright, the independence of religious institutions, and so on). Treating people the same as one another does not necessarily mean endowing them with political rights; on the contrary, to exalt an autocrat requires the leveling of his subjects. I see no reason to believe that the Yongzheng Emperor intended any departure from this tradition. As Kuhn observes, "formal commoner equality was right in line with the despotic and rationalizing style of [the Yongzheng Emperor]" (1990, 35).

In concluding this chapter, let me emphasize a deeper continuity. To lawmakers both before and after 1723, the trouble with prostitution was not that it made commodities of women's bodies, but rather that it constituted "illicit sexual intercourse"—conduct that threatened the family morality and structure essential to social order. (The institution of the official matchmaker is strong evidence that commodification in itself was not considered objectionable.) The Yongzheng extension of commoner norms to debased-status groups criminalized even their previously tolerated sex work as "illicit sexual intercourse," by widening the application of existing laws. But the complete prohibition of prostitution prompted no new penalties for the payment of money: extramarital intercourse in the context of sex work was never punished more severely than simple adultery.

To grasp this point, we must distinguish the sexual element from the commercial. In the United States today, for example, sexual promiscuity is not prosecuted except when it takes the commercial form of prostitution. Without payment there is no crime, and adultery now retains legal relevance only as an occasional factor in divorce proceedings. The law of imperial China reversed the formula: the commercial element was the *least* objectionable part of prostitution. This principle provided a deep continuity that underlay the innovations of the eighteenth century.

CHAPTER EIGHT

Conclusion

In the Tang code, offenses of "illicit sexual intercourse" were listed under the "miscellaneous statutes," and there were only a few of them. The Ming code contained many more statutes on illicit sex, and now the *substatutes* on this crime far outnumber even the Ming statutes. Those included in the present chapter [on "illicit sexual intercourse"] by no means exhaust the list—for example, the code's chapter on "forcing another person to commit suicide" does not hesitate to treat this crime in great detail. The vexatious pile-up of cases related to illicit sex may well be the result of this proliferation of laws; but also, *one can see in this phenomenon the condition of the present age.*
—Xue Yunsheng, late nineteenth century (DC, 375-04, commentary)

Qing-dynasty initiatives in the regulation of sexuality extended a uniform standard of sexual morality and criminal liability that had originally been narrowly associated with free commoner status. The most obvious way this extension was accomplished was by eliminating old status-based exceptions to the general prohibition of extramarital intercourse, namely prostitution and the sexual use of servile women by their masters. A parallel move was to assimilate homosexual sodomy to the previously heterosexual category of sex offenses. These expansions of the compass of "illicit sexual intercourse" (*jian*) were accompanied by the invention of new crimes against chastity and by the harsher punishment of such crimes generally. In addition, the Yongzheng regime launched an unprecedented propaganda campaign to promote female chastity among the common people: chastity honors were extended not only to chaste widows and martyred victims of attempted rape (as in the Ming), but also to wives who resisted family pressure to act as prostitutes, widows who died resisting forced remarriage, women who committed suicide in response to lewd propositions, and so on. Countless edicts spotlighted the sexual choices of poor women as questions of highest import, as if the state were enlisting them as guardians of the fragile boundaries of normative family order.

The results can be summed up as a shift in the basic organizing principle for regulating sexuality, from status performance to gender performance, whereby both males and females were held to fixed and idealized marital roles that applied to all. In part, this program simply updated the law to fit a changed social reality, to take account of both the expanding class of commoner peasants and the decreasing utility of fixed status labels. But more important, it represented an effort to cope with newly perceived dangers that threatened sexual anarchy.

The judicial constructs of the Qing must be understood against a social background in which, because men outnumbered women, patriarchal stability was perceived as under constant threat from a growing crowd of rogue males at the bottom of the socioeconomic scale. The numbers of such males were increasing, and their proportion in the overall population was probably increasing as well; but they loomed even larger in the collective consciousness of the Qing judiciary, given their disproportionate representation in the criminal caseload of both county and central courts. With few exceptions, it was these men who were prosecuted for heterosexual and homosexual rape, for consensual sodomy, and for adultery with widows. It was usually poor single males who bought the wives of even poorer men, who then became single themselves. It was poor men who pimped their wives, creating perhaps the only opportunity for heterosexual intercourse open to a great many other poor men (although, of course, women from the bottom of society performed sex work at all levels). In this sexual anarchy, many poor men shared a few promiscuous women, and they were feared to covet the wives, daughters, and young sons of better-established householders.

The Phallocentrism of the Law

The regulation of sexuality in late imperial law was framed by an absolute phallocentrism that defined the sexual in terms of a stereotyped act of penetration. Phallic penetration implied a number of things: most fundamentally, it initiated sexual partners into the hierarchy of adult gender roles, properly within the context of marriage, where male was assumed to dominate female. By extension, the act of penetration could imply initiation and domination in other contexts: for example, pirates sodomized male captives in order to initiate them into their ranks, or a widow might have her sexual partner rape her daughter-in-law to make her, in effect, a co-conspirator in their illicit affair.

In an important and profound way, sexual role gendered an individual as male (penetrator) or female (penetrated), and this division of roles far outweighed in importance the sex of one's object of desire. Thus, sexual union between males was understood not in terms of the polarity of sexual orientation, but rather in terms of the polluting gender inversion of the penetrated male. On this basis, Qing jurists conceptualized masculinity in terms of the dangerous predator outside the family order, the vulnerable adolescent of good family, and the polluted male who consented to penetration. Thus, the dangerousness, vulnerability, and pollution of males all derived from the threat of penetration *out of place*. A fourth figure, the normative male householder, was a penetrator harnessed to the social roles of husband and father, and disciplined by the filial duty to procreate and by sober fear of community sanction and imperial authority (Sommer, forthcoming).

The same basic logic framed thinking about female sexuality. Imperial law was utterly silent about female homosexual acts, on the apparent assumption that they were non-phallic and therefore non-polluting.[1] Instead, the judicial purpose was to protect the patrilineal family order against pollution by outside blood, whether that threat took the form of rape or of the treacherous adultery of women. Female sexuality was conceived as vulnerability to penetration; female *virtue* was defined ultimately in terms of how much a woman was willing to suffer in order to reserve that penetrability for her one husband and master.

Thus, penetration was understood (in both law and popular perception) as a potent and even dangerous act. Depending on context, this act could impose or overthrow legitimate hierarchies; it could reproduce or invert the normative gender order; it could initiate persons into social adulthood, or inflict a polluting stigma that provoked homicide and suicide. The imperative of sexual regulation throughout the imperial era was to guard against the multifarious threat of penetration out of place.

From Status to Gender, and the
New Focus on the Peasant Family

The underlying phallocentrism of the law underwent little or no change during the period covered by this study: penetration continued to imply a gendered hierarchy of domination, regardless of what else happened. What did in fact change was the judicial conceptualization of what kind of social order needed to be protected from the threat of penetration out of place, and what sort of outside male posed the greatest threat.

I should reiterate that a number of important changes well preceded the eighteenth century, although that era certainly witnessed rapid and transformative change. The exaltation of female chastity and fixing of gender roles accompanied the decline of fixed status categories in a gradual process that began long before. Indeed, the Yuan and Ming dynasties may also be considered watersheds in the regulation of sexuality. The Yuan established the basic system for honoring chaste widows on which the Ming and Qing cults were modeled; Yuan lawmakers also imposed death penalties for some scenarios of rape, and issued the first law that equated wife-selling with "illicit sexual intercourse." In addition, the Yuan attempted to quash an emerging commercial sex market that threatened to blur status boundaries, by issuing explicit prohibitions against commoner husbands prostituting their wives (or masters their slaves). (Actually, one edict to this effect had already been issued in the Southern Song.) Building on this foundation, the Ming dynasty extended chastity honors to martyred victims of attempted rape, expanded the death penalty to cover all rapes between status equals, imposed a stricter standard of evidence for rape conviction, and banned consensual homosexual sodomy for the first time. Qing jurists were well aware of what their predecessors had done, and they clearly perceived the general direction of change implied by that record. From this longer historical perspective, the remarkable and profuse initiatives of the High Qing judiciary can be seen as a logical outgrowth of all that had come before.

The classic organizing principle for regulating sexual behavior had been to uphold a *status* hierarchy rooted in an aristocratic vision of fixed social structure. What most worried Tang-dynasty jurists was the pollution of descent through the violation of free women by servile males, especially within a single household; in this context, "free" (*liang*) referred primarily to aristocratic women, since the typical peasant was not likely to own slaves (see Appendix A.1). The parallel with imperial Rome is striking: "What mattered to the ancient Roman when it came to sex was the status of the individual(s) engaging in sexual activity. Furthermore, Roman law with regard to sex ignored most of the population, since its purpose was to defend the values of the elite, ruling class. These values include the production of legitimate heirs and the protection of people with freeborn status from debasement" (Clarke 1998, 279). For most of the imperial era, the purpose of sexual regulation in China was never to ban any particular behavior altogether, but simply to confine it to its proper place. The absence of any mention of sodomy in early law reflects, I suspect, an aristocratic assumption that homosexual penetration was something one did to one's slave or servant as a pastime; in this context, the gender inversion of the penetrated male simply confirmed his subordinate position in the more important hierarchy of legal status.

In the Qing, however, the regulation of sexual behavior was reorganized to uphold a *gender* order defined in terms of strict adherence to family roles—and the family that jurists seem to have had in mind was the settled peasant family. The regulatory regime that took shape in the eighteenth century envisioned as its worst-case scenario the violation of chaste women and adolescent boys of *good yet humble family*, by males outside the family order altogether. The important cleavage was not between the elite and a servile labor force, but rather between the peasant family and the various antisocial individuals who supposedly threatened it from without. In other words, the shift from status performance to gender performance also involved a refocus downward toward the common people. From this perspective, the emergence of the penetrated male in late imperial legal discourse is a key mark of transition: it represents a shift in point of view, from the elite penetrator who is sure of his privileges, to the peasant householder anxious that sodomy was something a rogue male might do to his "son or younger brother."

Recent scholarship on gender in late imperial China has tended to focus on various concerns of the elite: dowry inflation, rising competition in the marriage market and in civil examinations, female literacy and education, women's poetry and publishing, the courtesan as symbol of loyalty and carrier of high culture, and so on. It is absolutely clear that elite gender discourse underwent major shifts in the eighteenth century—and these shifts must have affected legal developments, since the judiciary was staffed by degree-holding members of the elite. Specifically, the marginalization of the courtesan as a cultural ideal and the reaffirmation of wifely moral authority that occurred on the level of elite discourse (Mann 1997) coincided with the prohibition of prostitution and the extension of a *liang* standard of female chastity to all women. But key figures like the Yongzheng and Qianlong emperors and the veteran official Chen Hongmou[2] clearly saw the enforcement of normative gender roles as part of a larger civilizing project that targeted the common people (as well as the non-Han natives of new frontier territories—Rowe 1992). This new attention to gender performance among ordinary commoners went hand in hand with the project of status leveling, which extended what Kuhn (1992) has termed "formal commoner equality" to include practically everyone in the empire.

If we train our focus on the Qing judicial system, the centrality of non-elites becomes especially clear. For one thing, nearly all the people who appear in Qing legal cases (especially criminal records) are peasants, petty urbanites, or marginalized individuals of one kind or another; they possess at most only very modest means. These were the people that the eighteenth-century judiciary actually dealt with. In addition, Qing legislation appears to have been marked by what Kathryn Bernhardt (with regard to marriage and women's property claims) has called the "peasantization" of the law, namely a decisive shift away from the aristocratic priorities found in early codes toward those of the common peasantry (1996). Innovations in the regulation of sexuality seem to have been prompted less by any specific concern of (or on behalf of) the elite than by an imperative to strengthen the humble household seen as the foundation of late imperial order, and this urgency may have accurately reflected the anxieties and priorities of settled peasant householders themselves.

There has been a tendency to attribute Qing legislation against sodomy, in particular, to a disgusted reaction against "decadence" at court and among the elite in the late Ming (including rich men who patronized male prostitutes and actors, or installed catamites among their servants) (see especially Ng 1987 and 1989). This theory depends in part on mistaken chronology (since the prohibition of consensual sodomy predated the Qing conquest). But also, the disgusted reaction to "decadence" posited by this theory would seem more typical of a modernist, May Fourth–era perspective on sex (see Dikötter 1995) than of a seventeenth- or eighteenth-century perspective; the late Ming literatus Shen Defu, for one, seems to have been disgusted with excessive self-indulgence rather than with same-sex attraction or sexual acts per se.[3] In contrast, Ba Jin's 1931 novel *Family* (*Jia*) uses the lecherous patronage of effeminate actors by elderly Confucian scholars to symbolize the decadent hypocrisy of the doomed older generation. The novel's puritanical younger generation reacts with appropriate disgust to this and all other displays of carnal desire; the young people's relationships are characterized instead by fraternal solidarity and physical self-denial for the sake of a higher spiritual and political cause.[4]

Whether we look at the language of the substatutes, or at the actual cases to which they were applied, it is clear that Qing innovations on sodomy had nothing to do with the elite. Elite men who were disposed to patronize cross-dressing actors and male prostitutes continued to do so, regardless of the law; this fact reflects their practical privileges, but also, perhaps, the older aristocratic assumption that the gender inversion of the penetrated male was no cause for concern as long as it conformed to the proper order of status domination. The new Qing concern with vulnerable masculinity would seem to reflect not elite gender trouble, but commoner gender trouble—in other words, the anxieties of the peasant householder struggling against downward mobility and confronted by the specter of the rogue male who had already fallen through the cracks.

The ban on prostitution (like that on wife-selling) seems to have had nothing to do with elite tastes and practices either. The prohibition certainly included all prostitution, but none of the records of actual prosecution that I have seen involve anyone remotely connected with the elite. In fact, it may well have been the "democratization" of both the personnel and clientele in sex work, through the development of a pervasive commercial sex market by the end of the Ming, that prompted its total prohibition by the Qing. When the newly enthroned Qianlong Emperor exhorted his ministers to enforce this prohibition with renewed vigor, he characterized prostitution as a scourge on the lives of ordinary peasants. Practical enforcement at the county level involved punishing pimps, cracking down on husbands who pimped or sold their wives, and rescuing women who wanted to leave prostitution by marrying them off to proper husbands. These initiatives reflect not a crisis of *elite* mores, but rather an acute awareness of the growing number of people at the margins of society for whom sexual behavior criminalized by the state had come to play a basic role in survival.

The Changing Concept of *Liang*

~The shift from status performance to gender performance is clearly reflected in the changing meaning of the legal term *liang*. Jurists used this ancient legal term right down to the end of the imperial era, but its meaning changed significantly. As we have seen, from the Tang through the eighteenth century, the term's emphasis shifted from free commoner legal status to moral goodness, especially in a sexual sense. For example, where *cong liang* had originally meant for any servile laborer "to be freed to become a commoner," by the end of the eighteenth century it was used almost exclusively to mean a prostitute who "reformed" herself by taking up the normative female role of chaste wife. Similarly, as Angela Leung has pointed out, the usage in philanthropic discourse of the term *jian* (mean, debased) gradually shifted to emphasize moral degeneracy instead of legal status debasement (1993b).

In subtle ways, the legal category *liang* continued to change. We can even detect signs of a softening in the absolutism of chastity discourse, an even greater flexibility in who could be honored as exemplars of female excellence. During the Qianlong and Jiaqing reigns, chastity martyr eligibility was extended to new categories of women who had previously been excluded, further eroding long-standing distinctions between social groups in a logical continuation of Yongzheng policy.[5] For example, in 1746, reduced honors (money for a memorial arch, but no tablet in the temple of chastity and filial piety) were granted to chaste widows among a formerly debased servile group within the banner forces. The same policy was applied to domestic female slaves and wives of servants and hired laborers generally (QHS, 403/508, 513–14). In 1782 and 1783, the Qianlong Emperor granted canonization to chaste widows among non-Han tribes, singling out these "barbarian wives" (*fan fu*) for particular praise; these women received full honors (QHS, 403/513). An edict of 1793 canonized a woman who had died resisting rape, even though she was the wife of a yamen runner (long considered a debased-status occupation because of its historical roots in compulsory labor service);[6] the only concession to status considerations was the same reduction in her honors (QHS, 403/513). In 1806, a woman who died resisting her mother-in-law's pressure to submit to prostitution was canonized, in spite of the fact that she had married into a family of "local prostitutes" (*tu chang*); the only qualification was that the money for her memorial arch be awarded to her natal family instead of to her husband (QHS, 404/517).

The Jiaqing reign also witnessed an unprecedented blurring of the strict distinction between the penetrated and the chaste. In 1803, an edict extended chastity martyr eligibility for the first time to rape victims who had been penetrated, as long as their "intent to resist chastely" (*kang jie zhi xin*) was beyond doubt, and they had been overpowered by at least two attackers. If a woman had been polluted by a *single* rapist, then as long as she had been overpowered and tied up in advance, provincial governors could nominate them to the Board of Rites, which would decide each case on its own merits. This new policy appears to have been implemented for the first time in the following year, when a woman who committed suicide after being gang-raped was approved for chastity martyr status; however, her family received only half the usual grant of silver for her memorial arch. The same year saw the canonization of a woman who committed suicide after being raped by a single attacker; again, however, her family received only half the standard sum (QHS, 404/516–17). The memorialist who had advocated this change argued that an official captured by rebels might be forced to kneel, but that to do so would prove no disloyalty on his part; so too, a wife overpowered and penetrated by a gang of rapists should not necessarily be considered unchaste (HC, 92/33a–b).

In 1840, a "beggar girl with no name" (*wu ming gai nü*) who had been raped and murdered by a single attacker (another beggar) was approved for canonization, but again, only half the silver was granted, and no memorial tablet was set up at the local temple. In this final example the two trends intersected, when a female of the humblest possible station who had been penetrated qualified as a chastity martyr (QHS, 404/521).[7]

Each of these cases is recorded because it set a new precedent to be followed in subsequent decisions. In many instances, some reduction of honors preserved the sense that the woman was somewhat polluted, either by debased status or by penetration. Yet inclusion of these women at all suggests that purity of intent gradually came to outweigh absolute categories in determining what sort of woman could epitomize female excellence (Elvin 1984, n. 177; Sommer 1994, 415–19).

Another suggestive change was the introduction of the idea of reform into the judicial evaluation of individuals who had previously committed offenses of illicit sex. For example, a substatute of 1814 codified the traditional practice of reducing the penalty for gang rape if the victim had previously committed offenses of illicit sex. But the same substatute added a new qualification: if there was "definite proof" that the woman had "already repented and renewed herself (hui guo zi xin)" since committing such offenses, then she should be treated as a liang ren funü—that is, as liang in the sense of chaste—and her rapists should receive the full penalty of death (DC, 366-12). (Significantly, zi xin, "self-renewal," was the term used by the Yongzheng Emperor to characterize the second chance being offered to people formerly classified as yue households.) We find a comparable innovation in the law on "males who commit homicide in self-defense against rape": an amendment of 1824 mandated lenience for a male who had consented to being penetrated but later "repented" (hui guo) and rejected the penetrator's subsequent advances, finally killing him in order to avoid being raped (see Appendix B.1, final clause). Previously, self-defense against rape would have carried no weight with the judiciary in such cases, and the killer (that is, the victim of attempted rape) would have received the full penalty for homicide. The implication of these innovations was that a reformed attitude could cleanse a person of the pollution of having consented to illicit penetration, restoring her or him to liang status for purposes of penal law. (This recovery of virtue through willed self-reform follows the same logic as the post-Yongzheng usage of cong liang by ex-prostitutes.)

Increasingly, then, to judge someone as liang involved an evaluation of individual conduct and subjective consciousness. The shift is nowhere better illustrated than in an 1822 case from Shandong, reported by Conspectus of Legal Cases, in which a girl aged ten sui was abducted; she happened to be the adopted daughter of a prostitute. The governor of Shandong was not sure how to categorize the girl in order to fix the correct penalties for her abductors—as with rape, the penalty depended on whether the victim was liang, and this girl could hardly be considered a daughter of "good family." Moreover, prostitutes often adopted girls with the intention of inducting them into the same occupation. The governor asked the Board of Punishment for a ruling: specifically, how should the statutory requirement that the victim be liang apply in such a case? The board replied that the relevant law focused not on the victim's family background but on her own conduct and attitude: had she herself committed offenses of illicit sex? And if so, had she since repented and reformed herself? The victim in this case was young enough that these questions did not apply; therefore, even though she had been adopted by an unchaste woman, "her own body was pure" (*zi shen qing bai*), and she could be considered *liang*. Her abductors suffered the full penalty.

Before 1723, the mother's occupation as prostitute would have fixed the mean status of her entire household, and vice versa. But a century later, the Board of Punishment could assert that this girl's family background had no bearing on whether she was *liang*—so much had the legal sense of that term changed. All that mattered was the girl's own individual conduct and attitude (XA, 8/4b–5a). This reasoning parallels the 1806 canonization (cited above) of a woman who had married into a family of "local prostitutes" and died resisting her mother-in-law's pressure to sell sex.

The underlying logic of the changing interpretation of *liang* was that morality demonstrated in conduct should determine status before the law, instead of the other way around, as had long been the case. We can read this development as a logical outgrowth of the expansion of commoner legal standards in recognition of the increasingly fluid nature of social relations: for the Qing judiciary, willed conduct rather than the accident of birth or social position had become the most useful factor in distinguishing between most persons. One result was greater equality of individuals before the law. But we would be mistaken, I believe, to read this shift in terms of the Western paradigm of progress in the law.

William Rowe argues that the thinking of veteran official Chen Hongmou with regard to gender was characterized by a new, "early modern" individualism that downplayed old differences of status or class. But Rowe is careful to qualify this judgment: "He shares an emerging early modern valuation of the individual (female as well as male) within the family or household unit, at the same time that he views society as necessarily composed of households, not individuals, and thus fully endorses subordination to the patriarch's authority. The person embedded within the social role engages his sympathetic attention, but remains of secondary importance to the role itself" (1992, 34). This characterization is not what we think of as individualism in a modern, Western sense, but rather part of a broader leveling that asserted, in the place of anachronistic status labels, the importance of strict gender performance in subordination to family roles. The redoubled emphasis on normative gender performance went hand in hand with extension of the reach of penal law and of moral surveillance over the lives of common people.

All these changes aimed less to emancipate or repress individuals, I believe, than to clear away outdated distractions and to concentrate on new dangers. Much of the legislation and propaganda that we have examined was designed to exalt, empower, and protect the chaste wife of humble background, a category that became broader and more inclusive over time. The unprecedented importance attributed to the chastity of humble women—which implied that their own conscious choices with regard to sex actually mattered—signifies a new responsibility being imposed on such women. They stood on the frontlines to defend the normative family order, and the standard of chastity they maintained would determine its fate. Through their endurance and suffering they could preserve it; through promiscuity and sloth they might destroy it. Given our liberationist paradigm for thinking about women's history and gay-lesbian history, it is possible to miss the fact that Qing initiatives aimed not so much to *repress* women (let alone sexual minorities) as to strengthen an embattled peasant family against the moral implications of downward mobility and the possibly very real predations of a swelling underclass of "rootless rascals."

Survival Logic and Sexual Anarchy

The eighteenth century was a time of both hubris and paranoia, of both commercial expansion and overpopulation, when the numbers of both elite female poets and penniless male vagrants reached unprecedented heights. The paradoxical character of the century is clearly reflected in the Yongzheng edicts of "emancipation." Several of the edicts tended to confirm the market-driven spread of contractual relations of production, but the first and most important edict dramatically extended the reach of penal law and moral surveillance by mandating the extirpation of prostitution. This latter measure can be seen as a reaction *against* the market—that is, the commercial sex market that had displaced the old paradigm of sex work as hereditary penal servitude—and it suggests that Qing officials viewed socioeconomic change with very mixed feelings, at best. Indeed, the Qing founders (like the founders of every previous dynasty) had tried once again to fix people socially and geographically in place, according to an overly simplistic scheme that was a memory already by the Yongzheng era. Eighteenth-century initiatives in the regulation of sexuality were prompted not just by the anachronism of old status barriers, but also by growing anxiety at dangerous social and demographic trends.

Much of this study has been devoted to explaining judicial constructions and sketching the wider social context of Qing legislation. Chapters 3 and 4 stressed the basic congruence between the phallocentric assumptions of formal law and more widespread social norms and practices. In particular, I argued that the Qing judiciary's reconstruction of sodomy, while representing a departure from earlier practice, nevertheless made sense in terms of both legal tradition and widespread popular perceptions (especially among the settled peasantry); in effect, Qing sodomy law codified the contemporary common sense of what phallic penetration meant. Chapter 5 argued that even though not everyone may have "internalized" the moral agenda of the imperial chastity cult, that agenda was understood perfectly well by ordinary peasants, who adapted their lives and rhetorical strategies appropriately; this adaptation is particularly clear in the skillful way so many women performed the public role of "chaste widow." Chapter 5 ended by underscoring the function of litigation in disseminating official values, showing how different levels of patriarchal power reinforced each other. More generally, this book at many points has touched on the power of stigma and the threat of rogue males, suggesting that Qing legislation reflected the values and anxieties of the settled peasant community at least as much as those of the elite.

But I do not mean to imply the universal acceptance of officially mandated norms. On the contrary, the best scholarship on the Chinese peasantry tells us that much of peasant life was (and continues to be) dominated by a survival logic quite different from, and often at odds with, the priorities and pretensions of the state.[8] I believe that the gap between the mandated sexual order and sexual practice among the poor was growing over the course of the Qing dynasty.

One of the chastity cult's innovations was to honor wives who remained faithful for long periods under difficult circumstances even though their husbands had not actually died. In 1777, a wife separated from her husband for over 50 years was honored for remaining chaste; in the following year, a woman who remained faithful through 32 years of a marriage that was never consummated (because of the husband's long illness) was honored as well (QHS, 403/521). In both examples, the wife maintained absolute sexual loyalty to her one true husband, even when he did not play that role either sexually or economically. The unstated context for such heroism is the plethora of cases in legal archives in which women who had been abandoned or whose invalid husbands could not support them resorted to prostitution, adultery, or remarriage. The same context informed the honoring of women who resisted family pressure to become prostitutes.

Susan Mann has shown that over the eighteenth century, Qing officials promoted women's textile work with increasing urgency; they saw such work both as a means to shore up the peasant household economy and as "a check on female promiscuity" (Mann 1997, 163). Promoting women's work fit into the larger program of propagating female chastity among the poor: conscientious female commitment to handicrafts would strengthen both the household economy and wifely fidelity (the stereotype of the chaste widow had her spinning and weaving round the clock to support her children). Officials made this connection, I suspect, less on the basis of abstract morality or physiocratic economics than from their own concrete knowledge (as sitting magistrates charged with extirpating prostitution) that so many desperate people turned to strategies of sexual commodification in order to survive. The shrill, moralistic tone of officials who promoted textile work came from their understanding that the *realistic* strategy, for all too many women, was *sex* work.[9]

In the demonology of the Qing judiciary, the opposite of the chastity heroine (and also the female counterpart to the rogue male) was the *jian fu*: the treacherous promiscuous wife who flouted the disciplining bonds of family and of female chastity.[10] Fear of such women is reflected in the judicial treatment of practices of commodification like prostitution and wife-selling. The language used from Yuan through Qing to prohibit a husband from "abetting" (*zong*, "indulging," "unleashing") his wife's promiscuity implied the release of something wild; such language betrays a great fear of women who lost their sense of *yi*, the moral duty to submit to the normative role of chaste wife. The crime of "buying or selling a divorce" was imagined in the same way, the classic scenario being a husband's acquiescence to his wife's adultery by selling her to her lover. Jurists conceptualized these crimes not as wife abuse but rather as wifely licentiousness, and they sought to punish irresponsible husbands who betrayed the vital interests of husbands generally, by letting their wives get away with such disruptive promiscuity.

Perhaps such fears were not entirely misplaced. The Qing archives are full of cases showing that women who were pimped or otherwise sexually exploited by their husbands experienced a demystification, a "consciousness-raising," that could have radically subversive results. The wifely deference that helped induce some women to submit to such arrangements would itself be undermined by the disjuncture that sexual exploitation opened between mandated values and lived experience. In many examples, women ultimately chose the customer who could pay over the husband who could not—leading to elopement, murder, and other nightmarish ruptures of the mandated family order.

The long-term significance of the "moral transformation" envisioned in the Yongzheng reign remains an open question. By the Daoguang reign, the High Qing flood of sex-related legislation had slowed to a trickle, and we can detect a certain confusion in the judiciary. On the one hand, the chastity cult had opened up to an unprecedented degree, and memorial arches proliferated across the landscape; on the other hand, as Susan Mann has suggested, widows who did manage to remain chaste were being reduced from "symbols of community pride" to "objects of charity," and the entire chastity cult slowly began to lose its appeal for the elite (1987, 51–52). At the same time, the Board of Punishment had been forced to give up even the pretense of suppressing two widespread unchaste practices: widow remarriage during the mourning period, and wife-selling motivated by poverty (which includes nearly all wife-selling cases I have seen). The board authorized magistrates to let such illegal marriages stand, and also reduced the corporal penalties that applied—on the grounds that given their poverty, if the women in question were ordered divorced they would almost certainly end up losing their chastity by some other, even more unsavory means. By conceding this fact, the board had admitted the futility of the Yongzheng vision of enforcing female chastity among the poor (Sommer 1994, 388–94).

In the eighteen-forties, Bao Shichen (a former magistrate with a reputation for pragmatism) argued that poor people should not be punished for the moral compromises they found necessary for survival: "It is the *officials* who are responsible for teaching and nurturing the common people, and it is *they* who should be ashamed if poverty and hunger drive husbands and wives to separate in order to save themselves" (1968, 2138). This was an orthodox Confucian view with radical implications: the breakdown of family morality called into question the legitimacy of political leadership. If that is how a magistrate felt, we can only speculate on the cumulative subversive effect of the contradiction between normative values and lived experience for growing numbers of the poor.

The various unorthodox household patterns we have noticed in Qing case records (including those which involved sexual commodification) tended to mimic more typical marriages and households, in that the sexual bond was part of a more complex, hierarchical alliance of co-residence and economic interdependence, sometimes formalized by fictive kinship ties. Survival required alliance with others perhaps even more than it required property, and life outside the family and community order seems to have been a grim and brutish business; we can interpret unorthodox household patterns as attempts to reproduce, however imperfectly, the tenuous security that order provided. These survival strategies confirm, in an ironic sense, the hegemony of the normative values that subordinated the individual to hierarchical relations of reciprocal obligation within the family.

The likelihood remains, however, that people who could not buy into the normative pattern of marriage and household had less of a stake in it, and may have been less swayed by the moral system that legitimized it. Friction between dominant values and lived experience may help explain the mass appeal of heterodox sects whose novel approaches to sex and gender provoked such revulsion among Qing officials and other members of the elite. So many of the men who served as the cannon fodder for rebellion were "rootless rascals"—superfluous rogue males who could not hope to play the patriarchal roles honored and demanded by official family values. It may even be possible to trace a connection between unorthodox household patterns and the heterodox discourses articulated by sectarian rebels who fought the Qing. The classic association of *jian* with treason and rebellion derived not just from abstract moral concerns, but from realistic anxieties about the threat of sexual anarchy to social and political order.

This book has raised far more questions than it can answer. In my next book, I hope to address some of the unanswered questions by exploring in detail the range of survival strategies by which husbands pimped or sold their wives as assets of last resort. I believe these practices will prove critical to understanding how subsistence crisis and downward mobility undermined the foundations of late imperial order. This line of inquiry should help get us further beyond diehard stereotypes of "the Chinese family" and "Chinese values," revealing more of the diversity of strategies that enabled people to get by, and clarifying how the material conditions of life helped generate challenges to the mandated moral and political order.

Appendixes

Basic Legislation Against Sex Offenses

A.1: Tang Dynasty Statutes
Against Illicit Sexual Intercourse

1. Whoever engages in illicit sexual intercourse shall be sentenced to one and a half years of penal servitude; if the woman has a husband, the penalty shall be two years of penal servitude. If [a male of] *bu qu, za hu,* or *guan hu* status* engages in illicit intercourse with [a female] of commoner status (*liang ren*), then in either case [i.e., with or without a husband] the penalty shall be increased by one degree. If [a commoner male] commits illicit sex with a government or privately owned domestic female slave (*guan si bi*), the penalty shall be 90 blows of the heavy bamboo. (*If a male slave engages in illicit intercourse with a female slave [bi], the penalty shall be the same.*) Whoever engages in illicit intercourse with the wife of someone else's *bu qu,* or with a wife or daughter of *za hu* or *guan hu* status, shall be sentenced to 100 blows of the heavy bamboo. In every case, if coercion (*qiang*) is used, then the penalty shall be increased by one degree; if a bone or tooth is broken (*zhe shang*), then in each case the penalty shall be one degree more severe than that for the crime of breaking a bone or tooth in a fight.

2. [incest—omitted]
3. [incest—omitted]

---

* These were different categories of debased-status labor recognized by Tang and Song law. The *za hu* and *guan hu* were government slaves who had been "released" from the lowest-status level of slavery, that of *nu.* The *bu qu* were male "semi-slaves" held by private families; they could not be sold outright and hence enjoyed a status slightly superior to the ordinary slave, *nu,* who was considered his master's property. See Ch'ü 1965, 158–60.

4. Whoever engages in illicit sexual intercourse with a concubine of his father or grandfather (*that is, a concubine who has given birth to his father or grandfather's son*), his paternal aunt, his sister, the wife of his son or grandson, or the daughter of his brother, shall be sentenced to strangulation. Whoever engages in illicit intercourse with a female slave who has been sexually favored (*xing*) by his father or grandfather shall receive a penalty reduced by two degrees.

5. Any male slave (*nu*) who engages in illicit sexual intercourse with a commoner [female] (*liang ren*) shall be sentenced to two and a half years of penal servitude; if he uses coercion, then he shall be sentenced to life exile; if he breaks a bone or tooth, then he shall be strangled. If a male slave or *bu qu* engages in illicit intercourse with his mistress, or with the wife of his master or of his master's relative of the closest degrees (*ji qin*), then he shall be strangled; the woman shall receive a penalty reduced by one degree. If he uses coercion, then he shall be beheaded. If he engages in illicit intercourse with a relative or wife of a relative of fourth or higher degree [but not of the closest degrees], then he shall be sentenced to life exile; if he uses coercion, then he shall be strangled.

6. If any statute against consensual illicit intercourse does not specifically mention the female offender's penalty, then her penalty shall be the same as that of the male offender. If coercion is used, then the female offender shall not be punished. Any go-between who facilitates illicit intercourse shall receive a penalty reduced by one degree from that which the offenders themselves receive. (*If the male and female offenders' penalties differ, then the go-between's penalty shall be based on the more severe of the two.*)

7. Any official in charge of a jail who engages in illicit sexual intercourse with someone held inside his jail (*that is, someone of commoner status*) shall receive a penalty increased by one degree. Whoever engages in illicit intercourse during the mourning period for his or her father, mother, or husband, or any Daoist clergyman or nun who engages in illicit intercourse, shall each receive a penalty increased by one degree as well. [In such cases, the partner in illicit intercourse] shall be sentenced for the ordinary sex offense without any increase of penalty.

NOTE: These statutes are found in the chapter on "miscellaneous offenses" in the Tang code (TL, 26/15a–19a); the interlinear small character commentary is given here in italics, in parentheses. I have omitted two statutes that cover incest only. (For the Tang code, also see W. Johnson 1979 and 1997.)

A.2: The Basic Illicit Sex Statute
in the Ming and Qing Codes

Whoever commits consensual illicit sex (*he jian*) shall receive
80 blows of the heavy bamboo; if the woman has a husband, then
the offenders shall receive 90 blows of the heavy bamboo; if a man
lures a woman to another place in order to have illicit sex (*diao
jian*), they shall receive 100 blows regardless of whether the woman
has a husband.

Whoever commits rape (*qiang jian*) shall be strangled (*after the
assizes*); whoever attempts rape but does not consummate the act
(*wei cheng*) shall receive 100 blows of the heavy bamboo and life exile at a distance of 3,000 *li*.

(*In prosecution for rape there must be evidence of violent coercion [qiang bao], and the situation must have been such that the
woman could not struggle free; there must also be persons who
were aware and heard what happened, as well as physical injury to
skin and body, torn clothing, and other such evidence. Only then
shall the offender be sentenced to strangulation. If an offender joins
with a woman by coercion, but consummates the act by means of
her consent [yi qiang he, yi he cheng], then it does not count as
coercion.*

*If one offender seizes a woman by force, and a second has sex-
ual intercourse with her, then the one who has sexual intercourse
with her shall be sentenced to strangulation, and the one who
seizes her by force shall be sentenced to life exile for rape that is
not consummated.*

*If an offender, seeing a woman engaging in illicit sex with an-
other man, subsequently himself uses coercion to engage in illicit
sex with her, then because she is already a woman who has committed an offense of illicit sex [fan jian zhi fu], it would be inappropriate to sentence him to the penalty for coercion. Instead, the statute's provision on "luring a woman to another place for illicit sex"
should be applied.*)

Whoever engages in illicit sex with a girl of twelve *sui* or younger
shall receive the penalty for coercion even if she consents (*sui he,
tong qiang lun*).

In cases of consensual illicit sex (*he jian*) or illicit sex in which a
man lures a woman to another place for that purpose (*diao jian*), the
male and female shall receive the same punishment. Any son or
daughter born as a result of illicit sex shall be turned over to the
man who has engaged in illicit sex (*jian fu*) for him to raise. A wife

who engages in illicit sex (*jian fu*) may be sold in marriage by her husband (*cong fu jia mai*); if he is willing to keep her, then he shall be allowed to do so. If her husband sells her in marriage to the man who has engaged in illicit sex with her, then that man and the husband shall each receive 80 blows of the heavy bamboo; the wife shall be divorced and returned to her natal lineage, and the bride-price shall be confiscated.

In cases of rape, the woman shall not be punished.

[remainder omitted]

NOTE: This is the introductory statute in the chapter on "offenses of illicit sexual intercourse" (*fan jian*) in the Ming and Qing codes (DC, 366-00); the interlinear small character commentary, shown here in italics in parentheses, was added in 1646 in the first edition of the Qing code. This commentary was drawn from the *jian shi* commentary on the Ming code written by Wang Kentang (1549–1613) (Wu Tan 1992, 950, 954; Gao and Ma, eds., 1989, 348).

A.3: The Qing Substatute Against "Soldiers or Civilians Engaging in Illicit Sex" (*jun min xiang jian*)

If any official (*zhi guan*), or any soldier or civilian, engages in illicit sex with the wife of an official, then both offenders shall be strangled after the assizes.

If an official engages in illicit sex with the wife of a soldier or a civilian, then he shall be dismissed and shall receive 100 blows of the heavy bamboo to be carried out without the option of commuting the penalty into a cash payment; the woman who engages in illicit sex with him shall receive one month in the cangue and 100 blows of the heavy bamboo.

If soldiers or civilians engage in illicit sex, then both [the man and the woman] shall receive one month in the cangue and 100 blows of the heavy bamboo.

If slaves (*nu bi*) engage in illicit sex, they shall both receive 100 blows of the heavy bamboo, regardless of whether they share the same master or are of different masters; the same penalty shall apply to soldiers who have illicit sex with the concubines or female slaves of other soldiers or officials.

NOTE: This version of the substatute was entered into the Qing code in 1725 (DC, 366-01). The third clause was routinely cited to punish consensual heterosexual offenses for the rest of the Qing (for eighteenth-century examples, see XT, 75/QL 4.5.22; XT, 70/QL

4.8.18; XT, 187/QL 27.12.1). From 1734 on, the same clause was cited to punish consensual sex between males as well.

An earlier version of the substatute, first proposed in 1680 and officially codified in 1688, aimed primarily at disciplining banner forces, but it concluded by providing that "if civilians commit illicit sex (*min ren fan jian*), they shall also be punished according to this substatute"; it is my impression from case records, however, that in practice this law was not applied to civilians until the 1725 version was promulgated. The 1725 substatute superseded the original Ming statute against "consensual illicit sex" (*he jian*), which remained in the Qing code but was no longer cited in practice (see Appendix A.2). With the adoption of this substatute, the Ming statute's distinction in penalties based on the marital status of the woman disappeared from Qing law.

In the original 1688 version, the clause that corresponded to the third clause in the 1725 version reads as follows: "If a soldier engages in illicit sex with [the wife of another soldier] of the same rank, the man and woman shall each receive 100 blows of a whip and one month in the cangue, and the woman shall be returned to her husband [for his disposal]."

Although the 1725 version does not state it explicitly, in practice an adulteress' husband retained the option of keeping his wife or selling her off in marriage after she had been officially punished, as provided in the original Ming statute (see Wu Tan 1992, 951).

A.4: The "Substatute on Rootless Rascals" (*guang gun li*)

Evil rascals (*e gun*) who scheme to extort from officials or commoners; or who put up placards or make false accusations at any government office; or who extort loans by threat or blackmail; or who, because of a fight, gather a gang to seize someone, falsely accuse him of owing money, and force him to write a promissory note for the alleged debt; or who, having failed in an attempt at extortion, dare to beat or kill someone—in all such cases, if the circumstances are serious and the rootless rascals (*guang gun*) are truly to blame, then regardless of whether money was obtained, the leader shall be immediately beheaded, and followers shall be strangled after the assizes.

The head of the household of any such offender, as well as the offender's father and older brothers, shall each receive 50 blows of the light bamboo; if any are officials, their cases shall be referred to the Board [of Personnel] for disposition. If the head of an offender's household, or an offender's father or older brother, reports the offender, then he who made the report shall be spared, but the offender himself shall still be punished according to this substatute.

NOTE: This substatute in the "extortion" chapter of the Qing code was referred to simply as the "substatute on rootless rascals" (*guang gun li*). It went through a number of versions, the earliest being issued in 1656; the penalties of immediate beheading and strangulation after the assizes were fixed in 1680 (see DC, 273-07, and QHS, 794/692–703). The substatute originally related to extortion, but by the sixteen-seventies, jurists began to cite it by analogy to punish an increasingly wide range of crimes, including some variations of rape.

Qing Sodomy Legislation

B.1: The 1734 Substatute Against Sodomy

If evil characters (*e tu*) gather in a gang and abduct a young man of good character/commoner status (*liang ren zi di*—literally, "a son or younger brother of someone of good character/commoner status") and forcibly sodomize him (*qiang xing ji jian*), then the ringleader shall be sentenced to immediate beheading, according to the substatute on "rootless rascals" (*guang gun*); the followers, if they have also sodomized [the victim], shall all be sentenced to strangulation after the assizes; remaining offenders [who did not commit sodomy] shall be deported *to Heilongjiang to serve as slaves for the armored troops there*; these sentences shall apply regardless of whether the offenders have committed homicide in the course of the crime.

Even if he has not gathered a gang, whoever murders a young man of good character/commoner status for illicit sex (*jian*), or lures away a young boy of ten *sui* or under and forcibly sodomizes him, shall also be immediately beheaded according to the substatute on "ringleaders of rootless rascals."

Whoever rapes (*qiang jian*) a young boy of between ten and twelve *sui* shall be sentenced to beheading after the assizes; whoever consensually sodomizes (*he jian*) a boy of such age shall be sentenced to strangulation after the assizes according to the statute which provides that "whoever engages in illicit sex with a young girl shall receive the penalty for coercion even if she consents."

If one man by himself commits forcible sodomy (*qiang xing ji jian*) but has not injured the victim, then he shall be sentenced to strangulation after the assizes. If the offender injures the victim but the victim does not die, then he shall be beheaded after the assizes.

Whoever attempts rape but does not consummate the act, and does not injure the victim, shall receive 100 blows of the heavy bamboo and life exile at a distance of 3,000 *li*. If the offender injures the victim with an edged weapon but the victim does not die, then the offender shall be sentenced to strangulation after the assizes.

If a man consents to be sodomized (*he tong ji jian*), then the offenders shall receive one month in the cangue and 100 blows of the heavy bamboo according to the substatute on "soldiers or civilians engaging in illicit sex" (*jun min xiang jian*).

If someone falsely accuses another man of sodomy, or commits other such fraud, and the truth comes out in a court hearing, then the offender shall receive the penalty mandated for the crime he has falsely accused the other of committing, with the exception that death penalties shall be reduced by one degree; if the penalty mandated [for the sodomy falsely alleged] is immediate beheading, then the offender shall be deported into military exile at the farthest frontier at the maximum distance of 4,000 *li*, according to the substatute on "evil characters who cause trouble and commit violent acts" (*e tu sheng shi xing xiong*).

N O T E : This substatute was added to the Qing code in the second lunar month of 1734, in response to a memorial from Xu Ben, the governor of Anhui. Originally, the substatute provided that "someone of sixteen or seventeen *sui* can still be considered a child who misbehaves out of ignorance; if [a young man of such age] rapes a young boy or girl, then his penalty should be reduced from those mandated by statute for rape that is 'already consummated' or 'not consummated.'" Subsequently, senior officials protested that a male of sixteen or seventeen *sui* was already an adult and should be held accountable for his actions; in 1740 the provision was eliminated from the substatute. The brief portion in italics specifying the site of deportation was added in 1851. (See QHS, 825/989; DC, 366-03; and Wu Tan 1992, 951–52. For an alternative translation, see Hinsch 1990, 143–44.)

B.2: The Qing Substatute on "Males Who Commit Homicide While Resisting Rape" (*nanzi ju jian sha ren*)

If a male commits homicide while resisting rape, and he is fifteen *sui* or under, then he shall not be punished, regardless of whether he has committed planned (*mou sha*) or purposeful (*gu sha*) homicide or has committed homicide in a fight (*dou sha*), as long as all three conditions are fulfilled: (a) the dead man is at least ten *sui* older than the killer, (b) there is testimony and other proof at the scene to allow an accurate assessment of the facts of the case, and (c) the dead man, prior to death, confesses in a manner compelling enough to serve as proof, or his relatives testify in a reliable manner acknowledging his guilt; if the homicide was not committed immediately upon the rape attempt, then the offender shall be sentenced to 100 blows of the heavy bamboo, to be redeemed in cash according to the statute [on crimes committed by minors].

If the offender is at least sixteen *sui*, and he committed the homicide immediately upon the rape attempt, then he shall receive 100 blows of the heavy bamboo and three years of penal servitude; if the homicide was not committed immediately upon the rape attempt, then he shall receive 100 blows of the heavy bamboo and life exile at a distance of 3,000 *li*.

If one of the following three conditions is fulfilled: (a) the dead man provides no confession prior to death, but he is at least ten *sui* older than his killer, and it is clear that the homicide was committed while resisting rape and for no other reason; or (b) the dead man is not quite ten *sui* older than his killer, but there is compelling testimony and other proof that the homicide was committed while resisting rape; or (c) the dead man, prior to death, confesses in a manner compelling enough to serve as proof, or his relatives testify in a reliable manner acknowledging his guilt—then, as long as the offender is fifteen *sui* or under, and he committed the homicide immediately upon the rape attempt, he shall receive 100 blows of the heavy bamboo and three years of penal servitude; if he did not commit the homicide immediately upon the rape attempt, he shall receive 100 blows of the heavy bamboo and life exile at a distance of 3,000 *li*; the above penalties shall all be redeemed in cash according to the statute [on crimes committed by minors].

If the offender is at least sixteen *sui*, then regardless of whether the homicide was committed immediately upon the rape attempt, he shall be sentenced to strangulation after the assizes, according to the statute on "unauthorized homicide of a criminal" (*shan sha zui ren*).

If the dead man is the same age as his killer, or is only a few *sui* older,* or if interrogation proves there is some other reason for the homicide, and it has been falsely testified that the homicide was committed in resistance to rape in order to conceal this other reason, then the penalty shall be determined according to the basic [homicide] statutes, depending on whether it was premeditated or purposeful homicide, or homicide in a fight; in the Autumn Assizes,

---

* Literally, "three or five *sui* older."

the determination of execution or reprieve shall also be made in the usual manner.

If the offender testifies that he was resisting rape, but there is no witness or confession provided by the dead man prior to death [to confirm this], and interrogation produces no evidence of other reason for the homicide, then the penalty shall be determined according to the basic statutes on premeditated homicide, purposeful homicide, and homicide in a fight, and the offender shall be granted a reprieve in the Autumn Assizes.

If the offender was first sodomized, but later regretted this behavior and rejected [the sodomist's subsequent advances], and there is definite proof of his regret, and he killed the sex offender (*jian fei*) when again being forced to engage in sodomy, then he shall be sentenced to strangulation after the assizes according to the statute on "unauthorized homicide of a criminal," regardless of whether the homicide was premeditated, purposeful, or committed in a fight, and regardless of the relative ages of the offender and the dead man. If the homicide was committed for some other reason, then the offender shall still be sentenced according to the basic statutes on premeditated homicide, purposeful homicide, and homicide in a fight.

N O T E : This substatute was created in 1823 by combining earlier measures from the Qianlong and early Jiaqing periods. The final clause was added in 1824. (See DC, 285-33; Wu Tan 1992, 785; and QHS, 801/768–69. For an alternative translation, see Meijer 1985, appendix.)

Forced Remarriage of Chaste Widows

C.1: The Basic Qing Substatute on Forced Remarriage (DC, 105-01)

. . . If a widow is willing to maintain her chastity (*shou zhi*), but her natal family or husband's family abduct her and coercively marry her off (*qiang duo qiang jia*), so that she ends up being polluted (*wu*), then, if the offender is

a. her paternal grandparent or parent, or her husband's paternal grandparent or parent, the penalty shall be 80 blows of the heavy bamboo;

b. her senior relative of the second degree, the penalty shall be 70 blows of the heavy bamboo and one and one-half years of penal servitude;

c. her senior relative of the third or more distant degrees, the penalty shall be 80 blows of the heavy bamboo and two years of penal servitude;

d. her junior relative of the second degree, the penalty shall be 100 blows of the heavy bamboo and three years of penal servitude;

e. her junior relative of the third or more distant degrees, the penalty shall be 90 blows of the heavy bamboo and two and one-half years of penal servitude.

Furthermore, if the party taking the widow in marriage (*qu zhu*) does not know of the situation, then he shall not be punished; if he knows of the situation and participates in the abduction, then he shall receive 80 blows of the heavy bamboo, in a three-degree increase of the penalty of 50 blows of the light bamboo prescribed by the statute on "taking in marriage by coercion" (*qiang qu*).

If the woman does not end up being polluted, then the penalties for offenders—whether parent, parent-in-law, [more distant] relative, or the party taking the widow in marriage—shall be reduced by one degree.

The widow shall in every case be allowed to return home and maintain her chastity. If she is voluntarily willing to remain married to the new husband, then they shall be allowed to remain married according to statute, the bride-price shall be confiscated, and the offending relative(s) shall be sentenced to the heavy bamboo as appropriate according to statute.

If the widow is unwilling to lose her chastity (*bu gan shi jie*), and therefore commits suicide, then—regardless of whether or not she has already been polluted—if the offender is

a. her paternal grandparent or parent, or her husband's paternal grandparent or parent, the penalty shall be 100 blows of the heavy bamboo and three years of penal servitude;

b. her senior relative of the second degree, the penalty shall be 100 blows of the heavy bamboo and life exile at a distance of 2,000 *li*;

c. her senior relative of the third or fourth degrees, the penalty shall be 100 blows of the heavy bamboo and life exile at a distance of 2,500 *li*;

d. her senior relative of the fifth degree, the penalty shall be 100 blows of the heavy bamboo and life exile at a distance of 3,000 *li*;

e. her junior relative of the fifth degree, the penalty shall be military exile at a distant frontier;

f. her junior relative of the third or fourth degrees, the penalty shall be military exile at the farthest frontier;

g. her junior relative of the second degree, the penalty shall be strangulation after the assizes.

Furthermore, if the party taking her in marriage knows of the situation and participates in the abduction, with the result that she is caused to commit suicide, then he shall be treated as an accomplice and shall receive a penalty one degree lower than that of the relative [who was the ringleader], [according] in each instance [to the above schedule of penalties].

If the woman is willing to remain married to the new husband, but for some other reason commits suicide, then the penalties shall be determined with reference to the mourning system according to the statute on "marrying off [a widow] by coercion" (*qiang jia*), and not according to this substatute.

If a widow is willing to maintain her chastity, but someone uses coercion—without any [relative of the woman's] presiding over the marriage (*zhu hun*)—to seek her in marriage, forcing acceptance of the bride-price (*pin cai*), and for this reason she is caused to commit suicide, then he shall receive military exile at a nearby frontier, and in addition shall be forced to pay burial expenses; anyone who receives payment or commits homicide or battery because of such coercive abduction shall be punished according to the more severe provisions of the relevant basic statutes.

N O T E : This substatute was created in 1801 by combining and elaborating a Ming measure and a 1740 substatute (QHS, 756/335–36).

C.2: Forced Remarriage for Gain

A. If a woman's husband dies and she is willing to maintain her chastity (*shou zhi*), but someone uses coercion (*qiang*) to seek her in marriage and forces [her family] to receive the bride-price, without any [authorized] person presiding over the marriage, with the result that she ends up dying [by suicide] (*zhi si*), then he shall be sentenced to military exile on the frontier, in application of the statute [on "pressuring someone into suicide" (*wei bi ren zhi si*)], and he shall pay her burial expenses (ML, 19/37b).

N O T E : In the early Qing, this Ming substatute, preserved in the homicide chapter of the Qing code, was applied by analogy to punish family members who provoked a widow's suicide by forcing her to remarry for pecuniary gain (e.g., XT, 75/QL 4.5.30).

B. If a distant relative schemes for profit and therefore forcibly sells a woman (*tu cai qiang mai*), then the sentence of strangulation [after the assizes] shall be requested by memorial, in application of the substatute [on "using coercion to abduct a male or female of good character and to sell him/her to someone else as wife or concubine" (*qiang duo liang ren nan nü mai yu ta ren wei qi qie*)]. If [the offender] is a junior relative of the second, third, or fourth degree, who plots to seize property (*mou zhan zi cai*) or greedily schemes for bride-price (*tan tu pinli*), and therefore uses coercion to abduct and sell a paternal aunt or other senior relative, then he shall be beheaded after the assizes.

N O T E : This substatute was added to the Qing code in 1741 (QHS, 756/339).

C. If any junior relative of the second, third, or fourth degree plots to seize property (*mou zhan zi cai*), or greedily schemes for bride-price (*tan tu pinli*), and therefore uses coercion to abduct and sell (*yong qiang qiang mai*) a paternal aunt or other senior relative, then he shall be beheaded after the assizes. If any junior relative of the second, third, or fourth degree abducts and sells the wife of an older brother, [the wife of an older male cousin,] or his own older sister, or if any junior relative of the fifth degree uses coercion to abduct (*qiang duo*) a senior relative, or if any distant lineage relative outside the mourning system abducts and sells a senior or junior relative, then in each case the offender shall be sentenced to strangulation after the assizes.

If a senior relative schemes for material gain (*tu cai*) by coercively selling (*qiang mai*) a junior relative, then if of the second, third, of fourth degree, he shall receive 100 blows of the heavy bamboo and life exile at a distance of 3,000 *li*; if of the fifth degree, he shall be sent into military exile in a very near region.

If the marriage has not yet been consummated (*wei cheng hun*), then the penalties shall be decreased by one degree over those for offenders when the marriage is already consummated (*yi cheng hun*). If, en route, the woman is seized and taken back [before she arrives at the prospective husband's home], or if the party taking her in marriage voluntarily sends the woman back, and she has not yet been sexually polluted (*jian wu*), then all such cases shall be judged in the manner of a marriage not yet consummated.

If the woman is unwilling to lose her chastity (*bu gan shi jie*) and therefore commits suicide, then if the offender is a junior relative of the second or more distant degree, or is a distant lineage relative, he shall still be beheaded or strangled after the assizes according to the basic [provision of this] substatute; if the offender is a senior relative of the fifth degree, he too shall be sentenced to strangulation after the assizes; if the offender is a senior relative of the second, third, or fourth degree, he shall be sent into military exile at a nearby frontier. If the marriage is already consummated, and the woman commits suicide for some other reason, then the offender shall still be sentenced according to the [basic] provision on marrying [a widow] off by coercion in order to get property (*tu cai qiang jia*), and not according to this provision.

If the party taking the widow in marriage knows of the situation and participates in the abduction, or uses money in a scheme to buy the widow (*yong cai mou mai*) then in each case he shall receive a penalty one degree lower than that of the primary offender; if he is unaware of the situation, then he shall not be punished.

If a relative pressures a widow to remarry because the family is poor and cannot support her, or because of concern that she cannot maintain her chastity to the end (*zhong shou*), and there is truly no motive of greed for either property or bride-price, then all such cases shall be judged according to the substatute on "marrying [a widow] off by coercion" (*qiang jia*) [DC, 105-01]; the present substatute should not be cited in such cases, a mistake which would result in excessive penalties.

NOTE: This substatute (DC, 112-04) was promulgated in 1801 to expand and replace the 1741 measure.

Lü Kun's "Prohibitions Issued to *Yue* Households"

1. *Yue* households are distinguished from the common people as debased from commoners (*fen liang jian*), so it would be inappropriate to include *yue* households in the community covenant. But if no one is officially authorized to act as their leader, then what sort of persons might end up controlling them privately, without authorization? Therefore, in every department or county that has registered persons of *yue* status, two individuals with a reputation for justice and fairness, and who have been nominated collectively by the *yue* households, should be appointed to serve as *Yue* Headmen (*yue shou*). In every department and county, all *yue* households should be recorded in a register compiled for that purpose; it should be affixed with a seal by the official with jurisdiction and issued to [the *yue* headmen], who should be allowed to supervise them. Any *yue* persons who do not submit to these headmen's authority should be reported for punishment. If any headmen abuse their authority to practice extortion, the wronged party may file charges against them, and they shall be punished according to the amount of money they have extorted.

2. If any vagrant prostitute households migrate in from elsewhere (*liu lai shui hu*) and seduce or lead astray local people from commoner families (*liang jia zhe*), then the *yue* headmen may report these prostitutes to the authorities and expel them from the boundaries of the jurisdiction. Any *yue* headman engaging in extortion in league with an innkeeper who harbors such vagrants, or failing to report them out of fear of reprisal, shall be punished in the same manner [as those vagrants].

3. If any *yue* households harbor tax collectors (*da hu*),* gamblers, rootless rascals, or individuals of suspicious demeanor, then the *yue* headmen may investigate and report them to the authorities. If [*yue* headmen] fail to do so, then when [such violations of the rules] are discovered, the headmen shall be punished in the same manner as the offenders.

4. In regard to the thanksgiving processions and sacrifices held in Spring and Autumn, the worship of spirits and gods, the offering of libations and sacrifices at funerals, and the mourning of the dead— on all such occasions it is prohibited to gather together prostitutes and actors (*chang you*) who use licentious and irreverent language to desecrate (*luan*) these important rituals. If this prohibition is violated, then the party who summoned [the prostitutes and actors] and those who have answered that summons shall all be punished with equal severity.

5. Any member of a *yue* household who curses or exchanges blows with a commoner from an established household (*lao hu liang min*) shall be punished with extra severity, and in serious cases shall be exposed in the cangue.

6. Prostitutes (*chang fu*) shall not be allowed to adorn themselves in the same manner as members of commoner households (*liang jia*), nor shall they be permitted to wear clothing embroidered with gold thread or rich patterns, or to wear necklaces or jewelry of gold, pearls, or jade. In case of violation, the prohibited items shall be seized and liquidated by officials, and the proceeds used to benefit orphans and the aged.

7. Whenever prostitutes enter a home, the inevitable result is disaster between husband and wife. Henceforth, if a woman of prostitute household (*chang jia fu nü*) spends the night at a commoner's home (*liang min zhi jia*), or is retained to live in a commoner's home for his exclusive use, then the commoner who harbors the prostitute shall have his household's land tax liability raised by two degrees and shall be fined 30 *shi* of grain to be contributed for frontier defense. In addition, the prostitute shall be severely punished with the thumbscrew and a beating. If any *yue* headman fails to report such offenders, then he shall answer for it by being severely punished with a beating and the cangue. If a commoner wishes to take in marriage, according to proper ritual, a woman who has quit prostitution and been promoted to commoner status (*cong liang zhe*),

* For *da hu*, see Littrup 1981.

then he may be allowed to do so; he should not be harassed as if he had violated this prohibition.

8. If a *yue* householder buys a commoner, or lures a wife or daughter of commoner family (*liang jia fu nü*) to engage secretly in licentious evil, then in addition to being sentenced according to statute, he shall receive extra punishment with the cangue.

9. A husband and wife originally registered with commoner status (*yuan ji liang min fu fu*) who, being stupid and untalented, willingly sell illicit sex (*mai jian*) in order to make a living thereby insult their ancestors and dishonor their relatives, and are shameless to the extreme. When they encounter members of officially registered *yue* households (*guan yue hu*), they should kowtow and sit to one side, and if ridiculed or cursed, they should not be allowed to reply—the purpose of this policy is to provoke them to reform their conduct. If they come before a magistrate because of any offense, they should be punished more severely than members of officially registered *yue* households would be for the same offense.

10. [omitted]

11. *Yue* workers (*yue gong*) who own land shall pay taxes of grain and labor service. They should spend at least one month per year in government service, [performing] on such occasions as imperial celebrations (*chao he*), performance of sacrifices, and receiving officials. Those who receive no pay [for these services] shall be exempt from paying the head tax, just as ordinary households of the lowest three categories of tax liability are not required to pay both service and monetary taxes at the same time.*

N O T E : These rules are found in the instructions for community covenants (*xiang yue*) that Lü Kun issued as governor of Shanxi in the fifteen-nineties (Lü Kun 1971, 4/87a–89a; also see Handlin 1983; Goodrich, ed., 1976, 1007; Hansson 1996, 65–71; Littrup 1981, 165–68).

* For Japanese translation and discussion of item 11, see Terada 1959, 126–27.

Dynasties and Reign Periods

E.1: Major Dynasties Mentioned in the Text

Qin   221–206 B.C.
Han   206 B.C.–A.D. 220

Period of Division   220–589

Tang   618–907
Song   960–1279
(Southern Song 1127–1279)
Yuan   1264–1368
Ming   1368–1644
Qing   1644–1912
Heavenly Kingdom of Great Peace (Taiping Rebellion)   1851–64

E.2: Ming Reign Periods (each begins in the year given)

Hongwu   1368
Jianwen   1399
Yongle   1403
Hongxi   1425
Xuande   1426
Zhengtong   1436
(Emperor Yingzong)
Jingtai   1450
Tianshun   1457
(restoration of Yingzong)
Chenghua   1465
Hongzhi   1488
Zhengde   1506

Jiajing   1522
Longqing   1567
Wanli   1573
Taichang   1620
Tianqi   1621
Chongzhen   1628(–1644)

E.3: Qing Reign Periods (each begins in the year given)

Shunzhi   1644
Kangxi   1662
Yongzheng   1723
Qianlong   1736
Jiaqing   1796
Daoguang   1821
Xianfeng   1851
Tongzhi   1862
Guangxu   1875
Xuantong   1908(–1912)

Reference Matter

Notes

Chapter One   Introduction

1. See, for example, Hinsch 1990 and Ng 1987 and 1989; the quotation is from Elvin 1984, 112–14. On the decline of courtesan arts, see Yan Ming 1992 and Mann 1997; on the "religionization" of female chastity, see Liu Jihua 1991. For critique of Van Gulik from the perspective of traditional Chinese medicine, see Furth 1994.

2. See Appendix E for Ming and Qing reign periods and principal dynasties mentioned in the text.

3. The *locus classicus* for the paradigm of progress in Western law "from status to contract" is Sir Henry Maine's *Ancient Law* (1864). For discussion of the metanarrative of modernity, especially as related to gender history, see Hunt 1998.

4. See, for example, Ch'ü (1965, 282) and Jing Junjian (1993, 235). Debased-status groups were barred from the examinations, but it is a mistake to assume on that basis that commoner status implied a "right" to take them; civil examinations were an instrument of autocratic power, and men who took them did so at the imperial pleasure, without exception. As a practical matter, Qing courts enforced rights to property and person, but these could be exercised only against status equals, and they were by no means absolute (P. Huang 1996, 7–8, 108, 236). No rights could be asserted against the state; nor did the state formally recognize an individual's freedom of body and will to be the standard against which crime offends. Legal discourse included no word that carried the Western meaning of "right."

5. A growing body of scholarship questions the efficacy of Western models for understanding Chinese history. A useful overview of the problem is Cohen 1984; for the "civil society"/"public sphere" debate, see *Modern China*'s "Symposium . . ." (1993); for a critique of the "civil society" model from the perspective of women's history, see Mann 1997 (223); for the question of technological development, see Bray 1997 (introduction). Philip Huang has made the most thorough critique of the applicability of Western

models (Marxist, neo-classical, and Weberian) to Chinese socioeconomic and legal history (see especially 1990, 1991, and 1996). Bradly Reed (2000) provides a valuable new appraisal of Weberian theory in light of Qing administrative practice.

6. Jing Junjian (who, like Ch'ü, has made great contributions to legal history) embraces a different Western paradigm, Marxist stage theory, which has the similar effect of compelling him to dismiss change that did not lead to full-blown capitalism. See 1993 (conclusion) and 1994.

7. See the perceptive comments of Charlotte Furth (1991 and 1994) and Gail Hershatter (1996, 77–79).

8. Preliminary sketches of this argument can be found in Sommer 1994 and 1997b. Susan Mann (1991) was the first scholar to draw a clear link between the blurring of old status boundaries (reflected in the Yongzheng "emancipations") and a new discourse of gender in the eighteenth century; she highlights new debates on marriage and female literacy among the Yangzi Delta elite.

9. For a broad overview of this historical trend, see Hucker 1975, chaps. 7 and 12.

10. N.B.: for most of the pre-Qing era, I make no claim to explain judicial *practice*, which may be impossible to document since next to nothing in the way of legal archives survives. I refer, rather, to the judicial conceptualization that can be traced on the level of legal codes and official commentaries. The main exception can be found in Chapter 6, where I use published case summaries to discuss the local treatment of prostitution in the late Ming; I feel confident in doing so because late Ming practice corresponded closely to early Qing practice, which I *can* document with archival records.

11. Jing Junjian (1980 and 1993) has mapped a precise gradation of status levels defined by Qing law: the emperor, the imperial clan, officials, degree-holders not in office, commoners, and mean persons—with hired laborers occupying an ambiguous position akin to mean status. Their status gradually improved, and by the end of the eighteenth century most were treated as ordinary commoners. The commoner category included the vast majority of the population.

12. Angela Leung's study of Qing philanthropy traces how a new concept, "the poor" (*pin min*), emerged in contrast with the old concept of "mean people" (*jian min*). Elite commentators began to distinguish between people who were "debased" (*jian*) only in legal terms and those who were *morally* debased; and philanthropists discriminated against the latter category (e.g., prostitutes) in favor of the *virtuous* poor (e.g., chaste widows), who truly deserved charity. Leung's research highlights the key distinction between the *legal* and *moral* definitions of *jian*: as fixed status categories became anachronistic, this term came to imply stigma or disapproval more than the traditional legal meaning of mean status ([Liang Qizi] 1993b).

13. Mann notes a parallel shift in elite culture in which female writers played a key role: the courtesan (idealized by some in the late Ming as a

model of loyalty and carrier of high culture) was marginalized in favor of a narrower emphasis on the moral authority of the learned wife (1997, 121–22).

14. I base this count on Wu Tan's 1780 edition of the code (Wu Tan 1992).

15. For the changing legal status of agricultural laborers see Jing Junjian 1993 and P. Huang 1985.

16. My use of *gender performance* shares a certain amount with Judith Butler's concept of gender as "performativity" (1990)—i.e., as something not fixed in nature but coming into being through repetitive performance of roles to conform with (or subvert) social expectations. I am particularly concerned with Qing efforts to legislate and enforce normative gender performance among ordinary people, however, and I remain skeptical of Butler's postmodernist rejection of the "prediscursive subject," which would seem to undermine her account of the possibility of individual agency.

17. For an overview of state and society in the eighteenth century, see Naquin and Rawski 1987; Mann 1997 is the definitive study of women in this period (focusing on elite women of the Yangzi Delta) and also provides an excellent summary of recent scholarship on contemporary population and gender issues. For discussion of imperial government in the Yongzheng and Qianlong reigns, see Bartlett 1991; Kahn 1971; Kuhn 1990; and Zelin 1985.

18. For the problem of "downward migration" in the mid-eighteenth century, see Kuhn 1990; for the economic logic of this subsistence crisis, see P. Huang 1985 and 1990; for a case study of one region's long decline from the High Qing through the early twentieth century, see Friedman et al. 1991. A number of studies suggest that after about 1750, male life expectancy declined and average age of marriage for males rose, while early and universal marriage for females remained constant (Harrell, ed., 1995; Telford 1992). Kay Ann Johnson (1983) provides a useful overview of the "family crisis" of the peasantry in the early twentieth century. Recent research by Neil Diamant and Zhongqi Lu shows that in many liberated areas, wives and daughters of class enemies were redistributed as "fruits of struggle" to poor peasants who needed wives (personal communication).

19. In Tongcheng County (Anhui), the proportions of men never marrying and of wives being "recycled" through widow remarriage were both higher in the eighteenth than in the seventeenth century and higher still in the nineteenth century (Telford 1992). In the village of Daoyi (Liaoning) during the late eighteenth century, wives were in such short supply that "while almost all women over thirty years of age were married or widowed, as many as 20 percent of all adult men never married" (Lee and Eng 1984, 33–34). Susan Mann argues that rising competition in the marriage market affected all levels of society during the eighteenth century, and it helped drive shifts in elite gender discourse (1991 and 1997). For infanticide as a famine survival strategy, see L. Li 1991.

20. See Chen Baoliang's discussion of Qing stereotypes of the *guang gun* (1993, 272–76).

21. See Kathryn Bernhardt's appraisal of recent work by Dorothy Ko and Susan Mann (1996).

22. This was true in earlier periods as well: for example, Yuan-dynasty prohibitions against commoner husbands pimping their wives were prompted by reports from provincial officials that such practices had become increasingly widespread and threatened to blur status boundaries (see Chapter 6).

23. My Ba County sample includes 151 cases from the Qianlong reign, 138 from the Jiaqing, 137 from the Daoguang, and 74 from the Xianfeng; these are supplemented by a small volume of Qianlong cases published by the Sichuan Provincial Archives (HB).

24. The Danshui-Xinzhu Archive from northern Taiwan has not been a major source for this study. For a discussion of that collection, see Buxbaum 1971 and Allee 1994; for the Ba County Archive, see Sichuan Provincial Archives, ed., 1988; Zelin 1986; and Reed 1994, 1995, and 2000; for both of these and the Shuntian Prefecture Archive, see Huang 1982 and 1996.

25. For the Three High Courts of Judicature, see Bodde and Morris 1967, 116–17, 132–33.

26. These routine memorials should not be confused with the secret palace memorials (*zhu pi zouzhe*), which emperors read and commented on personally; see Silas Wu 1970. For the Qing review system, see Bodde and Morris 1967, 113–20, 130–42.

27. In the Qing code, the *statutes*—almost all carried over from the Ming code—generally remained unchanged even if obsolete; the law was kept current by adding new *substatutes* or amending older ones. Judges ignored obsolete statutes in favor of the relevant updated substatutes, even though the former remained formally in the code (see Bodde and Morris 1967, 63–68). The development of particular substatutes over the course of the Qing can be traced in QHS (section on Board of Punishment).

28. For the tradition of "private" commentary and a detailed study of Shen Zhiqi's influence on Qing adjudication, see Fu-mei Chang Chen 1980.

29. See Huang Jingjia's short biography of Xue Yunsheng in the first volume of DC.

30. Other scholars using large samples of Qing cases to study legal issues include Mark Allee, Kathryn Bernhardt, Thomas Buoye, Adrian Davis, Yasuhiko Karasawa, Melissa Macauley, Paola Paderni, Nancy Park, Bradly Reed, Janet Theiss, and David Wakefield.

31. Buxbaum (1971) was the first to make this point, based on the Danshui-Xinzhu archive.

32. The founding emperor of the Ming believed that the statutes he laid down should stand for all time. He once commented, "There are classic sources of law (*jing*) and there are tactics for particular situations (*quan*); the statutes are eternal, classic sources of law while the particular substatutes are merely the temporary tactics appropriate to a given situation" (cited by Huang Jingjia, introduction to DC, 1/3).

33. The profligate use of torture described by Kuhn (1990) was highly exceptional and probably derived from the political color of the soul-stealing

investigation. My own sense is that torture was usually reserved for extracting more information from individuals who had already confessed to capital crimes, and was threatened more often than actually employed.

34. My understanding of these questions has developed through many conversations with Karasawa Yasuhiko, whose own research on the subject is in progress (see Karasawa 1992 and 1993).

Chapter Two   A Vision of Sexual Order

1. As Francesca Bray points out, many classical terms for political order and disorder are metaphors related to cloth; one meaning of *luan* is to unravel a skein (1997, 190–91).

2. Proscribed works included such classics as *Peony Pavilion* (*Mudan ting*), *The Water Margin* (*Shui hu zhuan*), *Plum in the Golden Vase* (*Jin ping mei*), and *Dream of the Red Chamber* (*Hong lou meng*) (Li Mengsheng 1994; Wang Liqi, ed., 1981). For Qing edicts banning "licentious" books and songs, see QHS, 112/440–41; on the Qing "literary inquisition," see Guy 1987.

3. Fu Sheng was not defining the word *jian*, but late imperial jurists cite him to define that word (e.g., TM, 26/14b). Fu Sheng is also routinely quoted or paraphrased (sometimes without attribution) in later texts that discuss the penalty of *gong*—e.g., commentaries on the "Director of Punishments" section of *The Rites of Zhou* and on the "Five Punishments" chapter of *The Classic of Filial Piety*, as well as modern dictionaries of classical Chinese.

4. Paul Goldin, who is currently investigating sexual mores in the early empire, informs me that as yet he has found no prohibition whatsoever of male-male sexual acts.

5. The specific concept of the "six rites" apparently dates to the Han dynasty (Dull 1978), so Jia Gongyan's gloss on Fu Sheng involves a certain anachronism; still, Jia's basic point that Fu Sheng meant intercourse outside legitimate marriage is certainly correct.

6. Another example of "unfilial conduct" in Yuan law was to sleep with a prostitute during mourning for one's parent (*fu nei su chang*) (YD, 41/3a–4a).

7. This passage is one of several paradoxes proposed by the commentator in order to explicate deeper meanings in the law. The next proposition, for example, is that "there is no punishment for a son who murders his father"—an absurdity resolved by the explanation that none of the ordinary "five punishments" was sufficiently harsh to requite such a hideous crime; therefore, it deserved the extraordinary penalty of "death by slicing" (XF, ming li fu juan/13a–b).

8. Each "statute applied by analogy" (*bi yin lü*) applies a preexisting law to some offense not covered in the code proper (Huang Zhangjian, ed., 1979, 1027–69); another example is the Ming sodomy statute discussed in Chapter 4. For judgment by analogy generally, see Bodde and Morris 1967, 32, 175–78, and 518–30.

9. An adopted daughter-in-law (*tong yang xi*) was raised from childhood in her future husband's household. When she and her betrothed reached the appropriate age, they would be married without expense or fanfare. This practice is well documented for Taiwan (M. Wolf 1972; A. Wolf and Huang 1980) but appears in Qing legal cases from throughout the Han Chinese regions of the empire.

10. Ming and Qing law permitted women to redeem sentences of the light or heavy bamboo with cash payments, except when they were convicted of offenses of "illicit sex," unfilial conduct, or robbery; see DC, 001-14, 001-15, and 020-00.

11. See Gang Yi 1968, 2/58a–61b; Lin Enshou, ed., 1876, 4/6a–25a; DC, 411-7, commentary; Bodde and Morris 1967, 138.

12. For a detailed study of this law, see Meijer 1991.

13. This logograph must be distinguished from the one for "illicit sexual intercourse"—see Character List.

14. T'ung-tsu Ch'ü provides a good survey of masters' sexual privileges, but he downplays any change, as part of his larger thesis of stagnation in imperial law (1965, 198–99).

15. See Appendix A.1 for full text. In the Tang dynasty, *bu qu, za hu, guan hu,* and *nu bi* were different categories of servile people with debased status, akin to slaves or serfs. *Guan hu, za hu,* and *guan nu bi* were government-owned slaves who ranked in that order, from most "free" to least "free". *Bu qu* were male "semi-slaves" owned by private families, whose status was slightly superior to that of ordinary slaves (*nu* and *bi*) in that they could not be sold outright but only "transferred" to others. *Nu* (male) and *bi* (female) were considered the absolute property of their masters (Ch'ü 1965, 158–60).

16. Some scholars refer to *bi* as "maids." I fear this term may be ambiguous as to legal status, so I prefer to call them "domestic female slaves" or simply the Chinese term. For *bi* in the Song dynasty, see Ebrey 1993, 218–19 (Song law on this subject was taken from the Tang code); for early twentieth-century Hong Kong, see Jaschok 1988 and R. Watson 1991. Bray analyzes the politics of reproduction and motherhood in elite households that included a main wife (*qi*) as well as concubines (*qie*) and *bi* (1997, 351–68).

17. That is, reduced two degrees from the penalty of strangulation mandated for illicit intercourse with a concubine of his father or grandfather who has given birth to a son (see Appendix A.1).

18. This law was cited in 1739 to punish a Manchu bannerman from Beijing who murdered his manservant so as to enjoy unhampered sexual use of the servant's adolescent granddaughter (XT, 70/QL 4.9.12).

19. For judgment by analogy, see Bodde and Morris 1967, 175–78 and 518–30.

20. In fact, the woman in this case was punished more leniently than she would have been if defined as either a slave or a concubine. For degrees of mourning and explanation, see Bodde and Morris 1967, 35–38; for a con-

cubine's mourning relation to her husband's main wife, see Wu Tan 1992, 84–85, 125.

21. For example, in a 1745 case from Fugou County, Henan, one Chen Shi, wife of a worker-serf, was murdered by her master's younger brother when she resisted his attempt to rape her. She was canonized, although it was ordered that no tablet be erected in the local temple, and her attacker was sentenced to strangulation after the assizes for homicide (XT, 123/QL 10.6.10).

22. Chunmei ("Spring Plum Blossom") is also the name of Pan Jinlian's chambermaid in *Plum in the Golden Vase*; perhaps this *bi*'s master was a fiction buff.

23. Technically the girl had "consented" to intercourse, but if she were under twelve *sui* the act would be punished as "coercion" all the same (see Chapter 3).

24. For the scale of penalties in Qing law see Bodde and Morris 1967, chap. 3.

25. According to Rubie Watson, "maids" in early twentieth-century Hong Kong were treated as property but their masters had a clear obligation to arrange marriages for them, and these girls usually left servitude around age eighteen. Moreover, "like a daughter," a maid's "procreative life was supposed to start only when she left her master's house" (1991, 240). These expectations are radically different from those expressed in the Ming and earlier legal codes, and may reflect the impact of Qing judicial intervention.

26. For *yi jue* and compulsory divorce in Tang-Song law, see Niida 1943, 64–65, 683–85. The classic example of a non-sexual offense that indicated *yi jue* was if either spouse beat or killed the other's parent.

27. With regard to both wife-selling and relations between masters and servile women, Lei Menglin consistently advocates a strict approach that seems to anticipate High Qing orthodoxy; his views are frequently cited by Qing commentaries.

28. The original Ming statute had allowed the husband to sell her himself. The first edition of the Qing code (1646) ordered that the wife be "confiscated to become a government slave" (*ru guan wei nu*); sale in marriage "under official auspices" was substituted in 1740 (QHS, 801/762; Wu Tan 1992, 780).

29. Marriage among the poor involved little in the way of dowry (aside from a few simple items to save face) and generally amounted to sale of a daughter for cash (see Fuma 1993; Sommer 1994, 391–94). Of course that is what made dowry such a valuable status symbol for the upwardly mobile and the elite: dowry was a way to announce that you could afford not to sell off your daughters, the way the poor majority did. (The same logic applied to widow chastity.)

30. This is the fate of Ximen Qing's concubine Sun Xue'e, in the Ming novel *Plum in the Golden Vase*; after Xue'e is convicted of adultery, Ximen Qing's widow Wu Yueniang refuses to take her back into the household, so she is sold under official auspices as a kitchen slave and later resold to a

brothel as a prostitute (chap. 90). For a 1776 example from Ba County, see BX 1-1705.

31. In practice, magistrates sometimes waived the corporal penalty for sold wives, and sometimes imposed it; central cases show both approaches being approved without comment by senior reviewers, suggesting that the decision was left to the discretion of local courts.

32. Literally, "on the body (*shen*) of the wife." The term used here for "body" can mean "chastity"—as in *shi shen* ("to lose chastity").

33. For further elaboration, see Sommer 1994, 370–77.

Chapter Three   The Evolution of Rape Law

1. The Song penal code records an edict of A.D. 953, of the short-lived Later Zhou dynasty, mandating death for the rape of a married woman, but this edict does not seem to have been enforced by the Song dynasty (SX, 26/22a). An edict of the Qingyuan era of the Southern Song gives exile at a distance of 3,000 *li* as the penalty for rape without specifying the marital status of the victim (QY, 80/21a).

2. DC, 299-14 and 366-02, 04, 05, 08.

3. For detailed examples of how penalties were reduced, see XA, 52/1b–2a; and Ng 1987, 61–63.

4. Bannermen were treated as commoners for most judicial purposes.

5. Vivien Ng provides a somewhat different reading of this same case (1987, 66–67).

6. This prerequisite for canonization was relaxed somewhat in 1803; see Conclusion.

7. The same case is cited in Bodde and Morris 1967, 427.

8. See Appendix A.2; the specific language used here was drawn from the *jian shi* commentary of Ming jurist Wang Kentang (see Wu Tan 1992, 950; Gao Chao and Ma Jianshi, eds., 1989, 348). Vivien Ng is mistaken when she states that this "stringent definition of rape" was a radical innovation of the Qing (1987, 57–58).

9. For begging as a survival strategy in eighteenth-century China, see Kuhn 1990, 46–47.

10. As for incest, only rape within the very closest degrees of mourning would be punished by beheading in Tang law (TL, 26/15a–16b). Incest appears to have carried an importance more symbolic (given the ideological centrality of family order) than practical. With excruciating detail, each dynasty's code maps against the mourning chart all possible incestuous combinations, with penalties for each; nonetheless, if Qing archives are any guide, the vast majority of imagined offenses never appeared in court. The most we are likely to see is an affair between brother and sister-in-law (usually a widow), but even this scenario is unusual; I have yet to come across most of the combinations that lawmakers felt obliged to specify. Moreover, treatment of incest changed little over time, implying a lack of the friction between ideology and practice that seems to have driven much of the change in other areas of law.

11. On the evolution of the Qing code, see Zheng Qin 1995 and Bodde and Morris 1967, chap. 2. There exist two excellent English translations of the statutes in the Qing code—Staunton's (1966), first published in 1810, and Jones's recent edition (1994)—but unfortunately neither includes the substatutes.

12. As explained in the last chapter, this statute was amended in 1740 with an interlinear commentary to the effect that a commoner who raped another man's *bi* would henceforth be punished just as severely as one who raped a commoner wife (QHS, 825/994).

13. It is not a rape case, however. Ma Si, of Wuyi County, Zhili, had an affair with his master's daughter, who committed suicide when her pregnancy exposed their relationship; Ma was beheaded in 1651 (XT, 1042/SZ 12.6.7).

14. See Kuhn's analysis of popular and official suspicion of vagrants during the eighteenth century (1990, 41–48).

15. A series of Qianlong and Jiaqing era edicts imposed on local officials the duty of "prohibiting rootless rascals"—i.e., rounding up vagrant troublemakers and punishing them appropriately; these measures were closely associated with rules about arresting escaped convicts, and prohibitions against gambling, heterodox sects, and gathering large crowds (QHS, 130–32).

16. As Paola Paderni points out (1991, 1992), if a woman were attacked by an established member of her own community, concern to maintain social harmony might override outrage, militating against any publicity of the offense. Such incidents were often mediated privately and settled as quietly as possible (see, for example, XT, 181/QL 27.4.28).

Chapter Four   Qing Sodomy Legislation

1. For my preliminary attempts to answer these questions, see Sommer 1994 and 1997a.

2. See Hinsch's claim, based on a single fictional story by Yuan Mei, that "male marriage was prevalent enough in Fujian that the men of that region even felt compelled to sacrifice to a patron deity of homosexuality" (1990, 133). The deity is a rabbit, and since, as Hinsch notes, "rabbit" (*tuzi*) was derogatory slang for a male prostitute, it seems unlikely that Yuan Mei expected to be taken seriously. For a more sophisticated treatment of the discourse of "male marriage," see Volpp 1994.

3. See Hinsch 1990, 142–43. Harold Kahn has pointed out to me that there is probably no way to prove or disprove the rumors about these emperors' sexual predilections.

4. It is from this perspective that Meijer praises Qing law as "wiser and more moderate" than the harsh laws of eighteenth-century Europe against consensual sodomy (1985, 131).

5. The entire text of this memorial, from Anhui governor Xu Ben, is quoted in MQ, 59-10.

6. Here I use "homosexual" and "heterosexual" as adjectives, for their literal meanings of "same-sex" and "different-sex," and to characterize

practices or relationships only. I avoid speculating about any individual's sexual orientation or implying that the choice of partners marked one as "homosexual" or "heterosexual" in a profound and permanent way. Michel Foucault (1978), Robert A. Padgug (1979), and Jeffrey Weeks (1977) were among the first to argue that sexual orientation is fundamentally different from older ways of thinking about same-sex union; also see Halperin 1993. Judith Brown uses "lesbian" in her historical work, "for reasons of convenience," but she points out that the women in question did not see themselves and were not seen by others "as a distinct sexual and social group" (1986, 171–73). For an introduction to the social construction debate, see Stein, ed., 1992.

7. In classical Greece, legal codes used separate vocabulary to refer to penetrator and penetrated, but no clear equivalents for the nouns "homosexual" and "homosexuality." Sanctions of sex between males focused on maintaining proper hierarchy, not unlike Chinese codes' prioritization of legal status. On the other hand, there is evidence in Greek sources for about the same range of "sexual orientations" *in practice* as are familiar in late twentieth-century America. Orientation, in and of itself, was simply not granted the primacy many people now accord it. Indeed, perceptions today are by no means uniform around the world. In much of Latin America only the penetrated male is considered "a homosexual," while the penetrant role confers "macho" status (Boswell 1980 and 1992; Halperin 1993).

8. The famous stories of the "shared peach" and the "cut sleeve" both fall into this genre. Hinsch provides a good survey of such tales (1990).

9. Hinsch thinks he has found still earlier evidence. He quotes a law of the third century B.C. as mandating penalties for a servant who "forcibly fornicates with his master or mistress"; on this basis, he claims that "the Qin code lumps heterosexual and homosexual rape together" (1990, 142). In fact, the translations he cites render the law thus: "When a slave rapes his owner . . ." (Hulsewé 1985, 169) and "If a servant forcibly fornicates with a master . . ." (McLeod and Yates 1981, 116). The original Chinese, "*chen qiang yu zhu jian*," seems to stress status difference rather than the sex of the person raped. Chinese legal scholars interpret it to mean a male slave who raped a *female* of his master's household, and cite it as early evidence of the priority of status distinction (e.g., Zhang Jinfan et al., 1992, 424). This interpretation is much more plausible than Hinsch's; the term *zhu* (master, lord) is used in a Tang statute in a similar way, and the rest of the Tang statute and its official commentary make it absolutely clear that only females of the master's family are envisioned as potential rape victims (TL, 26/17b–18a).

10. Also known as *bi fu zafan zui lü, bi yin li, bi fu lü*, etc. (Huang Zhangjian, ed., 1979, 1027–69; Wu Tan 1992, 1142–44; DC, 52/bi yin lü).

11. Yang Shiwei adds that "the statutes include a measure against '*ji jian*'" (using the obscure logograph for *ji*); this appears to be a reference to the Jiajing "statute applied by analogy," which did not include the term "*ji jian*" (cited in Higashikawa 1979, 295; and Ci hai, 1/827). Yang may be re-

ferring to a Buddhist prohibition (also sometimes called "statutes," *lü*), but I have been unable to find *ji jian* in Buddhist reference works. The construction of the obscure logograph fits its meaning so conveniently that I suspect it may be an invention of Ming literati who aimed to show how sodomy *should* be graphically represented.

12. A substatute of 1727 codified the punishment of heterosexual gang rape by direct analogy to the substatute on rootless rascals, obviating this two-step process (DC, 366-02).

13. This substatute (DC, 366-01) superseded the Ming statute on consensual illicit sex (DC, 366-00) in 1725, being cited thereafter to punish consensual heterosexual offenses among civilians—see Appendixes A.2 and A.3.

14. Heterosexual offenses: DC, 366-00, 01, 02, 04, 07, 10, and 375-03, 04; homosexual offenses: 366-03, 07, 10, and 375-03, 04.

15. The cutting edge of research on homoerotic literature in late imperial China is the work of Giovanni Vitiello (1992 and 1994) and Sophie Volpp (1994 and 1995).

16. Meijer attempts to develop a concept of "male chastity," but the issue becomes confused because the parallel between the *"liang"* female and the *"liang"* male was in fact quite limited (1985, 129).

17. Guo's age is not given in the casebook's brief summary. He must have been over twelve *sui*, or the penalty would have been greater. But he must have been fairly young; otherwise his maturity would have made a judgment of rape by a single offender highly unlikely (see below).

18. This reasoning received formal codification in a substatute of 1775 (DC, 366-10).

19. A heated brick bed common in north China.

20. By "bisexual" I refer only to the fact that the rapists in question pursued members of both sexes. I mean to imply nothing about the *sexual orientation* of the individuals described in Qing sources.

21. Tingzhu ended up with a sentence of strangulation after the assizes for the "unauthorized killing of a criminal," but it was certain to be commuted, given the circumstances of the case.

22. For the erotic uses of bound-foot shoes, see Levy 1966.

23. See Roy's analysis of "the causes of social disintegration" in *Plum in the Golden Vase* (Roy 1993, xxix–xxxi), and Hanan's discussion of the fictional libertine (Li Yu 1996, vii–ix).

24. Translations from *The Carnal Prayer Mat* are Hanan's; those from "A Male Mencius' Mother" are Volpp's.

25. See Figure 2, and illustrations in Byron 1987 and Humana and Wu 1982.

26. Prohibitions of sodomy in the "laws" of Qing secret societies assume that hierarchies of age and sexual role conformed with each other, and portray "young and fair boys" and "younger brothers" as objects of sexual rivalry between older secret society "brothers" (Fei-ling Davis 1977, 147).

27. In a 1739 case from Shaanxi, a man propositions a young boy: "People say you're a 'rabbit.' Now, I want to have sex with you—are you selling?" (XT, 70/QL 4.9.5.). Also see Hinsch 1990, 133.

28. The surviving fragment of this memorial does not list the county where the case occurred.

29. For comparison, see Clarke's fascinating analysis of the Leiden gem (1998, 38–42).

30. Vitiello finds similar evidence in Daoist discourse on male homosexual relations (1992, 357).

31. Among pirates, anal penetration initiated male captives into the ranks and solidified fictive kinship/patron-client ties (junior pirates submitting to penetration by those whose favor they sought) (Murray 1987 and 1992). Fictive kinship could also frame homosexual relations among women outside the mainstream pattern of marriage and family (Topley 1975).

32. Dorothy Ko and Wai-yee Li inform me that these phrases originally refer to two modes of poetic expression, "emotions aroused by scenery" and "using one thing as an analogy for another." This word choice gives Shen's comments a mocking, amusing tone, while underscoring his assumption that homosexual acts were a poor substitute for heterosexual intercourse.

33. As Meijer points out, *Conspectus of Legal Cases* summarizes several cases involving male prostitutes who worked out of "barbershops"—it is not clear whether these men actually did any barbering along with the sex work (1985, 114). Barbering was also associated with some of the mean-status groups that traditionally provided entertainment services, including sex work (Hansson 1996).

34. In Qing law, the term *xia you*—literally, "improper intimacy with actors"—was a euphemism for engaging the sexual services of male prostitutes; see DC, 375-04.

35. In an earlier scene, Chen Jingji prepares to be fellated by Pan Jinlian: "He manipulated his penis until it was very hard, a stick standing straight up" (*ba nahua nong de ying ying de, zhi shu de yi tiao gun*) (82/5b); later, the very same words are used to describe Jin Zongming's preparation to penetrate Jingji's anus (93/10a). Such strategic repetition of words and images is a standard device in the novel, an internal echo that underscores parallels between characters, and links cause with effect (Roy 1993, xxvii–xxix). Here, it adds ironic emphasis to Jingji's role reversal. What is now being done to him is precisely what he himself has done to others in the past.

36. See citations in Dai Wei 1992; Hinsch 1990, appendix; Li Mengsheng 1994, 256–58; Topley 1975; and Van Gulik 1974.

37. *Hairpins Beneath a Cap* (*Bian er chai*), a collection of homoerotic stories from the late Ming, includes a variation on the tale of "the country of women" (a fantasy land where gender roles are reversed), in which the "king" (a female in drag) makes a young boy who visits his "queen." The (female) king consummates this marriage by penetrating the (male) queen anally with a dildo: since the substitute phallus preserves the proper rela-

tions of domination, the hierarchy of penetration conforms to the inverted hierarchy of gender roles (Vitiello 1994, 164–73).

38. One recalls Jia Baoyu—hero of the eighteenth-century novel *Dream of the Red Chamber*—whose ambiguous gender performance acts out his reluctance to grow up (see Edwards 1994 and McMahon 1995).

Chapter Five   Widows in the Qing Chastity Cult

1. An early version of this chapter was published in *Late Imperial China* (Sommer 1996). The classic studies of the late imperial cult of widow chastity are Elvin 1984, Liu Jihua 1991, Mann 1987, and Waltner 1981. For a provocative argument that "male anxiety" over tougher competition in civil exams led to an increase in widow suicide, by "a psychological mechanism of vicarious morality," see T'ien Ju-k'ang 1988. Unfortunately, T'ien fails to prove any causative link between the phenomena he correlates. More likely, as Susan Mann suggests (1993), *female* anxiety is a better explanation of widow suicide than male anxiety.

2. Many scholars have discussed different aspects of this economic logic: e.g., Fuma 1993; Holmgren 1985; Mann 1987; Waltner 1981; and Wolf and Huang 1980.

3. Prior to the Song dynasty, lineage and ancestor worship were organized according to the aristocratic value of primogeniture. The Neo-Confucian reformulation of kinship principles included all family branches in a more egalitarian system that made every male the ancestor of his own line of descent. From the Song on, a growing proportion of the population was incorporated into such kinship networks and embraced the related ideology (Ebrey 1986; Furth 1990).

4. Fuma (1993) argues that a young widow with no sons would be most vulnerable to such pressure, because in-laws would see getting rid of her as a way to avoid morselization of family property; also see Holmgren 1985. On the vulnerability of Song-dynasty widows, see Ebrey 1993, 190–94.

5. See Susan Mann's discussion of this debate (1987). Elvin argues that the Yongzheng Emperor's initiative to propagate the chastity ideal among ordinary commoners met with considerable success: ". . . the virtues of the elite, and especially the fidelity of widows, gradually became 'democratized'" (1984, 123); Sweeten agrees that by the late Qing, "the ideal of widow chastity had percolated down to the village level" (1978, 52). In contrast, Arthur Wolf asserts that "the ideal of the virtuous widow exerted no influence whatsoever" on the behavior of ordinary people (1981).

6. For the Song-dynasty origins of late imperial chastity discourse, see Ebrey 1993; for overviews of canonization, see Elvin 1984, Liu Jihua 1991, Mann 1987, Otake 1936, and Zeng Tieshen 1991; for Qing rules, see QH, 30/254–55; for successive edicts that developed the Qing system, see QHS, 403 and 404.

7. For the Ming cult of female virtue, see Carlitz 1994; also see Mann 1987 on the ways gazetteers represented the hardship of chaste widowhood.

8. As Mann observes (1985 and 1993), Qing emperors tried to discourage widow suicide and praised as a higher level of chastity a widow's resolve to remain alive to serve the living. Nevertheless, it appears that they were often willing to make exceptions, and the successive edicts on the canonization system (QHS, 403 and 404) include many instances of widow suicide's prompting canonization. The same is true of "liver-cutting"—using part of one's own body to make medicine for a sick parent (see T'ien Ju-k'ang 1988, 149–61)—which also was honored on repeated occasions, in spite of formal prohibition.

9. This rule was relaxed in 1803, so that a woman might qualify even if penetrated, as long as she had been attacked by two or more men. In exceptional circumstances, even a woman raped by one attacker might qualify for *reduced* honors, but only if she had been overpowered and tied up prior to the consummation of rape (QHS, 404/516). The memorialist who advocated this change argued that an official captured by rebels might be forced to kneel, but that that would prove no disloyalty on his part. So too, a wife overpowered and penetrated by a gang of rapists should not necessarily be considered unchaste (HC, 92/33a–b). The change indicates a shift from chastity as objective status to chastity as purity of intent (Elvin 1984, n. 177; Sommer 1994, 415–19); see Conclusion.

10. Early on, there appears to have been some difference of opinion on this point. In 1758, the judicial commissioner of Jiangsu proposed that the Qianlong Emperor clarify the rules for nominating chastity martyrs by formally excluding remarried widows, but the emperor at first demurred (QHS, 403/510). Still, I find no evidence that any remarried widow was ever actually nominated, let alone canonized. And in 1792, the same emperor explicitly forbade lower officials from recommending remarried widows for chastity honors (QHS, 403/513). I have seen several memorials from the late Qianlong, Jiaqing, and Daoguang reigns which note that a woman who died resisting rape had been remarried, in order to explain why canonization is *not* being requested.

11. For the alternate stereotypes in nonlegal discourse, see Waltner 1981 and Mann 1987.

12. For this purpose, chastity could be lost only through what was seen as willful misconduct on the part of a widow. For example, having been penetrated by a rapist would disqualify a dead woman from chastity-martyr status, but it would not deprive a surviving widow of her rights.

13. The definitive study of laws and customs pertaining to family property is Shiga 1967; also see Wakefield 1992 and Jing Junjian 1994.

14. For details, see QHS, 756; and Xue Yunsheng's commentaries on DC, 105-01 and 112-04.

15. The most thorough treatment of economic imperatives in forced remarriage is Fuma 1993. Also see Holmgren 1985, 11–14.

16. This example shows that on occasion, even very poor widows might refuse to remarry. In other words, our generalizations about the economic logic of remarriage, although probably correct in the aggregate, cannot explain actual behavior in every individual case.

17. Refusing meals played a key symbolic role in delayed transfer marriage in Guangdong (Stockard 1989, 20). On the strategy of cutting off hair or otherwise disfiguring oneself, see T'ien Ju-k'ang (1988, 37) and Carlitz (1994, 113–14).

18. For gazetteer hagiography, see Ebrey, ed., 1993, 253–55; Mann 1985 and 1987; Elvin 1984; and Spence 1978, chaps. 3 and 5. On the value of independence for its own sake, see Waltner 1981, 141–42, and Wolf 1981, 142.

19. An alternative for some was prostitution—e.g., BX, 3-8768 and 4-4881. Starting in the seventeen-seventies, local gentry and officials in some regions set up charitable widow homes in an attempt to make chastity an option for at least some of the poor (Leung 1993a; Fuma 1991; Mann 1987).

20. On the original document, this phrase is written in very large characters.

21. For children following widowed mothers into a second marriage, see Waltner 1981, 143–45.

22. His focus on her ethnicity may have been informed by anxiety about the supposed assertiveness and sexual power of Miao women (Diamond 1988). Attributing her defiance to a specifically Miao "temper" implied that it was part of a "barbarian" refusal to conform to "civilized" norms of human relations (*li*). But the evidence suggests that she was assimilated to Han culture: both her husbands were Han, she had a Chinese name, and her marriage was arranged according to Chinese custom.

23. Fuma (1993) makes a similar distinction between rich, poor, and "fairly prosperous" families in his analysis of the economic logic of in-laws' and natal families' attitudes toward widow remarriage, but he makes the widow herself appear to be an entirely passive object of manipulation by others.

24. Mann 1987, 46–47; also see A. Wolf 1975, 108. A case cited earlier in this chapter, of the widow Wu Shi, who was punished for adultery but not expelled, would seem to confirm this point. She had no brothers-in-law, her parents-in-law were dead, and the more distant members of her husband's lineage were sufficiently disinterested to testify on her behalf (XT, 185/QL 27.4.20).

25. Oddly, Wolf notes that in the same Taiwan community, a "common image of the widow is that of the young woman who is forced to remarry by her husband's brothers, who want control of her share of the estate." He does not explain why the threat of forced remarriage would be a problem, if adultery and uxorilocal marriage were not (A. Wolf and Huang 1980, 227–28).

26. There is evidence that the same had been true in Taiwan—e.g., an 1881 case from Xinzhu County, in which Lin Hong had his widowed daughter-in-law prosecuted for adultery (DX, 35401).

27. Qing law set strict limits on who might kill a couple caught in adultery, and authorized only a woman's husband and immediate relatives to seize her and turn her in for prosecution. But it explicitly excused "persons who are not authorized to seize adulterers" (*fei ying xu zhuo jian zhi ren*) from punishment for *beating* a couple caught in adultery, as long as no

"breaking injury" was inflicted (see DC, 285-00 and related substatutes; also see Meijer 1991).

28. For inheritance by adopted sons, see Wakefield 1992, 110–14.

29. For abortion in traditional Chinese medicine, see Bray 1997, 321–34.

30. One can interpret this episode as a conflict of interest between two separate "uterine families" within a single patriarchal family. A "uterine family" consists of a mother and her own children (see M. Wolf 1972).

31. Cf. Huang Liu-hung 1984, 278–79. Philip Huang cites Hu Shi's case as an unusual example of "magistrate as arbitrator" (1994, 173).

32. A story by Pu Songling (late seventeenth century) tells of a chaste widow who became pregnant but managed to dispel the scandal by proving that she had been impregnated by her husband's ghost (see Waltner 1981, 134).

33. As Susan Mann has commented, "even 'Neo-Confucian puritanism' could provide the basis for empowerment" for at least some women (1997, 225).

Chapter Six   The Regulation of Prostitution Before 1723

1. Sue Gronewald suggests incorrectly that the Qing never banned prostitution (1985, 27–28); her pioneering study lacks Chinese language sources, depending for the Qing code on Staunton's translation, which omits the substatutes. But no less an authority than Jing Junjian makes the same error, perhaps because he does not use archival records of criminal cases (1993, 231).

2. The foundational studies of status distinction in imperial law are Niida 1943 and 1962; Ch'ü 1965; and Jing Junjian 1993. Also see *Shinkoku*, 2/104–10, and Hansson 1996.

3. As explained in the introduction, the original meaning of *liang* was "free," where *jian* (debased, mean) meant "unfree" in the sense of owing labor service. Late imperial legal texts use a number of terms to refer to free commoners: Ming and Qing sources use *liang min* (the good or respectable people); *fan ren*, *chang ren*, and *ping min* (the ordinary or common people); and simply *min* (the people); earlier sources often use *shu min* (the common people), especially in contrast with aristocrats. For a general discussion of commoner status in Qing law, see Jing Junjian 1993, 20–35.

4. The classic study of the Yongzheng "emancipation edicts" is Terada 1959; for a recent view, see Hansson 1996. I present my own interpretation in Chapter 7.

5. In contrast with the previous era of "slave prostitution" and the subsequent era of "private enterprise prostitution" (Wang Shunu 1988, 7–8); for prostitution in modern Shanghai see Hershatter 1997.

6. E.g., *Jiu Tang shu*, 1838–39. On the penal origins of *yue hu*, see Higashikawa 1979, 157; *Shinkoku*, 2/107–8; Wang Shunu 1988, 193–95; Yan Ming 1992, 25–28; Yu Zhengxie 1964, 485–86.

7. For Zhu Di's *coup* and the dynasty's subsequent problems of legitima-

tion, see Elman 1993; for the fate of martyrs' dependents, see (in addition to sources cited above) Goodrich, ed., 1976, 1285; Mei Dingzuo 1910, 6/4b–5a; Yan Ming 1992, 93–95.

8. E.g., DC, 254-00, 255-00, and their respective substatutes.

9. The double meaning of *jian* is relevant here: the Jianwen loyalists were branded *jian chen* ("treasonous ministers"), while a commoner adulteress was termed a *jian fu* ("wife who has committed illicit sexual intercourse").

10. See the Ming dynasty's regulations on "Provision of Music and Dance by the Bureau of Instruction" in *Collected Statutes of the Ming Dynasty*; this section is followed by the "Prohibitions on *Yue* Households," some of which relate to prostitution (MH, 104/569–71). An office by the name "Bureau of Instruction" first appeared in the Tang dynasty; according to Yan Ming, the private management of brothels was prohibited during the Tang, and thus official prostitutes served both officials and ordinary commoners (1992, 54–55).

11. Until the late seventeenth century, when the Qing prohibited the custom, it was common for local officials to include prostitutes and other *yue* personnel as performers in local festivals (Mann 1997, 126–27; Hansson 1996, 65–68).

12. WX, ming li/18a; also see ML, 25/14a, and MH, 105/571.

13. For detailed discussion of these groups, see Jing Junjian 1993; Terada 1959; *Shinkoku*, 2/108–9; and Hansson 1996. For the moral significance of women's textile work, see Bray 1997 and Mann 1997.

14. A further source of complication is that *yue*, *chang*, and *ji* were used to denote women at all levels of the sex trade hierarchy, including elite courtesans, most of whose work consisted of less carnal forms of entertainment, as well as the most mundane sort of sex workers servicing a peasant clientele. Literary sources describe the high end of the scale, but in legal texts (especially criminal records) these terms nearly always refer to sex workers. See Wang Shunu (1988, 1–5) and Yan Ming (1992, 1–6) for discussion of the various terms used for courtesans and prostitutes throughout Chinese history.

15. If an offender was liable for punishment under more than one law, only the law that prescribed the most severe penalties would be applied.

16. Although by the Qing dynasty, homicide of a debased-status person by a commoner had come to be punished in the same manner as homicide of a status equal, unless the victim were a subordinate member of the killer's own household (Jing Junjian 1993, 44).

17. In addition, the Yuan, Ming, and Qing dynasties all prohibited members of prostitute households from taking civil examinations or becoming officials (YD, 31/15b; MH, 77; DC, 76-06 and 19).

18. For imperial sumptuary law in general, see Ch'ü 1965, 135–54.

19. Other terms of abuse based on the color green's association with prostitution are "turtle" (*wangba* or *wugui*, meaning "pimp" or "cuckold"), "turtle head" (*gui tou*, meaning the same thing), and "turtle's egg" or "turtle's son" (*wangba dan*, etc., meaning "bastard"). See Zhao Yi 1957, 849–52;

Ren Cheng 1991, 234–35; Wang Shunu 1988, 247–48. "Green chamber" (*qing lou*) was a common euphemism for a brothel (Mann 1997, 98).

20. See Jing Junjian 1993, 10–16.

21. Xie Zhaozhe 1959, 225–26. Jiang Mingshu is cited in Wang Shunu 1988, 197. Also see *Ming shi*, 4185.

22. It is not clear what this penalty was.

23. See Hinsch 1990, 72. Wang Shunu notes that in early texts, *chang* and *you* were synonyms (1988, 1). In Ming-Qing legal texts, *you* often serves as a euphemism for a male prostitute; for example, see DC, 375-04.

24. *Ling* is ambiguous, it can mean both "to force" and "to allow."

25. In this instance and many others, Ming lawmakers simply rounded off the number of blows prescribed in the Yuan statute to the nearest multiple of ten; thus 87 blows became 90.

26. Other texts contain slightly different versions of this measure; see Huang Zhangjian, ed., 1979, 946–47.

27. For the career of Lü Kun (1536–1618) see Handlin 1983 and Goodrich, ed., 1976, 1006–10. These prohibitions are also discussed by Terada (1959, 126–27) and Hansson (1996, 65–71).

28. See Littrup 1981, 165–68; and Goodrich, ed., 1976, 1007.

29. Zhang Kentang (*jinshi* 1625) later served the Ming as censor, governor of Fujian, and assistant minister in the Court of Judicial Review. He hanged himself in 1651 rather than submit to the Qing conquest (Zhang Kentang 1969, preface).

30. Apparently, the prefect (of Daming Prefecture) referred the case to the magistrate of Wei County, which lay close to the prefectural seat, instead of trying it himself; Anyang County was across the provincial boundary, and Changtan and Jun Counties, though both in Daming Prefecture, were much farther away than Wei County. The pimp later filed suit in Jun County because that was where he lived. Today, Daming Prefecture is part of Henan Province, but in the Ming, it was part of the Northern Metropolitan Province (present-day Hebei). See Tan Qixiang, ed., 1982, 44–45.

31. Zhang Kentang gives no information on the earlier prosecution of the woman's husband and Prostitute Li in the other jurisdictions.

32. Qing law mandated strangulation after the assizes for intercourse with a brother's concubine, be it consensual or coerced (DC, 368-00).

33. In the end an imperial amnesty voided these sentences.

34. For example Hansson 1996, 59; and *Mathews' Chinese-English Dictionary*, 1020.

35. See Niida 1943, 959, 963–64; 1962, 1/16. *Collected Statutes of the Yuan* spells out how *liang shu* were to be drafted (YD, 18/8a–b). For an example in the Ming code of *"fang cong liang"* referring to the manumission of slaves, see Huang Zhangjian, ed., 1979, 835. This statute was preserved in the Qing code, but later largely superseded by new substatutes (DC, 314-00).

36. See Dorothy Ko's analysis of "following" (*cong*) and "thrice following" (*san cong*) (1994, 6, 251–53).

37. The source does not say if Le'an County is the one by that name in Shandong or the one in Jiangxi (see Ko 1994, 119–20, nn. 11 and 12). Lü Kun's rules for *yue* households grant an exception to the ban on intermarriage and on prostitutes entering commoner homes by permitting commoner males "to take in marriage, according to proper ritual" prostitutes who *"cong liang"* (see Appendix D).

38. E.g., Feng Menglong 1990, 12/6a–b; Mei Dingzuo, ed., 1910, 8/4a–b. Such fantasies persisted into the High Qing—see Mann 1997, 134–35, 138.

39. For example, one prostitute refused to testify falsely against her patron, in spite of being imprisoned and tortured. Another, having been rescued from prostitution by her patron, committed suicide to follow him in death (Feng Menglong 1910, 1/33a–34b, 4/18a–b). For the idealization of courtesans as models of loyalty and virtue in the seventeenth century, see Carlitz 1994; Ko 1994; and W. Li 1997.

40. Feng Menglong 1990, 12/6a–b; Mei Dingzuo, ed., 1910, 3/4b–5a, 4/12b, 8/4a–b, 6b. For the general theme of boundary transgression in seventeenth-century literature, see McMahon 1988.

41. On the commercial publishing boom and emergence of a reading public in the late Ming, see Ko 1994.

42. Mei Dingzuo, ed., 1910, 6/4b–5a; also see Goodrich, ed., 1976, 1285; Yan Ming 1992, 94; and Yu Zhengxie 1964, 486.

43. On Ming amnesties, also see Terada 1959, 368 and Hansson 1996, 59.

44. Because only the first part of this memorial survives, we do not have the full details of their sentencing, but no doubt the couple was ordered divorced as well.

45. Because of an amnesty, their penalty was reduced by one degree and they were allowed to remain married; Fu Rong was sentenced to beheading. The judgment received imperial approval. I know more about this case than about most of my early Qing examples because three related memorials survive (MQ, 20-86; XT, 802/SZ 11.10.10 and 1041/SZ 12.6.4). Unfortunately, since for the other three cases recounted in this section one brief memorial each is all that survives, some details are lost.

46. We have already seen one example of such lenience in Ming law: unlike a commoner woman who committed adultery, a prostitute who slept with an official was allowed to redeem her beating with a fine, or, if unable to afford the fine, to refrain from stripping when receiving punishment.

47. Several documents related to this case survive, most of them in fragments: XT, 1701/SZ ?, 600/SZ 10.5.8, 1024/SZ 12.4.21 and 1695/SZ ?; MQ 22-37.

48. *Xun an Shanxi jian cha yu shi*; the office of regional inspector seems to have played a key role in the review of capital cases during the early Qing, but not in the eighteenth century.

49. *"Cong liang"* here implies the promotion Hou Shi would achieve by quitting sex work, abandoning her husband and his debased status, and marrying commoner Liu Qi. Presumably Liu did not intend to petition

a magistrate for some official change of registry but simply to move far enough away that in their anonymity, they would be taken for an ordinary couple.

50. The surviving record does not say which statute was cited to justify this penalty, but it was probably the catch-all law against "doing inappropriate things." Her penalty was too light to have been based on the sub-statute against "consensual abduction" (*he you zhi qing*) routinely cited to punish commoner women who ran off with lovers (DC, 275-02).

51. At the opposite extreme of the status hierarchy, officials and higher degree holders were above many of the laws binding on commoners (Jing Junjian 1993, 3–19).

Chapter Seven   The Criminalization of Prostitution

1. E.g., the Board of Household's 1723 policy statement on *yue* households: "Actually, they are descendants of loyal and righteous [martyrs]: their ancestors were harmed for refusing to submit to the usurpation of the throne at the end of the Jianwen era . . . and so they met this bitter insult, and were registered as *yue* households. For generations, their sons and grandsons have been unable to raise themselves up to commoner status. All jurisdictions are hereby instructed strictly to prohibit and change this [status registration], and to order [the *yue* households] to change their occupations and renew themselves (*gai ye zi xin*), so that they can become commoners" (QHS, 185/1007).

2. Both of these arguments are recapitulated by Hansson (1996, 165–68); he gives particular weight to the political factor as a motive for the 1723 edict, arguing that rectifying the Ming injustice was designed to demonstrate the moral superiority of the Qing.

3. Throughout his article, Terada uses two different characters interchangeably to represent the *"kai"* in *"kaihō"*: in Chinese, they are pronounced *"jie"* (to release) and *"kai"* (to open)—see Character List. Following Terada, Western historians generally use the English "emancipation" to refer to the Yongzheng initiative (e.g., Hansson 1996; Hucker 1975, 335; Mann 1997, 43; Naquin and Rawski 1987, 117).

4. In 1694, Huang Liuhong derided the "ridiculous" spectacle of prostitutes and actors (*chang you*) participating in the welcoming of spring, which he believed should properly be a solemn occasion, as prescribed by *The Book of Rites* (1973, 24/16a–17b).

5. Terada (1959), Jing Junjian (1993), and Hansson (1996) catalogue the relevant edicts, including those that affected groups not associated with prostitution; also see Mann 1997, 37–43. The original texts of many can be found in QHS, 158. The mean-status group "nine surnames fishing households"—Zhejiang boat people who lived by fishing and prostitution—was not specifically addressed in the Yongzheng edicts, but a law of 1771 enabled them to register and change their status, as long as they conformed to *"liang"* standards of occupation and conduct (Terada 1959, 131–32; Jing Junjian 1993, 217).

6. YZ, 56/27a–b. This translation is a slight modification of Philip Kuhn's rendering (1984, 22–23). For a Japanese translation see Terada 1959.

7. A search of the dynastic histories on the Academia Sinica's website database (www.sinica.edu.tw/) provides many similar examples.

8. Similar statements appear in the "Great Preface" to *The Book of Songs, The Book of Rites*, and elsewhere (Owen 1992, 37–56). Translations from Xunzi are Watson's, and those from *Analects* are Waley's; I have supplied the Chinese terms from the original texts.

9. Cited in Wang Shunu 1988, 261. In 1724, the Yongzheng Emperor also prohibited officials from maintaining troupes of actors (*you ling*); this ban was reiterated in 1769 (QHS, 117/723).

10. Also see Hansson 1996, 71. Wang Jingqi's journal of his travels became the focus of a celebrated literary inquisition case, and he was beheaded for sedition in 1726 (Hummel 1970, 812–13).

11. The final form of this law, DC, 285-07, is an amalgam of this measure and later amendments; see Wu Tan 1992, 782 and QHS, 801/766.

12. In a variation on this theme, the Jiaqing Emperor in 1806 canonized a chastity martyr from Zhili who was beaten to death by her mother-in-law for refusing to submit to prostitution. In this case, too, the prize money for the arch went to the martyr's natal family (QHS, 404/517). A substatute of 1792 mandated strangulation after the assizes for any woman who provoked her daughter-in-law's suicide by trying to force her into prostitution (DC, 299-17).

13. The term "unlicensed individual" is meant to contrast with the substatute immediately prior to this one (DC, 375-01), which prohibits pimping on the part of official matchmakers authorized by magistrates to sell women in marriage (see below).

14. This measure reached final form in 1767; see DC, 375-02.

15. I translate as "yue pimps" a colloquial term, *hang yuan*, that referred to a person of *yue* status (ZD, 8/562).

16. Here I have slightly modified Djang Chu's translations (Huang Liuhung 1984, 500–501). Huang also warned about the problems caused by prostitutes who operated at the stations on imperial postal routes (1973, 29/15b–16a). His concerns were shared by other officials; see HB, 97; and Li Yu, ed., 1996, 14/17a–18a.

17. In 1740 the site of deportation was changed; see DC, 375-01.

18. Also see a 1724 regulation that addresses *guan mei* (QHS, 99/271). References to official matchmakers can be found in the Ming novel *Plum in the Golden Vase* (90, 11b), and in eighteenth- to twentieth-century case records from Ba County, Baodi County, and the Board of Punishment itself (Sommer 1994, 395–407). A Ba County case from 1800 mentions that an official matchmaker named Song had been fired for taking advantage of his position to engage in illegal trafficking in women (BX, 2-4140).

19. The men were sentenced according to substatute no. 9 in Wu Tan 1992, 782; this measure was later subsumed by DC, 285-07.

20. See substatute no. 11 in Wu Tan 1992, 782 (later subsumed by DC, 285-07).

21. The memorial notes that because the crimes had occurred before "the new substatute" had been received, the innkeepers should receive only 100 blows of the heavy bamboo. The new law (DC, 375-02) added three months in the cangue.

22. Even the Board of Punishment did not always enforce this policy consistently. In "immediate examination" cases of prostitution from Beijing, the board sometimes cited local officials for "failing to detect" prostitutes (e.g., XB, ZL 01123), but sometimes did not (e.g., XB, JS 09324).

23. Adoption and sworn sisterhood were common among prostitutes and courtesans in late imperial and early twentieth-century China; see Mann 1997, 139–40; M. Wolf 1972, chap. 13.

24. This substatute (DC, 375-02) is a 1760 amendment of the 1736 substatute on "harboring" prostitutes cited above.

25. Reminiscent of the strategy used by a pimp in a case judged by Zhang Kentang; see Chapter 6.

26. BX, 4-4918; for other examples, see BX, 3-8621 and 3-8730.

27. It is not clear whether they first filed charges at the county yamen, but it was not uncommon for plaintiffs to go straight to the Chongqing Prefectural yamen (though the practice was discouraged): the two compounds were right next-door to each other.

28. For yamen corruption and Ba County runners in particular, see Reed 1994, 1995, and 2000.

29. For Qing opium policy in the eighteenth century, see Howard 1998, 75–92.

30. Xue also claimed that the failed policy had stemmed from a foolish misunderstanding of the Yongzheng Emperor's true intent: "When the present dynasty abolished the Bureau of Instruction and changed the *yue* households of the various provinces into commoners, the original purpose was to eliminate the evil policies of the former Ming dynasty. It was not to eliminate prostitutes altogether!" Xue's claim is disingenuous. He could hardly condemn the Yongzheng edicts themselves, and thus in order to criticize prohibition, he prudently disassociated that policy from the imperial will. The "evil policies" he had in mind were Zhu Di's use of *yue* status and the Bureau of Instruction to persecute the dependents of the Jianwen martyrs (DC, 375-04, commentary).

Chapter Eight   Conclusion

1. In fiction female homosexual acts are generally represented as a substitute for, or imitation of, heterosexual intercourse; often dildoes are used, implying that male writers had difficulty imagining sexual activity in other than phallic terms even when no men participated (for example, see Li Mengsheng 1994, 256–58). In the Greco-Roman world, too, male authors consistently imagined female-female lovemaking as involving penetration with dildoes (Clarke 1998, 227–29).

2. Chen Hongmou (1696–1771) held many important posts (including

the governorship of seven provinces) under the Yongzheng and Qianlong Emperors—see Hummel 1970, 86–87.

3. See Shen Defu's statement quoted in Chapter 4.

4. See Dorothy Ko's important discussion of how May Fourth–era nationalism has distorted historical understanding of gender relations in late imperial China (1994, 1–7).

5. Elvin (1984) cites this inclusion of women of humble background as evidence for the "democratization" of elite virtue.

6. On the mean status of runners, see Hansson 1996, 48–50. Over the course of the Qing, yamen runners gradually evolved into a professional group made up of people from various backgrounds—yet another example of how socioeconomic change blurred what had long been considered fixed connections between legal status, family background, and occupation (Reed 1994 and 2000).

7. Indeed, prior to the Yongzheng reforms the "beggar households" (*gai hu*) of some regions were officially registered with mean status.

8. For example Friedman et al. 1991; P. Huang 1985 and 1990; Perry 1980.

9. See especially the statement by Hubei official Zhou Kai (quoted by Mann 1997, 163–64). An 1803 magistrate's handbook makes a similar argument in order to impugn the virtue of wives who were sold by their husbands: "If a wife is properly diligent at spinning and sewing, and she and her husband get along in harmony, then in spite of poverty, it will never occur to him to sell her" (Sommer 1994, 390).

10. The term *jian fu* does not appear in the Tang code, but it acquired an increasingly central role in legal discourse over the Yuan, Ming, and especially Qing dynasties. After the Yongzheng reforms, this term applied to any woman who engaged in intercourse outside marriage (barring only acts that met the strict definition of rape). The classic image of the *jian fu* in literature is Pan Jinlian, heroine of *Plum in the Golden Vase*, who murders her first husband in order to become Ximen Qing's concubine and later betrays him as well with Chen Jingji; in fact, one of Ximen's favorite bedroom names for her is *yin fu*—"licentious wife"—which amounts to the same thing.

References

Sources Cited by Abbreviation

BX Ba County Archive, Sichuan Provincial Archives, Chengdu. Each case is identified by serial number.

DC Xue Yunsheng. 1970 (Qing). *Du li cun yi* (Lingering Doubts After Reading the Substatutes). Edited and punctuated by Huang Jingjia. Taibei: Chinese Materials and Research Aids Service Center. Each statute, substatute, or passage from Xue's *jin an* commentary is cited by serial number.

DX Danshui-Xinzhu Archive. Available on microfilm at the UCLA East Asian Library (and elsewhere). Each case is identified by serial number.

HB Sichuan Provincial Archives, ed. 1991. *Qing dai Ba Xian dang'an huibian (Qianlong juan)* (Compendium of Qing Dynasty Documents from Ba County—Qianlong Period). Beijing: Dang'an Chubanshe.

HC *Huang chao jing shi wen bian* (Collected Essays on Statecraft). Taibei: Guofeng Chubanshe, 1963.

MH *Ming hui dian* (Collected Statutes of the Ming). 1988 (1587). Beijing: Zhonghua Shuju.

ML *Da Ming lü jijie* (The Ming Code with Collected Commentaries). 1991. Beijing: Zhonghua Shuju (reprint).

MQ Chang We-jen [Zhang Weiren], ed. 1986. *Zhongyang Yanjiuyuan Lishi Yuyan Yanjiusuo xian cun Qing dai Neige Daku yuan cang Ming-Qing dang'an* (Ming-Qing Documents from the Qing Dynasty Grand Secretariat Archive in the Possession of the History and Language Research Institute, Academia Sinica). Taibei: Academia Sinica. Each case is identified by serial number.

QH *Qing hui dian* (Collected Statutes of the Qing). 1991 (1899). Beijing: Zhonghua Shuju (reprint).

QHS *Qing hui dian shi li* (Collected Statutes of the Qing, with Substatutes Based on Precedent). 1991 (1899). Beijing: Zhonghua Shuju.

QM   *Ming gong shu pan qing ming ji* (Perspicacious Judgments by Famous Magistrates). 1987 (Song). Beijing: Zhonghua Shuju.

QY   *Qingyuan tiao fa shi lei* (Laws of the Qingyuan Period). 1990. Beijing: Zhongguo Shudian.

SF   Shuntian Prefecture Archive, held at the First Historical Archives in Beijing (most cases are from Baodi County). All cases are from the category "marriage, sex offenses, and family disputes"; each is cited by number of bundle and the Chinese date of the earliest dated document.

SX   *Song xing tong* (The Song Penal Code). 1990. Beijing: Zhongguo Shudian (reprint).

TL   *Tang lü shu yi* (The Tang Code with Commentary). 1990. Beijing: Zhongguo Shudian (reprint).

TM   Xue Yunsheng. 1990 (late Qing). *Tang Ming lü hebian* (A Combined Edition of the Tang and Ming Codes). Beijing: Zhongguo Shudian (reprint).

WX   Gu Yingxiang et al., eds. Ming, Jiajing period. *Wen xing tiaoli* (Substatutes for Assigning Penalties). No publisher.

XA   *Xing an hui lan* (Conspectus of Legal Cases). 1834? (Edition in UCLA East Asian Library.)

XAX   *Xing an hui lan xu bian* (A Continuing Edition of the Conspectus of Legal Cases). 1970. Taibei: Wenhai Chubanshe.

XB   Board of Punishment Archive (*Xing Bu dang*). Held at the First Historical Archives, Beijing; all citations are cases from Beijing referred to the provincial bureaus of the board for "immediate examination" (*xian shen*). Each is identified by bureau and serial number (GD = Guangdong Bureau; FT = Fengtian Bureau; JS = Jiangsu Bureau; SC = Sichuan Bureau; ZL = Zhili Bureau).

XF   *Xing tai falü* (Laws of the Judicial Bench). 1990 (Ming, Wanli period). Beijing: Zhongguo Shudian (reprint).

XT   Grand Secretariat memorials on criminal matters (*Neige xingke tiben*). Held at the First Historical Archives, Beijing. Shunzhi and Yongzheng cases are cited by microfilm serial number and Chinese date; all are from the category "criminal punishment." Qianlong, Jiaqing, and Daoguang cases are cited by the number of document bundle, and the memorial's Chinese date. All are from the category "marriage, sex offenses, and family disputes."

XZ   *Xu zeng xing an hui lan* (Supplement to the Conspectus of Legal Cases). 1840? (Edition in UCLA East Asian Library.)

YD   *Yuan dian zhang* (Collected Statutes of the Yuan). 1990. Beijing: Zhongguo Shudian (reprint).

YZ   *Da Qing lichao shi lu* (Veritable Records of Successive Reigns of the Great Qing Dynasty). Yongzheng Reign.

ZD   *Zhongwen da cidian* (Great Dictionary of the Chinese Language). 1976. Taibei: Zhonghua Xueshuyuan.

Other Sources

Academia Sinica. Online database of dynastic histories. Available on the World Wide Web at http://www.sinica.edu.tw/.

Allee, Mark A. 1994. *Law and Local Society in Late Imperial China: Northern Taiwan in the Nineteenth Century*. Stanford, Calif.: Stanford University Press.

Bao Shichen. 1968 [1888]. *An Wu si zhong* (Four Treatises on Governing Wu). Taibei: Wenhai Chubanshe.

Bartlett, Beatrice S. 1991. *Monarchs and Ministers: The Grand Council in Mid-Ch'ing China, 1723–1820*. Berkeley: University of California Press.

Berman, Harold J. 1983. *Law and Revolution: The Formation of the Western Legal Tradition*. Cambridge, Mass.: Harvard University Press.

Bernhardt, Kathryn. 1996. "A Ming-Qing Transition in Chinese Women's History? The Perspective from Law." In G. Hershatter et al., eds., *Remapping China: Fissures in Historical Terrain*. Stanford, Calif.: Stanford University Press.

Blond, Neil C., et al. 1991. *Blond's Criminal Law*. New York: Sulzburger and Graham Publishing Ltd.

Bodde, Derk, and Clarence Morris. 1967. *Law in Imperial China, Exemplified by 190 Ch'ing Dynasty Cases*. Cambridge, Mass.: Harvard University Press.

Boswell, John. 1980. *Christianity, Social Tolerance, and Homosexuality: Gay People in Western Europe from the Beginning of the Christian Era to the Fourteenth Century*. Chicago: University of Chicago Press.

———— 1992. "Categories, Experience, and Sexuality." In Edward Stein, ed., *Forms of Desire: Sexual Orientation and the Social Constructionist Controversy*. New York: Routledge.

Bourdieu, Pierre. 1976. "Marriage Strategies as Strategies of Social Reproduction." In R. Forster and O. Ranum, eds., *Family and Society: Selections from the Annales*. Baltimore and London: Johns Hopkins University Press.

———— 1990. *The Logic of Practice*. Stanford, Calif.: Stanford University Press.

Bray, Francesca. 1997. *Technology and Gender: Fabrics of Power in Late Imperial China*. Berkeley: University of California Press.

Brown, Judith C. 1986. *Immodest Acts: The Life of a Lesbian Nun in Renaissance Italy*. Oxford: Oxford University Press.

Brundage, James A. 1987. *Law, Sex, and Christian Society in Medieval Europe*. Chicago: University of Chicago Press.

Brunnert, H. S., and V. V. Hagelstrom. 1912. *Present Day Political Organization of China*. Shanghai: no publisher (Taiwan reprint).

Butler, Judith. 1990. *Gender Trouble: Feminism and the Subversion of Identity*. New York: Routledge.

Buxbaum, David C. 1971. "Some Aspects of Civil Procedure and Practice at the Trial Level in Tanshui and Hsinchu from 1789 to 1895." *Journal of Asian Studies* 30, no. 2.

Byron, John. 1987. *Portrait of a Chinese Paradise: Erotic and Sexual Customs of the Late Qing Period.* London: Quartet Books.

Carlitz, Katherine. 1994. "Desire, Danger, and the Body: Stories of Women's Virtue in Late Ming China." In C. Gilmartin et al., eds., *Engendering China: Women, Culture, and the State.* Cambridge, Mass.: Harvard University Press.

Chen Baoliang. 1993. *Zhongguo liumang shi* (A History of Chinese Hooligans). Beijing: Zhongguo Shehui Kexue Chubanshe.

Chen, Fu-mei Chang. 1980. "The Influence of Shen Chih-ch'i's *Chi-Chu Commentary* Upon Ch'ing Judicial Decisions." In J. Cohen et al., eds., *Essays on China's Legal Tradition.* Princeton, N.J.: Princeton University Press.

Ch'ü, T'ung-tsu. 1965. *Law and Society in Traditional China.* Paris: Mouton and Co.

Ci hai (Word Ocean). 1978. Taibei: Taiwan Zhonghua Shuju.

Clarke, John R. 1998. *Looking at Lovemaking: Constructions of Sexuality in Roman Art, 100 B.C.–A.D. 250.* Berkeley: University of California Press.

Cohen, Paul A. 1984. *Discovering History in China: American Historical Writing on the Recent Chinese Past.* New York: Columbia University Press.

Conner, Alison W. 1979. "The Law of Evidence During the Qing Dynasty." Ph.D. diss., Cornell University.

Dai Wei. 1992. *Zhongguo hunyin xing'ai shi gao* (A History of Marriage and Sexual Love in China). Beijing: Dongfang Chubanshe.

Davis, Fei-ling. 1977. *Primitive Revolutionaries of China: A Study of Secret Societies in the Late Nineteenth Century.* Honolulu: The University Press of Hawaii.

Davis, Natalie Z. 1987. *Fiction in the Archives: Pardon Tales and Their Tellers in Sixteenth-Century France.* Stanford, Calif.: Stanford University Press.

Dennerline, Jerry. 1986. "Marriage, Adoption, and Charity in the Development of Lineages in Wu-hsi from Sung to Ch'ing." In P. Ebrey and J. Watson, eds., *Kinship Organization in Late Imperial China, 1000–1940.* Berkeley: University of California Press.

Diamond, Norma. 1988. "The Miao and Poison: Interactions on China's Southwest Frontier." *Ethnology* 27, no. 1.

Dikötter, Frank. 1995. *Sex, Culture, and Modernity in China: Medical Science and the Construction of Sexual Identities in the Early Republican Period.* Honolulu: University of Hawai'i Press.

Dull, Jack L. 1978. "Marriage and Divorce in Han China: A Glimpse at 'Pre-Confucian' Society." In D. Buxbaum, ed., *Chinese Family Law and Social Change in Historical and Comparative Perspective.* Seattle: University of Washington Press.

Ebrey, Patricia B. 1986. "The Early Stages of Development in Descent Group Organization." In P. Ebrey and J. Watson, eds., *Kinship Organiza-*

tion in Late Imperial China, 1000–1940. Berkeley: University of California Press.

―――― 1993. *The Inner Quarters: Marriage and the Lives of Chinese Women in the Sung Period.* Berkeley: University of California Press.

――――, ed. 1993. *Chinese Civilization: A Sourcebook.* New York: Free Press.

Edwards, Louise P. 1994. *Men and Women in Qing China: Gender in The Red Chamber Dream.* Leiden: E. J. Brill.

Elman, Benjamin. 1993. "'Where Is King Ch'eng?' Civil Examinations and Confucian Ideology During the Early Ming, 1368–1415." *T'oung pao* 79: 23–68.

Elvin, Mark. 1984. "Female Virtue and the State in China." *Past and Present* 104.

Feng Menglong, ed. 1990 (Ming). *Qing shi* (Anatomy of Love). Shanghai: Shanghai Guji Chubanshe.

Foucault, Michel. 1978. *The History of Sexuality: An Introduction.* New York: Random House, Inc.

Friedman, Edward, et al. 1991. *Chinese Village, Socialist State.* New Haven: Yale University Press.

Fuma Susumu. 1991. "Shindai no 'xuli hui' to 'qingjie tang'" (Widows' Aid Societies and Chaste Widow Homes in the Qing Dynasty). *Kyôtô Daigaku Bungakubu kenkyû kiyô* 30:41–131.

―――― 1993. "Chûgoku Min-Shin jidai ni okeru kafu no chii to kyôsei saikon no fûshû" (The Position of Widows and the Custom of Forced Remarriage During the Ming-Qing Period). In Maekawa Kazuya, ed., *Kazoku, setai, kamon: kôgyôka izen no sekai kara.* Kyôto: Minerva Shobo.

Furth, Charlotte. 1988. "Androgynous Males and Deficient Females: Biology and Gender Boundaries in Sixteenth-and Seventeenth-Century China." *Late Imperial China* 9, no. 2:1–31.

―――― 1990. "The Patriarch's Legacy: Household Instructions and the Transmission of Orthodox Values." In K. C. Liu, ed., *Orthodoxy in Late Imperial China.* Berkeley: University of California Press.

―――― 1991. Review of Bret Hinsch. *Journal of Asian Studies* 50, no. 4:911–12.

―――― 1994. "Rethinking Van Gulik: Sexuality and Reproduction in Traditional Chinese Medicine." In C. Gilmartin et al., eds., *Engendering China: Women, Culture, and the State.* Cambridge, Mass.: Harvard University Press.

Gang Yi. 1968 (1889). *Qiu yan jiyao* (Collected Essentials of the Autumn Assizes). Taibei: Wenhai Chubanshe.

Gao Chao and Ma Jianshi, eds. 1989. *Zhongguo gu dai fa xue cidian* (Dictionary of the Study of Ancient Chinese Law). Tianjin: Nankai Daxue.

Gao Hongxing et al., eds. 1991. *Funü fengsu kao* (Customs Regarding Women). Shanghai: Shanghai Wenyi Chubanshe.

Ginzburg, Carlo. 1983. *The Night Battles: Witchcraft and Agrarian Cults in the Sixteenth and Seventeenth Centuries.* Baltimore: Johns Hopkins University Press.

Goodrich, L. Carrington, ed. 1976. *Dictionary of Ming Biography.* New York: Columbia University Press.

Gronewald, Sue. 1985. *Beautiful Merchandise: Prostitution in China 1860–1936.* New York: Harrington Park Press.

Guy, R. Kent. 1987. *The Emperor's Four Treasuries: Scholars and the State in the Late Ch'ien-lung Era.* Cambridge, Mass.: Council on East Asian Studies, Harvard University.

Halperin, David M. 1993. "Is There a History of Sexuality?" In H. Abelove et al., eds., *The Lesbian and Gay Studies Reader.* New York: Routledge.

Handlin, Joanna F. 1983. *Action in Late Ming Thought: The Reorientation of Lü K'un and Other Scholar-Officials.* Berkeley: University of California Press.

Hansson, Anders. 1996. *Chinese Outcasts: Discrimination and Emancipation in Late Imperial China.* Leiden: E. J. Brill.

Harrell, Stevan, ed. 1995. *Chinese Historical Microdemography.* Berkeley: University of California Press.

Hershatter, Gail. 1996. "Sexing Modern China." In G. Hershatter et al., eds., *Remapping China: Fissures in Historical Terrain.* Stanford, Calif.: Stanford University Press.

———— 1997. *Dangerous Pleasures: Prostitution and Modernity in Twentieth-Century Shanghai.* Berkeley: University of California Press.

Higashikawa Tokuji. 1979 (1929). *Chûgoku hôsei dai jiten* (Dictionary of the Chinese Legal System). Tôkyô: Ryogen.

Hinsch, Bret. 1990. *Passions of the Cut Sleeve: The Male Homosexual Tradition in China.* Berkeley: University of California Press.

Ho, Ping-ti. 1959. *Studies in the Population of China.* Cambridge, Mass.: Harvard University Press.

Holmgren, Jennifer. 1985. "The Economic Foundations of Virtue: Widow-Remarriage in Early and Modern China." *The Australian Journal of Chinese Affairs* 13:1–27.

Howard, Paul W. 1998. "Opium Suppression in Qing China: Responses to a Social Problem, 1729–1906." Ph.D. diss., University of Pennsylvania.

Huang Liuhong. 1973 (1694). *Fu hui quan shu* (A Complete Book Concerning Happiness and Benevolence). Introduction and index by Yamane Yukio. Tôkyô: Kyûko Shoin.

Huang Liu-hung [Huang Liuhong]. 1984. *A Complete Book Concerning Happiness and Benevolence: A Manual for Local Magistrates in Seventeenth-Century China.* Trans. and ed. by Djang Chu. Tucson: University of Arizona Press.

Huang, Philip C. C. 1982. "County Archives and the Study of Local Social History: Report on a Year's Research in China." *Modern China* 8, no. 1.

———— 1985. *The Peasant Economy and Social Change in North China.* Stanford, Calif.: Stanford University Press.

———— 1990. *The Peasant Family and Economic Development in the Yangzi Delta, 1350–1988.* Stanford, Calif.: Stanford University Press.

———— 1991. "The Paradigmatic Crisis in Chinese Studies: Paradoxes in Social and Economic History." *Modern China* 17, no. 3.

————— 1993. "Between Informal Mediation and Formal Adjudication: The Third Realm of Qing Civil Justice." *Modern China* 19, no. 3.

————— 1994. "Codified Law and Magisterial Adjudication in the Qing." In K. Bernhardt and P. Huang, eds., *Civil Law in Qing and Republican China.* Stanford, Calif.: Stanford University Press.

————— 1996. *Civil Justice in China: Representation and Practice in the Qing.* Stanford, Calif.: Stanford University Press.

Huang Zhangjian, ed. 1979. *Ming dai lü li hui bian* (Compendium of Ming Dynasty Statutes and Substatutes). Taibei: Zhongyang Yanjiuyuan Lishi-Yuyan Yanjiusuo.

Hucker, Charles O. 1975. *China's Imperial Past: An Introduction to Chinese History and Culture.* Stanford, Calif.: Stanford University Press.

————— 1985. *A Dictionary of Official Titles in Imperial China.* Stanford, Calif.: Stanford University Press.

Hulsewé, A. F. P. 1985. *Remnants of Ch'in Law: An Annotated Translation of the Ch'in Legal and Administrative Rules of the 3rd Century B.C. Discovered in Yun-meng Prefecture, Hu-pei Province, in 1973.* Leiden: E. J. Brill.

Humana, Charles, and Wang Wu. 1982. *The Chinese Way of Love.* Hong Kong: CFW Publications.

Hummel, Arthur W., ed. 1970 (1943). *Eminent Chinese of the Ch'ing Period.* Taibei: Chengwen Publishing Co. (reprint).

Hunt, Lynn A. 1998. "The Challenge of Gender: Deconstruction of Categories and Reconstruction of Narrative in Gender History." In H. Medick and A. Trapp, eds., *Geschlechtergeschichte und Allgemeine Geschichte: Herausforderungen und Perspektiven.* Göttingen: Wallstein Verlag.

Ingram, Martin. 1987. *Church Courts, Sex and Marriage in England, 1570–1640.* Cambridge: Cambridge University Press.

Jaschok, Maria. 1988. *Concubines and Bondservants: A Social History.* London: Zed Books Ltd.

Ji Xu et al. 1989 (1789). *Li dai zhi guan biao* (A List of Offices in Successive Dynasties). Shanghai: Shanghai Guji Chubanshe (reprint).

Jia Gongyan. 1966 (ca. 650). *Zhou li zhu shu* (Commentary on *The Rites of Zhou*). Taibei: Taiwan Zhonghua Shuju.

Jiao Hong. 1991 (1616). *Guo chao xian zheng lu* (Record of Verified Documents of the Present Dynasty). Taibei: Mingwen Shuju (reprint).

Jin Ping Mei ci hua (Plum in the Golden Vase). 1988 (1617). Hong Kong: Xianggang Taiping Shuju (reprint).

Jing Junjian. 1980. "Shilun Qingdai dengji zhidu" (A Preliminary Discussion of the Legal Status System in the Qing Dynasty). *Zhongguo shehui kexue* 6.

————— 1993. *Qing dai shehui de jianmin dengji* (Debased Legal Status in Qing Society). Hangzhou: Zhejiang Renmin Chubanshe.

————— 1994. "Legislation Related to the Civil Economy in the Qing Dynasty." Trans. by M. Sommer. In K. Bernhardt and P. Huang, eds., *Civil Law in Qing and Republican China.* Stanford, Calif.: Stanford University Press.

Jiu Tang shu (Former History of the Tang Dynasty). Searched on Academia Sinica. Online database of dynastic histories. Http://www.sinica.edu.tw/.

Johnson, Kay Ann. 1983. *Women, the Family, and Peasant Revolution in China.* Chicago: University of Chicago Press.

Johnson, Wallace. 1979. *The T'ang Code: Volume I—General Principles.* Princeton: Princeton University Press.

—— 1997. *The T'ang Code: Volume II—Specific Articles.* Princeton: Princeton University Press.

Jones, William C., trans. (with the assistance of Tianquan Cheng and Yongling Jiang). 1994. *The Great Qing Code.* New York: Oxford University Press.

Kahn, Harold L. 1971. *Monarchy in the Emperor's Eyes: Image and Reality in the Ch'ien-lung Reign.* Cambridge, Mass.: Harvard University Press.

Karasawa Yasuhiko. 1992. "Between Speech and Writing: Textuality of the Written Record of Oral Testimony in Qing Legal Cases." Unpublished seminar paper.

—— 1993. "Composing the Narrative: A Preliminary Study of Plaints in Qing Legal Cases." Presented at the conference on Code and Practice in Qing and Republican Law, University of California, Los Angeles.

Ke fa lin zhao tian zhu (Candles That Shine unto Heaven in the Forest of Law). Ming. No publisher (Library of Congress).

Ko, Dorothy. 1992. "The Complicity of Women in the Qing Good Woman Cult." In *Family Process and Political Process in Modern Chinese History*, vol. 1. Taibei: Academia Sinica, Institute of Modern History.

—— 1994. *Teachers of the Inner Chambers: Women and Culture in Seventeenth-Century China.* Stanford, Calif.: Stanford University Press.

Kuhn, Philip A. 1984. "Chinese Views of Social Classification." In J. Watson, ed., *Class and Social Stratification in Post-Revolution China.* Cambridge: Cambridge University Press.

—— 1990. *Soulstealers: The Chinese Sorcery Scare of 1768.* Cambridge, Mass.: Harvard University Press.

Lau, D. C., ed. 1994. *A Concordance to the Shangshudazhuan.* Hong Kong: The Commercial Press.

Lee, James, and Robert Y. Eng. 1984. "Population and Family History in Eighteenth-Century Manchuria: Preliminary Results from Daoyi, 1774–1798." *Ch'ing-shih wen-t'i* 5, no. 1:1–55.

Legge, James, trans. 1970 (1895). *The Works of Mencius.* New York: Dover Publications, Inc.

Leung, Angela [Liang Qizi]. 1993a. "To Chasten Society: The Development of Widow Homes in the Qing, 1773–1911." *Late Imperial China* 14, no. 2.

—— 1993b. "'Pin qiong' yu 'qiong ren' guannian zai Zhongguo su shi shehui zhong de lishi yanbian'" (Historical Evolution of the Concepts of 'Poverty' and 'the Poor' in China's Popular Society). In Huang Yinggui, ed., *Renguan, yiyi, yu shehui.* Taibei: Zhongyang Yanjiuyuan Minzu Yanjiusuo.

Levy, Howard. 1966. *Chinese Footbinding: The History of a Curious Erotic Custom*. New York: Walton Rawls.

Lewis, Mark Edward. 1990. *Sanctioned Violence in Early China*. Albany: State University of New York Press.

Li, Lillian. 1991. "Life and Death in a Chinese Famine: Infanticide as a Demographic Consequence of the 1935 Yellow River Flood." *Comparative Studies in Society and History* 33, no. 3:466–510.

Li Mengsheng. 1994. *Zhongguo jinhui xiaoshuo baihua* (One Hundred Tales from Prohibited or Destroyed Chinese Novels). Shanghai: Shanghai Guji Chubanshe.

Li, Wai-yee. 1997. "The Late Ming Courtesan: Invention of a Cultural Ideal." In E. Widmer and K. Sun Chang, eds., *Writing Women in Late Imperial China*. Stanford, Calif.: Stanford University Press.

Li Yu. 1996 (1657). *The Carnal Prayer Mat*. Trans. by Patrick Hanan. Honolulu: University of Hawai'i Press.

Li Yu, ed. 1667. *Zi zhi xin shu* (A New Book to Assist in Governance). Photocopy in UCLA East Asian Library.

Liao shi (History of the Liao Dynasty). Searched on Academia Sinica. Online database of dynastic histories. Http://www.sinica.edu.tw/.

Lin Enshou, ed. 1876. *Qiu shen shi huan bijiao cheng'an* (A Comparison of Autumn Assizes Cases Deserving Execution or Reprieve). Beijing. In Hoover Institute East Asian Collection, Stanford University.

Littrup, Leif. 1981. *Subbureaucratic Government in China in Ming Times: A Study of Shandong Province in the Sixteenth Century*. Oslo: Universitetsforlaget.

Liu Jihua. 1991 (1934). "Zhongguo zhenjie guannian de lishi yanbian" (The Historical Development of the Concept of Chastity in China). *Shehui xuejie* 8; reprinted in Gao Hongxing et al., eds.

Lü Kun. 1971 (1598). *Lü Gong shi zheng lu* (The Honorable Lü's Record of Practical Government). Taibei: Wenshizhe Chubanshe (reprint of 1797 ed.).

Lu Rong. 1965 (15th c.). *Shuyuan zaji* (Miscellaneous Records of the Legume Garden). Taibei: Shangwu Yinshuguan.

Lü Zhitian. 1893 (1803). *Lüfa xu zhi* (Necessary Knowledge of the Law). Guiheng Shuju (Hoover Institute East Asian Collection, Stanford University).

MacKinnon, Catharine A. 1989. *Toward a Feminist Theory of the State*. Cambridge, Mass.: Harvard University Press.

Maine, Sir Henry S. 1986 (1864). *Ancient Law*. Tucson: University of Arizona Press.

Mann, Susan. 1985. "Historical Change in Female Biography from Song to Qing Times: The Case of Early Qing Jiangnan (Jiangsu and Anhui Provinces)." *Transactions of the International Conference of Orientalists in Japan* 30:65–77.

——— 1987. "Widows in the Kinship, Class, and Community Structures of Qing Dynasty China." *Journal of Asian Studies* 46, no. 1:37–56.

———— 1991. "Grooming a Daughter for Marriage: Brides and Wives in the Mid-Qing Period." In R. Watson and P. Ebrey, eds., *Marriage and Inequality in Chinese Society*. Berkeley: University of California Press.

———— 1993. "Suicide and Survival: Exemplary Widows in the Late Empire." In *Chûgoku no dentô shakai to kazoku: Yanagida Setsuko Sensei koki kinen ronshû*, 23–39. Tôkyô: Kyûko Shoin.

———— 1997. *Precious Records: Women in China's Long Eighteenth Century*. Stanford, Calif.: Stanford University Press.

Mathews' Chinese-English Dictionary (Revised American Edition). 1975, Cambridge, Mass.: Harvard-Yenching Institute.

McLeod, Katrina C. D., and Robin D. S. Yates. 1981. "Forms of Ch'in Law: An Annotated Translation of the *Feng-chen shih*." *Harvard Journal of Asiatic Studies* 41, no. 1:111–63.

McMahon, Keith. 1988. *Causality and Containment in Seventeenth-Century Chinese Fiction*. Leiden: Brill.

———— 1995. *Misers, Shrews, and Polygamists: Sexuality and Male-Female Relations in Eighteenth-Century Chinese Fiction*. Durham and London: Duke University Press.

Mei Dingzuo, ed. 1910 (ca. 1600). *Hui tu qing ni lian hua ji* (Lotus in Dark Mud). Beijing: Ziqiang Shuju.

Meijer, Marinus J. 1981. "The Price of a P'ai-Lou." *T'oung pao* 67.

———— 1985. "Homosexual Offenses in Ch'ing Law." *T'oung pao* 71.

———— 1991. *Murder and Adultery in Late Imperial China: A Study of Law and Morality*. Leiden: E. J. Brill.

Michael, Franz. 1966. *The Taiping Rebellion: History and Documents*. Seattle: University of Washington Press.

Ming shi (History of the Ming Dynasty). Searched on Academia Sinica. Online database of dynastic histories. Http://www.sinica.edu.tw/.

Murray, Dian. 1987. *Pirates of the South China Coast 1790–1810*. Stanford, Calif.: Stanford University Press.

———— 1992. "The Practice of Homosexuality Among the Pirates of Late 18th and Early 19th Century China." *International Journal of Maritime History* 4, no. 1.

Na Silu. 1992. *Qing dai zhongyang sifa shenpan zhidu* (The Central Judiciary of the Qing Dynasty). Taibei: Wenshizhe Chubanshe.

Naquin, Susan. 1976. *Millenarian Rebellion in China: The Eight Trigrams Uprising of 1813*. New Haven: Yale University Press.

Naquin, Susan, and Evelyn S. Rawski. 1987. *Chinese Society in the Eighteenth Century*. New Haven: Yale University Press.

Ng, Vivien W. 1987. "Ideology and Sexuality: Rape Laws in Qing China." *The Journal of Asian Studies* 46, no. 1.

———— 1989. "Homosexuality and the State in Late Imperial China." In Martin Duberman et al., eds., *Hidden from History: Reclaiming the Gay and Lesbian Past*. New York: Meridian Press.

Niida Noboru. 1943. *Shina mibunhô shi* (A History of Chinese Status Law). Tôkyô: Sayûhô Kankôkai (reprinted in 1983 by Tokyo University Press as *Chûgoku mibunhô shi*).

—— 1962. *Chûgoku hôsei shi kenkyû* (Studies on the History of the Chinese Legal System), 3 vols. Tôkyô: Tôkyô Daigaku Shuppankai.

Ogawa Yôichi. 1973. "Kantsû wa naze zaiaku ka: *San yan er pai* no baai" (Why Was Illicit Sexual Intercourse a Crime?—The Case of *San yan er pai*). *Shû kan tôyô gaku* 29.

Ogyû Sorai. 1989 (18th c.). *Minritsu kokujikai* (The Ming Code, with Japanese Annotation). Tokyo: Sobunsha.

Ono Kazuko. 1989. *Chinese Women in a Century of Revolution, 1850–1950*, trans. by J. Fogel et al. Stanford, Calif.: Stanford University Press.

Otake Fumio. 1936. "Qingdai jingbiao kao" (Canonization During the Qing Dynasty), trans. by Bi Renyong. *Ren wen yuekan* 7, no. 1.

Owen, Stephen. 1992. *Readings in Chinese Literary Thought*. Cambridge, Mass.: Council on East Asian Studies, Harvard.

Pa Chin [Ba Jin]. 1972. *Family*, trans. by S. Shapiro. Boston: Cheng and Tsui.

Paderni, Paola. 1991. "Le rachat de l'honneur perdu. Le suicide des femmes dans la Chine du XVIII siecle" (The recovery of lost honor: Female suicide in eighteenth-century China). *Etudes Chinoises* 10, nos. 1–2.

—— 1992. "An Appeal Case of Honor in Eighteenth-Century China." In *Ming Qing yanjiu: Redazione a cura di Paolo Santangelo*. Rome and Naples: Dipartimento di Studi Asiatici, Istituto Universitario Orientale and Istituto Italiano per il Medio ed Estremo Oriente.

Padgug, Robert A. 1979. "Sexual Matters: On Conceptualizing Sexuality in History." *Radical History Review* 20:3–23.

Perkins, Dwight. 1969. *Agricultural Development in China, 1368–1968*. Chicago: Aldine.

Perry, Elizabeth J. 1980. *Rebels and Revolutionaries in North China, 1845–1945*. Stanford, Calif.: Stanford University Press.

Pound, Roscoe. 1954 (1922). *An Introduction to the Philosophy of Law*. New Haven: Yale University Press.

Qing shi gao (Draft History of the Qing Dynasty). Searched on Academia Sinica. Online database of dynastic histories. Http://www.sinica.edu.tw/.

Qiu Yuanyou. 1991. *Taiping Tianguo falü zhidu yanjiu* (A Study of the Legal System of the Heavenly Kingdom of Great Peace). Beijing: Beijing Shifan Xueyuan Chubanshe.

Reed, Bradly W. 1994. "Scoundrels and Civil Servants: Clerks, Runners, and County Administration in Late Imperial China." Ph.D. diss., University of California, Los Angeles.

—— 1995. "Money and Justice: Clerks, Runners, and the Magistrate's Court in Late Imperial Sichuan." *Modern China* 21, no. 3:345–82.

—— 2000. *Talons and Teeth: County Clerks and Runners in the Qing Dynasty*. Stanford, Calif.: Stanford University Press.

Ren Cheng. 1991. *Zhongguo minjian jinji* (Chinese Folk Taboos). Beijing: Zuojia Chubanshe.

Rowe, William T. 1992. "Women and the Family in Mid-Qing Social Thought: The Case of Chen Hongmou." *Late Imperial China* 13, no. 2:1–41.

Roy, David Tod, trans. 1993. *The Plum in the Golden Vase (or, Chin P'ing Mei), Volume One: The Gathering.* Princeton: Princeton University Press.

Ruggiero, Guido. 1985. *The Boundaries of Eros: Sex Crime and Sexuality in Renaissance Venice.* New York: Oxford University Press.

Shen Defu. 1976 (1606). *Wanli ye huo bian* (Private Gleanings from the Wanli Reign). Taibei: Yiwen Chubanshe.

Shen Jiaben. 1976 (late Qing). *Li dai lü ling* (Statutes and Edicts of Successive Dynasties). Taibei: Taiwan Shangwu Chubanshe.

Shi ji—Shiki kaichû kôshô (Records of the Grand Historian, Annotated). Ed. by Takigawa Kametarô. Tokyo: Tôhô Bunka Gakuin Tôkyô Kenkyûjo, 1932–34.

Shiga Shûzô. 1967. *Chûgoku kazukohô no genri* (Principles of Chinese Family Law). Tôkyô: Sôbunsha.

—— 1984. *Shin dai Chûgoku no hô to saiban* (Law and Justice in Qing China). Tôkyô: Sôbunsha.

Shinkoku—Rinji Taiwan kyûkan chôsakai (Provisional Committee to Investigate Traditional Customs in Taiwan), ed. *Shinkoku gyôsei hô* (The Administrative Law of the Qing State), 7 vols. Taibei: Nantian Shuju reprint, 1989.

Sichuan Provincial Archives, ed. 1988. *Sichuan sheng dang'an guan guan cang dang'an gai shu* (An Introduction to the Holdings of the Sichuan Provincial Archives). Chengdu: Sichuan Sheng Shehui-kexueyuan Chubanshe.

Sommer, Matthew H. 1994. "Sex, Law, and Society in Late Imperial China." Ph.D. diss., University of California, Los Angeles.

—— 1996. "The Uses of Chastity: Sex, Law, and the Property of Widows in Qing China." *Late Imperial China* 17, no. 2:77–130.

—— 1997a. "The Penetrated Male in Late Imperial China: Judicial Constructions and Social Stigma." *Modern China* 23, no. 2:140–80.

—— 1997b. "Banki teisei Chûgoku hô ni okeru baishun: Jûhasseiki ni okeru mibun pafômansu kara no ritatsu" (Prostitution in Late Imperial Chinese Law: The Eighteenth Century Shift Away from Status Performance), trans. by Terada Hiroaki. *Chûgoku—Shakai to bunka* 12:294–328.

—— Forthcoming. "Dangerous Males, Vulnerable Males, and Polluted Males: The Regulation of Masculinity in Qing Law." In S. Brownell and J. Wasserstrom, eds., *Chinese Feminities/Chinese Masculinities: A Reader.* Berkeley: University of California Press.

Song shu (History of the Song Dynasty). Searched on Academia Sinica. Online database of dynastic histories. Http://www.sinica.edu.tw/.

Spence, Jonathan. 1978. *The Death of Woman Wang.* New York: Penguin Books.

Staunton, Sir George T. 1966 (1810). *Ta Tsing leu lee, Being the Fundamental Laws and a Selection from the Supplementary Statutes of the Penal Code of China.* Taibei: Chengwen Publishing Co.

Stein, Edward, ed. 1992. *Forms of Desire: Sexual Orientation and the Social Constructionist Controversy.* New York: Routledge.

Stockard, Janice E. 1989. *Daughters of the Canton Delta: Marriage Patterns and Economic Strategies in South China, 1860–1930*. Stanford, Calif.: Stanford University Press.

Sweeten, Alan R. 1978. "Women and Law in Rural China: Vignettes from 'Sectarian Cases' (*chiao-an*) in Kiangsi, 1872–1878." *Ch'ing-shih wen-t'i* 3, no. 10:49–68.

"Symposium: 'Public Sphere'/'Civil Society' in China?" 1993. *Modern China* 19, no. 2.

Tan Qixiang, ed. 1982. *Zhongguo lishi ditu ji—Di qi ce: Yuan Ming shiqi* (China Historical Maps Series—Vol. 7: Yuan and Ming Periods). Shanghai: Ditu Chubanshe.

Telford, Ted A. 1992. "Family and State in Qing China: Marriage in the Tongcheng Lineages, 1650–1880." In *Family Process and Political Process in Modern Chinese History*, vol. 2. Taibei: Institute of Modern History, Academia Sinica.

Temkin, Jennifer. 1986. "Women, Rape, and Law Reform." In S. Tomaselli and R. Porter, eds., *Rape: An Historical and Cultural Enquiry*. Oxford: Basil Blackwell.

Terada Takanobu. 1959. "Yôseitei no semmin kaihôrei ni tsuite" (The Yongzheng Emperor's Edicts of Emancipation for Debased-Status Groups). *Tôyôshi kenkyû* 18, no. 3.

T'ien Ju-k'ang. 1988. *Male Anxiety and Female Chastity: A Comparative Study of Chinese Ethical Values in Ming-Ch'ing Times*. Leiden: E. J. Brill.

Topley, Marjorie. 1975. "Marriage Resistance in Rural Kwangtung." In Margery Wolf and Roxane Witke, eds., *Women in Chinese Society*. Stanford, Calif.: Stanford University Press.

Van Gulik, R. H. 1974. *Sexual Life in Ancient China: A Preliminary Survey of Chinese Sex and Society from Ca. 1500 B.C. till 1644 A.D.* Leiden: E. J. Brill.

Vitiello, Giovanni. 1992. "The Dragon's Whim: Ming and Qing Homoerotic Tales from *The Cut Sleeve*." *T'oung pao* 78.

——— 1994. "Exemplary Sodomites: Male Homosexuality in Late Ming Fiction." Ph.D. diss., University of California, Berkeley.

Volpp, Sophie. 1994. "The Discourse on Male Marriage: Li Yu's 'A Male Mencius's Mother.'" *Positions* 2, no. 1 (spring).

——— 1995. "The Male Queen: Boy Actors and Literati Libertines." Ph.D. diss., Harvard University.

Wakefield, David R. 1992. "Household Division in Qing and Republican China: Inheritance, Family Property, and Economic Development." Ph.D. diss., University of California, Los Angeles.

Waley, Arthur, trans. 1938. *The Analects of Confucius*. New York: Vintage Books.

Waltner, Ann. 1981. "Widows and Remarriage in Ming and Early Qing China." In R. Guisso and S. Johannesen, eds., *Women in China: Current Directions in Historical Scholarship*. Youngstown, N.Y.: Philo Press.

Wang Huizu. 1970 (1889). *Wang Longzhuang yi shu* (Writings of Wang Longzhuang). Taibei: Huawen Shudian (reprint).

Wang Jingqi. 1967 (1928). *Du shu tang xi zheng sui bi* (Jottings of a Western Journey). Hong Kong: Longmen Shudian (reprint).

Wang Liqi, ed. 1981. *Yuan Ming Qing san dai jinhui xiaoshuo xiqu shi liao* (Historical Materials on the Prohibition and Destruction of Novels and Plays in the Yuan, Ming, and Qing Dynasties). Shanghai: Shanghai Guji Chubanshe.

Wang Shunu. 1988 (1935). *Zhongguo changji shi* (A History of Prostitutes in China). Shanghai: Sanlian Shuju.

Watson, Burton, trans. 1963. *Basic Writings of Mo Tzu, Hsün Tzu, and Han Fei Tzu.* New York: Columbia University Press.

Watson, Rubie S. 1986. "The Named and the Nameless: Gender and Person in Chinese Society." *American Ethnologist* 13:619–31.

——— 1991. "Wives, Concubines, and Maids: Servitude and Kinship in the Hong Kong Region, 1900–1940." In R. Watson and P. Ebrey, eds., *Marriage and Inequality in Chinese Society.* Berkeley: University of California Press.

Weeks, Jeffrey. 1977. *Coming Out: Homosexual Politics in Britain from the Nineteenth Century to the Present.* London: Quartet.

Wei Qingyuan, Wu Qiyan, and Lu Su. 1982. *Qingdai nubi zhidu* (The Qing Dynasty System of Slavery). Beijing: Zhongguo Renmin Daxue Chubanshe.

Wei shu (History of the Wei Dynasty). Searched on Academia Sinica. Online database of dynastic histories. Http://www.sinica.edu.tw/.

Widmer, Ellen, and Kang-I Sun Chang, eds. 1997. *Writing Women in Late Imperial China.* Stanford, Calif.: Stanford University Press.

Wolf, Arthur P. 1975. "The Women of Hai-shan: A Demographic Portrait." In M. Wolf and R. Witke, eds., *Women in Chinese Society.* Stanford, Calif.: Stanford University Press.

——— 1981. "Women, Widowhood and Fertility in Pre-modern China." In J. Dupaquier et al., eds., *Marriage and Remarriage in Populations of the Past.* London: Academic Press.

Wolf, Arthur P., and Chieh-shan Huang. 1980. *Marriage and Adoption in China, 1845–1945.* Stanford, Calif.: Stanford University Press.

Wolf, Margery. 1972. *Women and the Family in Rural Taiwan.* Stanford, Calif.: Stanford University Press.

Wu, Silas H. L. 1970. *Communication and Imperial Control in China: Evolution of the Palace Memorial System, 1693–1735.* Cambridge, Mass.: Harvard University Press.

Wu Tan. 1992 (ca. 1780). *Da Qing lüli tongkao jiaozhu* (Corrected and Annotated Edition of [Wu Tan's] *Thorough Examination of the Qing Code*). Ma Jianshi and Yang Yutang, eds. Beijing: Zhongguo Zhengfa Daxue Chubanshe.

Xiao erya. Taibei: Yiwen Yinshuguan, 1965.

Xiao jing yi shu bu (The Classic of Filial Piety, Annotated). Edited by Ruan Fu. Taibei: Taiwan Shangwu Yinshuguan, 1966.

Xie Zhaozhe. 1959 (ca. 1600). *Wu za zu* (Five Miscellanies). Shanghai: Zhonghua Shuju.

Xu Fuzuo. 1970 (1610). *Hong li ji* (The Red Pear Blossom). Taibei: Taiwan Kaiming Shudian.

Xu Shen. 1994 (Han). *Shuo wen jie zi* (Dictionary of Written Characters). Beijing: Zhonghua Shuju (reprint).

Yan Ming. 1992. *Zhongguo ming ji yishu shi* (A History of the Courtesan's Art in China). Taibei: Wenjin Chubanshe.

Yao Run et al., eds. 1878. *Da Qing lü li zengxiu tongcuan jicheng* (Revised Comprehensive Compilation of the Qing Code). UCLA East Asian Library.

Yao Yuxiang et al., eds. 1987 (1873). *Da Qing lü li hui tong xin zuan* (Comprehensive New Edition of the Qing Code). Taibei: Wenhai Chubanshe (reprint).

Yu Zhengxie. 1964 (1833). *Guisi lei gao* (Drafts Written in the Year Guisi). Taibei: Shijie Shuju.

Yuan shi (History of the Yuan Dynasty). Searched on Academia Sinica. Online database of dynastic histories. Http://www.sinica.edu.tw/.

Zelin, Madeleine. 1985. *The Magistrate's Tael: Rationalizing Fiscal Reform in Eighteenth-Century Ch'ing China*. Berkeley: University of California Press.

——— 1986. "The Rights of Tenants in Mid-Qing Sichuan: A Study of Land-Related Lawsuits in the Baxian Archives." *The Journal of Asian Studies* 45, no. 3.

Zeng Tieshen. 1991 (1935). "Qingdai zhi jingbiao zhidu" (The Canonization System of the Qing Dynasty). *Zhongguo shehui* 1, no. 5; reprinted in Gao Hongxing et al., eds. 1991.

Zhang Jinfan and Guo Chengkang. 1988. *Qing ru guan qian guojia falü zhidu shi* (A History of the Qing Legal System Prior to the Conquest of China). Shenyang: Liaoning Renmin Chubanshe.

Zhang Jinfan, Wang Zhigang, and Lin Zhong. 1992. *Zhongguo xingfa shi xin lun* (A New Study of the History of Criminal Law in China). Beijing: Renmin Fayuan Chubanshe.

Zhang Kentang. 1969 (1634). *Xun ci* (Words of Good Government). Taibei: Taiwan Xuesheng Shuju (reprint).

Zhao Yi. 1957 (ca. 1775). *Gai yu cong kao* (The Step-by-Step Collection of Studies). Shanghai: Shangwu Yinshuguan.

Zheng Qin. 1995. "Pursuing Perfection: Formation of the Qing Code," trans. by Guangyuan Zhou. *Modern China* 21, no. 3:310–44.

Zhou, Guangyuan. 1993. "'Legal Justice' of the Qing: A Study of Case Reports and Reviews in the Criminal Process." Presented at the conference on Code and Practice in Qing and Republican Law, University of California, Los Angeles.

Zhou Mi. 1987 (Song). *Guixin zashi* (Miscellaneous Observations from the Year Guixin). Reprinted in *Qinding siku quanshu*, vol. 1040. Shanghai: Shanghai Guji Chubanshe.

Zhu Yu. 1987 (Song). *Pingzhou ketan* (Curious Observations from Pingzhou). Reprinted in *Qinding siku quanshu*, vol. 1038. Shanghai: Shanghai Guji Chubanshe.

Character List

an fen　安分

ba nahua nong de ying ying de, zhi shu tiao gun　把那話弄的硬硬的直豎一條棍

ba xiaode jian le　把小的姦了

ba zhangfu de hou dai dou jue le　把丈夫的後代都絕了

bao jia　保甲

bei ta jian xing le　被他姦醒了

beicheng lishiguan　北城理事官

ben fu　本夫*

ben fu　本婦†

ben jia men shou　本家門首

ben wu lun li　本無倫理

bi, bei　婢

bi fu lü　比附律

bi fu zafan zui lü　比附雜犯罪律

bi le　逼勒

bi nü　婢女

bi yin li　比引例

bi yin lü　比引律

bi zhong jiu qing　避重就輕

*"The original husband."
†"The wife."

Bian er chai　弁而釵

bici ji jian　比此雞姦

bing mei you he cheng de shi　並沒有和成的事

bu gan shi jie　不甘失節

bu he li　不合理

bu he, wei zhi qiang　不和謂之強

bu li yu guan　不隸於官

bu li yu guan, jia ju er mai jian zhe　不隸於官家居而賣姦者

bu nan　不男

bu qu　部曲

bu ren zhui qi jia sheng　不忍墜其家聲

bu shen lan gei gong ju　不審濫給公據

bu shou fu dao　不守婦道

bu shou zei wu　不受賊污

bu shou zei wu zhen lie funü　不受賊污貞烈婦女

bu shun　不順

bu si chang jia nü　不似娼家女

bu wu zheng ye　不務正業

bu xiao　不孝

bu xiao e tu　不肖惡徒

bu xing hun jia 不行婚嫁

bu xu yu shu min qi tong 不許與庶民妻同

bu zhengjing de nüren 不正經的女人

ceng wei shen po 曾未身破

chang 倡, 娼*

chang fu 娼婦

chang fu yu liang ren you jian 娼婦與良人有間

chang hu 娼戶

chang ji 娼妓

chang ji zhi jia 娼妓之家

chang jia 娼家

chang jia fu nü 娼家婦女

chang nü 娼女

chang ren 常人

chang shi jiao fang, yue shi yue fu 娼是教坊樂是樂婦

chang you 娼優

chang you yue ren 娼優樂人

chang you zhi jia 娼優之家

chang zhe yue ji fu nü ye 娼者樂籍婦女也

chao he 朝賀

chao wo 巢窩

Chen Hongmou 陳宏謀

chen qiang yu zhu jian 臣強與主姦

cheng 成

cheng hun 成婚

cheng jian 成姦

cheng le jian 成了姦

cheng qin 成親

chi gao 敕誥

chu ji 除籍

chu jia 出家

chu le yue ji ming zi 除了樂籍名字

chu ling 除靈

chu ming 除名

chu nü 處女

chu qi jian ji 除其賤籍

chu wai wei chang 出外爲娼

ci qi shou gua qingxing 此豈守寡情行

cong 從

cong fu jia mai 從夫嫁賣

cong jian 從賤

cong liang 從良

cong liang qu cheng liang kouzi ba 從良去成兩口子罷

cong liang shu 從良書

cong liang wen juan 從良文卷

cong liang zhe 從良者

cong liang zhi zhao 從良執照

cu chuan yifu 粗穿衣服

da hu 大戶

da shang feng hua 大傷風化

dai bi 代筆

dai lü maozi 戴綠帽子

dan hu 蜑戶

dan yi di jue 單衣的決

dang guan jia mai 當官嫁賣

dang yi fan jian zhi lü lun zhi 當以犯姦之律論之

dao le ni jia ni zheyang qiongku, wo jia ni zuo shenme, ni hai lai chan wo 到了你家你這樣窮苦我嫁你做甚麼你還來纏我

de gui bao bi 得規包庇

dian pu 佃僕

diao jian 刁姦

diao tu 刁徒

die 爹

dimu 嫡母

*Used interchangeably in late imperial sources to mean "prostitute" or "courtesan."

diu lian 丟臉

dou ou 鬥毆

dou sha 鬥殺

Du li cun yi 讀例存疑

duan ling cong liang 斷令從良

duo min 墮民, 惰民

e 惡

e gun 惡棍

e si shi xiao, shi jie shi da 餓死事小失節事大

e tu sheng shi xing xiong 惡徒生事行兇

fa 法

fa zai bi xing 法在必行

fan fu 番婦

fan gou he jie wei jian ye 凡勾合皆爲姦也

fan jian 犯姦

fan jian fu nü 犯姦婦女

fan jian zhi fu 犯姦之婦

fan ren 凡人

fang 放

fang cong bian 放從便

fang cong liang 放從良

fang liang 放良

fang shu 放書

fang wei liang 放爲良

fei jia qu zhi zheng 非嫁娶之正

fei jian xiong qie zhe bi 非姦兄妾者比

fei shi 匪事

fei ying xu zhuo jian zhi ren 非應許捉姦之人

fen liang jian 分良賤

feng gu shi shou ku ji 俸姑矢守苦積

feng hua 風化

Feng Menglong 馮夢龍

fu dao jia shui xing yang hua 婦道家水性楊花

fu fu 夫婦

fu nei su chang 服內宿娼

fu nü 婦女

funü nanzi 婦女男子

Fu Sheng 伏生, 伏勝

fu wei liang min 復爲良民

fu zhi si jian 夫之私姦

gai hu 丐戶

gai jia wei liang ren qi 改嫁爲良人妻

gai ye wei liang 改業爲良

gai ye zi xin 改業自新

gong 公*

gong 宮†

gong dao 公道

gou yin 勾引

gugongren 雇工人

gu nian funü wuzhi 姑念婦女無知

gu sha 故殺

guan hu 官戶

guan hua 官話

guan ji 官妓

guan ji ding sheng shidai 官妓鼎盛時代

guan li su chang 官吏宿娼

guan mei 官媒

guan mei po 官媒婆

guan si bi 官私婢

guan yuan shi shu 官員仕庶

guan yue hu 官樂戶

guang feng hua 廣風化

guang gun 光棍

guang gun li 光棍例

gui jian bu fen 貴賤不分

gui men 閨門

*"Public," the opposite of *si*.
†"Castration" or "sequestration."

gui tou 龜頭

gui zong 歸宗

guo qing bu 裹青布

guzhu 雇主

hai yao nong chou zui ma 還要弄臭嘴嗎

hai you shenme lianmian qu jian ren 還有甚麼臉面去見人

hang yuan 伉院

hao bu xiu kui 好不羞愧

hao dou 好鬥

he 和

he jian 和姦

he jian wei bici he tong zhe 和姦謂比此和同者

he li zhe 和離者

he qu ren qi 和娶人妻

he sheng 和聲

he sheng shu 和聲署

he tong 和同

he tong ji jian 和同雞姦

he tong zhe 和同者

he you zhi qing 和誘知情

Hong li ji 紅梨記

Hong lou meng 紅樓夢

hong niangzi she xiang shan 紅娘子麝香山

hong you 哄誘

huan su 還俗

huan wei liang 還爲良

Huang Liuhong 黃六鴻

hui guo zi xin 悔過自新

Hui tu qing ni lian hua ji 繪圖青泥蓮花記

hui wu guan ru ren kou 穢物灌入人口

hun bu yi li 婚不以禮

huo jia 火甲

ji 雞*

ji 嬰†

ji 妓, 伎‡

ji 籍§

ji ba 雞巴

ji jian 雞姦

ji lie zi yi 激烈自縊

ji nü 妓女

ji qi 繼妻

ji qin 期親

ji si 繼嗣

ji zi 繼子

jia mai 嫁賣

jia xia you fu zhi fu 家下有夫之婦

jian 姦, 奸¶

jian 賤**

jian bu de ren 見不得人

jian bu de ren de shi 見不得人的事

jian chen 姦臣

jian cong fu bu 姦從夫捕

jian dang 姦黨

jian fei 姦匪

jian fu 姦夫††

jian fu 姦婦‡‡

jian guo xiao de 姦過小的

---

*"Chicken."

†"To use a male as a female."

‡"Prostitute"/"courtesan."

§"Status registration."

¶Used interchangeably in late imperial sources to mean "illicit sexual intercourse" or "treason," "betrayal," etc. The first variant is more common.

**"Debased"/"mean" legal status.

††"Man who has engaged in illicit sexual intercourse."

‡‡"Wife who has engaged in illicit sexual intercourse."

jian jing sheng qing　見景生情

jian le ta shenmu yo mai ta jia de changdi
　姦了他嬸母又賣他家的場地

jian min　賤民

jian sheng　姦聲

jian shi　箋釋

jian su　姦宿

jian tong　姦通

jian wu　姦污

jian yin　姦淫

jian zhan wei qi qie　姦佔爲妻妾

jian zhen zhi li　荐枕之利

jiang er zi bei　降而自卑

jiang er zi jian　降而自賤

jiang hua　僵化

jiang jia qu　講嫁娶

jiang nan zuo nü　將男作女

jiang shenjing fang ru ren fenmen nei
　yin xi　將腎莖放入人糞門內淫戲

jiao fang ming ji　教坊名妓

jiao fang si　教坊司

jiao wo zenme jian ren, bu ru si le ba
　叫我怎麼見人不如死了罷

jie　解

jie cao　節操

jie chong ren ya　藉充人牙

jie fang　解放

jie fu　節婦

jie ji　解籍

jie she wu ci yi　結舌無詞已

jin changji ye yi yan jin　今娼妓業已
　嚴禁

Jin ping mei　金瓶梅

jin shen jia ju zhe bu lun　縉紳家居者
　不論

jin wei yue hu　今爲樂戶

jin yu yue hu　禁諭樂戶

jing　經

jing biao　旌表

jiu xing yu hu　九姓漁戶

jiu yi liang ren　究異良人

ju ren zhi yi chang jian ye　懼人之以
　娼賤也

juan　卷

juan qu　捐軀

jue　絕

jun min xiang jian　軍民相姦

kai　開

kai hō　開放, 解放

kang jie zhi xin　抗節之心

kong nan xing jian　恐難行姦

kong xia qu cai　恐嚇取財

kou　摳

ku shou　苦守

lao di　老弟

lao hu liang min　老戶良民

le　勒

le ling duo tai　勒令墮胎

Lei Menglin　雷夢麟

li　例*

li　禮†

li　立‡

Li Chang　李娼

li lian chi　勵廉恥

Li Yu　李漁

li yu guan zhe　隸於官者

li yu guan zhe wei yue hu, you wei shui
　hu　隸於官者爲樂戶又爲水戶

lian piao　戀嫖

lian shang hai xiu　臉上害羞

---

*"Substatute."

†"Rites," "ritual"; "normative moral standards of human relationships."

‡"To establish."

liang　良

liang jia　良家

liang jia fu　良家婦

liang jia fu nü　良家婦女

liang jia zhe　良家者

liang jia zi di　良家子弟

liang jian xiang jian　良賤相姦

liang min　良民

liang min zhi jia　良民之家

liang nan ji jian　兩男雞姦

liang ren　良人

liang ren fu nü　良人婦女

liang ren zi di　良人子弟

liang ren zi nü　良人子女

liang shu　良書

liang wei jian　良爲賤

liao ni tuzi ye bu gan　料你兔子也不敢

lie　烈

ling　令

ling chi chu si　凌遲處死

ling jiao fang jian ji chu zhi　令敎坊簡籍除之

ling ren chang fu　伶人娼婦

ling shen chen du　領身趁度

liu　流*

liu chang　流娼

liu lai shui hu　流來水戶

liu li　六禮

liu shui　流水

lü　律

Lü Kun　呂坤

lü qi jin yi shi ru　綠其巾以示辱

lü yi jian tiao yi yi yun xie fou hu　律以姦條抑亦允協否乎

luan　亂

luan chang　亂娼

luan lun　亂倫

luan nong　亂弄

*"Flowing"; "life-exile."

luan tong　孌童

lun jian　輪姦

luo ji　落籍

mai chang chang qu du ri　賣娼唱曲度日

mai jian　賣姦

mai liang wei chang　買良爲娼

mai qi　賣契

mai xiu　賣休

mai xiu mai xiu　買休賣休

mai xiu ren　買休人

mao jian　冒姦

Mei Dingzuo　梅鼎祚

mei he ren　媒合人

mei lianmian　沒臉面

mei you jian wan　沒有姦完

mian mu sheng de gan jing　面目生的乾淨

Miao qi　苗氣

min jian si zi mai jian zhe　民間私自賣姦

min ren　民人

min ren fan jian　民人犯姦

ming chang　名倡

mingfen　名份

ming fu　命婦

ming ji　名妓

ming shi you yi gouyin　明是有意勾引

ming sui fu fu, shi xi luan chang　名雖夫婦實係亂娼

mou sha　謀殺

mou zhan zicai　謀占資財

Mu dan ting　牡丹亭

nali deng de sangfu man, zhe xie ren dou hao e si le　那裡等得喪服滿這些人都好餓死了

nan 男

nan chang 男娼

nan nü bu yi li jiao, jie si 男女不以禮交皆死

nan nü bu yi li jiao, wei zhi yin 男女不以禮交謂之淫

nan nü bu yi yi jiao 男女不以義交

nan se 男色

nan yi ku shou 難以苦守

nan zhi you nü tai zhe 男之有女態者

nanzi ju jian sha ren 男子拒姦殺人

nanzi wei chang 男子爲娼

nanzi yu funü da xiang xuan shu 男子與婦女大相懸殊

Neige xingke tiben 內閣刑科題本

nei luan 內亂

ni xi 逆媳

ni yao sha jiu sha, ning si ye bu cong de 你要殺就殺寧死也不從的

nian lao jian wu you nü 年老姦污幼女

nian shao mei hao 年少美好

nian you 年幼

nong guo 弄過

nu 奴

nu bi 奴婢

nu pu zhi qi 奴僕之妻

nü 女

nü shi 女使

pai zhang 俳長

pan luan 叛亂

piao 嫖

pin min 貧民

ping min 平民

po 破

po nao 潑鬧

po shen 破身

pu fu 僕婦

Pu Songling 蒲松齡

qi 妻

qi bu liang bian 豈不兩便

qi jian 欺姦

qi nü 妻女

qiang 強

qiang bao 強暴

qiang bi cheng hun jian wu 強逼成婚姦污

qiang bi cheng jian 強逼成姦

qiang bi tong jian 強逼通姦

qiang duo 強奪

qiang duo liang ren nan nü mai yu ta ren wei qi qie 強奪良人男女賣與他人爲妻妾

qiang duo qi jie 強奪其節

qiang duo qiang jia 強奪搶嫁

qiang jia 強嫁

qiang jian 強姦

qiang jian cheng le 強姦成了

qiang lai he ying 強來和應

qiang mai 強賣

qiang qu 強娶

qiang xing cheng jian 強行成姦

qiang xing ji jian 強行雞姦

qiang xing ji jian wei cheng 強行雞姦未成

qiang xing jian wu 強行姦污

Qiaoyu 巧玉

qie 妾

qie yu liang fu bu tong 且與良婦不同

qin hou 親厚

qinshu 親叔

qing bai zi shou 清白自守

qing dou wei kai 情竇未開

qing fa yun xie 情法允協

qing jie nian xiao 清潔年小

qing jun guai jue 清俊乖覺

qing li suo wu 情理所無

qing lou 青樓

Qing shi 情史

qing yi 情意

qu ji 去籍

qu jiao ta niangrmen lai, wo gei ta yi ge
    ganjing ba 去叫他娘兒們來我給他
    一個乾淨罷

qu yi shou xing 去衣受刑

quan 權

quanli 權利

ren cai liang wang 人財兩亡

ren he 人合

rong ren 容忍

Rou pu tuan 肉蒲團

rou xing 肉刑

ru guan wei nu 入官爲奴

ru he bu ai 如何不愛

ru yuan su chang 入院宿娼

san cong 三從

San fa si 三法司

san yi qi chu ze wu ren zhi qi lai li yi
    三易其處則無人知其來歷矣

san yuan 三院

san yue 散樂

sang xin wang gu 喪心忘故

se zhang 色長

shan sha zui ren 擅殺罪人

shang de wei zhi jia shun hu 尚得謂
    之假順呼

shao ai 少艾

shao di 少弟

shen 身

Shen Defu 沈德符

shen jia 身價

Shen Jiaben 沈家本

Shen Zhiqi 沈之奇

sheng de bai jing 生的白淨

shi 氏

shi ceng po shen 實曾破身

shi cha 失察

shi cha liu chang 失察流娼

shi e 十惡

shi fu fu zhi lun 失夫婦之倫

shi hao hao lai de 是好好來的

shi hun yin zhi zheng 失婚姻之正

shi jing wu lai zhi tu 市井無賴之徒

shi qiang er zhong he 始强而終和

shi ren 仕人

shi shen 失身

shi wei liang min 使爲良民

shi yu cha cha 失於查察

shinposei 進步精

shou bei 守備

shou jie 守節

shou zhi 守志

shu jia 贖嫁

shu min 庶民

shu mu 庶母

shu shen 贖身

shui 睡

shui hu 水戶

shui jiao 睡覺

shui qin 睡寢

shun 順

shuo bu de ke lian 說不得可憐

Shuo wen jie zi 說文解字

si 私*

si 司†

si dao 私道

si kezi 私窠子

Sima Qian 司馬遷

si tong 私通

si tong he jian 私通和姦

     *"Private"; "illicit."
     †"Bureau"; "office."

si xia tong jian　私下通姦

si zi　私自

si zi mai jian　私自賣姦

song gun　訟棍

su chang xia you　宿娼狎優

sui　歲

sui bu zhi qing　雖不知情

sui he, tong qiang lun　雖和同強論

sui xi xia jian, nan mian zhan di　雖係
　下賤難免斬抵

Sun men Yu shi　孫門余氏

suo yan　瑣言

tan cai　貪財

tan se　貪色

tan tu pinli　貪圖品禮

Tang Ming lü he bian　唐明律合編

tidu yamen　提都衙門

ti tou xia jian　剃頭下賤

tian he　天合

tiao jian　調姦

tiao xi　調戲

tong jian　通姦

tong shui　同睡

tong xin xie li bang xiaode zuo ren jia
　同心協力幫小的作人家

tong yang xi　童養媳

tou jian　偷姦

tou sheng jia shun　偷生假順

tu cai　圖財

tu cai jia mai　圖財嫁賣

tu cai qiang jia　圖財强嫁

tu cai qiang mai　圖財强賣

tu chang　土娼

tu ji　土妓

tuzi　兔子

tuo ji　脫籍

tuo wu bi xing　託物比興

wan　剜

wan ju　完俱

wangba　王八, 忘八

wangba dan　王八蛋, 忘八蛋

wang fa　枉法

Wang Huizu　汪輝祖

Wang Jingqi　汪景祺

Wang Kentang　王肯堂

wang li nong　往裡弄

wang xing zhan duo　妄行佔奪

wei bi ren zhi si　威逼人致死

wei chang　爲娼

wei chang you　爲娼優

wei cheng　未成

wei cheng hun　未成婚

wei ye　猥業

wo chang　窩娼

wo de er　我的兒

wo dun　窩頓

wo dun liu chang　窩頓流娼

wo jian ni erzi, ni gan ba wo zenyang
　我姦你兒子你敢把我怎樣

wo liu　窩留

wu　污

wugui　烏龜

wu ji zhi tu　無藉之徒

wu jian　誣姦

wu mie　污衊

wu ming gai nü　無名丐女

wu qi ya liang wei jian　惡其壓良爲賤

wu shi jia zhe　無室家者

Wu Tan　吳壇

wu zhi ke shou　無志可守

xia liu　下流

xia liu ba gun　下流把棍

xia shen　下身

xia you　狎優

xia you yin jiu fan shi　狎優飲酒犯事

xia zhu yao jian 挾住要姦
xian 縣
xian qiang hou he 先强後和
xian shen 現審
xian wei 縣尉
xiang yu 鄉愚
xiang yue 鄉約
xiao dan 小旦
Xiao erya 小爾雅
xiao fu ren 小婦人
xiao ji 削籍
xiao ji gui jiu zong 削籍歸舊宗
xiao qu chang zhi ji 削去娼之籍
xing 幸
Xing an hui lan 刑案匯覽
xing jian 行姦
xing jian wan shua 行姦頑耍
xing jian zhe 行姦者
xiong 兇
xiong e gun tu 兇惡棍徒
xiong gun 兇棍
xiong ren 凶人
Xu Ben 徐本
xu jin gai zheng 許今改正
Xue Yunsheng 薛允升
xun an Shanxi jian cha yu shi 巡按山西監察御史
xun ge nü ren zuo sheng yi 尋箇女人做生意

yan jin yue hu 嚴禁樂戶
yang mei du 楊梅毒
ye ji 野雞
yi 義*
yi cai mai xiu 以財買休
yi Cai Shi tan chang ren chang tao mai 以蔡氏彈唱認娼討買
yi cheng hun 已成婚

yi fa luo jin zai guan 已發落今在官
yi fen 義忿
yi feng yi su 移風易俗
yi fu huan fu tuo ming gu shen zheng ye 以夫還婦托名固甚正也
yi fu yi fu 一婦一夫
yi he he, yi qiang cheng 以和合以强成
yi he qi sheng 以和其聲
yi jian lun 以姦論
yi jian zheng liang shi bi bu de 以賤爭良勢必不得
yi jian zuo liang 移賤作良
yi jing po shen 已經破身
yi jue 義絕
yi le 抑勒
yi le tong jian 抑勒通姦
yi li zi chi 以禮自持
yi lü zhi zui 依律治罪
yi nü 義女
yi qiang he, yi he cheng 以强合以和成
yi wei feng hua, yi wei you hun 以維風化以慰幽魂
yi yi jiao 以義交
yi yi ren ren zhi suo yin yi 抑亦仁人之所隱矣
yi zheng qi qie zhi ming 已正妻妾之名
yin 淫
yin ci 淫詞
yin dian 淫店
yin fu 淫婦
yin gun 淫棍
yin jian wei bi ren zhi si 因姦威逼人致死
yin sheng 淫聲
yin shu 淫書
yin xin 淫心
yin xin che qi 淫心轍起
yin xiong 淫兇

*"Morality," "righteousness"; "the bond of moral duty between spouses."

yin xiong zhi fan 淫兇之犯

ying ba xiaode jian le 硬把小的姦了

yong qiang qiang mai 用強搶賣

yongyuan wei zhao 永遠爲照

you dian jia sheng 有玷家聲

you fu zhi pu fu 有夫之僕婦

you ling 優伶

you nü 幼女

you nü, you tong, funü 幼女幼童婦女

you ren 優人

you wu jian wu 有無姦污

you xie zi se 有些姿色

yu liang ren you jian 與良人有間

yu min yi ti dang chai 與民一體當差

yu xin 慾心

yuan 院

yuan cong liang zhe 願從良者

yuan ji liang min fu fu 原籍良民夫婦

Yuan Mei 袁枚

yuan men shou 院門首

yuan xi min hu 原係民戶

yuan zuo ban chang nü 元做伴娼女

Yue bu 樂部

yue fu 樂婦

yue fu chang tai 樂婦常態

yue gong 樂工

yue hu 樂戶

yue ji 樂妓*

yue ji 樂籍†

yue ren 樂人

yue ren nai jiao fang si ji zhe 樂人乃教坊司妓者

yue shou 樂首

yue yi 樂藝

yun 允

yun cheng qing fa zhi ping 允稱情法之平

za hu 雜戶

zai wei jing jinzhi changji yiqian 在未經禁止娼妓已前

zan liangge gan de goudang 咱兩個幹的勾當

zao le guan si 遭了官司

ze liang shi jia yan 擇良士嫁焉

zensei 善政

zha wu jian dian e yu 詐誣姦玷惡語

Zhang Fei 張斐

Zhang Kentang 張肯堂

zhang ze 掌責

zhao ji you shang 召妓侑觴

zhe shang 折傷

zhen 貞

zhen jie 貞節, 貞潔

zhen jie zhi cao 貞潔之操

zhen jie zi shou zhi nü 貞潔自守之女

zhen lie fu nü 貞烈婦女

zheng 正

zheng sheng 正聲

zheng yao xing jian 正要行姦

zhi guan 職官

zhi guan jian jun min qi 職官姦軍民妻

zhi ruo chang fu bu ze yi yi 致若娼婦不責以義

zhi shu yi tiao gun 直豎一條棍

zhi suan zuo le yi jian hao shi 只算作了一件好事

zhi yu ru ci, liang min qi he dao yi tuo ci jing ye 至於如此良民其何道以脫此阱耶

zhong bu shou ru 終不受辱

zhong cheng jian cha yu shi 中城監察御史

zhong shen wei ru 終身爲辱

*"*Yue* prostitute."
†"*Yue* status registration."

Zhou Kai　周凱
zhu　主
zhu ban chu jing　逐搬出境
Zhu Di　朱棣
zhu hun　主婚
zhu pi zouzhe　硃批奏摺
zhuo jian　捉姦
zi di　子弟
zi gan wu jian zhe　自甘污賤者
zi shen qing bai　自身清白
zi xin　自新

zi xin zhi lu　自新之路
zi xing qi yi wei chang wei you mai
　　jian zhe　自行起意爲娼爲優賣姦者
zi xing zhu xu　自行主許
zi yuan shou zhi　自願守志
zong　縱
zong jian　縱姦
zong qi wei chang　縱妻爲娼
zong rong　縱容
zu xu　族序
zun　尊

Index

In this index an "f" after a number indicates a separate reference on the next page, and an "ff" indicates separate references on the next two pages. A continuous discussion over two or more pages is indicated by a span of page numbers, e.g., "57–59."

Abduction: chastity of victim and, 74; of daughter of prostitute, 314–315; marriage by, 43–45
"Abetting or tolerating illicit sexual intercourse," 223–230; language used for, 318; Ming law, 227–229; pimping a wife, 54–56; post-Yongzheng cases, 282–287; prosecution of, 243–247; Song law, 224; wife-selling, 59; Yuan law, 225–227
Abortion: forced on prostitute, 236–237; of pregnant widows, 202–204
Academia Sinica in Taipei, 19, 365
Actors: civil service examinations and, 271; female impersonators and *liang*, 129–130; male prostitution and, 157, 223, 356; Yongzheng reforms, 365. *See also* Yue households (*yue hu*)
Adopted daughter-in-law, 38, 350
Adoption (fictive kinship), 288, 366
Adultery: autonomy and, 190–192; gender performance and, 9; homicide over, 42, 62; masters' responsibility to female slaves and, 51; pregnant widows and, 202–207, 209; prostitu-

tion by adulterous wife, 229–230; prostitution vs., 224; "seizing" a widow in (*zhuo jian*), 194–195, 197–202; status performance and, 6–7; in the United States, 304; of widows, 173–175, 190–207; wife-selling and, 61–64, 351–352
Age difference: in legal treatment of homosexual rape resistance, 135–138; in sodomy cases, 28–29, 133–138, 144–145, 331–332, 355
Age of liability for consent, 85, 125
Ai Wenyi, 87
Amnesty, 363
Anachronism, "emancipation" as, 264
Analects of Confucius, 30, 32, 268
Anal intercourse, *see* Rape, heterosexual; Rape, homosexual; Sodomy or anal intercourse (*ji jian*)
Analogy: judgment by, in homosexual rape, 121–124; "statutes applied by," 37–38, 121–124, 349
Anatomy of Love (*Qing shi*), 237
Ancestor worship, 31, 357
Anglo-American common law, 111
"Annals of Emperor Wen the Filial," commentaries on, 35
Autumn Assizes, 41, 53, 189

Ba County Archives, 17, 289, 295
Ba County (Sichuan), 17, 20, 289–298
Bai Chengwen, 152
Ba Jin, 311

Chen Minggui, 41
Chen Qishier, 127
Chen Sanxi, 291
Chen Shang-er, 134–135
Chen Su Shi, 288
Chen Telou, 81–82
Chen Tianzhang, 95
Chen Zhiwan, 179
Cheng Shi, 241–242, 351
Chi Tingguang, 148–149
Chicken logograph, 121
Chongqing Prefecture (map), 290
Chun Mei, 159
Ch'ü, T'ung-tsu: on importance of
family in Confucianism, 30–31; "legal
modernization" and, 4; master's privi-
lege and, 350; status levels identified
by, 5, 45; Yongzheng edicts dismissed
by, 262–263, 264, 271–272
Civil service examinations, 270–272,
262f
Classic of Filial Piety, The (*Xiao jing*),
268
Clergy, *see* Buddhist clergy; Daoist
clergy
"Coercion" (*qiang*): burden of proof,
85–89; "coercion followed by
consent," 86; consent vs., 84–93;
consummation and, 77–79; evidence
for consummation, 79–84; evidence
for heterosexual rape, 87–89, 105–106,
107, 109–110; evidence for homosexual rape, 133–135; forced
remarriage of widows, 171–172,
177–184, 333–337; forcing wife to
have sex with another man and, 57;
homosexual rape and, 120; Huang
Liuhong on, 71; rape law and, 66–67,
68, 71, 84–93; within marriage, 38–43.
See also Rape, heterosexual; Rape,
homosexual
Collected Statutes of the Yuan (*Yuan
dian zhang*), 36, 47, 81, 217, 220, 86f
*Combined Edition of the Tang and
Ming Codes* (*Tang Ming lü he bian*),
23
Commodification of women, 63
Commoner status: "buying a commoner
to be a prostitute," 222–223, 228–229,
231–235, 237, 291; chastity honors
extended to commoners, 170; in

eighteenth century, 8–9; escaping
prostitute status, 235–241; extension
of commoner standards, 211, 265–272,
303, 305; female chastity and, 6–7; of
gentry, 8; as *liang*, 8, 71–72, 75, 211,
312, 360; marrying prostitutes,
219–220; pimping and, 7, 54–57;
prostitution and, 210–211; rape of
unchaste woman, 73–75; in status
hierarchy, 6, 45, 95–96; transfer to
prostitute households prohibited,
221–223
Communist neo-puritanism, 4
*Complete Book Concerning Happiness
and Benevolence, A* (Huang Liuhong),
68
Concubines: female slaves vs., 49–50,
51, 350; as widows, 197–198, 200–202
Confucianism: classical discourse of
music, 268–270; conjugal bed and, 38;
filial piety in, 30–31, 37; personal
relationships and political order in,
30–31; prostitution and, 227–228
Cong liang, 235–241, 251, 293, 312,
363–364
Consensual illicit sex: homosexual,
123–124, 355; Qing code changes,
25–26; rape vs., 66; wife-selling and,
64. *See also* "Consent" (*he*); Sodomy
or anal intercourse (*ji jian*)
"Consent" (*he*): age of liability for, 85,
125; burden of proof, 85–89; "coercion
followed by consent," 86; coercion
vs., 84–93; of father to woman's
marriage, 65; as guilt, 66, 67–68;
homosexual rape and, 120; rape law
and, 66–67, 74–75, 84–93; of wife to
being sold, 64
Conspectus of Legal Cases (*Xing an hui
lan*), 24; *liang* and, 314–315; rape
cases, 75, 89; sodomy cases, 151, 356,
128ff
Consummation of illicit sexual
intercourse: evidence for, 79–84;
homosexual rape, 126–128; penal and
ritual consequences of, 77–79. *See
also* Penetration
Consummation of marriage: marriage
by abduction, 43–45; mourning period
and, 36–37; prior to wedding, 37–38;
remarried widows' refusal of,

Office to Harmonize Sounds (*He Sheng Shu*), 269–270
Official matchmaker (*guan mei*), 282, 365, 295f
Officials: as above the law, 364; marrying prostitutes, 218–219; "officials sleeping with prostitutes" (*guan li su chang*), 220–221, 223, 287; remarriage of widows prohibited, 7; status performance and, 7
Ou Chaogui, 297
Outside male: clergy as, 99–100; "illicit sexual intercourse" as threat to family order, 65; stereotype of, 94, 96–101. *See also* Rogue males; "Rootless rascals"

Paderni, Paola, 353
Padgug, Robert A., 354
Pan Asan, 144
Pan Jinlian, 356, 367, 159f
Pan Maoniang, 81
Paradigms in law: gender performance, 8–12; progress (Western), 2–5, 345–346; status performance, 5–8
Parallel hierarchies, 144–145
Pariah status, *see* Debased (*jian*) status
Peasants: "ethnographic" evidence and, 15–17; new focus on peasant family, 308–311; official values and, 168, 357; "peasantization" of the law, 14, 112, 164, 310; subsistence crisis among, 12, 347
Penal system, sexual slavery and, 212–213
Penalties, change in: for forced remarriage of widows, 171–172; regarding masters' privilege, 48–57; regarding rape, 69–71; weight adjustment for, 21–22; Yongzheng reforms, 25–26
Penetrant role (in sodomy): change in adulthood, 145–148; in classical Greek legal codes, 354; hierarchical division and, 117; relative age of penetrator, 28–29, 133–138, 144–145, 355
Penetrated role (in sodomy): in classical Greek legal codes, 354; stigma of, 132, 148–154, 117f
Penetration: chastity martyrs and, 170, 313, 358; consummation of homo-

sexual rape, 126–128; evidence for consummation, 79–84; "false" males or females and, 117; importance in rape law, 77–84; manual, 80–81; meaning of, 162–165; penal and ritual consequences of, 77–79; phallocentrism and, 306–307; relative age of penetrator in sodomy, 28–29, 133–138, 144–145, 355; stigma of being penetrated (for a male), 118, 132, 148–154
Penis: consummation of homosexual rape and, 126; consummation of rape and, 79–84; female homosexual activity and, 163; in *Plum in the Golden Vase*, 159, 356
Peony Pavilion (*Mudan ting*), 349
Period of Division, status hierarchy in, 5–6
Perry, Elizabeth, 12
"Pettifoggers" (*song gun*), 168
Phallocentrism, 306–307
Pimps and pimping: demystification of women and, 318–319; marital prostitution, 248–255; "official matchmakers," 282, 365; post-Yongzheng cases, 287–288; relatives of prostitutes file charges, 289, 291–292; "sexual monopoly" of husband, 255; Song edict prohibiting, 224; status performance and, 7; of wife, 54–57, 224. *See also* Prostitution after 1723; Prostitution before 1723
Pirates, 307, 356
Plum in the Golden Vase, The (*Jin ping mei*), 128, 158–162, 349, 351–352, 365, 367, 141f
Pollution: of descent, 84, 308–309; female homosexual activity and, 307; by intercourse with prostitutes, 228; by rape, 67, 84; sodomy as pollution of masculine purity, 130–132; sodomy as pollution of status, 129–130, 307
Pornography ("licentious books"), 32, 349
Poverty: debased status vs., 346; widow chastity and, 167, 184–187, 358f
Pregnant widows, 202–207, 209, 360
Progress in the law, Western paradigm of, 2–5, 345–346
Propaganda, 305–306

Ritual, *see Li* (rites, ritual, normative standards of human relationships)

Rogue males: gender anxiety and fear of, 12–15, 306; gender performance and, 13–14, 10f; homosexual rapist, 138–141; Qing dynasty stereotype, 9–10, 11, 94, 96–101; shortage of wives and, 12–14; subsistence crisis among peasantry and, 12; Tang dynasty stereotype, 10, 93–96. *See also* "Rootless rascals"

Roman law, 309

Rome, 39, 309

"Rootless rascals": bisexual object choice of, 139–141, 355; edicts prohibiting, 353; entrance into legal discourse, 14; gang rape and, 125; gender performance and, 13–14, 10f; as homosexual rapists, 139–141; male clergy as, 99–100; Qing dynasty stereotype, 96–101; Qing substatute, 327–328; Yongzheng rape law and, 70. *See also* Rogue males

Routine memorials on criminal matters, 19

Rowe, William, 310, 315

Runaway prostitutes, 292–295

Same-sex union, female, 163, 307, 366

Same-sex union, male, *see* Homosexuality; Rape, homosexual; Sodomy or anal intercourse (*ji jian*)

"Seizing adulterers" (*zhuo jian*), 194–195, 197–202

"Self-renewal" (*zi xin*), 266–267, 314

"Selling a commoner to be a prostitute," 222–223, 228–229, 237, 291

"Selling a divorce" (*mai xiu*): authorized (of adulteress), 61–64, 351–352; illicit, 57–61, 318, 351, 367

Servants, female, *see* Female slaves or bondservants

Servants, male, *see* Male slaves or servants

Sexual anarchy, 316–320

Sexual contract, voiding by remarried widows, 187–190

Sexual morality: gender performance and, 8–12; status performance and, 5–8, 247, 255

Sexual offenses, definitions of, 33–36

Sexual orientation, "homosexual" and "heterosexual" terminology and, 116–117, 353–354

Sex work, *see* Prostitution after 1723; Prostitution before 1723

Shao Xing, 128–129

Shen Defu, 156

Shen Zhiqi, 22, 61, 64, 83

Shi Shi, 246

Shi Shikong, 153–154

Shiga Shûzô, 23

Shui hu, 216

Shuntian Prefecture Archive, 17

Shuntian Prefecture (Zhili), 18

Si, 31–32

Sichuan Provincial Archives in Chengdu, 17

Sima Qian, 35

Six rites of marriage, 34, 349

Slaves, female, *see* Female slaves or bondservants

Slaves, male, *see* Male slaves or servants

Sodomy or anal intercourse (*ji jian*): adaptation of heterosexual standards to, 126–132; before the Qing dynasty, 118–120, 354; between masters and servants, 128–129; in *Carnal Prayer Mat, The* (*Rou pu tuan*), 128, 141, 142–143; consensual, 123–124, 355; as "decadence," 310–311; early Qing law, 121–124; elite men and, 311; entrance into legal discourse, 14; heterosexual rape and, 83; hierarchies parallel to heterosexual relations, 144–145; Manchu libertine, 156–158; origins of term, 121; as personal indulgence, 156–158; in *Plum in the Golden Vase, The* (*Jin ping mei*), 128, 158–162, 141f; as pollution of masculine purity, 130–132; as pollution of status, 129–130; Qing legislation, 16, 329–332; rationale for prohibition, 114–116; relative age of penetrator, 28–29; sex as survival strategy, 155–156; status hierarchy and, 117–118; stigma and secrecy in consensual relationships, 151–154; stigma of being penetrated, 118, 132, 148–154. *See also* Rape, homosexual

Soldiers: gang rape of chaste woman by, 75–77; "soldiers or civilians engaging in illicit sexual intercourse" substatute (*"jun min xiang jian" li*), 25–26, 92, 287, 326–327

Song Chaohan, 150

Song Tiehan, 283–284, 285

Song Wu, 150

Song Xianye, 285–286

Song law: age of liability for consent, 85; aristocratic priorities of, 15; on male prostitution, 119; on pimping of wife, 7, 55, 224; prohibition of intermarriage with prostitutes, 218–219; rape law, 70, 77

Sources, 17–29; central case records, 18–19; comparison of local and central case records, 20–22; county case records, 17–18; "ethnographic" evidence, 26–29; late imperial legal commentary, 22–24; Qing legal archives, 24–26

Standards of evidence: for coercion, 87–89, 105–106, 107, 109–110; for consummation of rape, 79–84

Status performance: defined, 5f; female chastity and, 6–7; Jing Junjian's map of status levels, 346; paradigm of, 5–8; pollution of descent and, 308–309; regulation of prostitution and, 210–211, 218–255; shift to gender performance, 5, 9, 11, 309, 346

"Statutes applied by analogy" (*bi yin lü*), 37–38, 121–124, 349

"Stealing illicit sex" (*tou jian*), 106–108

Stereotypes: of dangerous male, 93–101, 132–143; of Miao women, 189, 359; of outside male, 94, 96–101; of rapists, 9–10, 11, 93–101; of "rootless rascals," 96–101

Stigma: of adultery, 204; of being penetrated (for a male), 118, 132, 148–154; of being raped (for a female), 84, 132; of mutilation, 266–267; of regional sub-ethnic groups, 214; of sex work, 210

Su Wang, 79–80

Sub-ethnic groups, 214

Substatute (*li*): on forced remarriage, 333–335; on forced remarriage for gain, 335–337; importance in Qing code, 25–26, 348; on "males who commit homicide while resisting

rape," 330–332; on "rootless rascals," 97–98, 327–328; on sodomy, 329–330; on "soldiers or civilians engaging in illicit sexual intercourse" substatute (*"jun min xiang jian" li*), 25–26, 92, 287, 326–327

Suicide: sexual slavery of criminals' wives and, 213; of widows, 170, 177–183, 357f

Sumptuary laws, 6, 218

Sun Ban'ge, 217

Sun Lejia, 177

Sun Mao, 295–296

Sun, monk, 146

Sun Shi, 299–301

Sun Wenbang, 184

Sun Xue'e, 351–352

Sun née Yu Shi, 184

Survival strategies, 12, 16, 155–156, 316–320

Sweeten, Alan R., 357

Sworn sisterhood, 366

Taiping Rebellion, 17, 33, 137

Taiwan, 196–197, 359

Tang code: aristocratic priorities of, 15; *Combined Edition of the Tang and Ming Codes (Tang Ming lü he bian)*, 23; on "consensual illicit intercourse," 86; on "illicit sexual intercourse," 305, 323–324; on illicit sex with female slaves of others, 46–47, 350; *jian* in, 35; on master's privilege, 47, 53; mourning period and, 36; rape law, 67, 69f

Tang dynasty, status hierarchy in, 5–6

Tattooing, 266–267

Taxation of government prostitutes, 213

Telford, Ted, 13

"Ten Abominations" (*shi e*), 32

Terada Takanobu, 261–262, 264, 271, 303, 360, 364

Tian Dong, 104–106

Tian Mei, 299–300

Tie Xuan, 240

T'ien Ju-k'ang, 357

Tong Tai, 299–301

Tongzhi Emperor, 115

Torture, extraction of confessions using, 28, 207, 348–349

Translation of testimony, 27

Library of Congress Cataloging-in-Publication Data

Sommer, Matthew Harvey
    Sex, law, and society in late imperial China / Matthew H. Sommer.
        p.   cm. — (Law, society, and culture in China)
    Includes bibliographical references and index.
    ISBN 0-8047-3695-2 (cloth : alk. paper)
    ISBN 0-8047-4559-5 (pbk. alk. paper)
        1. Sex crimes—China—History.   2. Sex and law—China—History.
    3. Sex customs—China—History.   I. Title.   II. Series.
    KNQ4200.S65   2000
    306.7'0951—dc21   99-41276

⊗ This book is printed on acid-free, recycled paper.

Original printing 2000

Last figure below indicates year of this printing:
09   08   07   06   05